Human Dignity and the Law

AF791746

This book reassesses the relationship between human dignity, law, and specifically the 'personalist' school of agency.

The work argues that a specific way of appreciating dignity is contained in how law understands the person, and so can be used to improve upon how we explain and interpret the law. Despite considerable differences between jurisdictions as regards human dignity in application, it is argued that the particular weight of human persons is the widely shared focal point. The central claim, therefore, is that the law recognises, and tries to foster, the status of personhood, and, drawing on the work of Karol Wojtyła, the author develops a 'Status of Personhood Theory'.

The book will be of interest to academics and researchers working in the areas of Legal Philosophy, Jurisprudence, Philosophy, Ethics and Political Theory.

Michał Rupniewski is Assistant Professor (adiunkt) at the University of Lodz, Faculty of Law and Administration, Department of Political and Legal Doctrines, Poland. He is Associate at the Alexis de Tocqueville Centre for Political and Legal Thought, Poland. Professor Rupniewski has participated in courses and stipends at the universities of Bonn, Strasbourg, and Fordham. He served as guest lecturer at the Universidad Panamericana in Mexico City. His chief scholarly interest is political philosophy's influence on legal interpretation and legislation. In particular, he specialises in political liberalism, personalism, human dignity and law, as well as in theory of legal change.

Routledge Research in Legal Philosophy

Procedural Justice and Relational Theory
Empirical, Philosophical, and Legal Perspectives
Edited by Denise Meyerson, Catriona Mackenzie, and Therese MacDermott

The Origin of Copyright
Expression as Knowing in Being and Copyright Onto-Epistemology
Wenwei Guan

Constitutional Imaginaries
A Theory of European Societal Constitutionalism
Jiří Přibáň

Human Dignity and the Law
A Personalist Theory
Michał Rupniewski

For more information about this series, please visit: www.routledge.com

Human Dignity and the Law

A Personalist Theory

Michał Rupniewski

Routledge
Taylor & Francis Group
LONDON AND NEW YORK

First published 2023
by Routledge
4 Park Square, Milton Park, Abingdon, Oxon OX14 4RN

and by Routledge
605 Third Avenue, New York, NY 10158

Routledge is an imprint of the Taylor & Francis Group, an informa business

© 2023 Michał Rupniewski

The right of Michał Rupniewski to be identified as author of this work has been asserted in accordance with sections 77 and 78 of the Copyright, Designs and Patents Act 1988.

All rights reserved. No part of this book may be reprinted or reproduced or utilised in any form or by any electronic, mechanical, or other means, now known or hereafter invented, including photocopying and recording, or in any information storage or retrieval system, without permission in writing from the publishers.

Trademark notice: Product or corporate names may be trademarks or registered trademarks, and are used only for identification and explanation without intent to infringe.

British Library Cataloguing-in-Publication Data
A catalogue record for this book is available from the British Library

Library of Congress Cataloging-in-Publication Data
A catalog record for this book has been requested

ISBN: 978-1-032-18075-5 (hbk)
ISBN: 978-1-032-18076-2 (pbk)
ISBN: 978-1-003-25273-3 (ebk)

DOI: 10.4324/9781003252733

Typeset in Galliard
by Apex CoVantage, LLC

To Monika, Zosia, and Janek

Contents

Preface x
Acknowledgements xiii

Outline 1
Chapter 1. Methodological credentials of human dignity in the law 2
Chapter 2. Philosophy: the personalist conception of human action and respect proper to persons 3
Chapter 3. Law: the status of personhood and the dignitarian moment 4
Chapter 4. Politics: institutions and the status of personhood 5

1 **Methodological credentials of human dignity in the law** 7
Introduction 7
1 Three methodological commitments as a point of departure 10
1.1 The prima facie *function of human dignity 10*
1.2 The problem of consensus and metaphysical parsimony in law 14
1.3 Law and reality 16
2 Defining and explicating human dignity in the law 21
2.1 The questions of definition 22
2.2 The rules of explication 26
3 The dignitarian moment in the law 31
3.1 The foundational function 32
3.2 The regulative function 34
3.3 The heuristic function 46
3.4 The meta-legal level 49
3.5 Toward interpretation of the dignitarian moment 52
Conclusion 56

2 Philosophy: the personalist conception of human action and affirmation proper to persons 65

Introduction 65

1 Mapping personalism: the Personalist Postulate 67

2 Securing personalism: empirical basis and empirical relevance 72

3 Ontology: human action as the actus personae *77*

3.1 Self-determination and vertical transcendence 79

3.2 Self-possession and self-governance as the experiential component of human freedom 82

3.3 Reference to truth as the condition of transcendence and fulfilment: the role of integration 87

4 Normativity: affirmation of persons 92

4.1 The personalist value of the actus personae *and dignity of the person 94*

4.2 The moral duty: source, content, and structure of moral judgement 98

Conclusion 104

3 Law: the status of personhood and the dignitarian moment 110

Introduction 110

1 The suppositum humanum *in legal inquiries 112*

1.1 The 'praxiological' and the 'ethical' interpretation of human dignity in the law 114

1.2 The praxiological reading and the autonomy of human dignity in the law 118

2 The realism of the SPT: the ontological referral and reflective equilibrium 121

3 Human dignity as the status of personhood 127

3.1 Dignitarian legal interests of the human person 127

3.2 The Principle of the Status of Personhood as an explication of human dignity in the law: the status of personhood as a status-expressing principle 152

3.3 The Principle of the Status of Personhood, wide reflective equilibrium, and the issue of explaining the dignitarian moment in the law 164

Conclusion 170

4 Politics: institutions and the status of personhood 176

Introduction 176

1 The status of personhood, participation, and the idea of decent law 180

1.1 The Principle of the Status of Personhood and genuine participation 180

1.2 Decency of law and the public order 185

2 Normative indeterminacy and the principles of adjudication 194
2.1 Basic assumptions concerning adjudication 195
2.2 The personalist meaning to equal dignity 197
2.3 Hard cases and easy cases: toward a theory of error 205
3 Decent law, social engineering, and the principles of legislation 222
3.1 Toward dignitarian unity of a legal system: legal personhood 223
3.2 Legislative standards for decent law and the threats of 'law as engineering' 226

Conclusion 232
Philosophical conclusions 234
Jurisprudential conclusions 234
Political conclusions 235

Information on the Alexis de Tocqueville Centre of Political and Legal Thought 237
Index 238

Preface

The topic of human dignity has drawn considerable scholarly attention in recent decades, and the international community of scholars and lawyers is certainly equipped with knowledge and reflection which were absent just 20 years ago. Yet, despite advances, many crucial interpretive problems remain unresolved, which is particularly problematic for legal theory and professional activity. The paradox of dignity's career in the legal sphere consists in the fact that while most people would claim to share a commitment thereto, they may differ – sometimes to the extreme – as to what it entails and requires. That is why we are still in need of further guidance and reflection that will hopefully lead to a more principled and intelligible application of human dignity as a legal concept.

This contribution aims at finding such guidance, in a way that focuses on a dimension of human dignity which has been left at the margin of discussions, at least in specifically legal contexts. What I have in mind is the sphere of personhood, elucidated by a phenomenological and ontological inquiry. In my view, before asking about particular exigencies of human dignity in the legal sphere, and even before asking what specific human capacities and characteristics are at play in that context, one should attempt to answer an even more basic question – how does and should the law treat human persons, in its own eyes? My answer is that the law's response to human personhood is expressed by a principle that is called the Principle of the Status of Personhood (the PSP). In this context, another question naturally comes to mind: does law simply construe legal subjects and entities, including the figure of the human person as the bearer of dignity? Or is it the other way round – is it the law's architecture which is deeply influenced by the real structures of the human person? My theory of human dignity in the law – which I call the Status of Personhood Theory (the SPT) – explores the second alternative, mainly because this is what law evoking human dignity seems to suggest. The SPT is therefore an attempt to better conceptualise the bond between human personhood and law, as manifested in the existing law related to human dignity.

It is important to note that the subject under scrutiny is not something completely new, to be discovered or established. It is, rather, already known, and my theory serves to highlight and interpret it with the help of a philosophical conception that potentially gives new insights in sorting out the subject matter.

Despite that familiarity, the bond I am examining is far from obvious, and thus proposing the SPT bears the burden of explaining why personhood is ascribed to humans, and why the dignity attributed to personhood is linked so strongly to law.

In my view, the philosophy that is particularly well-equipped for that quest is a stream of thought centred around *The Acting Person* (Wojtyła 1979, first published in Polish in 1969), the most important philosophical book of Karol Wojtyła (who became Pope John Paul II in 1978), written while the author was professor at the Catholic University of Lublin (Poland), and a cardinal of the Catholic Church. This conception was subsequently developed by others from the same university, such as Tadeusz Styczeń, SDS, from whom I also draw a great deal in this book. While the Lublin philosophical school was diverse, and many other philosophers could be named in addition to Wojtyła and Styczeń, I will focus on these two. Hereafter, I will refer to their thought (despite the differences they may have had) as 'the personalist conception'.

Although the personalist conception was not developed as a legal theory or reflection, I argue that it can be extremely helpful in developing an account of human dignity in the law. Wojtyła and Styczeń draw our attention to the self-determination and integrity of the person manifested in her actions, which reveal the uniqueness and dignity (i.e. entitlement to affirmation) equally possessed by all persons. More precisely, the dignity of the person as found in the law deeply corresponds to the fact that action, insofar as it constitutes genuinely human conduct, is a free response to (normative and factual) truths, as distinguished from a reaction to incentives. As a consequence, the central idea behind the PSP is that the human capacity to act – to be author and master of an informed and principled conduct not reducible to a passive reaction to stimuli – is something real, and bears an inevitable influence on legal activity, as a *sign* of the dignity of the person. The legal essence of human dignity, which is a privileged status or standing of each human individual in relation to the law, should be therefore conceived as the status of personhood. As I will argue, this is a matter of human reality that law does, and in fact should, take into account. The PSP, then, is not a straightforward implication of a set of theoretical assumptions about law. It is, rather, a consequence of the simple fact that law is ultimately made by, and addressed to, human persons.

It must be emphasised that this book applies the personalist conception in a manner and context fairly unusual for it. Obviously, arising from a Catholic school of thought, it has been interpreted first and foremost as a philosophical correlate of the moral theology and social teaching of the Catholic Church. The 'legal' issues examined in previous contributions have been limited, embracing mostly human rights. The 'political' part has been focused on selected principles of democratic order or economy (as exemplified by the social teaching of the Catholic Church in the second half of the twentieth century). Strictly speaking, the aim of this book is not to interpret the personalist conception for its own sake. It is, rather, to borrow from it, and to develop its philosophical tools in the service of a different sort of inquiry, namely, a legal one. Hence, I examine different matters from those traditionally connected to the personalist conception, and I do it from a somewhat 'secular' perspective (without direct references to a theological or religious background). According to my methodological commitments, the inquiry starts with the law related to human dignity, and the philosophical conception is introduced only to the extent that is necessary to explicate and explain the legal processes. The central claim is that the law recognises, and tries to foster, the status of personhood (this is what the PSP expresses). Despite considerable differences between jurisdictions as regards human dignity in application, the particular weight of human persons and their agency is the widely shared focal point. The PSP is considered a cosmopolitan principle, due to this very fact.

This book is an attempt to combine *law* (comparative legal interpretation and dignity jurisprudence), *philosophy* (the phenomenology and ontology of personhood), and *politics* (political philosophy of participation and the decency of law). I might have made mistakes in any one of these fields, or in the way I have attempted to integrate them. However, the complexity of the subject matter under scrutiny has required me to extend and broaden my inquiry, and also entails a readiness on my part to receive criticism and lessons from specialists in the fields I had to touch upon. In this context, there is consolation in the words of a medieval Polish scholar, Matheus de Cracovia (d. 1410). In the introductory remarks to his treaty on contracts, he said:

> if [your writing is] true, it is indeed good for others to know it; if different than true, it is useful as an exercise to others, [who may] notice and repeal [your errors], so that the simple folks don't follow. [It is likewise useful] for the one whose are the opinions, as he may recover his senses and abandon his mistakes.
>
> (Mateusz z Krakowa 2011, 70, translation by the author)

If I could ask something from you, the reader, it would be to adopt a similar attitude and take the thoughts in this book either as worth knowing or as an exercise showing what not to know. While that may be almost too benevolent toward me, the author, it is also quite appropriate for our common task, which is to find the truth to the extent we are able.

References

Mateusz z Krakowa. 2011. *De contractibus*. Edited by M. Bukała. Kęty: Wydawnictwo Marek Derewiecki.

Wojtyła, Karol. 1979. *The Acting Person*. Translated by A. Potocki. Dordrecht: D. Riedel Publishing Company.

Acknowledgements[1]

Writing this book was a demanding journey, and I would like to express my gratitude to those whose companion turned it into a marvellous intellectual adventure.

Firstly, a great opportunity for initial systematic engagement with the topic came with my visit at the Universidad Panamericana, CDMX, where I conducted a seminar on human dignity and the human person. The sessions with the amazing students with whom I could work there gave me the inspiration and power to write the book. I am grateful to all participants, as well as to Eduardo Charpenel and María Elena García Peláez for inviting me to Mexico.

During the time of writing, I benefited from the creative environment of my workplace, the University of Lodz. In particular, I would like to thank Zbigniew Rau, Ryszard Kleszcz, Maciej Chmieliński, Tomasz Tulejski, Marek Tracz-Tryniecki, and Kazimierz M. Ujazdowski for inspiring conversations.

My reflections on the final shape of the book were inspired by the discussions at the virtual meetings at the University of Leicester and at the SWPS University in Poznań. I am grateful to the audiences, as well as to Stephen Riley and Marek Piechowiak, who were kind enough to receive me respectively in Leicester and Poznań. The work of these two scholars had an important impact on my own thinking. I am also grateful to anonymous reviewers of the book proposal for Routledge, and to Alison Kirk, my acquisition editor in that publishing house, for her interest in the project.

During the preparations of the manuscript, the crucial help came from Amy Ross, who corrected my grammatical mistakes, but was also the first, and attentive, reader. In that very period, Eduardo Charpenel read the whole thing and provided me the priceless feedback, and Kamil Aksiuto provided his remarks on Chapters 1 and 2.

For the most part, I wrote this book during the hard and unsecure times of the Covid-19 pandemic. Support from the family became even more important than under usual circumstances. Hence, I thank wholeheartedly my parents, Jola and Darek, my grandmother, Danusia, as well as my parents-in-law, Halinka and Czesiek, for helping me to reconcile the scholarly work with my parental commitments.

1 This book presents research financially supported by the NCN (Poland), under the project no. 2016/23/D/HS5/02400.

Finally, I must express my deepest gratitude to Monika, my wife, who shared the hardships of writing this book with me, and to my children, Janek and Zosia. The everyday presence of my closest was a source of amazement that stimulated questions about human personhood, and conditions of its development. I dedicate this book to them.

Outline

The subject matter that this book puts under scrutiny is human dignity. It is not my intention to embrace comprehensively all its aspects: my focus is limited to *human dignity in the law*. As it will become clear in due course, even in that limited sphere my account does not claim exclusivity – the idea of human dignity is simply too rich to reasonably hope to catch all the meanings in one box. Nevertheless, I claim that my account captures the manifestation that is crucial to the proper understanding of both human dignity in the law, and the law in general. The theory I am proposing – the Status of Personhood Theory (the SPT) – explicates human dignity as a cosmopolitan, implicit *principle* found in modern law in different branches and at different levels. I call it the Principle of the Status of Personhood (the PSP), which stipulates that *before the law, each person equally must be respected as an integrated whole, radically capable of self-determination, and striving towards fulfilment*. Most likely, the PSP as presented right now speaks little or nothing to you, the reader. All the terms used in the PSP are technical – the elucidation of their meaning comes from an interpretation of law through the lens of a particular philosophical account of human personhood, offered by the personalist conception of Karol Wojtyła and Tadeusz Styczeń, which I talked about in the Preface. The PSP expresses the priority status of human persons towards the law, which translates into respectful relations between persons as such, *mediated by law*.

The central claim of this book is that the normative expression and prescription of such relations in the norms related to human dignity is not a mere historical contingency; *it is a consequence of the real connection between legal activity on the one hand, and natural human personhood on the other*. Despite its familiarity, this connection has not been recognised to a sufficient extent in modern legal theory. Perhaps the most important task of this book is to make it more explicit, and clarify its meaning with the help of the personalist conception. This main task is pursued through attaining four specific research objectives: (i) *identification* of the privileged position of human dignity in the law in the broad, globalised context post-UDHR (referred to as 'the dignitarian moment in the law'); (ii) *explication* of the concept of human dignity in the law as 'The Principle of the Status of Personhood', based on the dignitarian moment interpreted through the personalist conception; (iii) *explanation* of the PSP's presence in the law, made through

DOI: 10.4324/9781003252733-1

the lens of the personalist interpretation of dignity; (iv) *incorporation* of the PSP into a wider web of 'political-legal' ideas, especially in the fields of adjudication and legislation. These four objectives are pursued within the following structure:

Chapter 1. Methodological credentials of human dignity in the law

Given the complexity of the subject, the proper inquiry is preceded with a detailed methodological chapter. Methodology is crucial not only to organise the complex work to be done, but also to justify the endeavour itself. One of the gravest arguments against the relevance of human dignity as a legal term is an alleged fuzziness that makes *arbitrary application* a possibility. In the face of this, one should be mindful not to merely use human dignity as an empty vehicle for one's vision of a good or just society. If a political agenda behind the word 'dignity' was the whole story, the relevance of human dignity *for the law in general* could be easily questioned. A systematic and self-constraining methodology, by contrast, may make us consider human dignity as something real and legally relevant, transcending the day-to-day clashes of worldviews or interests.

Taking these factors into consideration, the chapter begins by setting forth the basic methodological commitments (not to be conflated with the methods themselves) that serve as a starting point. This is the subject of Section 1. The commitments are: (i) *the human condition*, (ii) *weak metaphysical parsimony*, and (iii) *sceptical realism*. Taken together, they urge us to keep in contact with the existing law, which should be treated as a starting point and a recurring point of reference. My further analysis in this section suggests that in the case of human dignity, standard legal interpretation should be complemented with analysing the experience of personhood, which may be reasonably expected to be able to reveal some important truths concerning human persons. At the same time, however, the methodological commitments urge us to refrain from seeking ultimate metaphysical explanations of the observed phenomena (this is unnecessary in law). The ontological claims should be introduced with care, only when really indispensable and in equilibrium with the data provided by legal interpretation. Section 2 is devoted to a closer look at the formal characteristics (not yet the content) of the concept of human dignity in the law. Since it is characterised as an *interpretative concept with a family-type meaning*, I argue that only a partial definition of it, working in a particular context or conditions, is possible. The most reasonable way of approaching such concepts is *explication*, which consists in examining the use of the relevant language hitherto, and then 'refining' it through scientific methods. Since in our case the relevant language is that of the law, Section 3 provides a brief exposition of most characteristic uses of dignity: its functions and aspects in the global context. I argue that if those divergent uses are considered together, they constitute a special phenomenon that shall be called 'the dignitarian moment'. I conclude the chapter by briefly characterising the theory that I will defend – the Status of Personhood Theory – and particular methods I will use, namely: reflective equilibrium, comparative legal interpretation, and phenomenology of human action (and more broadly, of human personhood). All this sets up the instruments that will be put to work in the subsequent chapters.

Chapter 2. Philosophy: the personalist conception of human action and respect proper to persons

According to the commitment to weak metaphysical parsimony, approaching the legal dimension of human dignity as something derived from a philosophy is considered doubtful. Therefore, the theory I propose is not a straightforward application of the personalist conception into jurisprudence. It is, rather, the other way round: my investigations make a start in the law, particularly, in the dignitarian moment set forth in Chapter 1. Philosophical conceptions come into play insofar as they are indispensable in interpreting and explaining law. It seems reasonable to expect that many questions about human dignity generated by the law may be properly answered only once a clear philosophical conception of the agent (that is, the human person acting as legal subject) has been worked up. But the question about the agent is asked as a result of the law speaking for itself. This is especially clear once we realise that the law, in the dignitarian moment, *refers to the peculiar, personal character of the human being*. Thus, the philosophy of the human person that I deal with in Chapter 2 is perceived as a set of tools that enable us to sort out the issues stemming from the dignitarian moment. Although the conception of human dignity I want to achieve (which is essentially the task of Chapter 3) is conceived as a legal doctrine, the necessary background for it can be found nowhere but in the philosophy of the human person.

Obviously, the philosophy of the human person is an extremely rich field, composed of numerous and often contradictory traditions of thought. Instead of conducting a comprehensive review of these traditions (a task with no clear end), my strategy is *to choose* – in particular, to choose the tenets that are vital to interpreting the dignitarian moment. These central tenets are, to my understanding: (i) the capacity of human persons for the (genuinely personal) action, which is simultaneously *a sign* of their inherent dignity; and (ii) affirmation proper to persons, which is tantamount to adequate responses to their inherent dignity. Here again, instead of examining details of the history of ideas, I choose to engage in dialogue with the two philosophers who have examined those issues in the most direct and exceptionally penetrating way. Karol Wojtyła and Tadeusz Styczeń are perfect interlocutors and teachers in this regard. On the one hand, using the phenomenological method allowed them to go 'directly to things' which were to be examined (persons in action and respect for persons). On the other, conducting their analyses in the realist, Thomistic framework kept them in contact with the rich philosophical tradition of Western classical philosophy, as well as with common sense and common experience. Choosing their conception(s), I have two important hopes in mind – first, that their insights will elucidate the dignitarian moment in the law, and second, that the results of the inquiry will form a theory capable of defending itself as true.

The structure of the chapter is as follows. In Section 1, I outline the personalist conception against the broader background of the competing and the parallel conceptions of the human person. Then, in Section 2, I point at the most solid basis of the personalist conception, which is that of *experience*, understood very broadly, far from narrow empiricism. In short, the relatively secure position of personalism is that instead of relying on speculation, it recurrently refers to human experience. Once this is done, I examine in more detail two substantive tenets of the personalist conception, ones that are crucial to the proper interpretation of the dignitarian moment in the law – the ontology of the human person in action (Section 3), and affirmation of persons for their own sake, as a universal normative requirement (Section 4). Finally, I present the path in which the personalist conception will be applied in developing the Status of Personhood Theory. Importantly, I am suggesting a path that does not treat dignity and respect as an exclusively moral notion. Instead, dignity of the human person will be regarded as an implicit commitment of *the human activity* in more general terms, which includes the law. I call it 'the praxiological reading' of the personalist conception, and develop it further in the following chapters.

Chapter 3. Law: the status of personhood and the dignitarian moment

In this chapter, I finally lay out my own theory – the SPT. As explained earlier, the SPT is rooted in the existing law – in the dignitarian moment described in Chapter 1, which is to be interpreted through the use of the philosophical conception presented in Chapter 2. Therefore, Chapter 3 is an attempt to integrate the preceding two. This task is fulfilled by explicating 'human dignity' in the legal sphere as 'the Principle of the Status of Personhood'. My further goal in this chapter is to demonstrate that this explication sheds new light on the dignitarian moment in law, and thus on the law in general. While I do not attempt to give an ultimate explanation of the sort that only metaphysics could offer, I nevertheless demonstrate that certain developments in the legal sphere are not mere historical contingencies or pure conventions; they have a solid ontic basis in the structure of the human action, as well as in inherent dignity that is a real standing of persons against one another. The PSP is a legal expression of this standing.

I begin with considering how the *suppositum humanum* – the person who is not reducible to her social or biological conditions, and is endowed with her own, internal subjectivity – can figure in legal inquires (Section 1). I argue that if the irreducible character of the human person (corresponding to the special entitlement to affirmation) is something real, it should spontaneously manifest itself in the sphere of law. The underlying respect for the personhood of everyone subject to the law, observable in the dignitarian moment, is precisely such a manifestation. In Section 2, I claim that only a realist theory can respond to the challenges that await human dignity in the law, and I explain in what sense the SPT is such a realist theory. I make use of the idea of wide reflective equilibrium. The consistency between legal judgements and principles, the experience of personhood in action, as well as the background personalist ontology of the person, allow me to claim the truth of the theory. Against this background, Section 3 explicates human dignity in the law as the PSP. I begin with identifying the dignitarian interests of the human individual which are protected by the law. I claim that there is no one such interest – there is an open-ended list of interests. The most important on this list are self-determination, integration, and freedom from degradation – the dignitarian protection in most cases concerns either one of these three or their combination. Examples from law are evoked in support of this thesis. The rest of the section is devoted to the actual explication of the PSP as a status-expressing principle, and making a case of the wide reflective equilibrium that the SPT seeks.

Chapter 4. Politics: institutions and the status of personhood

This final chapter serves to insert the key findings of the book presented in Chapter 3 into a broader context of basic 'political-legal' ideas, in order to make the highly abstract theory more concrete (and hopefully less equivocal). The chapter thus attempts to describe an ideal of a polity whose laws respect the PSP, at the most basic, relatively thin level. Instead of providing a comprehensive political doctrine based on the PSP, *my concern is the basic conditions of a rule of law which takes the status of personhood seriously.* The ideas I introduce are centred on the idea of decent law, that is, of a non-arbitrary legal order respecting the status of personhood of every affected person. Admittedly, this makes the scope of this chapter quite minimalistic, focused on the essential political commitments emerging from the SPT which may be taken up and developed in many alternative forms, in different legal orders or legal-theoretical proposals. However, this minimalism does not entail doctrinal emptiness or sheer abstraction. The idea of decency of law is integrated with the Wojtilian doctrine of participation, that is, acting together with others in a way which maintains one's subjectivity, and allows each participant to recognise everyone else as their neighbour. This is considered as the main feature of a public order respecting the PSP. This bears important consequences for two activities essential for the rule of law – adjudication and legislation.

Granted, Section 1 elucidates the idea of the decent law, as well as its connections with the personalist idea of genuine participation. The particular importance of this section is that it shows the PSP as expressing not only the independence of individual persons before the law, but also their ***mutual interdependence***. The decent law 'sees' humans in all their complex involvements in communities, with all their vulnerabilities. Section 2 deals with adjudication, particularly with the normative indeterminacy of human dignity in the law, which is sorted out in the spirit of the decency of law. First, I lay out the most important ideal for adjudication – the equality in dignity. Subsequently, I offer an account on the easy, and separately on the hard, cases. Section 3 briefly characterises the most important implications the PSP yields for legislation. In particular, I deal with the dilemmas connected to constructing the contours of legal personhood, as well with the problems connected to the 'engineering' role that the law plays increasingly in modern jurisdictions. I maintain that all the challenges emerging from this must be dealt with in the way which does not forget the status of the direct authors of the law, that is, the human persons.

Given the fact that the journey in this book is a long one, I close the book with a **Conclusion**, collecting the results I find most important.

1 Methodological credentials of human dignity in the law

Introduction

When approaching the issue of 'human dignity and law' today, one cannot escape thinking in terms of the international law developed after World War II, most eminently of the Universal Declaration of Human Rights (hereinafter UDHR 1948). In this well-known document, one reads that 'human beings are born free and equal in dignity and rights' (UDHR 1948, Article 1), which is commonly considered to be a recognition (and not an enactment) of a universal principle of egalitarian concern towards human beings *qua* human beings. This and other provisions of international law have led to, again, a quite common picture of human dignity as a *foundation of human rights*, which was perhaps most strongly expressed in the International Covenants on Human Rights, the ICCPR (1966) and the ICESCR (1966). The Preamble, identical in both, states that the 'inalienable rights of all members of the human family . . . derive from the inherent dignity of the human person'. Although the term 'dignity' (with or without the egalitarian adjective 'human') has a long and complicated history anteceding the emergence of human rights law, the direct sources of the still-growing jurisprudence and literature on human dignity must be associated with it, and placed exactly in the post-war period.[1]

This book takes a somewhat different tack. My commitment is to conceptualise and explain the bonds between human dignity and law that are both deeper and broader in scope than the aforementioned. The use of human dignity in contemporary law is not limited to human rights and constitutional rights, and one can find dignity being protected in more 'ordinary' areas, such as penal law (including criminal proceedings), private law (including civil lawsuits), or administrative law. Examples will be discussed throughout the book, with a view to demonstrating that the *foundational* role that human dignity plays can be conceived of as *relevant for the law in general*, not just a particular branch of law, no matter

1 For a comprehensive overview of the historical-philosophical-legal background of the contemporary discourse on dignity, see McCrudden (2013). For a detailed history of the term 'human dignity' in Western culture, see Lebech (2019).

DOI: 10.4324/9781003252733-2

how important. This is not yet a theoretical-legal claim. This is rather how the law appears to be, in contemporary jurisdictions. My inquiry is focused on the good reasons to think that dignity as a legal term does not simply pop up out of nowhere. There is the common denominator that unifies its divergent formulations and applications. This book goes in search of it.

One may certainly claim that the global development of law leading to the vast use (perhaps even overuse) of dignity has been historical and contingent – a different wording might have been used, or the emphasis might have been put on legal instruments other than human rights, constitutionalism, and judicial review. Also, given the political, technological, and environmental challenges to the present world order, the future of the project of human rights is uncertain, and so is the fate of human dignity as conceived after the UDHR. What I am striving to identify and examine, however, is above all this, or, better to say, *at the bottom of all this.* I am therefore not directly concerned with the historical/sociological side of human dignity's career in the law. Rather, much of my inquiry is *transcendental* in character, in the sense that the legal institutions I will examine will not be regarded as social conditions creating human dignity at the fundamental level. To the contrary: I will argue that human dignity is a constitutive element of at least some social relations and some legal institutions at the fundamental level. Despite this 'transcendentalist' tenet, my project is not fully idealistic, and it is not exclusively relying on *a priori* justifications. As this book hopefully shows, certain aspects of human dignity can be adequately captured only through the analysis of factual legal institutions and the way they work in practice – the transcendental manifests itself in the factual. Insofar as the latter is the case, my project has a *reconstructive* side, that is, it is drawing from the factual legal processes themselves. In my view, those two aspects (human dignity as a transcendental condition of law, and human dignity as reconstructed from the law that is) come together at the fundamental level of this inquiry, which is that of *explanation.* As we will see in due course, my theory hopes to offer an answer not only to the question of *how* human dignity has been so widely evoked in the law, but also *why* it has been evoked. With credible answers at hand, one might be able to discern the implementations that are wrong or elusive from these well justified. This brings another purpose of our inquiry to the table, namely that of *critique.* In order to show how those different aspects of our inquiry (the transcendental, the reconstructive, the explanatory, and the critical) work together, in a consistent and non-circular way, one needs to set the methodology, which is the main task of this chapter. Speaking metaphorically, then, this chapter is not playing any music yet: The first task is to set up the instruments.

Given the idiosyncrasy of the topic, as well as the strong tendencies in jurisprudence and political philosophy which go in exactly the opposite direction (and regard human dignity as more or less conventional), *methodology* is crucial not only to organise the complex work to be done, but also to justify the endeavour itself. As far as the latter aspect is concerned, the crucial reason why the 'methodological credentials' are presented in Chapter 1 is my willingness to separate *genuine examination* from *doing ideology*. This separation is certainly not fully possible, given the inevitable normative presuppositions and implications of human dignity. But the demarcation between ideology and examination should at least be problematised, particularly bearing in mind the critique that human dignity has received in recent years. Although I will not discuss the details of this critique now, one of the gravest arguments against the relevance of human dignity as a legal term is its fuzziness, and the possibility of arbitrary application following this fuzziness. In the face of this, one should be mindful not to use human dignity merely as an empty vehicle for one's vision of the good or just society. Admittedly, both progressive and conservative political agendas are being justified by human dignity talk, and I am not saying that this is necessarily a bad thing. But if political agenda were the whole story, the relevance of human dignity *for the law in general* could be easily questioned. A systematic and self-constraining methodology may allow us to consider human dignity as something real, and relevant in the legal context; something that helps legal actors *transcend* the day-to-day clashes of worldview or interest, rather than simply *amplify* them. If that task is successfully accomplished, the existing law pertaining to human dignity would be better interpreted, and, as a result of this, could be further developed in a principled and self-restraining manner.

Taking the aforementioned into consideration, this chapter is devoted to presenting the methodological credentials of human dignity in the law, which serves a dual purpose – to organise the more detailed procedure of examination that is to come afterwards, and to lay the foundations of it, so that the results are immune to charges of being mere 'ideological' assertions. I begin with setting forth some basic methodological commitments (not to be conflated with the methods themselves) that serve as a starting point (Section 1). Then, in Section 2, I consider the formal characteristics (and not yet the content) of the concept of human dignity in the law. Since human dignity is characterised as an interpretative concept with a family-type meaning, I argue that only a partial definition – a definition working in a particular context or conditions – is possible. The most reasonable way of approaching such concepts is *explication*, that is, examining the use of the relevant language up to now, and then 'refining' it with the use of scientific methods. I argue that since the inquiry in this book is focused on the law, the relevant language, the basis of explication, also should come from that sphere. Thus, Section 3 provides a brief exposition of the most characteristic uses of dignity: its functions and its aspects. I argue that if those divergent uses are considered together, they constitute a special phenomenon in the law which may be called 'the dignitarian moment'. Finally, as a conclusion, I briefly characterise the theory that I will defend – the Status of Personhood Theory – and the main methods I will use. These methods are the comparative legal interpretation, the phenomenology of human personhood, and the wide reflective equilibrium. All this sets up the instruments that will be put to work in subsequent chapters.

1 Three methodological commitments as a point of departure

1.1 The prima facie *function of human dignity*

In my investigations, I treat human dignity as a foundation of law. It is, though, important to emphasise that this foundational role is not considered as an implication or presupposition of some legal theory (in the sense of general reflection on the concept or nature of law). Quite the contrary, for now I am setting aside the purely legal-theoretical disputes, such as those between legal positivism and natural law theory, and I would like to ask the reader to do the same. In my view, if human dignity is to be relevant for law, it should be conceived, to a certain extent at least, in a way that could be widely shared among competing legal theories, rather than attached to a particular theoretical standpoint. Despite this, one question of a theoretical nature needs to be asked right now, in the methodological context: What kind of knowledge about law are we supposed to get through the examination of human dignity? In other words, I am now asking the 'So what?' question: If we were to say that freedom is at law's normative foundation, or common good, or justice, *but not human dignity*, what would it mean for the law? And what do we want to attain, what kind of understanding of law are we after, when we defend a *particular conception* of human dignity?

Of course, to presuppose the results of the inquiry at the outset resembles a fatal logical fallacy (*petitio principii*). Therefore, I am now asking what we should look for, rather than determining what we will find. I believe that a minimal assumption about human dignity in law should be made, as essential to *asking* the proper question, not to *begging* it. The assumption is the following: human dignity *serves as a bridge between the human condition and the law*. Consequently, particular conceptions of human dignity point at those aspects of our humanity that deserve special legal recognition and protection. It does not mean that human dignity jurisprudence is supposed to reveal the essence of being human in its entirety. This is obviously not a job that law may be reasonably expected to accomplish. Some of our distinctively human capacities – a sense of humour, or artistic appreciation, for example – rarely are of direct legal concern, and if they are, the law does not go into depths. A lot of the open-ended human reality is, and should continue to be, free from juridification. On the other hand, law simply cannot escape being engaged with *some aspects* of the human condition, or human reality, and this is for two reasons. One reason (internal to the law) is that the bodies engaged in legal activity inevitably produce a certain picture of the legal agent, in legislation or adjudication, and human dignity is often central to that picture. The other reason (external to the law) is that, regardless of what we think about the nature or definition of law, flesh-and-blood humans produce it, as addressed to other flesh-and-blood humans who are supposed to obey or to make use of it. Legal systems take the latter into account, at least insofar as the social efficacy of law is to be achieved. The human condition is therefore present in law both from the inside (law producing a picture, or multiple collateral pictures, of the human being), and from the outside (real human beings producing law and making sense of it). In my view, this is human dignity which is at work in the process of determining what aspects of this are particularly important in governing human affairs, and worthy of a special kind of respect.

Let me illustrate what I mean with examples. In *Obergefell v. Hodges*, the Supreme Court of the United States decided that a right to marry, derived from the Fourteenth Amendment (the Equal Protection Clause and the Due Process Clause) is to be conferred upon homosexual couples, as a constitutional right. Interpreting the Due Process Clause, the Court said that the liberties granted by this provision 'extend to certain personal choices central to individual dignity and autonomy, including intimate choices that define personal identity and beliefs' (Supreme Court of the United States 2015, opinion, 10). How this interpretation of the Fourteenth Amendment has been developed, and how the judgement affects the American law, is not of our concern at the moment. But if we look at the way in which the concept of dignity was used by the Court (despite not being explicitly invoked in the text of the U.S. Constitution), we will see the close bond between human reality and the law which I have in mind. The reasoning as a whole is quite controversial (as suggested by the dissenting opinions of four out of nine justices), but it rests on a quite uncontroversial premise, namely, that marriage is 'central to the human condition' (Supreme Court of the United States 2015, opinion, 3). According to the Court, the 'equal dignity in the eyes of the law' (Supreme Court of the United States 2015, opinion, 28), which same-sex couples enjoy, should be recognised in the form of allowing a marriage license as an option for them, precisely because of the centrality of marriage in human life. An additional tacit premise is that individuals are entitled to freely choose their intimate life partner regardless of their gender. More generally – one is entitled to a self-constitution through crucial choices shaping one's life, and these should be protected by the constitutional law. 'Dignity' is therefore closely connected to 'autonomy', and it is the latter that calls for the dignitarian recognition. Such connection is present in earlier jurisprudence of the U.S. Supreme Court, particularly in *Planned Parenthood v. Casey*, where the Court confirmed a woman's right to terminate her pregnancy (constituting the viability of the foetus as the main criterion). More specifically, this right was interpreted as part of the protected sphere of family life that is a matter 'involving the most intimate and personal choices a person may make in a lifetime, choices central to personal dignity and autonomy' (Supreme Court of the United States 1992, opinion, 851). The woman should not face 'substantial obstacles' (Supreme Court of the US 1992, opinion, 877) preventing her from deciding whether or not to obtain an abortion, and this is underlined by attributing to her the status of dignity-autonomy. As we will see in this book, neither a right to same-sex marriage nor freedom to terminate pregnancy can be reasonably considered self-evident derivations from human dignity. Also, making dignity tantamount to autonomy is doubtful, especially if the latter is to be understood as a strictly individual creation of 'one's own concept of existence, of meaning, of the universe, and of the mystery of human life' (Supreme Court of the United States 1992, opinion 851), without careful consideration of our dignitarian social bonds with all other persons who are our equals. The important thing for us now, however, is only that the Court conceives of *personal autonomy* as crucial to the human condition, and employs dignity to make the protection of this crucial aspect of life by the law justifiable.

Another example also comes from constitutional law, but of a considerably different legal culture. In the Polish 1997 Constitution (that is still in force today), human dignity is a foundational, explicit commitment. Article 30 stipulates that

> The inherent and inalienable dignity of the person shall constitute a source of freedoms and rights of persons and citizens. It shall be inviolable. The respect and protection thereof shall be the obligation of public authorities.
> (Constitution of the Republic of Poland 1997, Article 30)[2]

The interpreters of Article 30 do not put a very strong emphasis on personal autonomy, especially not in a manner characteristic of the U.S. Supreme Court. This includes the only *authoritative* interpreters, namely, the justices sitting in the Constitutional Tribunal.[3] It is true that autonomy-friendly interpretation also occurs, for instance in the context of freedom of conscience. According to the Tribunal's jurisprudence, everyone is entitled to develop and follow their worldview autonomously; thus, 'forcing anyone to act against their own conscience would constitute an infringement on the inalienable human dignity' (Constitutional Tribunal of the Republic of Poland 2015, justification, 4.2.4, translation by the author). But this statement is only a secondary conclusion from the more general grounding premise that dignity is foundational to *humanness and integrity of the person*, as protected by the Constitution (which, in principle, extends to prenatal humans). It is important to emphasise that Article 30 is situated at the outset of Chapter II of the Constitution that regulates basic liberties and rights, and therefore has a special status in the constitutional matter. As the Tribunal says in one of the judgements:

> taking into consideration the central and fundamental importance that the principle of protecting each person's dignity has for the whole system of constitutional axiology, one should assert that evoking Article 30 [in judicial

2 In the official English translation of the Polish constitution, the word *człowiek* is translated as 'person', although 'human being' would be a better translation. For consistency, in what follows, I translate the word *człowiek* appearing in the jurisprudence of the Constitutional Tribunal as 'person', unless otherwise indicated.

3 The Polish constitution adopts the model that is common in continental Europe, namely, the model under which a separate, specialised court (in this particular case, the Constitutional Tribunal) reviews the primary legislation in the abstract – not hearing a particular case, but 'judging' the provisions of the law with a view to their consistency with the norms higher in hierarchy. A typical judgement would, then, declare the non-constitutionality of a statute. Given the constitutional crisis that began in Poland in 2015, there is a growing controversy with regards to the legitimation of the Tribunal. As a reaction to that uncertainty, I will not quote the judgements issued after the beginning of the crisis.

> review] is appropriate whenever the assessed subject matter concerns legal protection connected to respecting *the most vital interests of every individual*, that is, those pertaining to life, health, or bodily integrity.
>
> (Constitutional Tribunal of the Republic of Poland 2006, justification, 6.2, emphasis added, translation by the author)

In other words, the Tribunal associates human dignity not with one particular capacity of the person (such as autonomy), but rather with multiple human characteristics, especially those strongly attached to *basic human fulfilment.* Interestingly enough, this implies an interest-based theory of rights. This differs considerably from the previously mentioned cases heard by the U.S. Supreme Court: The argument in *Obergefell v. Hodges* and *Planned Parenthood v. Casey* clearly rests on the legal relevance of a person's *choice*, and therefore, arguably, on a will theory of rights. As a consequence of the generality of the Article 30 clause in the Polish constitution, and the focus on interest rather than choice, the Polish Tribunal uses human dignity extensively in the judicial reasoning concerning the meaning and weighing of basic constitutional liberties, at least as a background heuristic principle. The point of reference of this principle is, to a certain extent, extra-legal – it is human beings themselves – or more precisely, those aspects of the human condition – that call for constitutional protection to which everyone is entitled equally. Sometimes this idea is framed in terms of Article 30 regarded as a bridge between the natural law and the positive law (Constitutional Tribunal of the Republic of Poland 2002, justification, 6.2).

I made the foregoing juxtaposition of Polish and American constitutional jurisprudence to highlight both substantive opposition and the common denominator that comes despite it. While in the case of the Polish Constitutional Tribunal, human dignity is linked to essential preconditions of human fulfilment, the U.S. Supreme Court – at least in the cases cited earlier – associates it with respect for autonomy and life-shaping choices.[4] The feature common to both jurisdictions, however, is easy to observe: human dignity is being put to work in establishing, and justifying, the connection between the law and the human condition. Insofar as the above examples can be generalised (and I will argue that they can), it renders our reflection focused on *bridging the gap between law and the extra-legal human reality of critical significance.* One could call it a function, but we must bear in mind that human dignity has many functions that can be variously classified (and I will propose a classification in due course). This one, however, is here adopted as the *prima facie* function, giving guidance to the intended research procedure and its method. And this yields my first methodological commitment, namely, *the commitment to the human condition.* Note that this is distinguishable from a possible commitment to human nature. I assume that while human nature

4 For a comprehensive survey of how human dignity is applied by the Supreme Court of the United States, see Urbańczyk (2019).

might be important in providing an ultimate explanation of human dignity, what suffices at the level of the interpretation of law is the human condition – all that which determines our existence in the world, and which is important to us.

1.2 The problem of consensus and metaphysical parsimony in law

The critical difficulty that needs to be problematised as a consequence of the commitment to the human condition is the undeniable fact that there is no simple answer to the question of what precisely counts as human reality of the highest relevance for law. It is very often a matter of one's broader worldview, and that tends to vary. Admittedly, in certain cases, such as those of degrading treatment or extremely cruel punishment, there is not much room left for reasonable disagreement with regards to what counts as a violation of human dignity. But there are also other highly divisive issues: the scope and form of proper legal recognition of privacy, conscience, or social needs, to name a few examples. Legal arrangements concerning these matters (despite being embedded in constitutional doctrines and procedures) require political-axiological *decisions*. Thus, for better or worse, judges, legislators, and public administration authorities have found themselves in a position of necessity to make such decisions. How are we to determine if those decisions were right or not? This problem may be well illustrated by a case that was already mentioned. Recall that in *Obergefell v. Hodges*, the U.S. Supreme Court stated that denying a marriage license to same-sex couples 'serves to disrespect and subordinate them' (Supreme Court of the United States 2015, opinion, 22), and extended the fundamental, constitutional right to marry to same-sex couples, partly on dignitarian grounds. However, as Chief Justice Roberts points out in his dissent:

> It is striking how much of the majority's reasoning [i.e. the opinion of the Court] would apply with equal force to the claim of a fundamental right to plural marriage. If '[t]here is dignity in the bond between two men or two women who seek to marry and in their autonomy to make such profound choices,' *ante*, at 13, why would there be any less dignity in the bond between three people who, in exercising their autonomy, seek to make the profound choice to marry?
>
> (Supreme Court of the United States 2015, Roberts C.J., dissenting opinion, 20)

This passage, regardless of what one thinks about homosexual or polyamorous marriage, clearly shows the troublesome position into which anyone is put when striving for a systematic, self-constrained and compelling legal application of human dignity. How should an advocate of the majority's opinion respond to Roberts? And is there any procedure to determine whether or not these and similarly controversial cases transgressed the proper meaning of dignity or its legitimate application? Any conception of human dignity in law should be able to give at least some guidance on this question, if not some definite answers.

Now, one might tend to think of particular and sometimes rival conceptions of human dignity as nothing but particular and sometimes rival conceptions of the human being as such. This leads to a vision of human dignity as covering all or most aspects of human life that are worthy of respect, and all or most ways to achieve a good life or the right conduct. Consequently, the correctness of legal applications of human dignity would be heavily dependent on the adequacy of adopted thick anthropology (or metaphysics, or ethics). But if human dignity in the law were exactly this, the law would be founded on the job normally being done somewhere else – as part of philosophical, rather than legal, activity. There are good reasons to see this possible outcome as a problem.

The first reason is mainly prudential. Although law has to have some metaphysical and ethical foundations, there are different conceptions of these foundations themselves, as well as of their relations with, or influence on, law. At the same time, when evoking human dignity in the legal context, we normally want to *achieve consensus* rather than cultivate disagreement. Philosophical discussions on foundations should not impede the potential for consensus to be achieved in legal or political practice. This will be further referred to as the problem of consensus.

The problem of consensus has also a moral side: Respecting our fellows means, among other things, being ready to accept that they might not share our worldview and may have sound reasons for it. Many philosophers agree that as a result of the 'burdens of judgement', or the inescapable imperfection of our moral cognition, even perfectly reasonable persons may disagree (Rawls 2005, 54–7). General clauses in the law, such as 'human dignity', are very much prone to this kind of disagreement, as they are indeterminate and can be interpreted through the lenses of divergent intellectual traditions. Failing to recognise and respect this diversity, one may be easily accused of 'imposing arbitrary dogmatism' (Maritain 1966, 76), which is a charge particularly strong in the legal context.

The third reason is the most relevant one from the perspective of this chapter – the methodological status of anthropology (or metaphysics, or ethics) in the law is contestable. Speaking more precisely, there is no commonly accepted procedure of embedding ethical and metaphysical claims into the justification of legal decisions. Some people – such as hard positivists – reject the very idea of such embedment, at least in adjudication by courts (Raz 1996, 326–40). On the other hand, at least one tradition provides a clear vision of the close interlink between law and other domains of reasonable reflection: It is, of course, the natural law theory. Human dignity could be seen as the pinnacle of the natural law projects (most of the different versions of it), particularly in the context of human rights and basic liberties. As mentioned, the Polish Constitutional Tribunal regards human dignity as providing the interlink between the natural law and the posited law, and that judicial body is probably not the only one following this path. However, in my view, given the problem of consensus mentioned earlier, a theory of human dignity in the law should 'take a step back'. What I mean by this is that we can set aside (which is not equal to rejection!) the issue of natural law when conceptualising human dignity as foundational for law. More generally, linking human dignity to a particular tradition of thought, to strong metaphysical or ethical assumptions, or to thick conceptions of humanity, should be avoided (Tiedemann 2013, 29). This boils down to *metaphysical parsimony* as the second metaphysical commitment. The underlying hope is that an 'overlapping consensus' may be possible among different legal theories, which differ with regards to the broader philosophical background.

To sum up: Any responsible conception of human dignity should be able to provide some guidance in determining the correctness of its application in legal reasoning. The commitment to the human condition tells us that this correctness must have something in common with the figure of the human embedded in the law or influencing the law 'from the outside'. On the other hand, however, the guidance we expect must rest on something different from simply applying a wider metaphysical or ethical worldview to the legal questions. Given the prudential and moral concerns that the problem of consensus yields, metaphysical parsimony comes into play as a reasonable response.

1.3 *Law and reality*

One may have a justified concern that the preceding considerations have brought us into a self-defeating reasoning. If one expects a theory of human dignity to build bridges between the law and the human condition, some tools to talk about the latter are needed, and these tools seem to come from metaphysics, philosophical anthropology, or ethics. But this is precisely what metaphysical parsimony puts into doubt. The crucial question in this context is how to maintain the human condition as an important point of reference *despite* metaphysical parsimony, which appears indispensable in the context of modern law in the circumstances of pluralism, within and across jurisdictions. To ask the same question the other way round: How can we avoid arbitrariness or dogmatism and still apply human dignity as closely intertwined with the human condition and not just, say, as a merely legal, or purely formal, artefact of the person and her dignity?

The importance of the latter doubt becomes especially clear if we examine a quite common reaction to the problem of consensus: a full separation of legal concepts and their philosophical analogues. For the purposes of this discussion, I will call it *strong metaphysical parsimony*. According to this strategy, human dignity is treated as a technical term within a given legal system or jurisdiction. Despite its foundational role, as proponents of this approach argue, its content and meaning should draw no more than absolutely necessary from philosophical conceptions. A strong metaphysical parsimony is presented in a particularly clear way by Kirste (2013):

> Person is a functional term. It has to be understood within the respective normative system as a focal point for the aspiration and imputation of norms. Each normative system has different criteria for attributing the status of a person. These criteria are not dependent upon arguments from natural

> conditions or other normative systems. These persons are not created out of bones and flesh; their body consists of rights and duties.
>
> (Kirste 2013, 77)

In a sense, then, Kirste advocates for eschewing the philosophical or theological content from legal considerations. Although he acknowledges the fact that a lot of contemporary legal vocabulary has roots in theology and metaphysics, he argues that once those doctrines have been 'transformed into legal arguments', we should not exceed the borders of the legal text (Kirste 2013, 80). Following this line of thought, he proposes to conceive of human dignity as something born in, and sufficiently explained by, the legal realm. As a right, human dignity gives everyone power to demand recognition as a legal subject, or, in other words, the claim to 'recognition of the legal capacity of each human being' (Kirste 2013, 78). This clearly goes against my commitment to the human condition, which requires incorporation of flesh-and-blood personhood into legal interpretation, application, and theory. Kirste's approach is also remarkably minimalistic. Although human individuals are entitled to equal protection and various equal rights, their dignity itself is sufficiently respected just by recognising their status as legal persons (Kirste 2013, 81).

Strong metaphysical parsimony has undeniable advantages. Particularly, it secures *the independence* of legal theory from other spheres of inquiry. The legal realm remains neither fundamentally attached to nor conditioned by religious commitments, scientific findings, or philosophical speculation. In the case of human dignity, it also yields certain limits imposed on the interpretation of human dignity clauses, which may be a good thing. The 'inflationary' or 'arbitrary' application that may happen when putting one's philosophical commitments into law becomes less likely.

In my view, despite the advantages, such an approach cannot work. First and foremost, it does not properly take into consideration the factual applications of human dignity made in the law, which are considerably wider in scope and not ontologically minimalistic. In other words, the minimalism of strong metaphysical parsimony goes too far, against what real legal processes look like. As we saw with the Polish Constitutional Tribunal and the U.S. Supreme Court, human dignity is being used to justify divergent, and competing, rights, instead of just one right, as proposed by Kirste. Furthermore, it is widely considered not only as a right, but a constitutional value or principle – which actually precedes any possible recognition of a right to human dignity. As the literature shows, the manifold legal structure (value, principle, right) may be considered universal (see e.g. Barak 2013; Botha 2009; Daly 2013). Granted, it would be quite artificial to fully eliminate the value or the principle of human dignity from considerations. The German jurisprudence (generally, quite positivistic in tenor) also acknowledges human dignity as a general constitutional principle that has a wide range of applications with regard to ultimate questions of human life and integrity (Dreier 2004, 171–202). In sum, even a quick glance at the factual legal processes shows that the law evokes human dignity as intertwined with the human condition, or at least different vital aspects of it. And the commitment to the human condition cannot merge with metaphysical parsimony in the strong version.

Another problem that strong metaphysical parsimony faces is that it is normatively inconclusive. If the notion of the human person as bearer of dignity is fully a legal artifice, there is no further guidance on what duties or rights that person should bear. Thereby, the problem of arbitrariness is not resolved but merely moved elsewhere: instead of debating on what constitutes the core of, and what is only a secondary conclusion from, human dignity, we engage in similarly indeterminate discourse on what counts as the indispensable implication of legal personhood. As it has been compellingly argued, the persistence of deep disagreements with regard to practical principles is grounded, among other things, in the *'opposing images of humanity'* (Knoll 2019, 42, emphasis original). Legal authorities, when applying basic practical principles, endorse, at least implicitly, a certain figure of humanity – one simply cannot escape it. Thus, if there is any hope of resolving the problem of consensus, the concepts of the legal and the real human person should be considered in interaction, not in separation.

Creating a gap between the legal and the real personhood bears another even more fundamental problem: an inability to determine who (or what) counts as persons. Should law treat all biological humans as subjects, or only those with fully developed capacities? And if all humans, then why not non-human animals, or robots? In the present day, computer algorithms are capable of fulfilling only relatively simple tasks involving interpersonal interaction, such as advertising a product or scheduling a meeting (Google Duplex 2018). But these already constitute a *legally relevant behaviour*. What should we then do about the reality that is very likely to come in the near future – robots capable of negotiating and drafting contracts, for example? The debate over the 'electronic personality' is already being held by the European Parliament (Delcker 2018), as well as among scholars. One argument against conferring a 'human-like' legal status on self-learning machines would be the following: what appears to be 'artificial agents' is in fact something critically different, that is, abstract patterns of imitating human behaviour (Steiger 2021 argues this compellingly, drawing on Michael Polanyi). On the other hand, however, a legal fiction of treating companies as legal persons has long been in place and has proven useful, and no one would reasonably oppose this idea in the contemporary world. So it is a possibility that another legal fiction of robotic legal agents would do more good than harm (Wojtczak 2021). These are crucially important issues that will have massive consequences for the legal realm and beyond. But to engage in a dispute about them, one must ask what constitutes *genuine personhood*, and what *humanity* means for the law. And that clearly requires going beyond the boundaries set by the strong metaphysical parsimony. Of course, one might argue that determining the criteria for legal personhood and legal capacity is left entirely to the discretion of the lawgiver, as a purely conventional matter. But this assumes an arbitrariness that was itself probably one of the main motivations to separate the legal and the moral person.

Taking these for granted, we may seem to be standing against a hopeless dilemma – *strong metaphysical parsimony* versus *arbitrary dogmatism and moralising law*. But I argue that we can kill the two birds with one stone: Theorise human dignity at the intersection of the legal and the natural–moral personhood in a self-constraining manner. The guiding idea is to base the theory of human dignity on *some important truths about persons, but not the whole truth about persons*, and to examine what this tells us about the law. Again, the result of the latter inquiry is not intended to cover the whole truth about law as such, but rather some important aspects of the legal phenomena under scrutiny. This leads us to the third methodological commitment I will adopt, which can be called *the commitment to sceptical realism*. According to sceptical realism, law and reality are not completely separate spheres: It is assumed that certain facts and circumstances in the real world should influence both making and interpreting law. On the other hand, sceptical realism neither requires nor presupposes the full knowledge about these circumstances or the ultimate explanation of legal, or legally relevant, facts. Therefore, a sceptical version of realism is unlikely to lead to a clash of metaphysical doctrines. If metaphysics is understood as a philosophical endeavour to provide *ultimate explanations*, or the whole truth about the world, sceptical realism adheres to metaphysical parsimony, although in the *weak* sense. Propositions or assumptions about persons that are implicit in the law (such as the autonomy of the legal agent, for example) are considered to be sensible, and true or false. Regardless of their being true or false, they may have different ultimate explanations, coming from religion, philosophical speculation, or science. And it is the ultimate explanations, not the propositions themselves, that should be avoided in law, according to sceptical realism and weak metaphysical parsimony.

In my view, the tension between metaphysical parsimony and commitment to the human condition can be resolved if the former is conceived as *weak metaphysical parsimony*, which avoids engaging ultimate explanations and the whole truth into the legal discourse. At the same time, it allows us to seek ontological explanations – they may be called *pro tanto* explanations, as opposed to *ultimate* explanations sought by metaphysics. This is what makes my case of metaphysical parsimony *weak*. Certain ontological commitments, that is, beliefs affirming the truth of certain propositions, such as the proposition saying that persons exist, and that their action has such and such structure, are considered to be relevant for law.[5] Law cannot work in an ontological vacuum.[6] For example, certain

5 The notion of ontological commitment has itself a rich history that starts with Willard Quine and unfolds in many debates at a highly technical level (Bricker 2016). For our purposes, the intuitive understanding of 'ontological commitment' that I just presented is sufficient.

6 Obviously, not everyone would agree with this claim. In the context of a specific debate, that concerning legal personhood, Ngaire Naffine identifies a strand in thinking characteristic of 'Legalists'. According to that strand, being a legal person is not determined by natural features (Naffine 2009, 21). In more general terms, some forms of legal positivism insist that there are no links of necessity between the legal and the extra-legal realities. This book will argue against such contentions.

findings of contemporary neuroscience suggest that in fact there are no such things as persons, in the classical sense of the word. If this were true, it would entail a necessity, in the long run at least, of the fundamental redefinition or perhaps even annihilation of human dignity as traditionally conceived both philosophically and legally. Human beings have been considered to be of special status or worth by virtue of having certain characteristics that transcend the naturalist-biological determinants. Without these characteristics being real, humanity's special status would be nothing more than institutionalised speciesism. The proponents of strong metaphysical parsimony will not agree with the latter statement. For them, what is decisive is the law itself. If determinate legal rules prohibit or require certain types of action toward human beings who have received a status of legal subjects, then one can say that the law is committed to human dignity independently of what humans really are. I think this will not do. For instance, if it is definitely proven that there is no free will, and human behaviour boils down to movements determined by exactly the same laws as movements of rocks or butterflies, then dignity is not only an artefact – it is a fiction. The obvious exigencies of morality and basic rationality will tell us the same – law cannot, in the long run, be based on commonly known fictions.[7] For this reason, certain propositions about human reality that make human dignity intelligible have to be treated as true, or rather as *making claims to truth*. We might have good reasons to assume they are true unless the opposite is proven, but once this happens, we must review our legal theories accordingly. This attitude may be distinguished as another methodological commitment, namely, a *commitment to sceptical realism*. Whereas the strong metaphysical parsimony eschews the general, non-legal facts about the world and the human being to the greatest possible extent, the *weak* metaphysical parsimony combined with sceptical realism invite us to form beliefs about facts, and treat them as relevant, *pro tanto* explanations. In short, sceptical realism is a commitment that urges us to take the ontological commitments of the law one examines seriously, being open to revising them when there is strong proof against them. Weak metaphysical parsimony imposes limits on such realism – it invites only these contentions or beliefs that are really indispensable to make sense of the law one examines.

The important implication of the latter postulate is the following: A legal theory of human dignity should be independent from non-legal disciplines or fields of

7 This contention should not be conflated with any strong assumptions about the nature of law. Particularly, it does not mean that the law, by its very nature, converges, or ought to converge, with the real nature of all things it regulates (for example, that the 'forest' as defined for the purposes of the law must converge with the real nature of forests). Quite to the contrary: Sceptical realism, especially when merged with weak metaphysical parsimony, could be consistent with a completely opposite view; that is, some form of conventionalism saying that law is a social artefact. The only claim here would be that the architecture of law-as-mere-artefact must still somehow fit to the external reality. An artefact such as a knife must be sharp enough to cut things we want it to cut. Likewise, the law must keep some form of concurrence with the things it is aimed to regulate or coordinate.

inquiry, in terms of having its own sources and methods. To explain: In Christian (or Jewish or, to some extent, Muslim) theology and revelation, human dignity is grounded in the doctrine of *imago Dei*, according to which man was created by God in His own image and likeness. It certainly constitutes a strong ultimate explanation of human dignity. But one should ask: What is the status of the *imago Dei* proposition within the law? If it functions as a necessary condition of the rights and principles derived from human dignity, then the truth of Revelation, or at least a belief in this truth, is a necessary component of legal arrangements of utmost importance, such as basic liberties. This, arguably, is an unwelcome consequence not only for unbelievers, but for everyone, even if the Revelation is true. The reason for this is that the commitment to Revelation is a matter of faith rather than of law. Human dignity in the law should be independent from religious commitments, that is, possible to derive from other (terrestrial) premises, and analysed in its own terms to be found within laws or jurisprudence. The best way to achieve this sort of independence is to allow the law to *speak for itself* – to listen to what the law says first, and then try to interpret it.

So far I have not referred to my own theory of human dignity in the law – the Status of Personhood Theory. Although it is not yet the proper time to introduce it, I should disclose that in the subsequent chapters I will claim that the SPT – a theory that refers to the reality of the person as an integral whole, and that draws full consequences thereof in the interpretation of the law – pursues the three methodological commitments in the most adequate way. Thereby, the SPT will be presented as neither a fully-fledged metaphysical account nor a natural law account. Rather, the theory will be defended on the slippery slope between the two 'extremes', conflating law with metaphysics, theology, or ethics on the one hand, and establishing a total separation of law and human reality on the other. In what follows in this chapter, I will make a further methodological ground. But the SPT will not yet be of direct concern there, and one should suppose that there are different conceptions also meeting the methodological criteria. Nonetheless, I think it is better to disclose that the background view is that of personalism.

2 Defining and explicating human dignity in the law

Having identified the *prima facie* function of human dignity which leads to basic methodological commitments (the human condition, weak metaphysical parsimony, and sceptical realism), we can now move forward. To recall: in this chapter, I will not be striving to achieve any particular conception of human dignity. Instead, I will present some basic methodological rules that in my view should be followed in any conception. At first, one should reflect on the very *concept* of human dignity: What type of concept are we working with, and what are its most general characteristics? This brings the problem of what *definition*, if any, is possible and needed in the case of human dignity. I will argue that one should strive for an explicative definition, the methodology of which is another part of this section.

2.1 *The questions of definition*

Definitions are common in science and in law, serving a similar purpose in both – refining ordinary language, avoiding fuzziness of the words that we use, and securing cohesiveness and predictability of our (legal or scientific) activity. Defining human dignity may thus seem an attractive thing to do. However, the concept itself, and the history of its use, bears critical difficulties that put the very possibility of providing a satisfactory definition into serious doubt. Recall that a traditional, full definition of a term is perfectly adequate, which means that the *definiens* (expression defining the term in question) may replace the defined term (*definiendum*) at all times; I will call these 'equivalency definitions'. A definition of 'square' in geometry, for example, which would be 'regular quadrilateral', is an equivalency definition, because having four equal sides and four equal angles is common to all squares, and to squares only. What is more, this definition provides a set of sharp criteria of applicability to the *definiendum*. Not only is the expression 'a square' equated by 'a regular quadrilateral', but also the latter points out at common characteristics which constitute *necessary and sufficient* conditions for using the term. Such adequacy and clarity is impossible in the case of concepts that have more complex meaning, are connected to emotions, evoke values, or depend on social practices and cultural contexts. Such concepts are often employed as central in humanities, social sciences, and jurisprudence. 'Beauty', 'art', 'law', or 'justice' constitute just a few examples. In these and similar cases, it is impossible to build a *definiens* that would always be perfectly equivalent to its *definiendum*. Despite this fact, there are still good reasons to employ one common term with regards to different, but *somehow similar*, objects or processes. These objects or processes, instead of sharing a set of exclusively common characteristics that would determine their definition, share features only in an overlapping or crisscrossing way. This was famously called 'family resemblances' by Wittgenstein in *Philosophical Investigations* – his famous example was that of a game.[8] Developing this, some speak of concepts that have 'family-type meaning', which is open-ended, more or less blurry, and often changing over time. At the same time, some authors argue, the usage of these concepts is not completely arbitrary and may be subject to scholarly examination (Pawłowski 1980a, 23–53).

8 As Wittgenstein wrote:

> 66. Consider, for example, the activities that we call "games". I mean board-games, card-games, ball-games, athletic games, and so on. What is common to them all? – Don't say: "They must have something in common, or they would not be called 'games'" but look and see whether there is anything common to all. – For if you look at them, you won't see something that is common to all, but similarities, affinities, and a whole series of them at that. (Wittgenstein 2009, 36[e])

In this sense, Wittgenstein says that different objects we call by some the same name do not constitute a rigidly defined class; the boundaries of a term are blurred, and what we point at when using the same term is similarity or affinity rather than a set of common characteristics.

In this vein, Ronald Dworkin argues that moral and legal discourse works chiefly with interpretative, as opposed to criterial, concepts. Using interpretative concepts requires no common criteria or a shared decision procedure determining their content in every crucial aspect. Instead, 'their correct application is fixed by the best interpretation of the practices in which they figure' (Dworkin 2011, 158). The latter is naturally debatable and open to persistent disagreement, and so is the content of interpretative concepts. We share a criterial concept of a square, for example, only insofar as we share criteria of its use – having four equal sides and four equal angles. We share an interpretative concept of justice not only when agreeing about the proper set of its principles, but also when engaging in a discourse of what is just and unjust and reaching no common conclusion. This is possible because despite disagreement with regards to specific principles of justice, we ascribe the same or similar functions to justice itself, and we are likely to agree at least about some 'paradigm cases' (everyone would agree that the Nuremberg Laws during the Nazi rule in Germany were gravely unjust, for example). According to Dworkin, our discourse on justice amounts to trying to find the most reasonable, true interpretation of the practices of justice and its paradigm cases. Although, in my view, a lot of Dworkin's moral epistemology is mistaken, his distinction between criterial and interpretative concepts tells us something important about the majority of concepts that are used as crucial in jurisprudence and legal activities. It is also true of the concept of human dignity, which appears to have these two crucial features: a family-type meaning, and an interpretative nature. And this puts the 'defining' issue into an unsecured position.

Even a short glance at different usages will confirm this. In Cicero, for example, dignity may be attached to the respect associated with an office, as well as reverence toward the virtue of temperance (for a helpful selection of Cicero's texts, see Lebech 2019, 27–55). For medieval philosophers, dignity is sometimes attached neither to virtue nor to office, but rather to the human condition itself (as stated in an anonymous treaty, *De dignitate conditionis humanae*, available in Lebech 2019, 75–80). In modern times, philosophers commonly understand dignity as the worth beyond all price (Kant 1998, 42), although the more contemporary accounts associate it with basic capabilities (Nussbaum 2008) or with the particular vulnerability of human beings that exposes them to humiliation (Margalit 1996). In the law and legal discourse, human dignity is regarded as a source of rights (a special property or status that each human being inviolably enjoys), or as imposing a negative duty of respecting a citizen's privacy, or as a positive duty to provide decent working conditions, to name only a few examples. The next section of this chapter will provide some details, and it will become obvious that a project of seeking one equivalency definition of human dignity must be wrongheaded, given the complexity and extreme richness of its meaning. In seeking to achieve a conception of human dignity, one must bear in mind the complexity of the web of the relevant ideas.

However, a family-type meaning and interpretative nature does not have to entail that no definition of human dignity is possible whatsoever. This would mean that there is no possibility of providing any criteria of its use, and, as a consequence, the term itself is too blurry to be of any scientific or scholarly use. But we are not that hopeless, in my view at least: an equivalence definition is nowadays only one among the commonly accepted types of definitions. In 1936, Rudolf Carnap famously argued that even the relatively simple predicate 'soluble in water' cannot be fully defined (there is no equivalency definition), and that it may be introduced merely through 'reduction sentences', in a non-universal, conditioned way (Carnap 1936, 443). The important impact of Carnap's paper (regardless of whether he was right or not about 'soluble in water') is that, as a reaction to his observation, other scholars proposed to *extend the very notion of definition*, and to allow 'partial definitions' that do not require equivalence between the *definiendum* and the *definiens.* Despite lacking universal criteria of applicability, those definitions may be used in case of fuzzy concepts, and make some instances of their usage sensible (Przełęcki 1958). Quite unsurprisingly, definitions of this type have been an object of particularly strong focus in the humanities and social sciences, as a possible way of defining concepts with a family-type meaning (Pawłowski 1980b, 125–56). Although Dworkin would probably not approve, I contend that partial definitions can be put to work also in dealing with interpretative concepts. Logical structures of partial definitions may vary. Setting the particulars aside, suffice it to say that instead of providing necessary and sufficient conditions of using the term (as equivalence definitions do), in the case of partial definitions only a sufficient, or only a necessary, condition is provided. In other words, they give some guidance on what the *definiendum* means, but they do not claim that it may be properly used *if and only if* the criteria set in the *definiens* are met.

As an example, let us consider the notion of 'world music'. Since the genre is eclectic, and the used term is fuzzy, our best hope with regards to its definition is to find some overlapping or crisscrossing elements characteristic of world music that are observable, say, in a particular set of records. We may legitimately use the term 'world music' according to the adopted definition and referring to those records, bearing in mind that the future research on the genre, or the development of the genre itself, may bring other definitions supplementing, modifying, or even nullifying our own – there is no universal and exclusive meaning of 'world music'. A partial definition is initially supposed to work only in a particular context or at a certain stage of research. Partial definitions may be thus provisional and open-ended, and may not provide perfectly sharp criteria for using the defined term. But that does not make them useless: they may provide the basic semantic core of the concept, or make our conceptions more consistent and self-restraining, which gives hope of progress in the research. 'Human dignity' and 'world music' may have a lot in common in this particular respect. And the best available option in defining human dignity is a partial definition, or a set of such definitions. With no definition at hand, any conception of human dignity could be prone to falling into nonsense.

However, the question of defining human dignity is even more complicated, for one reason: It is a legal term. The obvious, albeit troublesome, feature of legal language is the *normative* component inevitably coming into play: Legal norms forbid or authorise or require certain actions. Sometimes they do not regulate actions directly, but constitute conditions under which legal subjects enjoy power to demand something. All these authorisations or requirements are *hypothetical*, and thus the definitions used in law do not typically aim at *description*; rather, they are part of a *prescriptive utterance*. We can imagine a case in which a property was bought in 1967, in a remote forest, and since then nobody, including the owner, has performed any action that relates to that piece of land – and yet, the legal powers which constitute the ownership spectrum are still there; tacit, but granted and protected by the law. In this sense, there is no real-world object that could be called 'a property right'. Contrast this with the notion of 'property relations' that can be defined and examined by social science or economics as factual processes in a society. The very structure of definition seems to require something that social sciences have and legal sciences seem to lack, namely, an empirical object to be defined. Despite this apparent logical difficulty, in many jurisdictions (particularly those of civil law tradition), we often find a statutory definition of property appearing in a civil code. The explanation of this would be that law refers to facts indirectly, by setting standards and rules that are subsequently applied to real-life situations.

The hypothetical nature of legal language becomes particularly important in *testing* definitions – one should ask: What criteria, other than formal correctness, should be applied to assess definitions used in the legal text or discourse? The answer to this question will vary depending on who is defining. The situation is relatively simple when a definition is provided directly by a lawmaker. These definitions cannot be 'inadequate' in a sense in which those in natural or social science can be: When a particular meaning of a legal term is stipulated by the law itself, *the lawmaker is generally free to construct whatever definition he pleases*. For example, when a statutory definition of 'a building' is introduced, the purpose is to fix terms for administrative or tax law, and not to discover what 'building' really is. On the other hand, if for some reason the law provided a definition that would authorise officials to qualify as buildings something normally considered a mere installation (scarecrows, for instance), it would probably cause legitimate indignation or even disobedience, possibly on legal, and certainly on common-sense, grounds. The real essence of objects, or at least the linguistic practice outside the law, is therefore of some concern in legislation, despite the general freedom that the legislator enjoys.

The situation changes significantly when judges or scholars adopt a definition of a term that is not defined in the legal text. Judges rarely produce definitions explicitly, but they must work with them at least in an implicit way when interpreting the law they apply. Although there may be different variations among jurisdictions and doctrines, *judges are generally considered to be bound by the legal texts* (a broader normative context of the terms to be defined, and their ordinary meaning), as well as the basic *intent of the legislator*, should there be one possible to decode. On the other hand, especially when the legal text points at open-ended concepts or values, judges are considered to have some freedom to adjust the content of the provisions to the changing conditions in society. These issues, however, evoke theories of the judiciary, and theories of legal interpretation, and won't be examined at this moment (Greenawalt 2018 offers a helpful synthesis). What is of my direct interest now is the situation of a legal scholar, which is the situation of the least freedom compared to legislators and judges. When examining law from a scholarly perspective, one needs to take into account not only the legal text and its context, but also the practical legal (juridical and other) processes that apply the term one aims at defining. A scholar is therefore prone to producing 'inadequate' definition, when some important legal usage is disregarded: The definitions offered by a scholar should be assessed through the lenses of the legal texts and the legal practice. This is particularly important in the case of open-ended terms, those of family-type meaning and interpretative nature. And that is what 'human dignity' is like.

Taking the preceding for granted, I argue that the only sensible way of defining 'human dignity' in the legal sphere is that of explication. Explication is a procedure in which *an explicandum* (the term to be defined) is replaced by the *explicatum* (containing a conception and definition of *explicandum*). *Explicative definitions* are those which take the pre-existing usage into account (the reconstructive aspect) but at the same time strive to refine that usage and 'regulate' the terms so that they fit into a more general theory, which is their stipulative, and possibly critical, aspect (Gupta 2019). The *explicatum* is more exact and typically narrower in sense and extension. For example, the non-scientific term 'fish', once referring broadly to any animal living in water, was explicated by zoology; hence, 'Piscis' or 'fish' as a scientific term (*explicatum*) is much more precise (the set of criteria is based on systematic biological knowledge) and excludes certain creatures commonly called 'fish' before the explication (Carnap 1962, 6). Similar procedures can be applied in jurisprudence. Of course, given the interpretative nature of most concepts in jurisprudence, the result will not be as precise as it is in zoology. But there is at least a possibility of identifying some 'whales' that are not 'fish' along the way. The chapters that follow will be devoted to providing a careful, *personalist explication of human dignity*, and defending it as the best interpretation of some important extra-legal truths about human persons. In my view, one should do it with a view to the practice of legal authorities, by interpreting their use of language. We should now take a closer look at the procedure of explication fitting this particular purpose.

2.2 *The rules of explication*

The procedure of explication was originally proposed by Rudolf Carnap, as fitted for natural sciences working with scientific laws and theories in the strict sense, and he would probably not regard the explication I am planning to make as a sensible one (Carnap 1962). Nevertheless, Tadeusz Pawłowski argued that, after some adjustments, explication is also a legitimate procedure in the humanities and social sciences, and I am taking his views as a basis for the inquiry. My own modifications will consist of what is required by the peculiarity of legal sciences. According to Pawłowski (and Carnap), explication is a procedure that consists of the following steps: (i) choosing the *explicandum*; (ii) stating the research problem and providing a tentative clarification of the *explicandum*; (iii) transforming, refining, and replacing the *explicandum* by its precise reformulation, which takes the form of *explicatum*; and (iv) including the *explicatum* into the system of concepts and propositions, replacing the *explicandum*. (similarly: Pawłowski 1980b, 160–1). I will now briefly comment on those steps and the rules I am adopting for the explication that is to come in the subsequent chapters.

1. The chosen *explicandum* is of course 'human dignity', alongside all linguistically related expressions, as they appear in international law and constitutional documents (including but not limited to 'dignity of man', 'dignity of the human person', 'personal dignity', or 'dignity of the members of the human family'). I will also take into consideration situations when 'dignity' appears without the qualification 'human', particularly in private law, labour law, penal law, or procedural law in different jurisdictions. To be sure, it is not bare legal texts that are of interest, but the law in action and interpretation. Although the relation between instances of dignity in different legal spheres is far from clear, I am assuming that they may have something in common, or refer to some common foundation. Therefore, an *explicatum* that helps to integrate these different instances is considered better than one that does not. In order to combine a relatively wide view with simplicity, I will focus on the law in selected countries, which is in force at the moment of writing.

2. Although the *explicandum* is obviously fuzzy (which is the reason we start the very procedure), a tentative clarification should be provided as a starting point, before commencing the explication itself, to avoid the whole discourse being futile or misleading. Referring to this, Carnap wrote:

> It seems to me that, in raising problems of analysis or explication, philosophers very frequently violate this requirement. They ask questions like: 'What is causality?', 'What is life?', 'What is mind?', 'What is justice?', etc. Then they often immediately start to look for an answer without first examining the tacit assumption that the terms of the question are at least practically clear enough to serve as a basis for an investigation, for an analysis or explication.
> (Carnap 1962, 4)

Having worries similar to these, I must clarify what is the subject of investigations and what is the problem to be resolved. As I stated earlier, I think that human dignity serves as a bridge between the human condition and the law. This is a function and a meaning that not only *allows* but also *requires* explication. Thereby, I reject understandings of human dignity as a non-interpreted thesis or a placeholder. Broadly speaking, these accounts argue that human dignity is best understood when treated as a kind of mystery; something we all acknowledge despite no universally shared meaning being available.[9] This is not a proper moment to engage in a detailed discussion with the placeholder argument. For now, suffice it to say that the practices related to human dignity, *including* the adjudication of basic rights, have gone further than simply treating dignity as an empty space that should not be filled in authoritatively by legal actors. Rather, courts and other bodies recurrently associate human dignity clauses with concrete content, as a particularly weighty reason for their decisions (Baruah 2014, 337). Although these applications (within and among jurisdictions) are obviously far from consistent, it seems that courts will not simply cease to employ human dignity in this extensive way. It seems therefore reasonable to seek an explication that attempts to integrate these different usages and sort them out. In what follows, I will refer to the numerous (implicit and explicit) manifestations of dignity in the law as 'the dignitarian moment in the law'. Section 3 will be fully devoted to the task of mapping the dignitarian moment, which will be equivalent to a tentative clarification of our *explicandum*. The task of interpreting it further, along with an explication that helps to sort it out, is left to the subsequent chapters.

3. As already noted, the theory I am going to defend in this book is personalist in nature. At the heart of this theory lies the *explicatum* I will propose: *the Principle of the Status of Personhood (the PSP)*. To be sure, the rich family meaning of our *explicandum* is open to many alternative explications (dignity as fundamental value, as integrity, as autonomy, as vulnerability, as capabilities, to name examples). However, my explication will not consider these as necessarily rival, but rather as criss-crossing, and open to a reasonable integration in one theory, in our case, in the SPT. Although the PSP will be stipulated as a merely partial definition, it will be considered the focal idea that points at the most fundamental aspect of human dignity in law, and thus an especially important *explicatum* among many possible alternatives. The procedure itself is a task of Chapter 3. Here I will outline the most important rules and requirements.

As stated before, human dignity as a concept has a family-type meaning and is of an interpretative nature. Let us now briefly consider what that means for its explication. Some concepts in law are criterial. Again, the definition of a 'building' in administrative law may be considered an example. Polish law stipulates that a 'building' is a construction object which is permanently connected to the ground, separated in spatial terms by means of building partitions, with foundations and a roof (Building Law Act [Poland] 1994, Article 3). This definition provides a set of characteristics common to all buildings and only to buildings, for the purposes of the law. Some problems with applying such notions to practice may arise – for example, wooden cabins in some forms could constitute

9 As Dreier points out, the author of the expression 'non-interpreted thesis' was Theodor Heuss, who became president of West Germany shortly after the Basic Law came into effect (Dreier 2004, 166). The idea of human dignity as a placeholder is more recent. In a seminal paper, Christopher McCrudden argued that while playing important institutional roles, human dignity is in itself unable to guide adjudication of human rights (2008).

borderline cases of the proper application of the term 'building', and their status could be thus uncertain. But the law possesses a quite clear equivalency definition that is also relatively sharp. The explication of such a term would be quite simple: it would suffice to refer to the ordinary language use (perhaps with the help of a dictionary), and pieces of relevant legal interpretation by courts (although courts in Poland do not have the power to make new law, they set informal standards of interpretation that determine the meaning and application of statutes). Unfortunately, such a smooth procedure is not possible when it comes to human dignity: It is a different type of concept, and therefore different rules must be applied.

A legal term considerably different in nature would be that of 'reasonable care' that appears in the context of the tort of negligence, known to English common law. In the famous case heard by the House of Lords of the United Kingdom, *Donoghue v. Stevenson*, Lord Atkin stated the following:

> You must take reasonable care to avoid acts or omissions which you can reasonably foresee would be likely to injure your neighbour. Who, then, in law is my neighbour? The answer seems to be – persons who are so closely and directly affected by my act that I ought reasonably to have them in contemplation as being so affected when I am directing my mind to the acts or omissions which are called in question.
>
> (House of Lords 1932, 562)

As we see, Lord Atkin defines the duty of (reasonable) care that is a prerequisite of negligence liability. 'Reasonable care' is here closely intertwined with the 'neighbour test'. But what exactly does 'being reasonable' mean, and who counts as those 'closely and directly' affected by my actions? The criteria to determine these definitions are not simply descriptive: they involve *an application of an evaluative standard*. It is a feature that was absent in the case of applying the Polish definition of a building – in the latter case, it suffices to check the simple criteria that specify whether something is or is not a building. In order to determine what counts as reasonable care, on the other hand, one needs not only to check whether certain actions have been undertaken, but also whether enough care and prudence was shown in these actions. When using a term such as 'reasonable care' in the legal practice, one must therefore make an assessment with regards to a relevant standard one considers minimal in a particular case. The assessment is always 'provisional' in the sense that it is meant to be relevant with regards to the facts of a specific case. So, in terms of definitions, it is certainly a partial definition we will deal with here. In some legal contexts, 'human dignity' can be quite similar to 'reasonable care' in many respects. For example, the European Convention of Human Rights stipulates that '[n]o one shall be subjected to torture or to inhuman or degrading treatment or punishment' (ECHR 1950, Article 3). If we agree that this norm implicitly pertains to and protects human dignity (Webster 2011), then a similar evaluation is to be made when answering what amounts to a violation of duty of care as well as of human dignity. For the purposes of our inquiry, we can call concepts such as 'reasonable care' or 'degrading treatment' *criterial and evaluative.* Simpler concepts, such as 'building', are *criterial and descriptive*, and thus their content may be stipulated by equivalency definitions. Evaluative concepts, by contrast, can be defined only partially and always require some broader social context. Although they are still criterial, the assessment of the criteria requires interpretation. Hence, one may say that such concepts are borderline cases between criterial and interpretative concepts. Human dignity in some instances, such as prohibition of degrading treatment, is precisely like this.

Some legal expressions are even more complicated in structure. What I mean here are open-ended constitutional provisions referring, for instance, to equality, liberty, or justice. Those and similar concepts are *par excellence* interpretive: they evoke values that are best understood as lying at the intersection of morality, politics, and law. Generally speaking, no value of this kind functions only within its own terms: to make judgements about one of them, there is always a need to look into other related values. This inevitably involves not only *evaluation*, but also *philosophising*. Ronald Dworkin strikes me as right when saying that philosophising in the practical realm (which he calls conceptual interpretation) consists in attempts at 'forming a mutually supportive network of moral values' (Dworkin 2011, 184). There is no answer as to what constitutes religious freedom without a value judgement about religion and its place in human life; there is no answer as to what equality demands from public institutions without a simultaneous judgement with regards to the weight and scope of economic freedom; and *there is no answer as to what human dignity amounts to without a vision of humanness and its honourable manifestations.* The latter is true in most cases, as I will argue, and it makes the task of explicating human dignity difficult but not hopeless. On the one hand, it involves an interdisciplinary reflection, but on the other, it should adhere to weak metaphysical parsimony. In other words, to explicate human dignity in the law, one needs to engage with broader issues examined by anthropology and ethics, but it must be done with recurrent reference to the existing law. One should be careful not to impute some normative or ontological claims that come entirely from the outside of the law.

What exactly would such an explication look like? Certainly, starting from philosophy and then simply trying to match it with law would be futile: This approach does not legitimise the connection of philosophical and legal visions of human dignity but simply assumes it, against weak metaphysical parsimony. Therefore, the procedure of explication needs to start with the law. The philosophical component should be used only *insofar as it can be reasonably expected to provide an ample explanation of the legal substrate.* Therefore, the inquiry that I am pursuing starts with identifying the dignitarian moment in the law; it then moves to setting forth the philosophical background that I regard as providing an adequate foundation to the dignitarian moment; finally, it merges the two spheres by working up a juridical explication of *human dignity as the status of personhood*, as part of the SPT conception. Those tasks will be fulfilled respectively in Section 3 of this chapter (identifying the dignitarian moment in law), in Chapter 2 (containing the crucial insights into human personhood and dignity), and in Chapter 3 (the explication of human dignity in law as the PSP).

4. Sometimes including the *explicatum* into a theory is quite obvious and spontaneous (as including the *explicatum* 'Piscis' into zoology probably was). But this is not the case in jurisprudence or theory of law. In order to set forth the theoretical purpose that is served by the status of personhood, we need to consider this aspect separately. One problem appearing at first glance is that there is no such thing as 'theory of law' in the strict sense applied in natural sciences. Rather, there are multiple, simultaneous, and rival 'theories' of law, but 'theory' is meant here quite loosely, as a system of concepts and propositions referring to the nature or purposes of law. What should be done about this fact? After all, explication is something we do to enhance our theory of something. Are we then bound to choose one theory of law we want to enhance? Recall that I have explicitly refused to make a commitment to a particular legal theory, and I am going to maintain this. Chapter 3 will strive to maintain that the SPT can fit in many rival theories – or, in other words, that many rival theories of law must (and some of them already implicitly do) take the status of personhood into account. This means establishing the close relations of law and morality, and hence some form of non-positivism, but not in a form that would be acceptable only to a natural law theory.

In the face of this, our task resembles 'conceptual interpretation' as envisaged by Dworkin: It consists in developing a system or web of interrelated concepts and claims (Dworkin 2011, 157–188). Following this Dworkinian thought, human dignity as the Principle of the Status of Personhood will be grasped with other accompanying ideas. Unlike Dworkin, however, I will not develop an exhaustive system or a complete theory of law, morals, and politics. Although such work could, and perhaps should, be done, the direct aims of our explication are less demanding. Chapter 3 will present what the PSP entails for the law, but this will be done in terms of what the law does, and should further do, vis-à-vis the fact of human personhood. In addition to that, Chapter 4 will explore some possibilities of developing these insights in the broader institutional-political sphere, but I will pursue only a limited programme of such extension.

3 The dignitarian moment in the law

We have focused first on the issues of defining and explication, for one simple reason: Without a more or less sharp concept at hand, the whole inquiry is doubtful. However, explication is not the ultimate aim of the inquiry, and it is not the whole story. Quite the contrary: A successful completion of the explication procedure is a moment at which the story *begins*. After all, scientific concepts are not ends in themselves – they are heuristic tools to serve some purpose that is external to them. Likewise, the PSP is meant not only to be explicated and acknowledged, but also to be used in saying something important about law. Namely, I will claim that the PSP helps to *explain* and *sort out* the numerous appeals to human dignity and dignitarian commitments that I call 'the dignitarian moment'. Thus, I will claim that the PSP is a legal principle by which legal institutions respond, or should respond, to something real about persons. In this sense, my theory makes a claim to truth. This thought will be developed in due course, mostly in

Chapters 3 and 4. Therefore, the dignitarian moment I will set forth in this section has a twofold status: On the one hand, it serves as a basis for explication of human dignity in the law. On the other, it is a phenomenon that itself is to be properly interpreted and explained.

In what follows in this section, I will present a typology of most characteristic uses of human dignity which may be observed in law. At this stage (and for quite some time in this book), I will be ignoring the issue of what is the proper legal category for human dignity in the law. As we will see, it appears as a right in itself, as a foundation for rights, as a legal value, or as a legal principle. For now, we have no other choice but to let that cacophony sound. Only as late as in Chapter 3 will I be able to sort out the issue of the proper legal category, and give my reasons to treat human dignity primarily as a principle.

As in every typology, the functions and aspects of dignity I will characterise will overlap with each other. I will be brief, since most of what I will discuss is to be found in studies made by others. The functions of human dignity that I think can be identified, apart from the *prima facie* function that I already mentioned (bridging between the human condition and the law), are the foundational, the regulatory, the heuristic, and the meta-legal. This multiplicity amounts to the dignitarian moment. I will refer to different legal systems to emphasise that this phenomenon transcends the particularity of legal cultures. Although the details, scope, and factual observance must vary among legal systems (a more detailed comparison is a task for another study), the commitment to human dignity is a widely shared phenomenon. That is why some scholars talk about an emerging overlapping consensus on the meaning of human dignity in the law (May and Daly 2020, 40–57)

3.1 The foundational function

The idea that is perhaps most commonly associated with human dignity is that it is somehow *foundational to the political and legal order*, nationally and internationally. The UN Charter mentions human dignity in its Preamble, stating that the peoples of the United Nations are determined 'to reaffirm faith in fundamental human rights, in the dignity and worth of the human person, in the equal rights of men and women and of nations large and small' (UN Charter 1945, Preamble).[10] Following this, the UDHR's Preamble declares that 'recognition of the inherent dignity and of the equal and inalienable rights of all members of the human family is the foundation of freedom, justice and peace in the world' (UDHR 1948, Preamble), and Article 1 stipulates that 'human beings are born free and equal in dignity and rights' (UDHR 1948, Article 1). More specifically, human dignity is regarded as the foundation of human rights. As already mentioned, international law states this most explicitly in the Preamble to the International Covenants,

10 For a detailed historical note of the process of placing human dignity in the international law after 1945, see Tiedemann (2012, 9–48).

according to which 'inalienable rights of all members of the human family . . . derive from the inherent dignity of the human person' (ICCPR 1966 and ICESCR 1966, Preamble). Modern constitutions follow both tenets – human dignity as a foundational principle, and human dignity as a source of rights. Dignity is to be found in preambles as well as in the articles or charters containing basic principles or fundamental rights. If there is no explicit evocation in a legal text, the courts develop doctrines identifying the principle of dignity as implicit (the United States and Canada are examples of that). Sometimes a wording referring to 'foundations' is explicitly used, as in the case of the Spanish constitution, which stipulates that '[t]he dignity of the person, the inviolable rights which are inherent, the free development of the personality, the respect for the law and for the rights of others are *the foundation of political order and social peace*' (Constitution of Spain 1978, section 10, emphasis added). Historically speaking, the most important constitutional evocation is that from Article 1 of the German 1949 Basic Law, which reads: '[h]uman dignity shall be inviolable. To respect and protect it shall be the duty of all state authority' (Basic Law for Germany 1949, Article 1.1). The already-quoted formulation in the Polish 1997 Constitution (Article 30) is more specific and synthesises what is found in different places in international law, so I shall recall it here. It says: 'The inherent and inalienable dignity of the person shall constitute a source of freedoms and rights of persons and citizens. It shall be inviolable. The respect and protection thereof shall be the obligation of public authorities' (Constitution of the Republic of Poland, Article 30). Undoubtedly, the constitutional use of dignity is not univocal among jurisdictions (Christopher McCrudden points at important differences; see McCrudden 2008, 673), but certainly the aforementioned formulations constitute the focal class of ways in which the foundational role of human dignity is being stated by the law.

Although a detailed theorisation will be offered later (essentially in Chapter 3), for now we can make an attempt to decode the critically important elements to be found directly in the text. First, there is an ontological claim, or, better to say, an *ontological referral*. Of course, law is a normative utterance and as such does not assert facts. It can evoke them indirectly, though, especially in preambles referring to general historical background of the adopted act, or its commitments and principles. In this sense, a human dignity clause affirms something about human existence, or identifies a property of human beings that is inherent to them and gives them special worth and high status. As something 'inherent', it is not conferred by any social, political, or legal arrangements, but is something 'members of the human family' simply have, to an equal extent, by virtue of their existence (being 'born'). Also, human dignity is not something having been discovered or made up recently; rather, law aims at 'reaffirming the faith in' human dignity, which allegedly is something context-invariant or at least long-lasting in human history. At the same time, the substantive content of 'dignity' is not elucidated in any detail. The foundational use of human dignity is *referring to something*, though, and it would be unreasonable not to ask what that reference is about. Article 1 of the UDHR asserts that humans are 'endowed with reason and conscience', which strongly correlates with them having dignity. The often-repeated expression 'human family' seems to point at a common origin of all humans, without specifying what this origin would be. Some constitutions (such as the Constitution of Ireland) contain an *invocatio Dei*, but others emphasise the laicism or neutrality of the state, and still strongly affirm human dignity. Sticking to the bare legal text, then, there is no further guidance to the substantive content of the ontological referral.

Second, there is a moral claim. Human dignity clauses stipulate that the humanity in persons, or individual persons themselves, should be respected. Regardless of the level of inter-personal or social interaction, people 'should act towards one another in a spirit of brotherhood' (UDHR, Article 1). This moral rule is strongly connected to the idea of the intrinsic, and perhaps absolute, worth of human persons, and their equality. *Intrinsic worth* has been commonly understood to mean that the human person is an end in himself or herself, rather than a mere means to some external end. In other words, any action affecting human persons should take into account their good, or their legitimate interest.[11] *Equality* means that the respect shall not be conditioned by a position in the social hierarchy, or any morally irrelevant individual characteristics such as ethnicity, gender, or age. The characteristics of persons that come from their own self-constitution, such as their religion or a developed worldview, also should not influence the extent to which they are covered by the dignitarian concern. Additionally, insofar as dignity is 'inalienable', it cannot be lost by any action of human individuals, including a voluntary one, so the gravest criminals would also be deemed to have human dignity.

Finally, there is a political claim. The duty to respect and protect human dignity binds the political authority, and thereby becomes an indispensable condition of state legitimacy. At the same time, the inherent dignity of each person constitutes limits of state (or state-like) power, since any violation of human dignity at the institutional level is forbidden and may meet individual disobedience or international intervention. Since human dignity is a source of human rights, the political order that acknowledges human dignity becomes also human-rights-oriented. In this context, it is also worth mentioning that quite often an explicit evocation of human dignity is understood as a reaction to the past atrocity of war (Goos 2013), or as a basis of transition from a totalitarian toward a liberal political order (Dupré 2013). Again, the detailed content of these general commitments is to be revealed or constructed by adjudication, political practice, or political theory.

3.2 The regulative function

In its foundational function, human dignity is, in a sense, extra-legal. If this function were exhaustive, human dignity would probably be rarely evoked in

11 Very often, where the moral aspect of dignity is concerned, the interpreters almost automatically point to the Kantian idea of dignity (*Würde*) as value beyond all price (Kant 1998, 41). However, Kant was not mentioned in the *travaux preparatoires* in the case of either the UDHR or German Basic Law (for the latter, see Goos 2013). My identification of dignity as a moral idea is therefore intended to be more broad and loose in meaning than the technical meaning of value beyond all price that is found in Kant's Groundwork.

legal practice, perhaps only in extraordinary circumstances such as racial segregation or war crimes. It would be considered as a source of political and moral postulates toward law rather than part of the fabric of law itself. To the contrary, in modern legal orders, a situation in which *human dignity (or 'personal dignity' or plainly 'dignity') serves as a basis for authoritative legal decisions* is obviously far from being exceptional. Dignitarian clauses do not work only as a rhetorical tool or a moral memorandum: certain actionable rights, and legitimation for authorities to intervene and regulate people's lives, are being derived from dignity, as present in the legal text, or at least as an indispensable part of legal reasoning that justifies those rights and authorisations. Hence the regulative function that should be exposed and considered separately.

Before we get into details, one important reservation should be made: Unlike the case of the foundational function of dignity, the regulative function is too manifold and too inconsistent to identify a focal class or general direction of application of human dignity in this field. Sometimes in a single legal system we face inconsistency, and all the more across jurisdictions, where similar matters are sometimes regulated in directly opposing ways, despite references to dignity. Abortion is a famous and controversial example: Dignitarian grounds were employed in the justification of liberal as well as restrictive abortion laws, depending on the country (Bognetti 2005). As commonly recognised, then, human dignity in its regulative function suffers from *normative indeterminacy* (Carroza 2011, 460–6). Although I do consider it as a problem, I also think that some extent of indeterminacy is inescapably inscribed into the very nature of human dignity (and its connection to freedom). The SPT will propose how to deal with normative indeterminacy, in a way that leaves inevitable flexibility (see Chapter 4). This subsection is thus merely an outline of some indicative examples in selected fields, without claims to exhaustiveness or internal coherence.

3.2.1 The humanitarian aspect

The first field of application we will consider deals with bare human life, so to speak, and the human capacity for being humiliated, which is an inevitable element of human life (Margalit 1996). The prohibition of torture or degrading and inhuman treatment, universally recognised in numerous domestic and international regulations, can be understood as a response to this condition.[12] For the purposes of this outline, I will call it *the humanitarian aspect of dignity.*

I will not delve into differences in meaning among torture, degrading treatment, and inhuman treatment, but it is important to highlight *the degradation or humiliation* that is crucial to all three. It should be contrasted with *suffering*. Indeed, torture and degrading treatment certainly involve a great deal of suffering, which has been used to define what torture is in the United Nations

12 For a list of international law acts that contain this prohibition, see Weissbrodt and Heilman (2011).

Convention against Torture (UNCAT 1984).[13] However, according to an overwhelming majority of scholars, what makes these maltreatments such a grave violation of basic principles of any civilised legal order, and constitutes their essence, is the ***infringement of dignity of a person exposed to it*** (Tiedemann 2012, 332–43). Torture reduces the victim to a 'mere plaything',[14] deprived of a moral standing, put in circumstances in which 'another person has the absolute power to determine what happens without the slightest possibility to evade or resist the situation' (Maier 2011, 105). 'Degrading treatment' may be less harsh: Humiliating a person without direct intent to cause suffering, by disregarding her crucial needs, interests, or violability in particular conditions such as detention or imprisonment. As far as the latter is concerned, the jurisprudence of the European Court of Human Rights contains cases such as detaining a woman with disability with no proper facilities and making her sleep in a wheelchair (European Court of Human Rights 2001), or not taking into proper consideration other vulnerabilities, such as chronic hepatitis of a prisoner (European Court of Human Rights 2010). What all these (more or less severe) circumstances have in common is that they are properly regarded as mistreatment if we focus on what they violate. Namely, all these circumstances violate the integrity of a free agent capable of action on the one hand, and the self-authenticating claim to respectful treatment founded on the bare fact of existence on the other. It is perhaps best summarised in the judgement of the International Criminal Tribunal for the former Yugoslavia. Judging on the basis of the Geneva Conventions, in *Prosecutor v. Furundzija*, the Tribunal stipulated that the chief purpose of international humanitarian and human rights law, taken as a whole, is to 'shield human beings from outrages upon their personal dignity, whether such outrages are carried out by unlawfully attacking the body or by humiliating and debasing the honour, the self-respect or the mental well-being of a person' (United Nations International Criminal Tribunal for the Former Yugoslavia 1998, 183).

The clauses concerning torture and degrading treatment are chiefly of prohibitive character and are aimed mostly against abusive use of force by government agencies. The vast majority of cases decided by the European Court of Human Rights under Article 3 of the European Convention of Human Rights deal with ill-treatment of prisoners, detainees, or migrants. Regional bodies in the African human rights system have been considerably less active, and Article 5 of the

13 The UNCAT (1984) defines torture as 'any act by which severe pain or suffering, whether physical or mental, is intentionally inflicted on a person for such purposes as obtaining from him, or a third person, information or a confession, punishing him for an act he or a third person has committed or is suspected of having committed, or intimidating or coercing him or a third person, or for any reason based on discrimination of any kind, when such pain or suffering is inflicted by or at the instigation of or with the consent or acquiescence of a public official or other person acting in an official capacity. It does not include pain or suffering arising only from, inherent in, or incidental to, lawful sanctions' (UNCAT, Article 1).

14 A wording 'mere plaything' comes from a judgement of the Indian Supreme Court, quoted by Daly (2013, 39).

African Convention[15] is evoked almost solely in cases of war crimes or heavy abuse of prisoners (African Court Law Report 2019); it also serves as a basis to produce guidelines for the condition of arrest (African Commission on Human and People's Rights 2017). In this respect, the legal effect of human dignity is chiefly *the obligation of government to restrain from certain types of abusive activity when using state force*. Under the regime of Geneva Conventions (Additional Protocol II 1977, Article 4, 2e), it may also involve individual criminal responsibility for atrocities committed at war, as it was decided in *Prosecutor v. Furundzija*.

However, the purely prohibitive effect is not the sole one. For example, in *Assenov and Others v. Bulgaria* (1998a), the European Court of Human Rights established a *positive obligation* on the state to provide 'effective official investigation' to its citizens, particularly in the case of allegations against the police abusing their power (European Court of Human Rights 1998a, 102). In this vein, the Court stipulated in *M.C. v. Bulgaria* (2004) that the state authority has 'a positive obligation inherent in Articles 3 and 8 of the Convention to enact criminal-law provisions effectively punishing rape and to apply them in practice through effective investigation and prosecution' (European Court of Human Rights 2004, 153). Also, according to the Court's judgement in *A. v. The United Kingdom*, Article 3 obliges the signatory states 'to ensure that individuals within their jurisdiction are not subjected to torture or inhuman or degrading treatment or punishment, *including such ill-treatment administered by private individuals*' (European Court of Human Rights 1998b, 22, emphasis added). The case concerned ineffective criminalisation of domestic violence that the applicant had been subject to while a child. According to the judgement, the state should provide vulnerable individuals with effective protection 'against such serious breaches of personal integrity' (European Court of Human Rights 1998b, 22). Generalising these cases, one may identify an additional legal effect of human dignity in its humanitarian aspect, which is the state authorities (which may include even the legislative branch!) *being obliged to establish institutions and take effective actions to maintain the core aspects of bodily and personal integrity*, particularly in conditions of vulnerability such as detention, imprisonment, hospitalisation, or domestic violence (Mowbray 2004, 43–65). Although the European system has been the most developed, analogous examples may be found in the jurisprudence of the Inter-American Court of Human Rights, for instance, In *I.V. v. Bolivia*, the unconsented sterilisation of a woman in a public hospital was regarded as a violation of the dignity of the patient (Inter-American Court of Human Rights 2016, 270). More specifically, the state was considered responsible for not providing adequate protection against this practice, which was its obligation under

15 The Article stipulates the following: 'Every individual shall have the right to the respect of the dignity inherent in a human being and to the recognition of his legal status. All forms of exploitation and degradation of man, particularly slavery, slave trade, torture, cruel, inhuman or degrading punishment and treatment shall be prohibited' (African Charter on Human and Peoples' Rights 1981, Article 5).

the American Convention of Human Rights (1969), derived from personal dignity and personal integrity (Inter-American Court of Human Rights 2016, 267).

Since there has been enough legal material, we should now reflect on what the humanitarian aspect protects. The full answer will be given in Chapter 3, along with presenting the SPT. For now, suffice it to say that the prohibition of degradation is closely attached to 'bodily' or 'personal' integrity. The latter term, although it seems to better capture the essence of the humanitarian aspect, is far from being unequivocal. 'Bodily integrity' quite clearly points at purely biological conditions of human functioning. But this is not the main subject of the infringements we have talked about. As already stated, torture consists not only in causing pain but also, perhaps more importantly, in an outrage upon the victim's capacity to respond to the situation, to keep his or her convictions or commitments. It attempts to nullify the capacity to make free decisions at the most basic level of the functioning of the human body. In this sense, torture makes people helpless, and thus harshly violates, perhaps even nullifies, a delicate sphere of 'ownness' that each human being has. There is a quite easily observable analogy in other cases I have mentioned, such as conditions of detention or treatment in hospitals. Personal integrity perceived through this lens would amount to a sphere of self-awareness, internal consistency, and basic control over one's actions enjoyed by the human person in normal circumstances of life. I will come back to this in Chapter 3, where the relations between the prohibition of degradation and integrity within the SPT will be set forth with greater precision.

A good illustration of the stakes of the humanitarian aspect is the famous case before the German Federal Constitutional Court regarding the constitutionality of the Aviation Security Act (Federal Constitutional Court of Germany 2006). In this world-famous judgement, the court stated that the authorisation to shoot down a civil aircraft used as a weapon against human lives, which was granted as a last resort to the Federal Government, was inconsistent with the protection of rights to life and dignity of the innocent passengers and crew. According to the complainants, '[t]he value and the preservation of their lives are left to the discretion of the Federal Minister of Defense according to quantitative aspects and to the life span presumably remaining to them "under the circumstances"' (Federal Constitutional Court of Germany 2006, 37). As the complainants argued, a utilitarian calculus that the government would have to make before the decision to shoot the aircraft down would amount to making the passengers 'mere objects of state action', and thus depriving them of 'their human quality and dignity' (Federal Constitutional Court of Germany 2006, 39). The court agreed with these arguments and declared the contested statute unconstitutional. The complaint was quite complex, but I will focus only on the dignitarian argument. According to the court, human dignity requires an absolute prohibition of 'any treatment of a human being by public authority which fundamentally calls into question his or her quality of a subject, his or her status as a legal entity' (Federal Constitutional Court of Germany 2006, 121). According to the Court, the Aviation Security Act created precisely such a situation. A hypothetical case of innocent passengers and crew being used as a shield by a hijacker's terrorist attack has one common characteristic with torture, namely the helplessness and humiliation of the victim. Of course, it is the terrorists who would deny the intrinsic value and basic legal status of the passengers. But the state must not in any sense continue this denial. As the court says:

> The desperateness and inescapability which characterise the situation of the people on board the aircraft who are affected as victims *also exist vis-à-vis those who order and execute the shooting down of the aircraft.* Due to the circumstances, which cannot be controlled by them in any way, the crew and the passengers of the plane cannot escape this state action but *are helpless and defenceless in the face of it* with the consequence that they are shot down in a targeted manner together with the aircraft and as result of this will be killed with near certainty. Such a treatment ignores the status of the persons affected as subjects endowed with dignity and inalienable rights.
>
> (Federal Constitutional Court of Germany 2006, 124, emphasis added)

As we see, despite the close link between the two, human dignity in its purest form is not to be conflated with the right to life, which is a separate constitutional norm. Human dignity as such protects the intangible sphere of 'ownness', a self-validating claim to intrinsic value or basic status, which would be entirely denied by a legal authorisation to decide to kill innocent people.

3.2.2 The autonomy aspect

The Aviation Security Act case points at another aspect of human dignity in the legal sphere, which is that of 'autonomy'. By making the innocent people mere objects of the state acting, one is denying their agentic capacity and self-determination. While autonomy is part of personal integrity, it brings another tone to the dignitarian moment. For instance, forcing someone to act against her own considered judgement does not have to be harsh enough to be degrading and inhuman in the sense stipulated in the previous subsection; it may not completely deny one's capacity to decide for oneself, but it still would amount to a violation of one's dignity. As legal persons or citizens, human beings are authorised to follow their own conscience, worldview, or values, especially when this is not weighted against direct harm done to others. As already mentioned, dignitarian arguments were used by the U.S. Supreme Court to justify the permissibility of abortion, or freedom to choose an intimate life partner, but these examples are part of the vast tradition of the Court appreciating – as we read in judgements regarding freedom of speech – the 'individual dignity and choice upon which our political system rests' (Supreme Court of the United States 1971, 24). This strong autonomist mark, present in different legal orders (see Daly 2013, 27–34), has brought many scholars to conclude that *the right to individual freedom, or autonomy*, is the proper and exhaustive explication of human dignity in law (Jakl 2013, 100–4). For reasons to be explained, I think this would be too rushed. For now, suffice it to say that human dignity is also being used to justify the opposite: Under certain conditions, it serves as a ground for *legal paternalism*, which means protecting an individual *from their own choices.* Restricting the sphere of choice is considered justifiable despite the fact that it might not have any direct influence on the rights of others, precisely by virtue of the individual being characterised by dignity 'of which he is a repository but not a proprietor' (Hennette-Vauchez 2014, 372). Taking this into consideration, I will now outline the autonomy aspect of the regulative use of human dignity, both in cases when the law protects the sphere of autonomous choice as well as when it restricts or regulates its exercise.

Human dignity is commonly regarded as closely intertwined with liberty, or perhaps a vast menu of particular liberties. Freedom of religion and conscience (Riordan 2013), of speech (Heyman 2008), or of contract (Tiedemann 2012, 364–6), among others, are therefore regarded as concretisations of human dignity. Certainly, at least under a liberal-democratic reading, human dignity generally authorises the human person to perform all actions that are not explicitly illegal and forbids anyone (state or non-state institutions, as well as individuals) to arbitrarily impose their will on others. A free development and endurance of a personality, while respecting the equal freedom of all, is a strong entitlement based on dignitarian grounds. All this has a powerful background in the history of ideas, but as such, it is a matter of legal or political theory rather than of pure law itself. In other words, either in the case of the general presumption of liberty or in the case of particular liberties, human dignity is foundational but not regulative, at least not in a straightforward manner.

Given that, there is a limited scope of examples of dignity-as-autonomy being explicitly regulative, especially in black letter law. One example that should be considered, though, is the right not to be subject to involuntary medical (or other scientific) experiments, as stipulated in Polish constitutional law. In a 1993 resolution, the Constitutional Tribunal stipulated:

> Allowing a scientific experiment without consent of the person that is subject to it violates the principle of the democratic state ruled by law through a breach of human dignity. In such a case, the human being is treated as a mere subject of scientific experimentation.
>
> (Constitutional Tribunal of the Republic of Poland 1993, 9, translation by the author)

Following this important tenet, the framers of the 1997 Constitution ensured that a separate article deals with the issue. According to Article 39, 'No one shall be subjected to scientific experimentation, including medical experimentation, without his voluntary consent' (Constitution of the Republic of Poland, Article 39). Although the word 'dignity' is not used, the place of the article in the constitution shows its direct affinity with Article 30 that contains the dignity clause. As such, involuntary experimentation is closely related to degrading treatment,[16]

16 For example, the ICCPR regulates the issues of degrading treatment and involuntary experimentation in one article: 'No one shall be subjected to torture or to cruel, inhuman or degrading treatment or punishment. In particular, no one shall be subjected without his free consent to medical or scientific experimentation' (ICCPR: Art. 7.). In the case of the Polish

but quite clearly the protected sphere in the former case is that of autonomous choice, and not simply health or life (Królikowski and Szczucki, 2016, 957). As most commentators argue, the Polish constitution prohibits experiments on persons that are not able to give an informed consent, such as prenatal humans, children, or the mentally ill, regardless of the benefits that such treatment could yield (Bosek and Olejniczak 2012, 135). One can thus argue that in the case of experiments, the only factor that renders them consonant with human dignity is the consent of the person to be subject to it.

A similarly close connection between consent and dignity is made in the Charter of Fundamental Rights of the European Union (CFR 2012). The Charter not only recognises the foundational role of human dignity in the Preamble, but it also attributes the special place thereto in the authoritative part. Its Title I, 'Dignity', covers the rights to dignity, life, and the integrity of the person, alongside with prohibitions of torture, inhuman or degrading treatment or punishment, slavery, and forced labour. The right to integrity is declared in Article 3, in which we read that medical procedures must ensure, *inter alia*, 'the free and informed consent of the person concerned, according to the procedures laid down by law' (CFR 2012, Article 3).

Another common way in which dignity and autonomy are interlinked is that of judicial reasoning. Alongside the already mentioned jurisprudence of the U.S. Supreme Court, there are many analogous examples in numerous other jurisdictions. What is important in this context is that very often the use of human dignity in judgements goes beyond mere rhetoric: it is not simply a question of style. To the contrary, dignity becomes indispensable to the argument itself, even if the term is not present in the constitution, or the original complaint did not evoke it. If we recall *Obergefell v. Hodges*, for example, we see that the decision rests on the premises of marriage being fundamental to human life, and homosexual relations having equal dignity in comparison to heterosexual ones, because they equally come from autonomous choice or self-determination. The court employed dignity to link the due process and equal protection with the right to homosexual marriage, so that dignity itself is a part of the argumentation. The Fourteenth Amendment jurisprudence is, of course, much wider, and extends, *inter alia*, to issues of consent to medical treatment and assisted suicide. Although the Supreme Court did not accept the alleged 'right to die' or 'right to a physician-assisted suicide' as protected by the U.S. Constitution,[17] it was made explicit, in *Cruzan v. Director, Missouri Dept. of Health*, that 'A competent person has a liberty interest under the Due Process Clause in refusing unwanted medical treatment' (Supreme Court of the United States 1990, 262).

In the Fourteenth Amendment jurisprudence, though, the argument as a whole is always very complex, and dignity is only one line of reasoning among others. It is not an accident that in *Cruzan*, human dignity is evoked only in

constitution, the prohibition of torture follows it directly (Constitution of the Republic of Poland, Article 40).

17 In *Washington v. Glucksberg*, the Court sharply distinguishes between assisted suicide and refusing medical treatment, only the latter being protected as a constitutional right (The Supreme Court of the United States 1997, 703).

the concurring opinion of Justice O'Connor, and not in the majority opinion (Supreme Court of the United States 1990, 289). In such cases, then, perhaps simply too much is engaged to precisely determine the sense in which human dignity consists in or protects autonomy.

A particularly clear and instructive example comes from South Africa. In *Coetzee v. Comitis* (High Court of South Africa 2001), the court was addressed with a complaint of a young football player (Mr. Coetzee) who challenged the legality of the rules adopted by the National Soccer League (hereinafter NSL), the regulator of professional football in the country. In the applicant's view, the regulations (which every NSL player has no choice but to adhere to while entering professional soccer) infringed his rights, including that of human dignity, guaranteed in the South African constitution.[18] The complaint regarded the compensation regime: In order to start playing for a new club, a player needed to obtain a clearance certificate from his former club, which was entitled to a transfer fee paid by the new club, even though the contract between the former club and the player had expired (High Court of South Africa 2001, 15). In effect, the player was potentially put in a sort of a catch: He might no longer be considered a professional player (beyond a certain time after the contract with the former club expired), and in order to continue his career, he needed to conclude a new contract, which could not be done unless the clearance certificate had been issued. In the event of a dispute between the clubs, the settlement of fees must be submitted to arbitration. In a sense, then, the career of the player was either in the hands of the former club, which might grant him a compensation-free transfer, or the arbitrator, who might resolve a dispute in a manner charitable to the player. This mechanism excluded the player's influence on a dispute that affected himself in the first place (High Court of South Africa 2001, 24–9).

The court declared the NSL rules unlawful, chiefly on dignitarian grounds. Justice Traverso wrote:

> As pointed out above a player, in terms of the NSL rules, is helpless. He can give no input in respect of the transfer fee, and, if all else fails, he is at the mercy of an arbitrator who determines the compensation payable according to a formula for which there is no rational basis. The player would then be treated just like an object. His figures will be fed into the formula and an amount will pop up! Not very different from the manner in which the book value of a motor vehicle is determined! It is abundantly clear that the transfer fee thus determined bears no relation to any amount expended by the club in training the player.
>
> In my view, this procedure strips the player of his human dignity as enshrined in the Constitution.
>
> (High Court of South Africa 2001, 34)

18 'Everyone has inherent dignity and the right to have their dignity respected and protected' (Constitution of the Republic of South Africa 1996, s. 10).

The situation of Mr. Coetzee is considerably less harsh than that of the victims of torture, degrading treatment, or shooting down of a hijacked civil aircraft. Interestingly enough, though, the tone of 'helplessness' rings again. And this is what makes the case very instructive. The dignitarian norm is here applied as protecting *nothing but autonomy*: the unlawfulness of the NCL is a result of the fact that the player has no say in determining his future as a professional football player; that he is treated like a mere object of a bargain between disputing sport clubs.

Under this background, it seems quite obvious why autonomy probably will not suffice to do the main job in explicating human dignity. When we juxtapose the German Aviation Security case with *Coetzee v. Comitis*, it is really hard to argue that the former regards nothing but human autonomy, in the sense in which the latter does. Rather, we see that a somewhat 'mysterious' and intangible thing – the respect-bearing integrity that is peculiar to humans – is at stake when the humanitarian aspect of dignity is considered. It assumes autonomy, but is not equal thereto. At this point, it is too early to conceptualise this, but I think the subsequent conceptualisation must bear it in mind. The panorama will become even more complex, however, once we realise how dignity is used to regulate or restrict autonomy instead of fostering it. Namely, sometimes the law assumes that the person might violate her own dignity, or fall short in paying respect to herself.

The first fairly uncontroversial example is that of human trafficking, universally recognised as unlawful and prohibited. According to international law, human trafficking consists in any form of transfer, recruitment, or transportation of persons for purposes of exploitation, which means, 'at a minimum, the exploitation of the prostitution of others or other forms of sexual exploitation, forced labor or services, slavery or practices similar to slavery, servitude or the removal of organs' (Protocol supplementing the UN Convention against Transnational Organized Crime 2000, Article 3). Importantly, according to the said Protocol, Article 3 (d), '[t]he consent of a victim of trafficking in persons to the intended exploitation . . . shall be irrelevant'. One can quite easily imagine a situation in which a person, desperately looking for financial profit, explicitly agrees to sell organs, or engage in labour similar to slavery. And yet, the perpetrator will be held responsible for a crime, regardless of the victim's hypothetical willingness to engage in the trafficking. In the aforementioned Protocol, the word 'dignity' is not used. However, the Polish legislation, introduced in 2010 with a view of complementing the said convention as well as the relevant European law, embeds dignity into the very definition of human trafficking, which covers

> exploitation, *even upon consent of the person concerned*, in particular in prostitution, pornography, or other forms of sexual exploitation, in forced labor or services, in beggary, slavery or any *other forms of exploitation that degrade the dignity of the person.*
>
> (Penal Code [Poland 1997], Article 115 paragraph. 22, emphasis added, translation by the author)

This particular wording is underlined by the understanding of dignity as *inherent* and *inalienable*, which is in harmony with the Polish constitution. As inherent, dignity does not emerge as a product of social or legal conventions. As inalienable, dignity is not considered a quality depending solely on the individual will – and this opens the possibility of a justifiable constraint imposed on individual choices in disposing of one's own dignitarian interests. As commentators argue, the irrelevance of consent in cases of exploitation in the Polish penal code 'is a natural consequence of the inalienability of human dignity' (Daniluk 2018, 793, translation by the author). This example is uncontroversial given the fact that a genuinely voluntary exploitation, in the context of harsh human trafficking issues, seems hard to imagine. The legal protection regardless of consent seems natural here: it would appear counterproductive to introduce the lack of consent as something to be proven by the prosecutor, for example. It is also important to note that although the penal regulation assumes that the individual may will something that is against her own dignity, it does not penalise her conduct – she is considered a victim and never a perpetrator. As a part of the penal law system, the dignity clause must be narrow and strict in application: The courts of appeal have been careful not to allow an extensive interpretation of it, according to the basic principle *nullum crimen sine lege certa* (Królikowski and Zawłocki 2018, 108).

However, there have been famous cases in France and Germany in which human dignity was applied to limit conduct of the individual against his will, by means of administrative law, and that had a direct 'negative' effect, at least from the subjective individual perspective. What I mean here are the 'dwarf-tossing' shows that were banned by administrative authorities on the basis of contravening public morality, particularly human dignity. A 'dwarf-tossing' competition or show is a situation in which persons of very short stature are thrown by the competitors at landing areas or at a target. In Germany, a show of this kind was administratively banned in the federal state of Rhineland-Palatinate. The ban was upheld by the reviewing Neustadt Administrative Court, and the judgement was based directly on Article 1 of the Basic Law, obliging the authorities to protect human dignity (Mathis 2013, 132–3). In France, in a famous case, the mayor of Morsang-sur-Orge banned an analogous 'tossing' competition on the basis of article L. 131–2 of the Code of Communes (*code des communes*), which stipulated, at the time of issuing the decision: 'The city police is obliged to maintain the right order, safety, security, and public health' (Council of State of the French Republic 1995, translation by the author). After the ban was lifted by the Administrative Tribunal of Versailles, the case was heard by the Council of State (the supreme administrative tribunal), upon the mayor's complaint. In its judgement, the Council declared that 'the respect for the dignity of the human person is one of the components of public order' (Council of State of the French Republic 1995). The ban was upheld, since the spectacle of throwing people as missiles, which was possible only because of their physical handicap, contravened human dignity.

In both the German and the French case, the persons directly concerned – used as 'objects' in said competitions – were directly engaged in contesting the bans. In the French case, the affected person with dwarfism, Manuel Wackenheim, took pains to appeal to the United Nations Human Rights Committee, on the basis of the rights guaranteed by the ICCPR. The Committee, though, did not decide in his favour (The Human Rights Committee 2007, 5.2). There is no doubt, then, that in the dwarf-tossing cases, the authorities constrained the individuals' power of making decisions regarding themselves *against their will, and on dignitarian grounds.*

The legal construction in both cases is the following: general clauses (public order, public morality, human dignity) are applied by respective administrative authorities as a legitimation of constraint. The reviewing bodies upheld their decisions as remaining within the scope of the policy power vested in public administration. However, unlike in case of torture, inhuman and degrading treatment, or human trafficking, the circumstances of dwarf-tossing are considerably light, perhaps even silly. Although they may be found obnoxious, neither bodily harm nor a permanent rejection of autonomy is involved. Yet, it was legally confirmed (by national and international bodies) that human dignity constitutes a justifiable reason for an administrative ban of this kind of entertainment. The justification seems to depend on the assessment regarding 'honourable' ways of human conduct. Turning oneself into a 'missile' and being thrown by others, which is possible only because of a physical handicap, was considered undignified. Such application is clearly paternalistic as restricting or regulating autonomous choice, which is at least partly aimed against a harm done to oneself.

3.2.3 The social security aspect

Human dignity is not always equal to a prohibition of ill-treatment of some kind. *Positive obligations* of states or supra-national actors that have been derived from dignity go far beyond performing basic functions, such as protection from atrocious crimes, which we considered as the humanitarian aspect of dignity. According to the UDHR, domestic and international institutions are obliged to actively promote human dignity as integral to human fulfilment, at the level of social and economic rights, for example. Article 22 reads as follows:

> Everyone, as a member of society, has the right to social security and is entitled to realization, through national effort and international co-operation and in accordance with the organization and resources of each State, of the economic, social and cultural rights indispensable for his dignity and the free development of his personality.
>
> (UDHR 1948, Article 22)

This is the paradigm regulation, which has influenced and inspired many analogous solutions in different legal systems. At this point, we do not need to examine them, since the human dignity in these norms 'is regarded as part of the circumstances that are relevant to the content of a regulation' (Zieliński 2003, 48, translation by the author), but as such, it does not really regulate anything. To explain further: It is commonly accepted that 'the right to social security is of central importance in guaranteeing human dignity' (Economic and Social Council of the United Nations 2018, par. 11.1), which has been emphasised also by many constitutional courts (Daly 2013, 54–60). But human dignity does not constitute a separate norm that would say what precise conduct or threshold of welfare is required. Rather, it provides either *a reason* for maintaining social protection (which is the foundational function) or *general political guidance* to the standards that states should strive to achieve.[19] In the latter usage, it performs what I will call the heuristic function, to be set forth next.

3.3 The heuristic function

What I call the heuristic function of human dignity manifests itself in situations at which courts adjudicate claims based on some other specific legal provision or right, but they employ dignitarian considerations in an auxiliary way, as part of judicial argumentation. A similar working may be observed in legislation, when human dignity is considered as one of the reasons for changing the law. Taken in this function, human dignity is not part of the fabric of law as a free-standing rule; rather, it serves as an auxiliary principle in legal reasoning. Some constitutions say it straightforwardly – the Polish constitution calls everyone to apply its precepts 'paying respect to the inherent dignity of the person' (Constitution of the Republic of Poland 1997, Preamble). In the constitution of South Africa, we read: 'When interpreting the Bill of Rights, a court, tribunal or forum must promote the values that underlie an open and democratic society based on human dignity, equality and freedom' (Constitution of the Republic of South Africa 1996, s. 39.1a). In other jurisdictions, like Germany and Canada, courts have come to similar conclusions concerning dignity in the course of their judicial history (Grimm 2007).

The heuristic function has three major aspects: interpreting evaluative standards, weighting rights in case of conflict within the system of constitutional values, and developing them in case there is a reason for change. The reservoir of potential examples, from many jurisdictions, is bottomless. I will now set forth one for each aspect, just to avoid misunderstandings on what I am talking about.

As far as the first aspect is concerned, a good illustration will be the case *Trop v.* Dulles (1958) in which the U.S. Supreme Court had to decide whether revoking

19 Sometimes, the solutions are fixed by the law. For example, the ICESCR stipulates that 'education shall be directed to the full development of the human personality and the sense of its dignity', and further that 'primary education should be compulsory and available free to all' (ICESCR, Article 13). Free primary education, then, is clearly considered to be a required by human dignity.

citizenship, as a form of punishment for wartime desertion, violates the Eighth Amendment's prohibition of cruel and unusual punishment. The affirmative conclusion reached by the Court was backed by a dignitarian reasoning:

> The exact scope of the constitutional phrase 'cruel and unusual' has not been detailed by this Court. But the basic policy reflected in these words is firmly established in the Anglo-American tradition of criminal justice. The phrase in our Constitution was taken directly from the English Declaration of Rights of 1688, and the principle it represents can be traced back to the Magna Carta. *The basic concept underlying the Eighth Amendment is nothing less than the dignity of man.* While the State has the power to punish, the Amendment stands to assure that this power be exercised within the limits of civilized standards. Fines, imprisonment and even execution may be imposed depending upon the enormity of the crime, but any technique outside the bounds of these traditional penalties is constitutionally suspect.... The Court recognized in that case that the words of the Amendment are not precise, and that their scope is not static. *The Amendment must draw its meaning from the evolving standards of decency that mark the progress of a maturing society.*
>
> (Supreme Court of the United States 1958, 99–101, footnotes removed, emphasis added)

Arguably, human dignity in *Trop v. Dulles* constitutes neither a separate legal rule in itself nor a basis for radical modification of pre-existing legal institutions. In spite of that, it performs an important role in judicial reasoning by helping to make an assessment, on the basis of the existing constitutional provisions and jurisprudence. Depriving the convict of his citizenship does not involve pain and suffering in the way an atrocity such as torture does. However, being equal to 'the total destruction of the individual's status in organized society' (Supreme Court of the United States 1958, 101), it breaches an important dignitarian interest – a basic form of recognition of status, especially taking into account that the petitioner would have become stateless should the punishment be upheld. In this sense, human dignity, in cases like *Trop v. Dulles*, serves as a device for assessing standards.

Weighing rights, on the other hand, is tantamount to limiting some particular constitutional liberty out of consideration of legitimate and pressing reasons. As such, it must meet the requirements of proportionality, which, as reconstructed by Weinrib in a comparative study, 'coheres with the absolute duty of the state to realize a regime adequate to the dignity of all' (Weinrib 2016, 218). Dignity, then, appears as a heuristic tool that allows the interpretation of law that 'does not introduce exceptions to the duty of public justice, but formulates what this duty requires in cases in which conflicts arise between its specifications (Weinrib 2016, 218). An important example of this doctrine working in practice is the case of *R v. Butler*, heard by the Supreme Court of Canada, where dignity was applied to determine whether a challenged criminal legislation against obscenity constituted 'a reasonable limit prescribed by law', or an unconstitutional legislative assault on basic liberties (Supreme Court of Canada 1992). The appellant was convicted for selling pornographic materials depicting men and women in sexual acts involving violence and degradation, and claimed that the conviction violated the constitutional guarantee of freedom of expression (Canadian Charter of Rights and Freedoms, 1982, s. 2(b)). While agreeing with the appellant with regards to the fact of violation, the court determined that in this case this violation was legitimate: the right to freedom of expression was outweighed by pressing reasons to *prevent harm to society as a whole.* According to the court, the harm done by the appellant's activity consisted in the fact that 'degrading or dehumanizing materials place women (and sometimes men) in positions of subordination, servile submission or humiliation. They run against the principles of equality and dignity of all human beings' (Supreme Court of Canada 1982, 479). There is one element that makes this application of dignity considerably different from the previous example of *Trop v. Dulles.* Namely, in *R v. Bulter*, the Canadian court not only evokes dignity to develop a definition of some vague legal term, but also uses it in order to come up with a legitimate balance in the face of opposed reasons that are on par in terms of being embedded in the constitution.

Finally, it is worth mentioning that the heuristic function is not observable only in courts. As a political commitment, human dignity guides *legislation* in many areas: biolaw, social security issues, and fostering economic freedom are just a few examples. In this sense, human dignity helps to *develop the system of rights*, contributing to the way in which a community defines itself through lawgiving. Of course, the courts also may develop rights on a dignitarian basis (Carozza 2011, 466), but in my view, the role of the legislatures also should be kept in mind. A recent example from Poland is the official justification of a bill ('The law of entrepreneurs') aimed at extending the freedom of economic activity by facilitating cooperation between the economic entities and public administration. According to proponents of the bill:

> The 'law of entrepreneurs' act, likewise the Constitution, neither creates nor grants the freedom of economic activity. Rather, this freedom is an inalienable human right (enjoyed also by human associations) which is every person's due *because of her inherent dignity*.... What the Constitution and ordinary legislation create and should create, however, is the inevitable legal guaranties and security of economic activity, in the form of specified duties of public authority, and the correlational rights of entrepreneurs.
>
> (Sejm of the Republic of Poland 2017, justification of the bill, 4, translation by the author, emphasis added)

As we see, the legislator considers himself obliged to foster economic freedom – which is based on human dignity – by improving the legal framework related to entrepreneurship. Human dignity (considered an extra-legal principle as well as an inalienable part of the human condition) serves not only as a political inspiration, but also as *the crucial element of the normative framework that should be respected while making law.*

The heuristic function obviously overlaps with the regulative and the foundational. Sometimes interpreting the existing rights can hardly be discerned from creating new ones. If we reconsider *Trop v. Dulles* vis-à-vis *Obergefell v. Hodges*, it appears that in the latter case, the U.S. Supreme Court in fact creates a new constitutional right, a right to homosexual marriage (Greenawalt 2018, 121). In the former, it establishes only an extension of meaning of the pre-existing rights, a right not to be subject to cruel and unusual punishment. Despite this fuzziness, the heuristic function should be highlighted as posing, in a particularly strong way, the mentioned problem of normative indeterminacy that should be resolved by the planned explication of human dignity. We should ask how human dignity is to be employed in legal reasoning itself, and how its implications are determined, in contrast to the implications of other normative ideals such as equality or freedom.

3.4 The meta-legal level

The legal material presented so far may give the impression that the 'dignitarian moment' is something extraordinary or exceptional. After all, grave crimes such as torture, or complex constitutional cases catching the public eye worldwide, are not something that lawyers deal with on a daily basis. Perhaps one even could argue that 'the dignitarian moment' is therefore a narrative based on curiosities rather than something realistic and true about law in general. I would not go that far in scepticism, and some important observations made by Jeremy Waldron will help us to reject such doubts (Waldron 2011, 2012). He argues that in order to examine how law protects human dignity, one should avoid focusing exclusively on the particular provisions of international or constitutional law. There is also no need to start with the moral ideal of human dignity and make a way into jurisprudence from there. Instead, Waldron argues, one should reflect on the way law *works* – how legal procedures are being performed, how legal rules and standards are being addressed to people, and how the coercion that is sometimes involved with legal activity differs from bare violence. Once having done this himself, he concludes that '[t]here is an implicit commitment to dignity in the tissues and sinews of law – in the character of its normativity and in its procedures' (Waldron 2011, 25). What I call the *meta-legal level* draws from this: At the meta-legal level, human dignity is not always a distinct and separate norm, but rather the way in which the system of norms is being constructed and applied. Human dignity so conceived is the lifeblood of law rather than a symbol to put on its banners.

The Waldronian idea of human dignity is that of basic *status*. Focusing on this aspect of dignity, he advocates against the conventional, Kantian-inspired understanding of dignity *as absolute worth*. Not directly denying the possibility or importance of this moral commitment, he argues that lawyers should primarily examine the *inherently legal* construction of dignity, which has been, historically speaking, that of rank and status. Although the dignity as status has assumed social hierarchy and was used to make distinctions between people, the modern law ascribes a certain kind of high standing to all humans *equally*, as a result of historical processes of transition from aristocratic toward egalitarian society (Waldron 2012, 34–6). Human dignity so understood is perhaps never fully secured (Waldron 2011, 25), though legal systems generally do aspire towards it: Law treats human persons as rational, autonomous agents, enjoying capacity of understanding and following rules, as well as of self-control. The basic human standing involves interpreting the person's actions in good faith, unless the uncharitable reading is proven, and carefully listening to their own understanding of their factual and legal situation (Luban 2005). This is easily distinguishable from treating people as mere objects of legal regulation, as those who simply have to follow orders. And this is by no means something extraordinary. The law *normally* does not require obedience without simultaneously expressing respect – leaving room for reasonable response – to those who are to obey. According to Waldron, abandoning these ideas overall would amount to a situation in which a jurisdiction could hardly be called a 'system of law', and in this way human dignity becomes law's indispensable component (Waldron 2011, 17).[20]

The value-status controversy is important, and I will deal with it in subsequent chapters, aiming at integration of the two notions rather than highlighting their apparent opposition. But this belongs to a substantive conception, and not a methodology. For now, I will comment on those of Waldron's observations I find most instructive for the meta-legal level of human dignity, as a crucial supplement to what has been said so far about the dignitarian moment. Unless otherwise indicated, the examples are my own.

First, there is law's *argumentative structure* and the *use of standards* connected thereto. It is true that sometimes law works like a simple command – it obliges one to keep a speed limit, or imposes a duty to wear seatbelts when driving. In such cases, there is not much room left for interpreting the situation of the addressee, or assessing the reasonableness of the rules themselves (although in some instances of necessity, such reasoning could be necessary). Most norms, however, require 'genuine thought in the way we receive and comply with them' (Waldron 2012, 53). Recall the standard of 'reasonable care', as applied in the English law of torts: in order to determine whether or not a defendant is guilty of negligence, the court must hear the story of two opposing parties, carefully consider their situations and behaviour, and then make a legal decision in accordance with the relevant precedent and common sense (Waldron 2012, 53). In such a process, the parties normally have their voice, and the final decision is always informed by their argumentation. A universal feature of private law proceedings which reveals individual agency in a particularly strong way is therefore the *adversarial character* of the procedure. Whereas civil law countries commonly adopt adversariality as a principle of civil litigation (which has been often connected to the traditional Roman phrase *audiatur et altera pars*), in England and Wales it is

20 Although this idea is implicit, one may find its direct expressions. For example, according to ICCPR, 'Everyone shall have the right to recognition everywhere as a person before the law' (ICCPR, Article 16).

to be found, for instance, in the duty of the court to ensure 'that the parties are on an equal footing' (Civil Procedure Rules of England and Wales 1998, 1.1). In a sense, then, private law is a paradigm with regards to using general standards and argumentation in determining what the law is. And this is a dignitarian commitment, according to Waldron at least.

This brings another important factor into play – *the importance of legal representation* (mentioned by Waldron 2012, but fully inspired by Luban 2005). Seen through dignitarian lenses, the attorney's job does not simply consist in *defending the interest* of the client. The latter is of course the merit of each case. But its prerequisite, of which lawyers are in charge, is *to use the legal-procedural armoury in a way that assures the proper standing* of the client; that which interprets her story and makes her case in the way that is best for her in the eyes of the law. Law is very often formalistic, hard to understand, and very likely to be misused in court. A professional representation is aimed to ensure that a layperson is not impaired by his not being a lawyer or simply a smart litigant. As Luban writes, 'Just as a non-English speaker must be provided an interpreter, the legally mute should have – in the very finest sense of the term – a mouthpiece' (2005, 819).

However important private law may be for human dignity at the meta-legal level, it is not the only relevant sphere. For our purposes, it is enough to make only one more remark. In administrative law, which is commonly thought to be at the opposite angle vis-à-vis private law in terms of formality and rigidness, one may also trace implicit dignitarian commitments. For instance, administrative decisions, in European countries at least, are in principle accompanied by *justifying (factual and legal) grounds*, presented to the person concerned. Although administrative authorities exercise power that does not require the explicit consent of the governed, their conduct must not be arbitrary. Hence, The European Code of Good Administrative Behaviour (2002), an act that has a huge informal impact on legal systems across the EU, states that 'Every decision of the institution which may adversely affect the rights or interests of a private person shall state the grounds on which it is based by indicating clearly the relevant facts and the legal basis of the decision' (2002, Article 18.1). What is more, administrative decisions are always subject to some kind of judicial review, according to each member state system. This reveals an important aspect of administrative decisions generally, in a modern legal system: This type of legal activity does not boil down to a bare command, a mere *incentive* for action. Rather, they are understood as providing *legitimate reasons* that have at least a potential to make a reasonable citizen *feel obliged* to conform with the decision.

Now, in the aforementioned examples, human dignity *is not* directly evoked. What links them, both with human dignity and with one another, is that they allow us to interpret the idea of the rule of law in a particular way. As Waldron writes, legal systems operate:

> by using, rather than short-circuiting, the agency of ordinary human individuals. They count on people's capacities for practical understanding,

> self-control, self-monitoring, and the modulation of their own behavior in regard to norms that they can grasp and understand.
>
> All this makes ruling by law quite different from, say, herding cows with a cattle prod. . . . It is quite different too from eliciting a reflex recoil with a scream of command.
>
> (Waldron 2012, 52, footnotes removed)

Interpreted from this perspective, human dignity consists in law aspiring towards a reasonable order between autonomous, equal agents rather than simply a system of social cohesion stabilising people's behaviour. Although in his observations Waldron highlights autonomy (treating people as self-controlling bearers of reason and intelligence), I think that his observations touch upon something that is even more basic than this. Perhaps a good idea that could express the meta-legal level of human dignity is the idea that everyone, ordinary people in the first place, *should matter*. In other words, the law implicitly acknowledges the importance, or weight, of everyone.[21] This is a very egalitarian feature. It should matter, without discrimination, how people perceive themselves and their legal situation. It is a binding requirement even if, or especially when, people are not capable of expressing their views well. And if their power to produce such views is impaired, they also deserve special treatment from public officials. It also should matter whether or not people are likely to obey or bypass the law, not out of consideration for law's social efficacy, but because of its legitimation. And it should matter in what manner law governs the social relations, whether it is more like herding sheep, or more like coordinating the action of (at least potentially) rational agents (Riley 2017, 178). This is the essence of the meta-legal dimension that I have in mind.

The meta-legal level is crucial to the project I will pursue in this book, since it constitutes the reason to think that the other functions that were identified earlier have a common point of reference. This would mean that if the spheres of law other than human rights law or constitutions protect personal dignity (for instance, as a private interest protected by tort law or labour law or penal laws), there is indeed a common denominator. And this would make the dignitarian moment something real and indispensable in law.

3.5 Toward interpretation of the dignitarian moment

The preceding part of this chapter was focused on setting forth the 'dignitarian moment in law', not as a name for a point in time or an historical process, but as a transcendental aspect of the law in general. The focus on the modern

21 The metaphor of weight, coming from the Hebrew word *k'vod*, is explored in some detail by Moshe Halbertal in his Dewey lecture, available on YouTube (Halbertal 2015). Although he perceives the weight metaphor as somehow opposed from the 'rank' Waldron talks about, I think the two concepts are overlapping and mutually supportive.

law developed after the UDHR, and a limited number of legal systems evoked, was not to imply that the dignitarian moment is not present elsewhere. Quite the contrary: Particularly in the face of the meta-legal level, one can reasonably expect that surveys dedicated to different historical periods or other legal cultures would show different faces of the same phenomenon. In societies less egalitarian than ours, for example, some elements of the dignitarian moment would still be traceable – the Roman law could serve as an example. In legal cultures less concentrated on rights, the different wording and constructions could nevertheless show overlapping elements. For the purposes of this book, however, we will confine ourselves to what has been said to this point. It is important to recall that the identification of the dignitarian moment was made in the methodological context, as a tentative clarification of the *explicandum* (human dignity) rather than a complete survey. As such, then, it constitutes the basis for the explicative and explanatory efforts which may be reasonably expected to be sensible and conclusive. In other words, the dignitarian moment is a clearly identified phenomenon that should be explained and may serve as a linguistic-factual basis of constructing an explicative definition for the purposes of law. Since it has been quite a long trip, Table 1.1 provides a summary.

The biggest, striking question that results from this is whether there is unity to be found in the multifarious functions and aspects just outlined. To exaggerate a little, one could even ask: Is the entire enterprise hopeless? Are we perhaps standing against nothing but a normative cacophony with no prospect of consonance? The meta-legal level is crucial in this respect: If one agrees that human dignity is present 'in the tissues and sinews' of law the way Waldron argues, then we do have a good reason to assume that the law evoking 'human dignity', 'personal dignity', 'dignity', and so on, has some common, foundational point of reference. My hypothesis is that one may explicate a focal meaning for human dignity in the law if one follows the *ontological referral.* My own, personalist theory of human dignity, with the central idea of the status of personhood, will be defended as fulfilling exactly this task – finding a suitable bond between the law on one hand, and the natural human personhood on the other. This is quite ambitious and contradicts a lot of the current literature on the topic, which for the most part joins McCrudden in saying that 'dignity appears to become other than impossibly vague only when it is tethered to a coherent community of interpretation' (McCrudden 2008, 723). As mentioned earlier in this chapter, the SPT attempts to go beyond treating human dignity as a placeholder. My suggestion is that when we tether human dignity in the law *to that to which it refers* – to human personhood as such – we can arrive at some universal guidance in developing and adjudicating human dignity. Admittedly, there is some truth in sceptical claims: The family-type meaning and interpretive nature of the notion of human dignity excludes the possibility of a complete and universal definition. However, I will claim that the status of personhood captures something that different jurisdictions have in common, and to which different alternative explications of human dignity in law implicitly refer. That thing is simply *the human legal subject* – the 'natural' human person as someone to whom legal norms are addressed and who shapes these

Table 1.1 The dignitarian moment in the law: a summary.

Function	*Aspects*	*Examples in the law*
Foundational	1. Ontological referral: dignity inheres in all human beings equally and gives them special worth and high status 2. Moral claim: the human being as an end in himself or herself, never a mere means to some external end 3. Political claim: human dignity as a source of human rights, and a basis for the political order	• The UDHR, Article 1 • The UDHR, Article 1 • German Basic Law, Article 1
Regulative	1. Humanitarian aspect: human dignity protecting against grave ill-treatments and crimes (torture, inhuman or degrading treatment) 2. Autonomy aspect: human dignity either fosters autonomy and freedom of choice or imposes limits on it 3. Social security aspect: the authorities obliged to provide a minimum (dignified) economic standard	• The United Nations Convention against Torture • The Charter of Fundamental Rights of the European Union, Article 3: the right to informed consent on medical procedures (fosters autonomy) • The Council of State in France: the dwarf-tossing case (puts limits on individual choice) • The UDHR, Article 22: the right to social security
Heuristic	1. Interpreting evaluative standards 2. Weighing rights (in case of conflict within the system), 3. Developing rights	• *Trop v. Dulles* (The Supreme Court [United States] 1958) • *R v. Butler* (The Supreme Court [Canada] 1992) • *Obergefell v. Hodges* (The Supreme Court [United States] 2015)
Meta-legal level	1. Human dignity shaping the construction and application of a system of law 2. Human dignity as a mark of egalitarianism in the law	• Law using interpretative standards and argumentation • The ethics of legal representation as ensuring a proper standing of the litigant • Justification of administrative decisions (The European Code of Good Administrative Behaviour 2002, Article 18.1)

norms by his activity, either individual or communal. Before we arrive there, however, there is a long road to come: First, one should have some general, philosophical conception of the person at hand, to work up a figure of the human person as legal subject (Chapter 2 will deal with that). Second, one needs to face the inner diversity of the dignitarian moment. This diversity generates multiple problems that a successful explication should be able to tackle. Although I will try to actually resolve these issues in Chapters 3 and 4, for now we should indicate the most important of them.

In terms of the basis of human dignity, there is no *prima facie* coherence. Many influential dignitarian clauses, such as Article 1 of the UDHR, contain an ontological referral: They declare dignity as something inherent in each human being, implying equality in dignity, as well as excluding the idea that dignity can be *conferred* on someone by a legal arrangement (the latter only recognises something that exists independently). On the other hand, some applications of dignity in its regulative function appear to treat dignity as conferred by, or dependent on, social conditions. The most characteristic example is that of the Fourteenth Amendment jurisprudence of the U.S. Supreme Court (1992, 2015). Does this mean that in these and analogous cases, the court simply drifts away from the inherence of human dignity, and in this sense from the UDHR? This is what some have compellingly argued (Menuge 2021). Or perhaps those two different legal concepts – that of inherent, and that of conferred dignity – can be reasonably integrated in some way?

In terms of normative status or weight, there comes the question about the absolute versus limitable character of human dignity. For example, in Explanations Relating to the (European) Charter of Fundamental Rights, one reads that 'none of the rights laid down in this Charter may be used to harm the dignity of another person, and that the dignity of the human person is part of the substance of the rights laid down in this Charter. *It must therefore be respected, even where a right is restricted*' (2007, Article 1, emphasis added). A similar principle is often applied in constitutional interpretation – the courts strive to balance or limit basic rights in a way that, despite the limitation, does not undermine anyone's dignity as the bearer of rights, to recall Weinrib (2016). On the other hand, certainly not everything covered by the dignitarian moment may be considered absolute. Even in constitutional law, the absolute character of human dignity is either watered down by judicial practice and legal scholarship (for the case of Germany, see Enders 2019, 305–12), or explicitly rejected by law, like in the case of Israel or South Africa (both constitutions open their dignity clauses for balancing). In other spheres of law, the limitable character of dignity is more obvious: For instance, the protection of 'personal dignity' against libel or slander must be somehow limited by freedom of speech. The main question in this context concerns whether the human dignity one explicates is only that which is absolute, or only that which is relative. Or perhaps, one may arrive at a conception integrating some absolute core of normative implications, and some secondary rules that are limitable and open for change.

In terms of substance, or in terms of what is supposed to be protected by dignity under the law, we have observed at least three most important facets: human dignity as autonomy (exemplified by *Coetzee v. Comitis*), human dignity as bodily and mental integrity (exemplified by the German Aviation case or French judgements on dwarf-tossing), and human dignity as a recognition of the equally high rank, importance, or weight that legal agents should have (as exemplified by the meta-legal level). An explication of human dignity in the law should be able to show how these three work together, and to what extent, if at all, they are compatible.

Finally, in terms of the proper legal category, human dignity figures in the law in many forms – as a foundation, a fundamental value, a principle, a free-standing right, and so on. Given the family-type meaning of the very concept, one perhaps should not try to find the one and only admissible form. But one may at least hope for finding some paradigmatic, most important forms.

To answer the questions set forth, one can either take a 'reductionist' approach, oriented to find the shared minimum core of the idea, or a 'wide-view' approach that would seek to embrace and integrate many divergent manifestations of the dignitarian moment. This choice is of outstanding consequence. If one adopts the former strategy, one is entitled to exclude perhaps even the majority of the applications of human dignity as found in the law. Choosing the wide view means that as much as possible should be comprised by the theory one wants to work up. To speak metaphorically – after the explication of fish as 'Piscis', we know that dolphins are not fish. The approach one decides to take in explicating human dignity will determine how many fish there are in the sea, and how many non-fish creatures. 'The sea' in our case is, of course, those elements in the law that add up to the dignitarian moment. In this book, I am taking the wide-view approach, for reasons to be explained while working up the conception itself.

The wide-view approach brings one more critical question: How should one deal with normative indeterminacy, as far as the regulative and heuristic functions are concerned? In other words, this is a question about guidance in the scholarly, judicial, and legislative determination of what is to be counted as the normative implications of human dignity. The particular weight of this question results from the fact that, as we have seen, human dignity is often considered to have implications that directly oppose each other.

Conclusion

Although the methodological standards I have outlined in this chapter may possibly be met by various and rival conceptions of human dignity, it is a good moment to briefly characterise the theory I will present and defend in this book, namely, the Status of Personhood Theory. This theory finds its philosophical roots in the personalist conception in anthropology and ethics, and the main patrons of my approach are Karol Wojtyła and Tadeusz Styczeń, both of whom taught at the Catholic University of Lublin in the second half of the twentieth century. I will examine their philosophy with a view to the very specific purpose of interpreting the dignitarian moment. Although personalism is a well-established doctrine in philosophy, ethics, and social thought, it seems to have been a neglected path in jurisprudence. Thus, what I perceive as my most significant contribution is developing a theory of human dignity that would be *both personalist and legal*. Commitments to the human condition, weak metaphysical parsimony, and sceptical realism will guide these investigations, which will result in explicating human dignity as the status of personhood, and using this to explain and sort out the manifold appeals to human dignity in modern law (the dignitarian moment).

Two central ideas of the personalist conception are *human action* (as opposed to mere behaviour), and *entitlement to affirmation* that deeply corresponds to that radical capacity for action.[22] In other words, the personalist conception identifies a special kind of standing of human agents in relation to each other as well as in relation to the law as a system of intelligible rules assuming intentional agency of the addressee.[23] This special standing will be called 'the status of personhood', and the intended *explicatum* of human dignity in the law is a cosmopolitan principle of law stipulating such status. The personalist conception seeks to reconcile certain ontological statements with the sphere of legal norms, as well as with basic postulates concerning institutional arrangements. In other words, the status of personhood, which is at bottom a *philosophical concept*, should be consistent with statements about the aspects of personhood relevant for *law*, and answer what it means to have this status in terms of *politics*. Hence, the three chapters that are the road that is left to come in this book each regard one of these different spheres: philosophy (Chapter 2), law (Chapter 3), and politics (Chapter 4).

Now, the results in all three spheres of inquiry should remain in reflective equilibrium, which is the ultimate method of this inquiry, embracing and integrating all others. Reflective equilibrium is a method that has gained a wide interest as presented by Rawls. He adopted reflective equilibrium as a method of justification, or more precisely, a description and refinement of our sense of justice, which consists in finding coherence between considered moral judgements or intuitions and general moral principles (Rawls 1971, 48–51). Here, I am interested in a much *wider* version of reflective equilibrium, proposed by Norman Daniels, who envisaged it as 'an attempt to produce coherence in an ordered *triple* of sets of beliefs held by a particular person, namely, (a) a set of considered moral judgments, (b) a set of moral principles, and (c) a set of relevant background theories' (Daniels 1979, 258, emphasis added). Unlike Daniels, I will defend an interpretation of reflective equilibrium, which can be called *truth-seeking*. Some

22 The notion of radical capacity, important for my conception of human dignity, is borrowed from Finnis (2011, 8). Its meaning will be explained in more detail in Chapter 2. For now, suffice it to say that radical capacity is not just one of many possibilities (in this sense, I have a capacity to finish writing this book, and you have a capacity to read it), but something essential (in this sense, you and I have a radical capacity to write and read, which was there 'in us' from the outset, even before we learned how to read and write).

23 At the same time, it is assumed that there is no earthly creature known to us that resembles human agency in a way yielding the status equal with humans. But such possibility is not excluded *a priori* – the existence of such creatures is a matter of experience.

further details of this method will be presented along with its direct application in Chapter 3. For now, suffice it to say that Daniels's scheme should be adjusted to jurisprudence, that is, seeking consistency between the status of personhood, particular normative judgements of what human dignity requires, and background theory of the human person. The latter will be considered as making a claim to truth (possibility of falsification being still open). When reflective equilibrium is so conceived, it does not exclusively serve the justificatory role. It may also have a theoretical impact: It allows us to better conceptualise, understand, *and explain* the phenomena under scrutiny.

Adopting reflective equilibrium in a jurisprudential inquiry, one should ask what sources of the 'input' to the reflections are eligible. According to the commitment of weak metaphysical parsimony, the legal material must be conceptually prior to philosophical intuitions or speculation. What I mean is the requirement that the conception of human dignity should result from a reconstruction; something drawn from the law itself, and not merely implanted to the law from elsewhere. While credibility of intuitive moral judgements in reflective equilibrium has been put into doubt (Singer 2005), our reliance on considered *legal* judgements seems to discharge us from these worries. Since the judgements about dignity have been made by the legal authorities in reality, a theorist is certainly not moving back and forth between his or her own biased views or doubtful appearances. The initial 'considered judgements' are the *datum* drawn from external, social reality – they should be taken from the dignitarian moment as has been set forth in this chapter. This renders the law speaking for itself, and a philosophical conception of human dignity providing a basis of a principled interpretation of the law that is. In this sense, the personalist conception of human dignity will be reconstructive. The key method in this context is *comparative legal interpretation*. In further steps, however, according to the commitments to the human condition and to sceptical realism, the interpretation remaining only within the law should be complemented by some source of information about the human subjects (to which it refers). The reconstructive side must be corrected by the critical thinking with a view to identifying misinterpretations of the concept of dignity. This is when *phenomenology* enters into play: a great deal of work in this book will be a juridical application of the phenomenological analysis of personhood. However, reflective equilibrium allows one to correct the phenomenological insights vis-à-vis the considered judgements, and the other way round, when they are confronted.

I admit that all this is quite far from what reflective equilibrium was originally intended to be. According to Rawls, it was a formal device that, at bottom, was seen as 'investigating an aspect of human psychology, the structure of our moral sensibility' (1999, 288). In this context, a legitimate question is that of the cognitive status of the results. Are the judgements we reach true? Or perhaps the best we can achieve is consistency within a system of statements, but we cannot say anything about the truth of these statements? The commitment to the human condition obliges us to offer *a realistic interpretation of reflective equilibrium* and to interpret the results as making a claim to truth. I will not say merely that the personalist conception provides the most reasonable interpretation of the dignitarian moment. Rather, I will claim that the interpretation of the dignitarian moment says something true about different legal practices, and about extra-legal reality. As such, the results of this last step of my inquiry (the explanation of the dignitarian moment) are open to refutation through the findings of some other disciplines, such as natural sciences. For example, if natural sciences prove that there are no such things as persons, the dignitarian moment can no longer be reasonably explained in the way I am proposing, and the Status of Personhood Theory is plainly wrong.

To sum up: The personalist conception of human dignity, with the PSP at its core, connects comparative legal interpretation with phenomenology of action and person, as well as moral or practical principles that are correlative thereto. In this sense, the reconstructive and the critical, as well as the transcendental and the explanatory, may come together in one inquiry. These are the instruments that this chapter was intended to set up. And now we shall start playing.

References

Barak, A. 2013. 'Human Dignity: The Constitutional Value and the Constitutional Right'. In *Understanding Human Dignity*. Edited by Christopher McCrudden. Oxford: Oxford University Press, 361–80.

Baruah, Pritam. 2014. 'Human Dignity in Adjudication: The Limits of Placeholding and Essential Contestability Accounts'. *Canadian Journal of Law & Jurisprudence* 27(2): 329–56.

Bognetti, Giovanni. 2005. 'The Concept of Human Dignity in European and US Constitutionalism'. In *European and US constitutionalism*. Edited by G. Nolte. Cambridge, UK: Cambridge University Press, 95–107. DOI: 10.1017/CBO9780511493904.007

Bosek, Leszek and Olejniczak, Dorota. 2012. 'Opinia w sprawie projektu rozporządzenia Parlamentu Europejskiego i Rady w sprawie badań klinicznych produktów leczniczych stosowanych u ludzi oraz uchylenia dyrektywy 2001/20/WE. [Opinion on the proposal for a regulation of the European Parliament and of the Council on clinical trials on medicinal products for human use, and repealing Directive 2001/20/EC [COM (2012) 369 final]'. *Zeszyty Prawnicze Biura Analiz Sejmowych* 4(36): 118–48.

Botha, Henk. 2009. 'Human Dignity in Comparative Perspective'. *Stellenbosch Law Review* 20(2): 171–220.

Bricker, Phillip. 2016. 'Ontological Commitment'. In *The Stanford Encyclopedia of Philosophy (Winter 2016 Edition)*. Edited by Edward N. Zalta. https://plato.stanford.edu/archives/win2016/entries/ontological-commitment/.

Carnap, Rudolf. 1936. 'Testability and Meaning'. *Philosophy of Science* 3(4): 419–71.

Carnap, Rudolf. 1962. *Logical Foundations of Probability*. Chicago: University of Chicago Press.

Carroza, Paolo G. 2011. 'Human Dignity in Constitutional Adjudication'. In *Comparative Constitutional Law*. Edited by T. Ginsburg and R. Dixon. Cheltenham, UK, Northampton, MA: Edward Elgar, 459–72.

Daly, Erin. 2013. *Dignity Rights*. Philadelphia: University of Pennsylvania Press.

Daniels, Norman. 1979. 'Wide Reflective Equilibrium and Theory Acceptance in Ethics'. *Journal of Philosophy* 75(5): 256–82. DOI: 10.2307/2025881.

Daniluk, Paweł. 2018. Commentary on Article 115. In *Kodeks karny. Komentarz.* [*Penal Code: a Commentary*]. Edited by Ryszard A. Stefański. Warszawa: C.H. Beck.

Delcker, Janosch. 2018. 'Europe Divided over Robot "Personhood"'. *Politico*, 11 April 2018. www.politico.eu/article/europe-divided-over-robot-ai-artificial-intelligence-personhood/

Dreier, Horst. 2004. 'Menschenwürde'. In *Grundgesetz Kommentar, Band I: Article 1–19.* Edited by Horst Dreier. Tübingen: Mohr Siebeck, 139–231.

Dupré, Catherine. 2013. *Importing the Law in Post-Communist Transitions The Hungarian Constitutional Court and the Right to Human Dignity.* Oxford and Portland: Hart Publishing.

Dworkin, Ronald. 2011. *Justice for Hedgehogs.* Cambridge, MA and London: Harvard University Press.

Enders, Christoph. 2019. 'Human Dignity in Germany'. In *Handbook of Human Dignity in Europe.* Edited by P. Becchi and K. Mathis. Cham: Springer, 281–318. DOI: 10.1007/978-3-319-28082-0_14.

Finnis, John. 2011. *Intention and Identity. Collected Essays, Volume 2.* Oxford: Oxford University Press.

Google Duplex. 2018. *A.I. Assistant Calls Local Businesses to Make Appointments.* YouTube video. www.youtube.com/watch?v=D5VN56jQMWM&t=00s.

Goos, Christoph. 2013. '*Würde des Menschen*: Restoring Human Dignity in Post-Nazi Germany'. In *Understanding Human Dignity.* Edited by Christopher McCrudden. Oxford: Oxford University Press, 79–94.

Greenawalt, Kent. 2018. *Realms of Legal Interpretation.* Oxford: Oxford University Press.

Grimm, Dieter. 2007. 'Proportionality in Canadian and German Constitutional Jurisprudence'. *University of Toronto Law Journal* 57: 384–97.

Gupta, Anil. 2019. 'Definitions'. In *The Stanford Encyclopedia of Philosophy.* Edited by E.N. Zalta. https://plato.stanford.edu/archives/win2019/entries/definitions/.

Halbertal, Moshe. 2015. *Three Concepts of Human Dignity.* YouTube video. www.youtube.com/watch?v=FyEvREFZVvc&t=0s.

Hennette-Vauchez, Stéphanie. 2014. 'Human Dignity in French Law'. In *The Cambridge Handbook of Human Dignity.* Edited by M. Düwell, J. Braarvig, R. Brownsword, and D. Mieth. Cambridge, UK: Cambridge University Press.

Heyman, Steven J. 2008. *Free Speech and Human Dignity.* New Haven and London: Yale University Press.

Jakl, Bernhard. 2013. 'Human Dignity as Fundamental Right to Freedom in Law'. In *Human Dignity as a Foundation of Law.* Edited by Winfried Brugger and Stephan Kirste. Stuttgart: Franz Steiner Verlag, 93–104.

Kant, Immanuel. 1998. *The Groundwork for the Metaphysics of Morals.* Translated and edited by M. Gregor. Cambridge, UK: Cambridge University Press.

Kirste, Stephan. 2013. 'A Legal Concept of Dignity as a Foundation of Law'. In *Human Dignity as a Foundation of Law.* Edited by Winfried Brugger and Stephan Kirste. Stuttgart: Franz Steiner Verlag, 63–81.

Knoll, Manuel. 2019. 'Deep Disagreements on Social and Political Justice: Their Meta-Ethical Relevance and the Need for a New Research Perspective'. In *New Perspectives on Distributive Justice.* Edited by M. Knoll, S.

Snyder, and N. Simsek. Berlin and Boston: Walter de Gruyter, 23–51. DOI: 10.1515/9783110537369-003.

Królikowski, Michał and Szczucki, Krzysztof. 2016. Commentary on Article 39. In *Konstytucja RP. T.1. Komentarz do Art. 1–86*. Edited by Marek Safjan and Leszek Bosek. Warszawa: C.H. Beck.

Królikowski, Michał and Zawłocki, Robert. 2018. *Prawo karne*. [*Penal Law*]. Warszawa: C.H. Beck.

Lebech, Mette. 2019. *European Sources of Human Dignity: A Commented Anthology*. Oxford: Peter Lang.

Luban. David. 2005. 'Lawyers as Upholders of Human Dignity (When They aren't Busy Assaulting It)'. *University of Illinois Law Review* (3): 815–45.

Maier, Andreas. 2011. 'Torture'. In *Humiliation, Degradation, Dehumanization: Human Dignity Violated*. Edited by P. Kaufmann, H. Kuch, Ch. Neuhäuser, and E. Webster. Dordrecht: Springer.

Margalit, Avishai. 1996. *The Decent Society*. Translated by N. Goldblum. Cambridge, MA and London: Harvard University Press.

Maritain, Jacques. 1966. *Man and State*. Chicago: University of Chicago Press.

Mathis, Klaus. 2013. 'Human Dignity as a Two-Edged Sword'. In *Human Dignity as a Foundation of Law*. Edited by Winfried Brugger and Stephan Kirste. Stuttgart: Franz Steiner Verlag, 131–44.

May, James R. and Daly, Erin. 2020. *Advanced Introduction to Human Dignity and Law*. Cheltenham and Northampton: Edward Elgar Publishing.

McCrudden, Christopher. 2008. 'Human Dignity and Judicial Interpretation of Human Rights'. *The European Journal of International Law* 19(4): 655–724. DOI: 10.1093/ejil/chn043.

McCrudden, Christopher. 2013. 'In Pursuit of Human Dignity: An Introduction to Current Debates'. In *Understanding Human Dignity*. Edited by Christopher McCrudden. Oxford: Oxford University Press, 1–59.

Menuge, Angus. 2021. 'The New Dignity Jurisprudence: A Critique'. In *The Inherence of Human Dignity, Volume 2: Law and Religious Liberty*. Edited by B.W. Busey and A.J.L. Menuge. London and New York: Anthem Press, 75–92.

Mowbray, Alastair. 2004. *The Development of Positive Obligations under the European Convention on Human Rights by the European Court of Human Rights*. Oxford and Portland: Hart Publishing.

Naffine, Ngaire. 2009. *Law's Meaning of Life*. Oxford and Portland: Hart Publishing.

Nussbaum, Martha. 2008. 'Human Dignity and Political Entitlements'. In *Human Dignity and Bioethics*. Edited by Barbara T. Lanigan. New York: Nova Science Publishers, 245–64.

Pawłowski, Tadeusz. 1980a. *Concept Formation in the Humanities and the Social Sciences*. Dordrecht, Boston, London: D. Reidel Publishing Company.

Pawłowski, Tadeusz. 1980b. *Begriffsbildung und Definition*. Translated by G. Grzyb. Berlin and New York: Walter de Gruyter.

Przełęcki, Marian. 1958. 'W sprawie terminów nieostrych. [On Fuzzy Terms]'. *Studia Logica* 7: 313–17.

Rawls, John. 1971. *A Theory of Justice*. Cambridge, MA: Belknap Press of Harvard University Press.

Rawls, John. 1999. *Collected Papers*. Cambridge, MA and London: Harvard University Press.

Rawls, John. 2005. *Political Liberalism*. New York: Columbia University Press.

Raz, Joseph. 1996. *Ethics in the Public Domain: Essays in the Morality of Law and Politics.* Oxford: Oxford University Press.
Riley, Stephen. 2017. *Human Dignity and Law.* London and New York: Routledge.
Riordan, Patrick. 2013. 'Which Dignity? Which Religious Freedom?'. In *Understanding Human Dignity.* Edited by Christopher McCrudden. Oxford: Oxford University Press, 421–34.
Singer, Peter. 2005. 'Ethics and Intuitions'. *The Journal of Ethics* 9(3/4): 331–52.
Steiger, Andy. 2021. 'Artificial Dignity: The Humanizing and Dehumanizing Implications of Polanyi versus Turing's Ontology'. In *The Inherence of Human Dignity. Volume 1: Foundations of Human Dignity.* Edited by B.W. Busey and A.J.L. Menuge. London and New York: Anthem Press, 217–33.
Tiedemann, Paul. 2012. *Menchenwürde als Rechtsbegriff.* Berlin: Berliner Wissenschafts-Verlag.
Tiedemann, Paul. 2013. 'Human Dignity as an Absolute Value'. In *Human Dignity as a Foundation of Law.* Edited by Winfried Brugger and Stephan Kirste. Stuttgart: Franz Steiner Verlag, 25–40.
Urbańczyk, Michał. 2019. *Idea godności człowieka w orzecznictwie Sądu Najwyższego Stanów Zjednoczonych Ameryki* [*The Idea of Human Dignity in Supreme Court of the United States of America Case Law*]. Poznań: Wydawnictwo Naukowe UAM.
Waldron, Jeremy. 2011. 'How Law Protects Dignity'. NYU School of Law, Public Law Research Paper No. 11–83. DOI: 10.2139/ssrn.1973341.
Waldron, Jeremy. 2012. *Dignity, Rank, and Rights.* Edited by M. Dan-Coen. Oxford and New York: Oxford University Press.
Webster, Elaine. 2011. 'Degradation: A Human Rights Law Perspective'. In *Humiliation, Degradation, Dehumanization: Human Dignity Violated.* Edited by P. Kaufmann, H. Kuch, Ch. Neuhäuser, and E. Webster. Dordrecht: Springer.
Weinrib, Jacob. 2016. *Dimensions of Dignity.* Cambridge: Cambridge University Press.
Weissbrodt, David and Heilman, Cheryl. 2011. 'Defining Torture and Cruel, Inhuman, and Degrading Treatment'. *Law & Inequality* 29: 343–94. http://scholarship.law.umn.edu/faculty_articles/366.
Wittgenstein, Ludwig. 2009. *Philosophical Investigations.* Translated by G.E.M. Anscombe, P.M.S. Hacker, and J. Schulte. Chichester: Willey-Blackwell.
Wojtczak, Sylwia. 2021. 'Endowing Artificial Intelligence with Legal Subjectivity'. *AI & Society.* DOI: 10.1007/s00146-021-01147-7.
Zieliński, Adam. 2003. 'Pojmowanie godności ludzkiej w świetle praw ekonomicznych i socjalnych. [Understanding human dignity in the light of economic and social rights]'. In *Godność człowieka a prawa ekonomiczne i socjalne* [*Human Dignity and Economic and Social Rights*]. Warszawa: Biuro Rzecznika Praw Obywatelskich, 47–57.

Cases

Constitutional Tribunal of the Republic of Poland. 1993. 17 March 1993. W. 16/92.
Constitutional Tribunal of the Republic of Poland. 2002. 15 October 2002. SK 6/02.
Constitutional Tribunal of the Republic of Poland. 2006. 1 September 2006. SK 14/05.
Constitutional Tribunal of the Republic of Poland. 2015. 7 October 2015. K 12/14.

Council of State of the French Republic. 1995. Conseil d'Etat. 27 October 1995, no. 136727.

European Court of Human Rights. 1998a. *Assenov and others v. Bulgaria*. 90/1997/874/1086.28 October 1998.

European Court of Human Rights. 1998b. *A. v. The United Kingdom*. 100/1997/884/109623. September 1998.

European Court of Human Rights. 2001. *Price v. the United Kingdom*. 33394/96. 10 July 2001.

European Court of Human Rights. 2004. M.C. v. Bulgaria. 39272/98. 3 April 2004.

European Court of Human Rights. 2010. *Florea v. Romania*. 37186/03. 14 September 2010.

Federal Constitutional Court of Germany. 2006.15 February 2006.1 BvR 357/05. Official translation. www.bundesverfassungsgericht.de/SharedDocs/Entscheidungen/EN/2006/02/rs20060215_1bvr035705en.html.

High Court of South Africa. 2001. *Coetzee v Comitis and Others*. 2001 (1) SA 1254 (C).

House of Lords. 1932. *Donoghue v Stevenson* UKHL 100. 26 May 1932.

Inter-American Court of Human Rights. 2016. *I.V. v. Bolivia*. 30 November 2016.

Supreme Court of Canada 1992. R v. Butler. 1 S.C.R. 452.

Supreme Court of the United States. 1958. *Trop v. Dulles*, 356 U.S. 86.

Supreme Court of the United States. 1971. *Cohen v California*, 403 U.S. 15.

Supreme Court of the United States. 1990. Cruzan v. Director, Missouri Dept. of Health, 497 U.S. 261.

Supreme Court of the United States. 1992. *Planned Parenthood of Southeastern Pennsylvania v. Casey*, 505 U.S. 833.

Supreme Court of the United States. 1997. *Washington v. Glucksberg*, 521 U.S. 702.

Supreme Court of the United States. 2015. *Obergefell v. Hodges*, 135 S. Ct. 1732, 576 U.S.

The Human Rights Committee of the United Nations. 2007. Selected Decisions Of The Human Rights Committee Under The Optional Protocol. V. 8. New York and Geneva: United Nations. Communication No. 854/1999: 110–114.

United Nations International Criminal Tribunal for the Former Yugoslavia. 1998. *Prosecutor v. Anto Furundzija*. IT 95 17/1 PT. 10 December 1998.

Legal and political documents

Additional Protocol II. 1977. Protocol Additional to the Geneva Conventions of 12 August 1949, and relating to the Protection of Victims of Non-International Armed Conflicts (Protocol II). 8 June 1977.

African Charter on Human and Peoples Rights. 1981. OAU Doc. CAB/LEG/67/3 rev. 5, 21 I.L.M. 58 (1982). 27 June 1981.

African Commission for Human and Peoples' Rights. 2017. Guidelines on the Conditions of Arrest, Police Custody and Pre-Trial Detention in Africa. Luanda Guidelines Toolkit.

African Court Law Report. 2019. Report of Judgments, Advisory Opinions and Other Decisions of the African Court on Human and Peoples' Rights, Volume 1 (2006–2016). Pretoria University Law Press.

American Convention On Human Rights. 1969. Adopted at the Inter-American Specialized Conference on Human Rights. 22 November 1969.

Basic Law for Germany. 1949. Basic Law for the Federal Republic of Germany. Adopted 8 May 1949. Official translation available at: www.gesetze-im-internet.de/englisch_gg/.
Building Law Act [Poland]. 1994. Ustawa Prawo Budowlane. Adopted 7 July 1994. Dz. U. 1994 Nr 89 poz. 414.
Canadian Charter of Rights and Freedoms. 1982. Enacted as Schedule B to the Canada Act 1982, c. 11 (U.K.).
CFR. 2012. Charter of Fundamental Rights of the European Union. 2012/C 326/02. 26 October 2012.
Constitution of Spain. 1978. Adopted at the Congress of Deputies and the Senate. 31 October 1978. Official English translation. www.lamoncloa.gob.es/lang/en/espana/leyfundamental/Paginas/index.aspx.
Constitution of the Republic of Poland. 1997. Adopted by the National Assembly. 2 April 1997. Official translation available at: www.sejm.gov.pl/prawo/konst/angielski/kon1.htm. Accessed 28 January 2020.
Constitution of the Republic of South Africa. NO. 108 OF 1996. 18 December 1996.
ECHR. 1950. Convention for the Protection of Human Rights and Fundamental Freedoms (ETS No. 005). Rome. 4 November 1950.
Economic and Social Council of the United Nations. 2018. Committee on Economic, Social and Cultural Rights. Views adopted by the Committee under the Optional Protocol to the Covenant concerning communication No. 10/2015. E/C.12/63/D/10/2015.
Explanations Relating To The Charter Of Fundamental Rights. 2007. The Presidium of the European Convention. 2007/C 303/02.14 December 2007.
ICCPR. 1966. International Covenant on Civil and Political Rights. United Nations General Assembly resolution 2200A (XXI). 16 December 1966.
ICESCR. 1966. International Covenant on Economic, Social and Cultural Rights. United Nations General Assembly resolution 2200A (XXI). 16 December 1966.
Penal Code [Poland]. 1997. Ustawa z dnia 6 czerwca 1997 r. kodeks karny. Dz. U. 1997 Nr 88 poz. 553. Last amended 2021.
Protocol Supplementing the UN Convention against Transnational Organized Crime. 2000. Protocol to Prevent, Suppress and Punish Trafficking in Persons Especially Women and Children, supplementing the United Nations Convention against Transnational Organized Crime. General Assembly resolution 55/25.15 November 2000.
Sejm of the Republic of Poland. 2017. Uzasadnienie projektu ustawy prawo przedsiębiorców z dnia 10.02.2017 r. Druk sejmowy nr 2051. 21 November 2017.
The Civil Procedure Rules of England and Wales. 1998. No. 3132 (L. 17).
The European Code of Good Administrative Behaviour 2002. www.ombudsman.europa.eu/en/publication/en/3510.
UDHR. 1948. The Universal Declaration of Human Rights. United Nations General Assembly resolution 217A (III). 10 December 1948.
UNCAT. 1984. Convention against Torture and Other Cruel, Inhuman or Degrading Treatment or Punishment. United Nations General Assembly resolution 39/46. 10 December 1984.
UN Charter. 1945. The Charter of the United Nations. Adopted at the United Nations Conference on International Organization. 26 June 1945.

2 Philosophy

The personalist conception of human action and affirmation proper to persons

Introduction

According to my commitment to weak metaphysical parsimony, approaching the legal dimension of human dignity as something *derived from philosophy* must be considered doubtful. Therefore, the SPT is not a straightforward application of the personalist philosophy into jurisprudence. It is, rather, the other way round: my investigations have made a start in the law, particularly in the dignitarian moment set forth in Chapter 1. Philosophical conceptions are now coming into play as indispensable when interpreting and explaining law (in this case, the law evoking human dignity). Recall that weak metaphysical parsimony does not consist in completely eschewing broader ontological or axiological statements. Quite to the contrary: They must be introduced, as part of the human condition, that which human dignity serves to tie up with the law. The notion of wide reflective equilibrium likewise suggests that it is not reasonable to *a priori* exclude a possibility of finding sufficient reasons for legal arrangements, or developments within law, in truths external to the law. Law is obviously unexplainable through the recourse to the law only, especially when legal provisions themselves refer to extra-legal reality, as in the case of the ontological referral that is made as part of the dignitarian moment. In this context, one must agree that metaphysical parsimony does not predetermine how deeply or how broadly one needs to engage with ontological or metaphysical issues. It merely asks the researcher to be cautious, and it all depends on how much the inquiry itself will demand. In the case of our inquiry, we may expect that many questions about human dignity generated by the law will be properly answered once a clear philosophical conception of *the human legal subject, and that subject's legal personhood*, has been developed. Although the conception of human dignity I want to achieve (which is essentially the task of Chapter 3, with the necessary supplement in Chapter 4), is conceived as a *legal doctrine*, the necessary background is found in *a philosophy of the human person*.

However, an important reservation is that the methodological credentials of human dignity encourage one to abstain from looking for a comprehensive or exhaustive figure of the human being which would provide an interpretation of human dignity as one among many of its implications. Instead, *one should*

DOI: 10.4324/9781003252733-3

directly examine, with philosophical tools, both human personhood and dignity as they appear in the law. The philosophy of the human person that I will deal with in this chapter is then perceived as a response to challenges generated by the law itself. A set of interpretative guidelines, available in the personalist conception, offers prospects to sort out the issues directly stemming from the dignitarian moment. The underlying question is how to conceive of the person to whom the ontological referral appeals, and on which aspects, out of the open-ended palette of features, narratives, capacities, and the like, one should put special attention.

The hope underlying this book is that a philosophical reflection of a particular kind, namely, *phenomenology of the human person* alongside *phenomenology of normativity*, is well-suited for the job of answering this question. For now, from the perspective of the reader, it cannot be perceived otherwise than as an assumption, and I ask the reader to make that assumption with me. What additionally justifies the choice of the personalist conception is the peculiar character of this philosophy itself. Namely, one of the distinguishing features of this approach is to 'go directly to the things examined', rather than focus on their conceptualisations hitherto. In other words, both Wojtyła and Styczeń are, in the first place, committed to reflecting directly on the phenomenon or reality they intend to examine. Instead of discussing the history of ideas, they apply the phenomenological method in order to describe things as they appear in perception and in reality. I am attempting to do something similar in this book.

I started with a raw mapping of dignity usages in the law (Chapter 1), which leads me to the problem of personhood (as the ontological referral suggests, it is reasonable to search for 'the who': the person at whom the human dignity clauses point). Given the fact that law is often the domain or frame of human action, an account which tries to examine personhood through actions seems an appropriate candidate to engage with in this chapter, along with the normative side of personhood – that is, the respect or affirmation that is the person's due. My engagement with these topics, as analysed within the personalist conception, leads to certain insights, which are then tested, adjusted, and put in equilibrium with the legal usages of human dignity and its political and institutional implications (Chapters 3 and 4). As we will see, the phenomenology I am dealing with is of a particular, radically realist kind. It claims to be able to examine something more than mere appearances as objects of consciousness – the real things themselves. This is why the equilibrium that is to be reached at the end of our inquiry is to be understood in a realistic manner – as an equilibrium that does not seek mere consistency but simply truth.

The central tenets that I will be occupied with in this chapter are: (i) the capacity of human persons for the (genuinely personal) action, which is simultaneously a sign of their inherent dignity; and (ii) affirmation proper to persons, which is tantamount to adequate responses to their inherent dignity. As explained earlier, instead of examining details of the history of ideas, I choose to engage in dialogue with the two philosophers who have examined those issues in the most direct and exceptionally penetrating way. Karol Wojtyła and Tadeusz Styczeń are perfect interlocutors and teachers in this regard. Applying phenomenological methods allowed them to directly engage with the phenomena they wanted to examine. On the other hand, conducting their analyses in the realist, Thomistic framework kept them in contact not only with the rich philosophical tradition of Western classical philosophy, but also with common sense and common experience. Choosing their conception(s), I have two important hopes in mind – first, that their insights will elucidate the dignitarian moment as it appears in the law, and second, even if some important competing accounts were not examined, the truth of the results will speak for itself, and defend the theory against competing accounts when necessary.

The structure of this chapter, which serves a bridge or middle step between the dignitarian moment and its proper interpretation, is as follows. In Section 1, I outline the personalist conception against the broader background of the competing and the parallel conceptions of the human person. Then, in Section 2, I point at the most solid basis of the personalist conception, which is that of experience, understood very broadly, far from narrow empiricism. In short, the relatively secure position of personalism is that instead of relying on speculation, it recurrently refers to human experience. Once this is done, I examine in more detail two substantive tenets of the personalist conception, ones that are crucial to the proper interpretation of the dignitarian moment in the law – the ontology of human persons in action (Section 3), and affirmation of persons for their own sake, as a universal normative requirement (Section 4). Finally, as a conclusion, I present the path in which the personalist conception will be applied in developing the Status of Personhood Theory. Importantly, I am suggesting a path that does not treat dignity and respect as an exclusively moral notion. Instead, dignity of the human person will be regarded as an implicit commitment of human activity in more general terms, which includes the law. I call it 'the praxiological reading' of the personalist conception, and I will develop it further in the following chapters.

1 Mapping personalism: the Personalist Postulate

The term 'personalism' may be misleading, and thus some initial clarification is needed. First, it may be associated with the continental-European disputes held in the nineteenth century, concerning pantheism versus theistic personalism (Bengtsson 2006, 33). Theological issues are obviously beyond the scope of this study, but it must be recalled that both Wojtyła and Styczeń were Catholic philosophers, which obviously makes them stand in the latter (theistic) camp. In terms of the history of ideas, the personalist conception should be situated in the context of Catholic philosophy developed after the Second Vatican Council. An important mark of that particular stream in Catholic philosophy is that it focuses on the human person, combining the ancient and medieval classics (*philosophia perrenis*) with certain elements of modern thought, especially that of phenomenology. In particular, Wojtyła (and Styczeń after him) was strongly inspired by, and critically engaged with, the thought of Max Scheler.[1]

Before getting into any detail of the personalist conception, it seems expedient to situate it within the panorama of commonly known (and competing) conceptions of human personhood. For the sake of clarity, I will situate the personalist conception between two extremes. According to one extreme, being a person is tantamount to having self-awareness that continues over time. This thinking has a long tradition, starting perhaps with John Locke's thought that the word 'person' stands for a being which 'can consider itself as itself, the same thinking thing, in different times and places' (Locke 1999, 318). According to this thought (which, when understood broadly, still enjoys quite common appeal among philosophers), a continuing stream of consciousness, manifested in having memories of the past and plans for the future, the picture of one's own self, as well as meaningful social relations, is that which ultimately constitutes personhood (McMahan 2002, 6). According to the other extreme, being a person means primarily belonging to a class of entities with a special kind of nature. Although that nature is rational – which implies a continuing self-awareness and a general picture of oneself – being a person ultimately consists in being a substantial entity of a particular, rational kind. This position dates back to Boethius, who famously defined 'person' (having in mind the Divine persons in the first place) as an individual substance of a rational nature. In contemporary debates, a similar position is attached to affirming that the organic human life (a dynamic functioning of bodily elements, trackable from the very moment of fertilisation of a human ovum) is at the same time the personal life (Finnis 2011a, 284). Whether or not, and in what sense, being a person involves having or being a soul, is another, separate question, one that we do not have to consider here. The controversy I am now referring to is whether human personhood boils down to consciousness, or rather to the substantial form, that is, the very essence of the human being.

Now, the personalist conception is obviously closer to the second position. Although Cardinal Wojtyła focuses largely on a paradigmatic, adult, and well-developed human being who is at the same time an acting person, he also mentions that personhood is attributable to the human being from the moment of conception (Wojtyła 1979, 180). Tadeusz Styczeń, also a Catholic priest, argued forcefully for the full recognition of the unborn humans as human persons (Styczeń in Moń 2019, 183–90). Thus, one should note that the personalist conception should never be conflated with an idealist, metaphysical standpoint characteristic of American personalism, 'wherein being is defined as personal consciousness' (Williams and Bengtsson 2020, s. 4). To the contrary, both Wojtyła and Styczeń were metaphysical realists, and they claim that human personhood has a real,

1 Colosi (2008) highlights the fact that the idea of the uniqueness and worth of persons, manifesting itself in experience, which is the central tenet in Wojtyła's thought, was a positive inspiration he took from Scheler (1973), despite all criticism, expressed in his habilitation (Wojtyła 1959).

substantive basis in the biological human life, which nevertheless is marked with a spiritual aspect. However, despite realism, there is one important tenet which differentiates the personalist conception from simple neo-Aristotelianism, or a restatement of the conventional scholastic metaphysics (or, rather, what scholastic metaphysics is conventionally taken to have been). Namely, according to Wojtyła, examination of the content of consciousness by means of phenomenology is fully legitimate, as *supplementing* (and not opposing) the objectivistic, Aristotelian framework of substantial forms. While Wojtyła appreciated that framework (1979, 63), he also thought that it might lead to failing to discern and recognise the irreducible, individual character of the human person (2008a). According to Wojtyła, *human reality in itself*, as an object of inquiry accessible in experience, transcends each philosophical tradition taken separately, and calls for integrating different traditions rather than going for one or the other (Wojtyła 2008a, 210). Thus, on the one hand, although he rarely uses the term 'human nature', he does not reject the Thomist view on essence – human beings do have real essence, according to Wojtyła (2008b, 182). With this realistic basis in mind, he explicitly argues that personal consciousness should not be conflated with the human subject considered as a whole (Wojtyła 1979, 34). On the other hand, Wojtyła believes that the lived experience of personal consciousness is critically important for really understanding the person as a person, and not merely as an instantiation of the human species. This is what fundamentally differentiates Wojtyła from philosophers such as John Finnis or Ralph McInerny, who claim the reflection on basic human goods (Finnis 2011b) or human nature (McInerny 1992) suffices to establish an adequate picture of the human being for practical purposes. According to the personalist, by contrast, the phenomenological analysis of consciousness reveals that there is something irreducibly subjective in the human person; something which cannot be captured by traditional, objectivising categories dating back to Aristotle or Boethius (Wojtyła 2008a, 211).[2] The personalist 'fusion' of the perennial philosophy and phenomenology allows us to examine personhood *from within*, by analysing the content of conscious acts in a subjective perspective. But these analyses are made on the objectivist plane – a broadly Thomistic background, with the special affinity for existential Thomism, established by Etienne Gilson, and widely accepted in Lublin (for details, see Kupczak 2000, 49–57). Tadeusz Styczeń, whose work focused mostly on meta-ethics, was also a metaphysical realist. His *opus magnum* (2012a) sought for a universally valid basis for ethics, which he found in moral experience, which

2 In fact, it is highly debatable how precisely the relation of Thomism and phenomenology is set in Wojtyła's work. I will not examine this issue here, but it is worth mentioning that the first (Polish) edition of *The Acting Person*, published in 1969 was more Thomistic in tenor. The English translation, and the subsequent Polish editions (released in 1985, 1994, and 2011) that follow it, highlighted the phenomenological aspects, at the expense of the Thomistic traits, in quite a few passages. For a detailed tracking of the changes, see Jałocho-Palicka (2016). For the controversy over the English edition, see Weigel 2005, 174–175).

appears, when examined without bias, as a 'specific, direct cognitive contact with morality as a distinct fact' (Styczeń 2012a, 116).

In spite of the importance of the context and background just indicated – the Catholic thought after the Second Vatican Council, perennial philosophy, the existential Thomism, and (realistic) phenomenology – the approach taken in this chapter distances itself from all this, in a certain sense. Namely, according to the commitment to sceptical realism, I examine the personalist analyses as relatively independent from the context in which they emerge. By consequence, their results are treated not as a product of their époque, but rather as simply true or false contentions; adequate or misleading insights into the real structures of personhood. In short, the examined elements of the personalist conception will be regarded as *objectively valid* statements, rather than as historically expressed opinions or conjectures.[3] We can now present these statements.

The focal and organising thought, which most adequately characterises the personalist movement (conceived broadly, also beyond Wojtyła and Styczeń), says the following: Each human person – or, rather, each human being as a person – must be respected as a free, conscious, and self-constituting agent who belongs to himself or herself, and is not fundamentally ordered to some end that is external to them. The term *incommunicabilitas* – incommunicability – is sometimes used to express this fundamental condition of personal existence (Richard of St. Victor 2011, 101). In contemporary anthropology, a synthetic formulation of this by John F. Crosby says the following:

> Persons do not exist as replaceable specimens or as mere instances of some ideal or type, but exist rather for their own sakes, each existing as incommunicably his or her own.
>
> (Crosby 1996, 41)

For the purposes of our discussion, this may be called *the principle of incommunicable personhood*. The theory of human dignity in the law that I am pursuing in this book may be read as a legal reinterpretation of this principle. Acting properly to persons, and giving them the respect that is their due, constitute the field in which incommunicability manifests itself in the most instructive way, and this has been made explicit by Wojtyła and Styczeń. My aim is to highlight the implications for law which come once we take the personalist conception seriously.

The incommunicability of persons in the sense adopted by medieval theology, and twentieth-century anthropology, affirms the reality of a particular kind of

3 In context of the worldviews which claim that the human being is fully explainable in materialistic, scientific (biological or social) terms (Churchland 2008), the possibly fundamental challenge for the personalist conception would be that it is based on either false premises or attempts to build 'a science-like' reflection on a somehow irrational basis. Against this, we must say that reality and relevance of features of human conduct such as consciousness (Gallagher 2018) or intentional agency (List 2019) have not yet been completely dismissed as irrelevant, or 'folk' and prescientific. The ball is still in play.

existence that human beings have, which is 'personal and not merely individual in the sense of individuation of nature' (Wojtyła 1979, 73, translation modified). This statement could be understood as calling for something more than an ontological contention or an experiential observance – a metaphysical, ultimate explanation of personal existence, saying what it consists of and what its ultimate source is. As extensively explained beforehand, our inquiry into human incommunicable subjectivity will be limited by the very purpose of that inquiry. Since law does not necessarily need ultimate metaphysical explanations, we will also stay within the boundaries of the practical. In this context, Crosby's principle may be reformulated in a manner pertaining to the sphere of legality, in the form of the Personalist Postulate (PP):

> PP. *Before the law, persons are not regarded as replaceable specimens or as mere instances of some ideal or type, but rather as having intrinsic importance, each standing as incommunicably his or her own.*

My theory of human dignity in law, with its central concept of the status of personhood, should be read as a specification of the PP, by reaching equilibrium with the dignitarian moment in the law.

Of course, this view of persons stands on the shoulders of giants. Recalling them all here would be counterproductive, but I must emphasise the importance of one historical *legal* contribution, namely, that of the Roman law. In the Digest of Justinian, one finds the idea of a person as central for law as such. In the opening chapters, we read that 'all law is established for the sake of the human beings', and thus the status of persons is something which 'we shall speak first of' (Digest of Justinian, 1.5.2, translation modified). This commitment means that the human person is placed as law's chief purpose (*causa omne ius*), and thus as something one always should bear in mind while considering more particular legal cases. But persons are not simply passive units that law should take care of. Free persons – those who are *sui juris* – are subject to *their own jurisdiction*, and not somebody else's (Digest of Justinian, 1985, 1.6.1).[4] A *sui juris* person is therefore endowed with certain intrinsic importance, enjoying freedom within the framework of laws. This idea was particularly strong in the civil law tradition (which originated in continental Europe), and thus Patrick Glenn is right to emphasize that this tradition has been marked by 'the centrality of the person' (2010, 148–51). The SPT attempts to provide a secure basis of renewing this old thought in modern circumstances, on the personalist grounds. The underlying belief is that

4 As commonly known, Roman law ascribed such status only to some human beings, those who were free men (*liberi*), as opposed to slaves (*servi*), and those of status of *alieni juris* (such as those having status of sons and daughters, subject to paternal authority). Although such fundamental differentiation of legal status is no longer present in modern law, that basic construction of free persons as being *sui juris* is persistent, and enjoyed, in principle at least, by everyone.

the roots of the SPT itself are more solid than simply an historical exigence to renew that thought.

2 Securing personalism: empirical basis and empirical relevance

Before dealing with the substance of the personalist conception, I shall set forth its most important meta-theoretical, or plainly epistemological, claim. Namely, both Wojtyła and Styczeń are univocal with regards to the source and starting point of their theories, which they see in *experience*, thereby making claim to the empirical foundation of the personalist conception, and its empirical relevance. One could even say that their project as a whole stems from a particular view of 'experience' and rests on a particular view of what 'empirical relevance' means. This is extremely important for my inquiry, too – the requirements of metaphysical parsimony and sceptical realism may be met precisely because of the way in which the personalist conception is grounded in experience. To be exact: The personalist conception itself is not metaphysically parsimonious in the sense I have adopted in Chapter 1 of this book (Taylor 2009).[5] But its special recurring engagement with the data given in experience allows me to develop the Status of Personhood Theory in a metaphysically parsimonious, albeit personalist, manner.

First and foremost, the personalist conception strongly rejects empiricism, that is, a reductionist standpoint wherein experience is nothing but *observation or perception* of that which appears *in sense* (Wojtyła 1979, 8). Instead, what is considered to be 'at the very heart of experience' is *phenomenon* – 'something that "manifests itself" to us, something that affects our cognitive powers in a perceptible way' (Wojtyła 2008c, 114). Such a view is clearly inspired by Husserl's phenomenology – the personalist conception seems to implicitly accept Husserl's *principle of all principles*, according to which '*everything originarily* (so to speak, in its "personal" actuality) *offered* to us *in "intuition" is to be accepted simply as what it is presented as being, but also only within the limits in which it is presented there*' (Husserl 1983, 44, emphasis original). The notion of phenomenon is then tethered to individual consciousness – phenomena appear in mental processes as objects accessible in an intuition or perception. Every cognitive contact with phenomena which the human being experiences is 'always associated with the

5 It is particularly well observable in the case of Styczeń. In his view, the analysis of the moral duty that constitutes the foundation for ethics, understood as a science, must be complemented by an ultimate explanation – without one, ethics is not possible as a science. In this sense, the 'explicative ethics' (making explicit the character and content of the moral duty) must be subsequently developed into a 'metaphysics of morals', explaining not only the duties in relation towards, but also the very existence of, persons (Styczeń 2012a, 198–235). Our inquiry is of a different character: We will use philosophical conceptions to *explain* the law, it is true, but the explanation will be offered on a lower level of *pro tanto* explanation – without recourse to ultimate explanations of metaphysical nature, strictly speaking.

experience of himself' (Wojtyła 1979, 3). Experience, in the sense adopted by the personalist conception, must be then something broader than merely the data apprehended by the senses, although it must be something directly accessed by the cognising subject (and not a result of mere speculation).

As an example, let us consider Wojtyła's approach to human freedom. As he writes, freedom is an indispensable element of action, and as such, it also allows one to morally qualify one's conduct, and moral character, as 'good or bad' (Wojtyła 1979, 98). He observes:

> When we search deep into the integral structure of moral conduct and becoming, into the integral structure of man's becoming morally good or morally bad, we discover in it the proper moment of freedom. 'Moment' is here understood in the phenomenological sense – in the structure of man's becoming morally good or bad through his actions, freedom manifests itself most appropriately.
>
> (Wojtyła 1979, 99, translation modified)

As one may infer from this passage, freedom certainly is not something to be cognised through sense perception or falsified through experimentation. Nonetheless, freedom (as something which is one's own) is directly accessible to the individual by means of inner experience. The latter reveals freedom as a real characteristic or structure of human conduct, rather than a merely mental process (lived experience of 'feeling free'). The example of freedom is instructive, as one clearly sees a twofold stance that fundamentally characterises the personalist conception: The subjective, phenomenological examination of inner experience is integrated with an objectivist orientation in epistemology. According to Wojtyła, freedom is not only a piece of consciousness which can be described through the phenomenological method. Although it certainly is intuited as a phenomenon, at the same time it 'forms a real and inherent component of the [human] structure' (1979, 99). Importantly, the belief that freedom is real is not gained through metaphysical speculation about human nature. Rather, it is directly given as something real in experience of the person in action. The most direct source of knowledge about freedom, and the basis for philosophising about or further conceptualising freedom, is therefore the experience of one's own freedom.

Speaking more generally, Wojtyła aims at integrating different ways in which the experience of the human being as acting person occurs. That includes not only empirical knowledge gained by methods of natural science (boiling down to sense perception) but also other elements, such as experience of one's own efficacy, one's own ego, or interiority (inner experience). Also not excluded are some ways (although not fully problematised or explicated) in which the knowledge, and thus some form of experience, of the peculiar interiority of *other persons* is accessible to us (Wojtyła 1979, 7). Of course, at least since the establishment of logical empiricism, this inclusiveness has been widely considered doubtful, and the broader experience has been excluded from having *scientific* relevance, as not eligible for intersubjective or experimental control.[6] Wojtyła does not share this scepticism. Although he does not reject the direct relation of senses and the grasped object, and he does not deny that sense observation may tell us a lot about the human person, he argues that other aspects of human reality, aspects which manifest themselves to our cognitive capacity as related to the human being, should be taken into account. It is 'the total experience of man', rather than some arbitrarily chosen and absolutised aspect, that should constitute material for philosophical interpretation (Wojtyła 1979, 8). Styczeń shares this approach when arguing that the moral experience must be taken into account as a whole, in its entirety, in developing a satisfactory theory of ethics (Styczeń 2012a, 114–18).

Another important mark of experience, according to the personalist conception, is its inevitable connection to comprehension (Kupczak 2000, 70). It does not mean merely that we subsequently tend to interpret, or strive to understand, that which we have experienced. The bond is even more fundamental – the affective or sensual side of experience is always accompanied by an intellectual act of comprehension. As Wojtyła writes about the intuition of our subjectivity: 'Here the understanding springs directly from the experience without any intermediate steps, without inference' (Wojtyła 1979, 57, translation modified). To be sure, Wojtyła does not say that nothing at all is to be inferred, or that the full comprehension is inherent in the experience alone. What he means is that the material that is given in experience, and already comprehended to some degree, must be subsequently subject to philosophical examination, which makes the comprehension deeper. But the fundament of that philosophical examination is experiential, in a recurrent way. As Wojtyła explains:

> For our position is *that action serves as a particular moment given in an intuition – that is, in experiencing – the person.* Undoubtedly, this experience yields at the same time a substantively determined understanding, which consists, as already mentioned, in an intellectual apprehension grounded on the fact that man acts in its innumerable recurrences. The datum 'man-acts', with its full experiential content, now opens itself for being comprehended as a person's action.
> (Wojtyła 1979, 10, emphasis original, translation modified)

In Wojtyła's view, then, the philosophical conceptualisation of personhood is not superfluous – through philosophy, one may achieve an adequate interpretation of the data given in experience, finding sufficient reasons, or necessary conditions

6 Moritz Schlick's position is very characteristic of such an approach. He writes, not without irony, about the phenomenologists:

> According to them we possess the capacity of determining the existence of a value in much the same way as we are acquainted with the presence of a material object by means of perception. The role here played by sensation is there taken over by a specific experience, which one may call the feeling or experience of value, insight, or what not; without of course contributing anything to a closer description by this naming(Schlick 1939, 105).

thereof (Styczeń 1973). Philosophical reflection is perceived as interpretation, 'uncovering all the aspects' of the examined issue (Wojtyła 2011, 21), although it should keep recurrent references to the sourcing understanding, presenting itself in the primordial experience (Wojtyła 1979, 14–16; 50). On the other hand, conceptualisation or interpretation of that which is given in experience leads to better understanding and, consequently, to more adequate experience of the objects under scrutiny.[7] Thus, one may describe a philosophical inquiry as a *sequence of comprehensions* (Wojtyła 1979, 182). Primordial philosophical insights, based on initial experiences that the inquiry starts from, gradually get improved by means of analysis and interpretation. The intellectual apparatus and knowledge of sufficient reasons enhance the experience and comprehension at the same time, uncovering 'deeper aspects' of that which is under scrutiny (Wojtyła 1979, 136). The final result of that scrutiny is *reduction*, by which he means grasping the content that is given in experience in the most adequate way possible – 'revealing the most fundamental principles of an experienced object' (Kupczak 2000, 73).[8]

Last but not least, one should emphasise that the personalist conception regards experience in radically realist terms. One could say that this realism is an assumption, but this assumption is arguably not arbitrary – it is deeply rooted in the very structure of experience. As we have seen earlier in the example of freedom, experience pertains to something that exists, externally to the experiential act, and independently of such an act. In particular, experience contains two important moments – the sense of knowing, and the sense of reality (Wojtyła 2008c, 115). The latter points exactly at the realist assumptions. As will see in detail later, the crucial consequence of these assumptions is that the category of *truth* gains fundamental importance in analysis of person and action (Wojtyła 1979, 159–62). This is clearly a strongly Thomistic mark, opposing transcendental idealism characteristic of phenomenology.[9] Styczeń's path is very similar to that of Wojtyła. When reflecting on the experiential basis for ethics, Styczeń rejected the Husserlian idea of phenomenological reduction almost as strongly as he rejected positivistic empiricism. More precisely, he rejected the phenomenological reduction

7 A helpful metaphor is offered by Weigel, according to whom Wojtyła's method should not be conflated with traditional deduction from first principles. Rather, it 'was circular, but in the manner of walking down a spiral staircase, not going round-and-round a closed circle. He, too, would begin by identifying a problem: for example, what constitutes a just act? Then he would walk around the problem, examining it from different angles and perspectives. When he had gotten back to the starting point, he and his students would know a little more, so they would start walking around the problem again, reexamining it from this angle or that, but now at a deeper level of analysis and reflection' (Weigel 2005, 139).

8 It is worth noting that Wojtyła's understanding of reduction should be discerned from that of Husserl's 'eidetic reduction'. In the latter, one arrives at an essence, or *eidos*, of that which is given in experience. For Wojtyła, reduction consists not only in grasping a bare essentiality of the experienced object, but also in understanding the experienced object in the most adequate way, in its entirety irreducible to something else (compare Wojtyła 1979, 15–16).

9 While there were some realists standpoints in the phenomenological movement, most of its members follow Husserl's idealistic turn (Ingarden 1975).

insofar as it suspends judgement about the fact of existence of the experienced phenomena – in his case, the moral duty. According to Husserl, that which is given in experience should be examined as pure data of consciousness, and thus 'the natural attitude' – the tendency to treat it automatically as real – should be suspended, or 'parenthesized' (Husserl 1983, 61). For Styczeń, at least in the case of morality, this kind of suspension is arbitrary, since the realness of duty (i.e. its independence of conscious acts of comprehension) is given in experience itself. In other words, moral experience itself, when examined without bias, inevitably pertains to *concrete* and *really binding* duty (Styczeń 2012a, 141). Suspending the realness of the moral duty would be equal to suspending the judgement about its binding force, which would be a self-defeating intellectual operation, far from keeping contact with the experiential data (2012a, 143). Therefore, according to Styczeń, the experiential basis for ethics must fulfil not only the requirement of being *directly accessible*, but also the requirements of *concreteness* and *realness*.

Bearing in mind the chief aim of my inquiry in this book, which has to do with the law pertaining to human dignity, we should recall what has been said in Chapter 1 about the methodological credentials. The findings about the dignitarian moment allow us to consider precisely the sphere of the *factual legal practice as the experiential basis and starting point*. The idea underlying this chapter, however, is that the knowledge that is helpful in sorting out the dignitarian moment also may come from other sources. As indicated already, the peculiar character of the law related to human dignity allows us to scrutinise 'natural' human personhood, that is, the personhood that is independent from the law. Subsequently, in Chapters 3 and 4, we will juxtapose and check the results of our legal mapping of human dignity in the law with the inquiry into natural human personhood present in this chapter.

Taking the preceding into consideration, I will now examine the personalist conception – or, rather, the aspects of it that are indispensable for interpreting the dignitarian moment – with particular questions in mind. Firstly, to what extent may the experience of a person, theorised in the personalist manner, be considered relevant for law? In other words, one should ask what the insights into the structure of the person and the act are able to tell us about law – how they elucidate the dignitarian moment. The second question we should bear in mind is the following: To what extent is the content which is given in moral experience (or the experience of morality), as examined by the personalist conception, relevant for law in general, and for the dignitarian moment in particular? Note that this question must be distinguished from the more conventional one, which asks if and in what sense morality is necessary for legality. I have deliberately set aside the theoretical-legal debate of positivism versus natural law, and I intend to keep that judgement suspended as long as possible. The question I am now asking, in a more careful formulation, is this: Is there anything in moral experience that is eligible for generalisation, that is, pertaining also to experience of normativity in general, and perhaps of legality in particular? With these specific questions in mind, I will now begin presenting and analysing the substance of the personalist conception.

Before we proceed further, one important methodological remark must be made. As the reader may have noticed, the personalist conception neither uses nor discusses the method of wide reflective equilibrium. Recall that this has been depicted as the master method for our inquiry, developing the Status of Personhood Theory. The reliance on reflective equilibrium is, admittedly, a moment in which I step away from the original personalist conception. Nevertheless, wide reflective equilibrium, especially in the truth-seeking interpretation I am adopting, is not totally alien or contradictory to the personalist conception. The idea of a sequence of comprehensions, presented earlier, suggests a similar approach – the issues under scrutiny should be regarded from different angles, different aspects of them should be examined, and the final results should take these different insights into consideration, presumably striving for coherence between them. This is not very far from wide reflective equilibrium. However, it seems that the ultimate method for Wojtyła is *reduction*, understood as grasping the real essence of the examined object in the Aristotelian manner. In my inquiry, by contrast, it is assumed that the results of reduction may always be potentially verified and modified in case there is pressing evidence from elsewhere (say, natural sciences or legal practice). This difference does not nullify the fact that the personalist insights into the structures of personhood and the affirmation proper to persons are of decisive importance in interpreting the dignitarian moment.

3 Ontology: human action as the *actus personae*

The original Polish title of Wojtyła's main philosophical work, *Osoba i czyn*, translates more accurately as 'Person and Act'. The notion of act – deliberate action – is close in meaning to the classical term *actus humanus*, as distinguished from *actus hominis* (Wojtyła 1979, 25).[10] Referring to this classical distinction, alongside the whole philosophy of man developed by Thomas Aquinas, which remains an important background, Wojtyła analyses deliberate action as revealing the human being as *author and master* of his own acting (Wojtyła 1979, 69). As an agent, one is also conscious of his own acting, of his own subjectivity in acting, which renders the perspective oriented on the *personal* dimension of human existence. Therefore, the best expression to denote the object that will be under scrutiny in this section is *actus personae* – action of the person, which has a slightly different meaning from the act of the human being, to be explicated in due course. Throughout all the analysis, however, it is important to bear in mind the Thomistic, realistic 'anchoring' of Wojtyła's conception, according to which performing particular deliberate actions neither conditions nor creates the personhood of the agent. It is, rather, the other way round: *The real structure of the agent himself or herself* conditions his acting as a person (*operari sequitur esse*). To use a language alien to Wojtyła, but pointing at the same reality: Deliberate action is *a radical*

10 This distinction is fundamental also for Wojtyła's later work (2008e).

capacity (capacity 'at the root') of the human subject, which means that it characterises her 'from the outset of her existence as such' (Finnis 2011a, 35; compare Wojtyła 1979, 180).

Wojtyła's emphasis on the real structure of persons as the ground for action has a strongly 'individualistic' hue. As a comparison, it is worth recalling that Hannah Arendt's account of action assumes human *plurality* as its fundamental prerequisite (Arendt 1998, 175). As she writes:

> The realm of human affairs, strictly speaking, consist of the web of human relationships which exist wherever men live together. The disclosure of the 'who' through speech, and the setting of a new beginning through action, always fall into an already existing web where their immediate consequences can be felt. Together they start a new process which eventually emerges as the unique life story of the newcomer, affecting uniquely the life stories of all those with whom he comes into contact.
>
> (Arendt 1998, 184)

This is not necessarily in full contradiction with Wojtyła, but it is important to note that Arendt seems to claim priority of plurality over action, the latter not being 'not a dormant set of agentic capacities but rather individual's distinctive interventions in the public sphere' (Riley 2017, 75). Wojtyła argues for a reversed picture: It is the inherent structure of the human person, the 'who' that is irreducibly inscribed into each individual, that fundamentally constitutes the genuine plurality of persons, as manifested in their joint acting. The personhood of the agents can be grasped and analysed without direct recourse to their plurality.

On the other hand, the plurality of the acting persons, and their community, plays an important role in Wojtyła's philosophy – his 'individualism' must not be conflated with a libertarian stance, according to which every individual has full ownership over themselves, acting in full independence and solely on the basis of their own preference or will (Rothbard 1998, 45–7). There are two important points with regards to this. First, in Wojtyła's view, every deliberate action should be perceived in its *constitutive relation to truth*. The choice that always proceeds action does not boil down simply to turning 'toward one value and away from others' (1979, 137). Rather, 'to choose' means to make judgements 'about the objects presented to the will in intentionality, according to the principle of truth' (1979, 137, translation modified). A choice fundamentally disregarding the truth (including the moral truth about value pursued within the action) would be futile – not in the sense of not gaining what was intended by the agent, but in the sense of *failing to fulfil the agent as a person*, which occurs in performing genuine action (Wojtyła 1979, 154). Thereby, the arbitrariness in choosing values – grounding the genuine choice in the bare willing – is excluded. Secondly, although individual capacity to act is inherent in the agent himself or herself, *the personalistic value* of his action may be revealed only in a particular, concrete community in which he acts together with others (Wojtyła 1979, 271). This reveals both the possibility and critical importance of genuinely interpersonal relations exercised through *participation* (Wojtyła 2008d, 240–6). In this sense, the plurality that Arendt talks about seems inescapable for a normal fulfilment of action. But this is valid only in the secondary order, so to speak, as a requirement necessary for the action to fully bear fruit in a community of persons. I come back to this issue in some more detail in Chapter 4.

All the above preliminaries will be analysed further in what directly follows. The problematic relation of the notion of radical capacity (and its fulfilment through action) to the more traditional, and straightforwardly metaphysical, notions of human nature and its actualisation will be examined in Chapter 3. For now, suffice it to say that – according to Wojtyła's method – radical capacity for action is revealed in experience (inner experience of myself, and outer experience of others when acting together with them), and is then subject to philosophical interpretation. These phenomenological insights into human dynamism uncover only *some aspect or elements of the totality of human reality and experience.* For some of Wojtyła's colleagues at the Lublin School, particularly for Albert Krąpiec, this was problematic – if phenomenological analysis is always aspect-oriented, it may fail to grasp some important truths that come from the more comprehensive picture (Krąpiec 1973). For our purposes, however, this limited or aspect-related scope of Wojtyła's inquiry is a crucial *advantage.* The phenomenological method is able to reveal these facts which are particularly relevant for our task, while the full metaphysical-anthropological interpretation of these experiential facts may be suspended, to the degree which is desirable from the perspective of the commitments to the human condition on the one hand, and metaphysical parsimony on the other. Taking these for granted, the conception of *status of personhood* that I will develop in Chapter 3 has limited focus. A fully metaphysical account of the human being would have to be much more holistic, and certainly would not concentrate on action exclusively. *The status of humanness* – a possible 'comprehensive' conception of human dignity – could follow from such an account. But this is not the point of this book. In the face of the methodological credentials outlined in Chapter 1, it is reasonable to limit the legal doctrine of human dignity to those aspects of human reality (or, indeed, the human condition) that are most important for interpretation of the dignitarian moment in the law. With this in mind, we may move forward to presenting the structure of action in detail.

3.1 Self-determination and vertical transcendence

The strong association of the word 'action' (Polish '*czyn*') with the Latin term *actus humanus*, which is employed in *The Acting Person*, excludes a lot of human activity from the scope of direct interest at the outset. For some linguistic sensitivity, it may even appear as violating the intuitive understanding of the term. In ordinary speech, we sometimes talk of 'action' referring to almost any sort of external movement of the agent (or internal move within the agent) which has some visible effect. This understanding seems to underlie modern cognitive science as well (Jeannerod 1997). Some scholars also adhered to this wide understanding around the time of Wojtyła writing *The Acting Person*. Tadeusz Kotarbiński, for example, when developing a philosophical praxiology *as a theory of efficient action* (Kotarbiński 1965), used the Polish term *czyn* to denote the central subject under scrutiny. And although it is the very same term as Wojtyła uses, likewise translated into English as 'act' or 'action', its meaning was considerably different, intended to cover any sort of intentional activity which effectuates in reaching a goal of the agent. In this sense, an event as trivial as pressing a button to call a lift, for example, counts as a 'simple act' and, as such, is fully eligible for praxiological analysis (Kotarbiński 1965, 14). A similar understanding of action seems to underlie the economic analyses of Ludwig von Mises. According to him, action is tantamount to any purposive behaviour of the agent, or any 'conscious adjustment to the state of [the] universe that determines his life' (Mises 1966, 11). In contrast to these, Wojtyła analyses action as something much more specific, which reveals the deep, personal structure of the acting agent himself or herself. Therefore, according to Wojtyła, the best formulation of the object of his theory is not even the Thomistic *actus humanus*, but rather *actus personae* – the action of the person (Wojtyła 1979, 27).[11] I will use the latter as a technical term, to denote the specific meaning that Wojtyła gives to the notion of action. It emphasises that the reality under scrutiny is not simply an activity that is proper to the human being because of its nature, by virtue of *what* the human being is. Rather – given the peculiarity of inner experience that is at hand here – the focus is on the unique and unrepeatable act, performed by 'someone' – as a result of *who* the agent is. This signifies that the action is performed by an incommunicable person (and not merely by member of a species capable of action; see Wojtyła 2008a, 212). If this is accepted, then certainly only a particular kind of human activity, with a complex inner structure, counts as *actus personae*.

If the alternative, purely praxiological notion of action were assumed, perhaps the analysis would be futile in revealing anything meaningful about the human person as such. After all, pursuing goals by individual and somehow 'purposive' activity may be purely 'schematic', unengaged, or even unconscious – as in the case of pressing a lift button when going for a coffee break during work, for example. One may also argue that action conceived praxiologically, in effect-oriented terms, is quite common among non-human animals, too, and one does not have to engage analysis of personhood in order to analyse this activity. As Kotarbiński writes:

> I am convinced that the chimpanzee which wields a stick to get a banana, the dog which takes a stranger's coat in its teeth, the bird which puts the food into the open beaks of its little ones – all of these perform certain simple acts,

11 In the English edition, the Latin phrase *actus personae* was translated into English, which was not the case in any of the Polish editions.

> and that in general animals do act, and occasionally happen, in their work, to achieve a mastery often not easy to equal.
>
> (Kotarbiński 1965, 22)

From this perspective, in which efficiency (bringing about a relevant effect) is the main focus, there is no need to find something particularly human about human action, or something presupposing the peculiarity of the human condition in the action. By the same token, there is no need to fundamentally distinguish between genuine action and other forms of human purposive activity, such as labour and work, which was Hannah Arendt's famous achievement in *The Human Condition* (Arendt 1998). As we have seen, Wojtyła does strive to find that peculiarity – the inherently human, personal structure of acting, and in this respect his project is much closer to Arendt's than to those of Kotarbiński or von Mises. What is characteristic of the approach taken in *The Acting Person* is that the scrutiny is focused not only on deliberate action in itself, but also in its dynamic relation to the agent, to '*inner and intransitive consequence of a person's efficacy*' (Wojtyła 1979, 150, emphasis original). According to Wojtyła, there are two distinctive elements that constitute genuine *actus personae*, in its relation both to the external world, and to the agent himself or herself: self-determination and transcendence.

Self-determination relies on the fact that the agent is in possession of his own person, and enjoys genuine governance over that dynamic whole which is herself of himself. And that makes the agent the real author of his or her own action. As Wojtyła writes:

> Every actual act of self-determination makes real the subjectivity of self-governance and self-possession. In each of these structures that are inherent to the person, the person-as-subject (as the one who governs and owns) obtains the insight into his own person as the object: as one that is governed and owned. This objectiveness is, as may be seen, the correlate of the person's subjectivity, and moreover, seems to bring to light subjectivity in itself, in a particularly strong way.
>
> (1979, 108, translation modified)

As we see, the *actus personae* is an activity which can be, without doubt, described as one's own – efficacy is achieved through objective control that the person enjoys over himself. The acts fully exercising one's capacities as a person consist in determining one's own activity. Thereby, the chain of particular activities adds up to a kind of 'continuity of guidance' that was freely chosen and may be called 'conduct' (Wojtyła 1979, 254). As Wojtyła specifies:

> In this sense, we may speak of an 'objectification' that is introduced together with self-determination into the dynamism that is proper to persons. The objectification means that in every actual self-determination (that is, in every act of 'I will') your own 'I' is the object, indeed the primary and nearest object. This is contained in the very notion of self-determination, and in

> the term expressing it – 'self-determination' means that someone is determined by oneself. The subject and object are simultaneously and correlatively evoked. And both of them are your own 'I'.
>
> (Wojtyła 1979, 108–9, translation modified)

The factual exercise of self-determination is conditioned by two crucial structures: the person being in possession of herself (self-possession), and the person governing her own self (self-governance).

The second distinctive feature of the *actus personae*, namely, the 'transcendence' in action, means that the human person 'goes beyond oneself', in the twofold sense of 'going beyond'. In the 'horizontal' sense, the agent is directed toward an object, in his intentional acts of cognising or willing *something external.* In the 'vertical' sense, which Wojtyła considers the more important for his analysis,

> the person transcends his structural boundaries through the capacity to exercise freedom; of being free in the process of acting, and not only in the intentional direction of willings toward an external object. (Wojtyła 1979, 119)

> [Continuing in the footnote]: This is not transcendence 'towards something', transcendence directed toward an object (value or end), but one within the frame of which the subject confirms himself by transgressing (and in a way outgrowing) himself.

The transcendence in action, particularly the vertical transcendence, supplements self-determination and puts it into the context of truth and fulfilment. In other words, it shows that self-determination should not be exercised for its own sake, for the sake of one's bare preferences, but rather always in the light of truth about the world, about the human persons concerned by the action, and the rightness of human conduct.

In what follows, we will take a closer look at the distinctive features of the *actus personae.* To start with, we will examine self-possession and self-governance as structures conditioning self-determination in action. Once this has been done, we will move forward to transcendence in action (in the context of truth and fulfilment).

3.2 Self-possession and self-governance as the experiential component of human freedom

Self-determination, present in the structure of the *actus personae*, requires that action is always somehow *accompanied by consciousness.* The agent is someone who is conscious of his own acts, and also conscious of his own consciousness in acting (Wojtyła 1979, 28). Not all forms of human activity share this. For example, when routinely picking up berries, or driving a car, one may or may not actively realise what is really being done at a particular moment. In the personal acting, which involves the moment of willing (the 'I will' lived experience), consciousness must activate, at least at the very moment of choice that conditions genuine willing. Essentially, consciousness has a twofold job. On one hand, it reflects manifold processes that happen in the agent, as well as the moment of his action itself (the mirroring function; see Wojtyła 1979, 30). On the other hand, it is not merely an epiphenomenal 'echo chamber'. Rather, consciousness also allows one to assign all the activities of a concrete human subject to oneself – to make them one's own (this is called the reflexive function of consciousness; see Wojtyła 1979, 43). In this particular sense, consciousness constitutes the *actus personae* together with self-possession and self-governance, as an important aspect of both.

Of course, the problem of consciousness in itself is bottomless, and – at least since Descartes has been examined from countless perspectives, including philosophy of mind, phenomenology, and cognitive science. In this context, one may argue that Wojtyła's examination of consciousness is far from exhaustive. However, the non-exhaustiveness might have been deliberate – according to Wojtyła's analyses, consciousness is merely an aspect, and not the essence, of the *actus personae*, and he examines it only as such. As Wojtyła writes, 'Looking at consciousness . . . we see it not as a separate and self-contained reality but as the subjective content of the being and acting that is conscious, the being and acting proper to man' (1979, 33). The awareness of (and in) action is thereby put in the broader context of a concrete agent, a concrete human person, whose existence and structure is independent from his actual state of consciousness.

Having remarked on the importance of consciousness for self-determination, we may now turn to presenting its *distinctive* features, that is, those of self-possession and self-governance. As Wojtyła writes:

> The two objective structures, 'man-acts' and 'something-happens-in-man', determine the two fundamental lines of the dynamism proper to man. Their directions are mutually opposite, so far as man's 'activeness', that is, his acting, is made accessible to experience – and actualized – in the former, while certain passiveness of man, and his passivity, is [present] in the latter.
>
> (Wojtyła 1979, 61–2, translation modified)

Needless to say, the *actus personae* (conditioned by self-possession and self-governance) has the 'man-acts' structure, which Wojtyła considers something real and ontologically independent of consciousness, but at the same time accessible only through it, given to the subject as a lived experience. This experience suggests that *the acting person is endowed with genuine efficacy* – that our 'I will', our choice, is really the efficient cause of our action. For example, there is an enormous and easily observable difference between entering into marriage and falling asleep. The reason for the difference in experience is the underlying difference in structure. While falling asleep (when healthy) depends almost entirely on our internal physiology, that is, on something that merely happens in humans, entering into marriage is one of the most momentous realisations of our ability to choose and sustain the choice – that is, to our self-determination.

As we see, consistently with his own methodology, Wojtyła analyses efficacy starting from the first-person experience of being active and efficient, setting aside the broader speculation about causation. Of course, one may always legitimately ask about the adequacy of this approach – description of experience is not, in any sense, close to demonstrating the truth of its ontological commitments or metaphysical implications. Instead of providing a full defence of efficacy, however, Wojtyła refers to the *self-evident* character of the causal bond between person and act:

> The one who acts, having the experience of himself as the agent, discovers himself to be the origin of his acting . . . . To be the cause means to produce an effect and to sustain its existence, its becoming and its being. Man is thus in a wholly experiential way the cause of his acting. There is between person and action a sensibly experiential, causal relation, which brings the person, that is to say, every concrete human ego, to recognize his action to be the result of his efficacy.
>
> (Wojtyła 1979, 67, translation modified)

One could legitimately ask, then – is efficacy simply a 'take it or leave it' statement, a matter of belief in the truth of something that experience merely suggests, no matter how strongly? Or, perhaps, does Wojtyła leave space for others to develop a metaphysical (ultimate) interpretation of experience, alongside the defence of its plausibility? Something like this seems to be suggested by the final remarks in *The Acting Person*:

> Finally, there is still one more disturbing question that demands consideration. It concerns man's 'existential status', the status of his being or existing, the whole truth about his limitations and his ontic contingency. Is this truth sufficiently built into the analyses of the person and the action?
>
> . . .
>
> In the introduction we stated that our aim was to extract from the experience of the action everything that would shed some light on man as the person, that would help to obtain some insight thereto; but our aim was not to build a theory of the person as a being, to develop a metaphysical conception of man.
>
> (Wojtyła 1979, 356–7)

Although the direct subject matter of this passage is the contingency of the human being, when read in broader context, it confirms what I have said about the limitation of the inquiry – its aspect-oriented scope which was criticised by Krąpiec (1973). A full account of the acting person, then, would provide an ultimate metaphysical interpretation of the *ontological* structures that appear directly in experience. As such, it would not only involve the most fundamental questions about being as such (God, the human soul, and the world), but would also require one to embrace the newest results of the natural sciences, such as neurology or cognitive science.

My own inquiry deliberately escapes this. My direction of demonstrating the adequacy of this account is much humbler; namely, it is intended to work in *application to the interpretation of law*. A kind of 'verification' will thus come alongside the interpretation of the dignitarian moment. If this interpretation turns out to be successful, in terms of an explication of human dignity, and an explanation of the dignitarian moment as it stands in the law, one can consider the truth of the personalist conception as 'highly supported' by this, if the word 'demonstrated' appears too strong. This is the context in which the personalist conception is being set forth.

According to Wojtyła, self possession and self governance determine the structure of willing, insofar as it is freely chosen. As he writes, '[e]very authentically human "I will" is an act of self-determination' (Wojtyła 1979, 106). Here, Wojtyła confirms the traditional assumption of the Roman law, that which we have mentioned earlier, saying that *persona est sui juris* – Wojtyła's conception can be regarded as another formulation of that well-established contention.[12] To put this in first person: I must have myself at my own disposal, in order to genuinely act; only to the extent to which I do have myself at my own disposal, I perform an *actus personae*. And this is not merely a purely logical postulate, but rather an experiential *fact of self-possession* that is discernible in the inner lived experience of my own acting. Further, and likewise discernible in experience, I must effectively exercise that possession of myself, when choosing to act in this or that way, and that is pursued in *self-governance*. As Wojtyła writes, 'the person is, on the one hand, the one who governs himself and, on the other, the one who is governed' (Wojtyła 1979, 106). These two facts or structures add up to the *freedom of the person* – they reveal what freedom consists in, with regards to conscious experience, as well as the structure of the subject.

In order to highlight these, Wojtyła distinguishes between two types of volition, one characteristic of 'man-acts' structure, the other of 'something-happens-in-man':

> Volition as an intentional act is embedded in the dynamism of the will only to the extent self-determination is contained in it. Introspection informs us of various types of volition that arise in man's interior life and are authentic intentional acts but which are not embedded in the dynamism proper to the will. We may then say that some kind of volition is 'happening' in the subject even when man does not will – it does not emerge with the experience 'I will'.
>
> (Wojtyła 1979, 110)

12 See Wojtyła (1979, 106). The English translation omits the Latin phrase '*sui iuris*' in favour of the expression 'the person is his own judge'.

Here, Wojtyła appeals to an opposition that is very clear to a speaker of the Polish language, but any direct English translation must lack that clarity. In order to explicate the crucial intuition that underlies Wojtyła's analysis of self-determination – and certainly transcends mere linguistics – I must appeal to the peculiarity of the Polish language. Namely, an expression widely used in Polish ordinary speech is that of '*chce mi się*', which can be translated as 'I am willing'. So, for example, one may say '*chce mi się spać*', to say 'I am willing to sleep'. In the functional translation, so to say, one could simply say 'I'm sleepy'. The latter is perhaps even more adequate a translation, since it expresses the passiveness of the subject which is also made clear in the Polish '*chce mi się*'. If one were to look for a strictly literal formulation, it would go something like: 'it makes me want to sleep' or 'it happens to me that I want to sleep'. Here, we will go for the second, and the opposition of '*ja chcę*' versus '*chce mi się*', will be translated as 'I will' versus 'It happens to me that I want'. The latter is also a type of volition, but one which is lacking the fundamental moment of self-determination – the active choice and authority exercised over one's own person. 'It happens to me that I want' is therefore not tantamount to action, but to 'activation' – a process that happens in man as passive subject (Wojtyła 1979, 69). Getting sleepy, or growing old, are examples of this. To the contrary, the 'I will' is an act, or action, in which the person becomes an active agent, genuinely influencing the external world (as referred to in an intentional act of volition), as well as himself, by his own efficacy (self-determination and transcendence). All that normally stands behind the statement 'I will to marry you' is an example of a situation of genuine human volition and thus personal action.

Taking this into consideration, one may say that the fundamental distinction within human activities is that of *action* versus *activation* (Wojtyła 1979, 69). Activations are characteristic of human dynamism in which the human being is moved or triggered, but the whole process is guided by factors other than her own choice and will. These factors, however, are not external to the person. Quite the contrary: they are definitely subjective, and in this is sense personal. Depending on particulars, they may boil down to either somatic reactivity (Wojtyła 1979, 216) or emotivity (1979, 227). As opposed to all that, action (in the technical meaning of the *actus personae*) occurs if and only if the activity in question constitutes a result of self-determination – of exercising one's will and authority over oneself.

One bothersome question appears here: How do we distinguish between the two forms of dynamism, in ordinary life as well as within philosophical reflection, given the fact that no action can be taken without some emotions taking part in it, and the work of the somatic basis is likewise necessary? Does the difference between action and activation consist in consciousness? As we have already seen, it does not – one may easily give examples in which we are aware of internal processes in which something merely happens in us. We are also aware of our 'I will' acts, in which a course of conduct is freely chosen. Therefore, Wojtyła's answer is that it is not consciousness which distinguishes the *actus personae*. It is something else – namely, its fundamental or constitutive kinship with assessment and affirmation of truth. As mentioned, the *actus personae* is never based on bare preferences – it is never simply taking this or that course of action, to achieve something that simply *happens* to be wanted. Instead, it is choosing a particular kind of conduct with regards to the truth that this conduct embodies, or responds to, as presented to the judgement of the agent – the judgment that one must follow. This 'must', however, is not simply coercion – it presupposes that the agent is always capable of *acting otherwise*, that the option to do otherwise is real (or, at a minimum, that is what experience strongly suggests). In this sense, the *actus personae* is always a free response to the relevant truth, and thus a source of *responsibility*. And precisely as such, it is an act of *self-determination*, not merely *self-coercion*. As a consequence, truthfulness is the necessary condition of the *transcendence* of the person, as well as the distinguishing characteristic of the *actus personae*. Since this is a separate group of issues, we shall focus on them in a separate section.

3.3 *Reference to truth as the condition of transcendence and fulfilment: The role of integration*

In the Introduction to *The Acting Person*, the author writes:

> Our experience and also our intellectual apprehension of the person in and through his actions are derived in particular from the fact that actions have a moral value: they are morally good or morally bad. Morality constitutes their intrinsic feature and what may be viewed as their specific profile, which is not to be found in acting that assumes agents other than a person. Only the acting, in which the agent is assumed to be a person . . . has moral significance.
>
> (Wojtyła 1979, 11)

However important morality is for action, Wojtyła decides to 'factor it out' from his analyses; 'by an analogy to operations in algebra', he places morality 'before brackets' (Wojtyła 1979, 13). In other words, he sets aside the moral dimension (that is nevertheless common to all genuine human actions) in order to show the person-action dynamic 'in its own reality', that is, as discernible from the dynamics of person-action and morality-of-action taken together (1979, 14). It seems quite paradoxical, and one could ask what the purpose is of examining the *actus personae* as something distinguishable from moral facts, or rather something that does not boil down to moral facts only. In other words, one should ask why Wojtyła suspends the well-established bonds between anthropology and ethics.

Certainly, the right answer must be as far as possible from saying that Wojtyła wants to split the two spheres for good. *The Acting Person* does not undermine the crucial significance of the moral aspect of human conduct. Actually, the interdependence of personal action and morality works both ways. On one hand, persons and their actions are necessary for morality to come into real existence, since moral facts ('a living morality') are the good, or the evil, deeds of persons (Wotjyła 2011, 28). On the other, morality shapes the very identity of persons themselves, the 'unfolding ontological reality' of personal self-determination (Wojtyła 1979, 152). The answer to the paradox of suspending the inherence of morality in action is therefore not substantial, but methodological – the suspension of the moral dimension is a strategy which may help to examine the dynamics of the person and act independently from the morality of actions, and then, on that basis, to examine the moral significance of action in relation to the acting persons (and not only to norms or goods that these persons pursue).

This strategy has advantages. Firstly, it helps to examine the *actus personae* in situations in which the moral aspect is not of first importance. After all, human efficacy is manifested in contexts that yield moral good or evil in the background, rather than as something that is directly at stake. Designing and constructing a building may be one such example: It would be hard to deny that it requires many human actions (as opposed to activations), but at the same time the moral qualification of the process is secondary, and heavily dependent on external conditions. As I will suggest in Chapter 3, a lot of legal activity is like this – it assumes self-possession and self-governance of the human legal subject, but it may or may not engage moral values as the main purpose or problem. In such cases, though, thanks to Wojtyła's method, one may obtain insight into human agency as such, not only its relation to particular moral norms or goods. The second advantage comes from the first one: Highlighting agency 'in its own reality', and examining it in its own terms, reveals its peculiar kind of worth. While in the overwhelming majority of cases the agency is exercised for some external goods, at the same time it has the 'intransitive' effect, namely, it leads to *fulfilment* of the agent – the confirmation of his own identity. The *actus personae* is therefore of autonomous, 'personalistic' value (Wojtyła 1979, 264). This section will explain the concepts that underlie that value of action – transcendence and fulfilment. Those two aspects complement our understanding of self-governance and self-possession and lay the foundation for the personalistic value of action, to be examined in the next section.

The *actus personae* is grounded in the fact that the human person 'outgrows himself' therein – this is the moment of *transcendence*, which is explainable only insofar as the action is related *to truth.* As mentioned already, transcendence has two different modes: the horizontal one, which is tantamount to intentional reference towards some external object (good or aim); and the vertical one, which signifies the dynamic relation within the acting person himself – 'the highly specific structure of self-governance and self-possession' (Wojtyła 1979, 179).

At first glance it might appear unclear why Wojtyła connects self-determination with the *vertical* rather than *horizontal* transcendence. After all, self-determination is connected to the will – it is manifested in the 'I will' experience, distinct from 'It happens to me that I want'. As such, it must obviously be connected to external objects that one strives for or pursues in acting. In my view, the key element of vertical transcendence is its dynamic relation to truth. As Wojtyła writes in his essay 'The Person: Subject and Community':

> Truth presents itself as a constitutive condition of the freedom proper to action, in which this freedom manifests itself as the self-determination of the person. To be free means not only to will, but also to choose and to decide, and this already suggests a transcendent subordination of the good to the true in action.
>
> (Wojtyła 2008d, 234)

For Wojtyła, then, the *actus personae* is an act that must be performed with a view to the truth that it embodies, confirms, or respects. This is the moment at which the notion of *conscience* comes into play: An action must contain some affirmation of truth, or subordination thereto, which is the domain of conscience (Wojtyła 2008d, 234). As a consequence, it is not just any good or aim that can be wanted (as the notion of horizontal transcendence could suggest) – it is rather the true or suitable good (*bonum honestum*) that should be *chosen*, the good in the case of which 'truth presents itself as the source of moral duty, or "categorical" duty (as Kant would say)' (Wojtyła 2008d, 234). In this sense, truth 'presents itself as a constitutive condition of the freedom proper to action' (Wojtyła 2008d, 234). An activity that lacks this element whatsoever cannot be properly called action or act. An activity in which the agent is aware of the truth but disregards it counts as action, but one that is morally wrong, leading to disintegration and despair.

By the same token, self-determination should be distinguished from autonomy (a word that Wojtyła deliberately avoids), insofar as the latter is conceived in purely constructivist terms – as a sort of 'creation' of norms or values that is subordinated to nothing that is external to the agent.[13] For Wojtyła, freedom does not consist in creating one's goals and values solely by means of deciding to act;

13 Although it is not the proper moment for a detailed discussion that would compare the personalist conception to alternatives, such as that of liberalism, it is perhaps worth mentioning that there is a certain kind of overlap, as well as the crucial disagreement, with the liberal view. On the one hand, some liberal theories acknowledge that 'we act freely only when the desire that moves us to act is one we approve being moved by' (Haworth 1991, 129), which seems to assume a structure similar to that of self-determination, and some kind of vertical transcendence. On the other hand, the liberal doctrine of autonomy cannot accept the binding force of truth, so important for Wojtyła. For a liberal theory, it suffices that the agent 'has a preference about his preferences, a desire not to have or to act upon various desires' (Dworkin 1988, 15). That latter, higher-order desire, however, does not seem to be subordinated to truth in any significant sense. It is the agent herself, and not some truth external to her, that constitutes the necessary condition of freedom. This difference will be developed in Chapter 3.

rather, it consists in deciding to act in the face of the truthfulness of the goals and values one is to pursue:

> Freedom is expressed by efficacy and efficacy leads to responsibility, which in turn reveals the dependence of freedom on truth; but this relation of freedom to truth constitutes the real significance of the conscience as the decisive factor for the transcendence of the person in his actions. It is in this way that transcendence determines that special structural trait of man as the person which consists in his specific superiority over himself and his dynamism. This superiority above his actual being that the person exhibits leads to self-governance and self-possession.
>
> (Wojtyła 1979, 180)

This quote shows clearly in what sense, when choosing, the acting person transcends himself in the vertical sense: he is oriented not simply toward some goal, but also towards the truth or goodness that this goal stands for. It can be a simple factual truth, as well as 'the normative truth', in the sense of the rightness of the intended action. The truth is 'above' the agent and his situation, in the sense that the agent considers himself obliged to respect or follow it. By choosing to do so, he 'outgrows himself', transcends the boundary of merely subjective wants and 'opinions' – that is the meaning of vertical transcendence.

To sum up this part of the inquiry: The genuinely personal mode of human action, which has the structure of self-determination and thus is characterised by transcendence and freedom, assumes a 'man-acts' structure, connected to the 'I will' experience, as opposed to 'it happens to me that I want' that is characteristic of *activations.* 'To act' is then not simply 'to strive towards something'. Rather, performing human actions is preceded by a free decision based on the real duty to respect that which is true. The action-activation distinction should be understood exactly in these terms. When one is simply 'activated' by some external incentives or internal processes, we may say that he *works*, in a machine-like-manner. When one genuinely 'acts', on the other hand, one cannot be sensibly perceived as a human-machine, because her acting is rooted in affirming the truth *in conscience.* By the same token, the acting person is not simply an instantiation of species – an individual or a specimen – but she constitutes the incommunicable, or the irreducible, subject – the *suppositum humanum* (Wojtyła 2008d, 235).

These considerations have led us to another element of Wojtyła's doctrine of human action, namely, to *fulfilment.* Since performing actions does not consist simply in attaining the intended goals or values, but also in affirming their truth and subordinating oneself thereto, it leads to affirming the agency of the person herself. The human being, in experiencing her own acting, simultaneously cognises her own essential structures as a person (self-possession and self-governance, alongside conscience). Thereby, the person is addressed with a certain 'calling' to perform actions, particularly, good deeds (Wojtyła 1979, 167). In this sense, efficacy does not only have an upshot in the external world, but also bears *the intransitive*, internal effect – fulfilment of the agent, that is, confirming her identity as a person, a human subject (Wojtyła 1979, 149). In other words, the *actus personae* is connected not only to truths about the external world, but also the truth about the agent herself. Becoming morally bad (a bad person), that is, continuously performing actions that disregard or disrespect truth, or contravene duty, leads to a loss of identity (Wojtyła 2008d, 234). Wojtyła calls it 'disintegration', which ultimately results in personal despair, as opposed to flourishing (1979, 176, 193–5).

The latter aspect of human action refers to another important element of the dynamic structure of action, namely, to *integration*. Integration is understood by Wojtyła primarily as complementary to the transcendence in action (1979, 190). As Acosta and Reimers emphasise, integration is 'attainment and manifestation of a whole and a unit that is constituted by certain complexity' (2016, 188). Human life in general is characterised precisely by certain unity that comes despite complexity (Wojtyła 1979, 191). Wojtyła offers a detailed analysis of the integration of the person in action – the somatic and the emotional dynamisms become subject to, and are determined by, self-determination in relation to truth, which is a sign of the special, spiritual nature of the human being (1979, 256). All these aspects are in constant, dynamic mutual interplay, which is different from simply the body working as the instrument of the person (Acosta and Reimers 2016, 195). It is a complex process in which the soma and the psyche both condition the action and become determined by the acting person himself or herself. Additionally, integration is a feature of the person who is indeed capable of a principled action and in this sense possesses virtue (Wojtyła 1979, 253). Along with this most important aspect, Wojtyła observes that the body as such has its own, distinctive dynamism of reactivity, which is also marked by a special kind of spontaneous integration (1979, 208). He does not regard these two dynamisms as necessarily in tension, and certainly not as mutually exclusive. In short, the analysis of integration reveals the human person as a complex, corporeal being which possesses characteristics that transcend corporeality, and as a spiritual being which is inevitably centred in the person's own body.

For now, we can pause our study of the doctrine of the acting person. There is one important ambiguity we need to disentangle before we move any further. On the one hand, one may have the impression that the only sphere proper to the *actus personae* is that of morality. Certainly, morality constitutes the focal point or paradigm of acting. The figure of Socrates, who refuses to escape prison and decides to die in order to fully affirm the moral truth of his life, is certainly one of the most universally appealing figures of humanity, and of the acting which is proper to persons (Styczeń 2012a, 50). On the other hand, as we have seen, Wojtyła decides to factor out morality from action and to examine its connection to the person in its own reality. The two rival interpretations may appear here. One is *ethical* – it asserts that, at the end of the day, morality turns out to be not only the *focal* but also the *exclusive* sphere in which the person fulfils himself or herself. The other interpretation – the one that I have tacitly assumed – is *praxiological*. It does not deny the key position of morality in acting. Indeed, it is hard to imagine truthfulness or self-determination in a situation which is completely morally irrelevant (if we assume that such situations may appear). Rather, the praxiological reading says that one can point at many situations in which morality is not of the first concern, and yet, the *actus personae* occurs (as the previous example of constructing a building suggests).

The inquiry conducted in this section was intended to reveal crucial elements of the ontology of the human action, and thus of the human person. The human person was depicted as capable of vertical transcendence, that is, of 'outgrowing oneself' in acts of self-determination, performed in a dynamic relation to truth. That is the essence of the *actus personae*, and, as one may conclude, a remarkable sign of the special status or value of these acts. Persons are not passive subjects, merely following various 'activations' or drives; nor are they perfectly isolable individuals, ultimately governed by nothing but their own conscious willing. According to the personalist conception, human persons are free agents, but are fully engaged with the external world and possibly with other persons who are equal to them. This entanglement is possible through judgement affirming the truths about both the external world and other persons.

These results constitute the ontological commitments of the status of personhood conceived in personalist terms. However, status is a normative notion. Human dignity in the law, which I will explicate as the Principle of the Status of Personhood, is likewise a normative provision which cannot be conceived simply as a derivation from facts (that is, from the ontological structures of human acting reconstructed earlier). Rather, the status of personhood must find its own, independent normative expression and foundation. This is where the notion of *respect* comes into play. Although Wojtyła and Styczeń use different words to denote the proper person-to-person relation, namely either *love* (Wojtyła 2013, 25; Styczeń 2012a, 216) or *affirmation* (Styczeń 2012b, 329), I take the liberty of using the term 'respect' to denote this, in order to emphasise the different sphere in which my theory is situated, namely, the sphere of *legal* norms. As I intend to show, respect toward persons finds its foundation in a particular experience, namely, in the intuition of the dignity of the person.

4 Normativity: affirmation of persons

As commonly known, the idea of dignity of persons, and of respect towards persons as a moral demand, was highlighted particularly strongly by Immanuel Kant. As he declared in *Metaphysics of Morals*:

> [M]an regarded as a person, that is, as the subject of a morally practical reason, is exalted above any "price" for as a person (*homo noumenon*), he is not to be valued merely as a means to the ends of others or even to his own ends, but as an end in himself, that is, he possesses a *dignity* (an absolute inner worth) by which he exacts *respect* for himself from all other rational beings in the world.
>
> (Kant 1991, 230)

Although it is highly debatable whether Kant himself really considered dignity to be the basis of ethics,[14] the personalist conception says exactly this – the prohibition on treating a human being primarily as contributing to the realisation of ends external to that being is considered the touchstone of ethics based on human dignity. As Styczeń writes, certain acts constitute our moral duties precisely because they 'express affirmation that is due to somebody or something by virtue of the inner worth, that is, in case of a person, by virtue of his dignity' (Styczeń 2012b, 261). The role of Kant's thought in making this vision of dignity widely recognised among philosophers is fully acknowledged (Wojtyła 2011, 37). On the other hand, the personalists have their differences with Kant, which I will not discuss at length. Just one particular disagreement should be mentioned here: For Kant, what is ultimately worthy of respect is either the moral law in itself, as he explicitly writes in the *Groundwork* (Kant 1998, 13), or the humanity (*Menschheit*) in one's own person, although the latter demands respect only because this is what the moral law in itself demands (Kant 1991, 230). As a consequence, the concrete, empirical persons have dignity somehow indirectly, as 'rational beings' – by virtue of their being capable of understanding morality and complying therewith. The person as such, in her entirety and concreteness, is considered by Kant as remaining 'beyond what is given to knowledge' (Casas 2017, 629), and therefore somehow beyond his ethical theory. In the personalist conception, as quite clearly stated in several places, *the concrete, particular persons with whom we interact in any possible way* are the proper object not only of our knowledge, but also, most importantly, of unconditional love and affirmation (see e.g. Styczeń 2012a, 166).[15]

Given the last point, it is important to bear in mind that the personalist emphasis on action *does not* intend to show action as a *condition* or *prerequisite* of the persons' dignity. According to the personalist conception, dignity is an irreducible, existential condition of the person. Action serves only as a sign or

14 As Oliver Sensen compellingly argues (2011), the requirement to respect others – according to Kant – is justified by the law of (one's own) reason, and not by the inner worth of human persons that is external to the moral law (see especially Sensen 2011, 107–18).

15 Wojtyła's critique of Max Scheler, despite that the latter theory was largely a negative reaction to Kant, points at a similar problem. According to Wojtyła, Scheler falls short of recognising the foundational role of human efficacy exercised by concrete persons which is played in the domain of morality. In Wojtyła's reconstruction of the Gospel message in this regard, good and evil are 'real and objective' characteristics of persons performing good or evil acts (Wojtyła 1959, 51). Despite having an objective normative basis (God's law), the moral values of good and evil always have a very concrete, personal embodiment (Wojtyła 1959, 62). Wojtyła's later theory of the human person and morality, while setting aside the theological questions, remains committed to the concreteness and agency of persons. When confronted with the Wojtilian view, both Scheler and Kant seem to put too much emphasis on the abstracts or generalities, such as moral values, humanity, or moral law. This leads, among other things, to a radical separation of personal fulfilment and the moral duty. In fact, as Wojtyła argues, the two are not opposed to each other and are being integrated in ordinary human practice (Wojtyła 2006, 280–4).

manifestation of dignity, but not as a basis from which it would flow. In this sense, the account on affirmation of persons that I will present next should be regarded as autonomous from the earlier account on action.

4.1 *The personalist value of the* actus personae *and dignity of the person*

According to Wojtyła, human capacity for action, the structure of which is accessible through experience and which has been the object of analysis in the *Acting Person*, reveals something even more fundamental – a particular kind of value, pertaining exclusively to persons. As Wojtyła writes:

> [T]he performance itself of an action by the person is a fundamental value, which we may call the *personalistic* – personalistic or personal – value of the action. Such a value differs from all moral values, which *belong* to the nature of the performed action and issue from their reference to a norm. The personalistic value, on the other hand, inheres in the performance itself of the action by the person, in the very fact that man acts in a manner appropriate to him.
>
> The 'personalistic' value of the human action – that is, the personal value – is a special and probably the most fundamental manifestation of the worth of the person himself.
>
> (Wojtyła 1979, 264, emphasis original)

Although he does not use the word 'dignity' here (and nowhere in *The Acting Person*), we may be quite sure that 'dignity' is in fact meant. In his later philosophical work, Wojtyła writes:

> The 'dignity' of man as a person means above all property or fundamental quality – and in this sense the 'value' of the person as such: a value which belongs to man because he is a person and for which, therefore, man ought to strive.
>
> (Wojtyła 2011, 36)

Although the dignity of the person is directly accessible in experience of morality, certain human capacities are foundations of that morality and thereby 'correspond' to human dignity (Wojtyła 2011, 44). These are, in the first place, '*the capacity* for cognition, choice, and the *realization of the suitable good (bonum honestum)*' (Wojtyła 2011, 43, emphasis original). The latter would be impossible, or even simply inconceivable, without the structure of self-determination that was presented in the previous section and that makes the *actus personae* possible – and the performance of actions is a remarkable sign of dignity. As Wojtyła contends, 'man realizes that dignity through his actions – precisely through the values which he makes an object of pursuit in those actions' (Wojtyła 2011, 38).

Two points are crucial not to overlook here. First, as already noted, the performance of action (or the capacity thereto) *is not* something on which the worth of the person would *supervene*, at least in the ontological sense. In most general terms, supervenience is a relation between properties or entities such that 'the A-entities supervene on the B-entities just in case there cannot be a difference in the A-entities without some difference in the B-entities' (Kovacs 2019, 1968). By 'ontological supervenience', as applied to moral considerations, I mean a thesis saying that if a thing or state of affairs has a base property B, it also has an ethical property E, and that all things or states of affairs having B also have E (I am drawing from McPherson 2019). This is precisely the bond between action and dignity *that I deny here*, and Wojtyła seems to do so, too. In the previously quoted passage, he does not say that the person's fundamental value or dignity (which would stand for E) *supervenes* or *is grounded* on capacity to perform actions (which would stand for B). Rather, what is stated in the passage is that *performance of actions serves as a manifestation or sign* of dignity that pertains to the acting person. Certainly, *not only* persons with a fully developed capability to act, or factually exercising this capability, have dignity. Likewise, persons acting more sustainably or intensively than others certainly do not have 'more dignity' than others who act more poorly. According to Wojtyła:

> In virtue of his self-governance and his self-possession man deserves the designation of 'somebody'; regardless of whether he has this distinctive structure actually or only virtually. Thus man is somebody from the very moment of conception as also when and if something intervenes and prevents his fulfillment of himself in actions, that is to say, if his mature actualization of self-governance and self-possession was to be prevented. That the designation 'somebody' is appropriate to man can be deduced also in an analysis of man's being and not only from the experience of the person's transcendence.
> (Wojtyła 1979, 180, translation modified)[16]

The idea of 'sequence of comprehensions' finds its application here. Experience of the person in action, which reveals the ontological structure of (vertical) transcendence, allows one to say something about the human existence as such, namely, that it is a personal existence. The issue of *equality* of dignity, which is presupposed here, will be analysed more thoroughly in due course.

16 In the English 1979 edition, the sentence 'from the very moment of conception' was translated as saying 'from the very moment of his coming into existence'. However, both the 1969 and 2011 Polish editions I am using to verify the English translation, read '*już więc w chwili poczęcia*'. This expression is without doubt better translated as 'from the very moment of conception'. It quite clearly points at the moment of two gametes' fusion.

The second important point connected to the personalistic value of action is that it is not simply one among many moral values. According to the previous quoted passage, moral values in the strict sense are realised (or even, in some weak sense, 'created') in the course of performing actions in which the agent affirms the truth of the good (rightness) of a certain conduct, which she ascribes thereto on the basis of a general moral norm. For example, the moral value of helping the poor is realised in performing particular acts of mercy, on the basis of the general norm 'one should help the poor'. As Wojtyła seems to claim, in this very situation of someone helping the impoverished, we may discern an additional point – the personalistic value of this deed as a genuinely personal action, as the *actus personae*. In a certain sense, this 'value' is situated 'above' the particular moral value of benevolence – it is its prerequisite. Acknowledging this does not mean that the acting person is somehow 'beyond good and evil', or that she creates the values 'out of nowhere', solely by her individual decision or by virtue of some norm-creating power of her reason, for example. What Wojtyła says here is rather that in performing an action, irrespectively of that action fulfilling a particular norm, one can discern another morally relevant moment – that of choice and self-determination. Wojtyła explains:

> As a specific structure of self-governance and self-possession, the person fulfills himself most adequately through duties. He realizes himself neither by the intentionality of volitions nor even through self-determination in itself, but rather through *his sense of duty, as the peculiar modification of self-determination and intentionality.*
>
> (Wojtyła 1979, 169, translation modified, emphasis original)

In this sense, the personalistic value of action is not opposed to moral values, but rather stands as their 'inherent substratum'; something 'upon which [moral values] take root and are developed' (Popović and Maj 2016, 364).[17] To be more exact, one may speak of two distinctive aspects in the personalistic value of action. One of them is fulfilment of the agent (mentioned in the previous section); the other is '*the agency itself*', which is of fundamental value because it allows human persons to genuinely choose the course of their conduct. And that genuine choice of conduct is necessary to act morally, *which is something different from mere behaviour in accordance with moral norms.*

Human agency, manifested in the structure of the *actus personae*, corresponds to human dignity, understood as inherent and absolute worth. Although, again, it does not constitute the base or the ground for human dignity, the personalist value of human action is quite clearly the moment in which the normative considerations come into play. For Wojtyła, human conduct that affects other persons

17 The two authors rightly emphasise that although *evil acts* are conditioned by the ontological structure of self-determination, they do not have the personalistic value – it is pertinent only to the good ones (Popović and Maj 2016, 367).

(or our own person) must be guided by love, which he understands, generally speaking, in the biblical sense, as revealed by the commandment to love. The principle expressing that commandment in philosophical terms (or constituting a certain axiological basis to understand it) is called *the personalistic norm*:

> As a principle formulated negatively, this norm states that the person is a kind of good that is incompatible with using, which may not be treated as an object of use and, in this sense, as a means to an end. Hand in hand with this goes the positive formulation of the personalistic norm: the person is a kind of good to which only love constitutes the proper and fully-mature relation. And this positive content of the personalistic norm is precisely what the commandment to love brings out.
>
> (Wojtyła 2013, 25)

Although the personalistic norm was proposed in an early work of Wojtyła, *Love and Responsibility*, dealing with a particular problem in applied ethics (a Catholic vision of sexual and marital morality), one may say that it is of great importance for the rest of his philosophical work, as well as his ecclesiastical writings and documents as Pope John Paul II. Given the limited focus of my inquiry, I will be interested only in how the principle may influence our understanding of law in general, and the dignitarian moment in law in particular. Namely, I will attempt to examine how the personalistic norm merges with what I have called the Personalistic Postulate (drawing from Crosby 1996), according to which *before the law, persons are regarded not as replaceable specimens or as mere instances of some ideal or type, but rather as having intrinsic importance, each standing as incommunicably his or her own.*

As I intend to show, the works of Wojtyła's disciple, Tadeusz Styczeń, SDS, are of great importance in this context. In his philosophy, Styczeń accepts the personalistic norm as the most fundamental principle of morality. In his formulation, the norm says that 'every person, considered as person, is to be affirmed for her own sake, which is her due from every other person' (Styczeń 2012c, 379). Or, in a simpler form: 'a person unconditionally owes love to other persons' (Styczeń 2012a, 216). In his work, Styczeń puts the personalistic norm in the context of very detailed, meta-ethical analyses. The dignity of the human person is in the centre of these analyses, as we shall see in detail shortly. As I will attempt to demonstrate, this dignity-oriented meta-ethical approach proposed by Styczeń allows something more than he originally intended – it allows one to reflect not only on ethics, but also, more broadly, on *the phenomenon of normativity*. In other words, I will attempt to show that dignity of the person is important not exclusively for morality, but also for normativity. In what follows, I will outline the most important elements of Styczeń's theory of the moral duty (Subsection 4.2), and subsequently show the main lines of how to *generalise* this towards a theory of normativity applied to legal considerations (Conclusion). This will serve as a bridge that will bring us to my own theory, the SPT.

4.2 *The moral duty: source, content, and structure of moral judgement*

As already noted in Section 2 of this chapter, the personalist conception assumes experience, broadly understood, as the starting point of all philosophical theorising. The case of ethics is no different. According to Styczeń, ethics (as a science of morality irreducible to the sociology of morality, psychology, or any other discipline) is possible only insofar as it has its own, separate object of scrutiny. He argues that there is such an object, namely, the moral duty, perceived in experience. In his view, the moral duty is fundamentally related to *dignity of the human person*. As he writes:

> There are three possible ways in which a human act is determined as a duty. Namely, an act is considered morally required by duty for the reason that: (1) it is a necessary condition of the flourishing of the acting subject; or (2) the act was commanded by the proper norm-giving authority, or finally (3) the act embodies the affirmation which is due to somebody or something as a result of an inherent value of this somebody or something. This inherent value shall be called dignity when pertaining to persons.
>
> (Styczeń 2012b, 261, translation by the author)

Styczeń strongly argues that only the third way of determining duty allows us to preserve ethics as an independent discipline (not reduced to something else). Going for the flourishing/moral perfection of the agent, one would conflate or substitute ethics with 'eudaimonology' – a philosophy of happiness, not of morality (Styczeń 2012b, 272–80). On the other hand, reducing morality to a bare commandment of authority would annihilate genuine freedom of the agent, and thereby morality itself (Styczeń 2012b, 289). If morality is dependent solely on God's command (without objective reasons for the command that he would give), then there is no reasonable difference between following orders and acting morally, the latter being reduced to the former.[18] If the norm-giving authority is placed within the agent himself or herself – as in the case of practical reason and a good will in Kant – the situation does not change. If the moral imperative is merely formal, then it boils down to 'unconditional or categorical *pressure* on the freedom of the agent' (Styczeń 2012b, 301, emphasis added). Although in my view, Styczeń's reconstruction of Kant is fundamentally wrong in several respects,[19] what is more important here is the personalistic belief that genuine moral action is *a free response of the will to reasons*, which should be distinguished

18 On that occasion, Styczeń offers an interesting interpretation of the biblical story of Abraham and Isaac. In Styczeń's view, Abraham's decision to obey God's request and kill his son Isaac must not have been blind obedience. Rather, Abraham must have believed in some objective, morally relevant reasons for God's request. (Styczeń 2012b, 291–4).

19 There is no need to provide a detailed argument against Styczeń's reconstruction. It is perhaps worth mentioning, though, that Kant's question about possible *universalisation of*

from an 'automatic' observance of norms by the agent forced by an imperative. According to Styczeń, ethics may be established only having this at the background: the structure of the agent responding to relevant and real *reasons for action*. And the primary reason for action affecting persons is their dignity.

At this point, it is important to emphasise one modification of the classical natural law theory that the personalist conception brings. In natural law theory, reasons for action are tantamount to the (common) good, or a list of basic goods. Life, knowledge, or friendship may serve as examples (Finnis 1998, 79–85). Although the personalist conception does not reject the idea of natural law, it emphasises dignity, which *is not* one among such basic goods or values. Dignity – the basic reason to affirm persons, and the fundamental guidance as to what should be done – is rather the fundamental characteristics of persons themselves, equal for all. As the most basic feature of persons' existence, dignity is deeply intertwined with the moral duty, that is, *the duty to affirm persons for their own sakes in all actions*. As Styczeń writes:

> So, what is this duty-bearing 'thing' that serves both as subject and grounding of the duty judgement? What can be the adequate reason to 'transcend oneself', which is the underlying commitment in every moral judgement? This par excellence duty-bearing 'thing' is the dignity of the person. One does not need to look elsewhere, in order to take notice of a moral obligation, and the very same dignity of the person contains everything that constitutes the moral duty, and gives it a mark of unconditionality. The person, by the very fact of being what she is, is the one that should be affirmed for her own sake.
>
> (Styczeń 2012b, 312, translation by the author)

As one may infer from this quotation, the experience of personhood, or simply 'looking at a person', is enough to obtain an intuition into that person's dignity, and to form a moral judgement requiring an unconditional affirmation of that very person. This may sound quite mysterious, or simply too prone for a sceptical shrug of the shoulders – Styczeń is well aware of that 'moral daltonism' often being the case (Styczeń 2012a, 39). Thus, on several occasions, our author offers additional arguments that show the moral duty – which he calls *datum morale* in more technical contexts[20] – as something commonly known to humanity, and implicitly accepted. First, there is fictional literature and drama, which may be considered as highlighting the real, acute concerns in human lives, the 'sourcing moral situations' in the first place (Styczeń 2012a,

maxims at the background of action, which is one that every moral agent must ask, is tantamount to the question about the underlying reasons for action, and its moral plausibility.

20 Styczeń distinguishes the *datum morale*, which is the moral duty directly given in moral experience, and the *datum ethicum* – the judgement universalising our moral experience (Styczeń 2012a, 184–98).

38). Styczeń is probably right to claim that the stories of Sophocles' Antigone, or Dostoyevsky's Raskolnikov, would not have touched so many readers if they had not described something that those readers had experienced in their own lives (Styczeń 2012a, 41–52). Reflection on real historical experience yields a similar conclusion – the atrocities of wars, World War II in particular, would not be so obviously wrong and terrifying, if human dignity were simply a matter of convention (2012b, 257). Finally, the proclamation of human rights, with its vast universal career and activism, points at the realness of human dignity, and the personalistic norm as the most adequate expression of its content (Styczeń 2012c, 379). Styczeń claims:

> A discovery of the personal dignity of the human being remains what it is: an insight into his rank among beings, that is, an act that merely *reveals* the dignity which is proper to the human being as person. The act of comprehension certainly does not *establish* that truth, but *merely confirms* it. Affirmation is each person's due *because of her dignity, and not because of anyone taking notice of that dignity!*
>
> (Styczeń 2012c, 382, translation by the author, emphasis original)

According to Styczeń, then, human dignity is real and accessible through intuition. The only thing that can be done for a sceptic to help him obtain such an intuition is an indirect argumentation referring to different human practices and moral dilemmas marking human life. As such, this indirect argumentation must be something similar to the 'midwifery' work of Socrates (Styczeń 2012c, 384). Once intuited, the judgement of dignity as something proper to persons is accompanied by a strong feeling of realness (Styczeń 2012a, 65).

Let us tentatively, but for a moment longer, take the sceptical position seriously. Does the certainty of an intuition, as moral experience suggests, really end the controversy? It does not seem so. I may be certain, for example, that I have just seen an alien spaceship. A given configuration of flashing lights, clearly visible in the night sky above me, appears as such, since it is not similar to the behaviour of any natural or human-made objects that I know. Does this mean that the alleged alien spaceship must be real? Of course not, and my subjective feeling of certainty does not change anything in reality – I might simply have seen a new human-made satellite in action, hitherto unknown to me. One should ask whether or not *the intuition of a person's dignity* could be similarly misleading. Even if we agree that experiences of the categorical duty to affirm persons are accompanied by particularly strong certainty that is subjectively felt, reality still may be different. For example, the certainty of categorical duty may be a result of certain biological/evolutionary mechanisms that make me think or feel in a particular way (Singer 2005). What is more, I may be quite certain about the rightness of a particular action that, if pursued in reality, would do much more harm than good. Do these counterexamples suffice to refute the dignitarian intuition?

In my view, they do not. Let us assume that my sense perception was not distorted by anything and was not illusory – the flashing lights really appeared in the night sky, caused by a new human-made satellite. In such a situation, it was *my interpretation of sense perception* that failed, but the perception itself was quite real. Likewise, I may be wrong about the content of moral duty (of what exactly should be done) or may err fundamentally about its metaphysical grounds (I may consider morality epiphenomenal to biological evolution, while in reality it has a divine source). But being wrong or having doubts about the proper interpretation of the *datum* only confirms the realness of *the datum* itself. According to Styczeń, dignity of persons is such a *datum*. Therefore, to suspend or reject the realness of moral duty would be analogical to suspending the realness of the very act of *perceiving lights* in the spaceship case, *not of perceiving a spaceship*. In this context, mistakes about morality are for the most part mistakes about the proper interpretation of the moral duty – but not about the realness of duty itself.

In order to make this contention clearer, let us consider an important example that Styczeń gives to analyse *the structure of a moral judgement*. Namely, we may imagine that

> two friends, *A* and *B*, dispute before entering the hospital and visiting their friend, *C*, who is terminally ill. The friend *C* is not aware of his terrible condition, and he will certainly ask his friends about it. *A* claims that they should tell *C* the truth, as only the truth can bring the good for *C*. *B* understands the argumentation of *A*, however claims the opposite: they should do their best to hide the truth from *C*, the truth about his health condition, as only this serves his good. This is a difficult dispute. Might seem a hopeless one. However, we should not overlook one important thing, which is indisputable in this dispute, to the extent which makes it the condition of this dispute being held and being sensible: the disputing friends implicitly agree that they should perform an action affirming *C*, and that *C* should be affirmed. Then and only then they can dispute on what can and what cannot affirm *C*.
>
> (Styczeń 2012b, 328, translation by the author)

The two friends disagree with regard to what should be done, and probably one of them is wrong. However, they are on the same page with regards to the attitude of affirmation which they both have toward their friend, and both of them are right. By the very fact of their moral disagreement, they indirectly confirm the very basis of any moral judgement concerning the disputed case, namely, the dignity of their friend, *C*. If we take that example for granted (I see no reason to do otherwise), dignity appears to play a very peculiar role. In a way, it is analogous to the personalistic value of human action that Wojtyła talks about. Recall that the personalistic value of action is not to be too easily conflated with moral values. In the debate between *A* and *B*, the dignity of the friend who is ill – the duty to do the right thing for him – is somehow discernible from the question of what actually is that right thing to do. But how is this possible? Styczeń's answer is that one may discern two separate dimensions, or different aspects, of the same moral judgement requiring affirmation of the ill friend. As he writes:

> As far as the indisputable part of the dispute about the ill friend was crucial to our characteristics of ethics, we must not overlook that which is a subject matter of the genuine dispute. The dispute concerns the issue of what affirms *C* and what does not so. . . . Therefore it is not a dispute whether or not *C* should be affirmed, but about the substantive determination of a moral duty to affirm *C*, its 'specification' or perhaps 'concretization'.
>
> (Styczeń 2012b, 340–341, translation by the author)

In my view, one should interpret these two different aspects – the indisputable and the disputable – in terms of a *prima facie* distinction between *dignity* and *the good*. While *dignity* stands for the duty to affirm *C*, at the most general level of affirming persons for their own sakes, the judgement concerning the *good* determines the course of action that best serves this very purpose.[21] While dignity is not really justified, but – as I have explained earlier – a kind of intuited axiom of human practices, the substantive determination concerning the good of the person certainly needs a justification and opens a possibility for reasonable disagreement. Styczeń proposes to call these two different aspects of morality 'the duty dimension' (regarding the duty to affirm persons) and 'the rightness dimension' (concerning the issue of what exactly should be done) (Styczeń 2012b, 341).[22] While the former is of purely moral character – fully exhausted in the duty to affirm – the latter requires not only value judgement (although this, too), but also additional knowledge. In this sense, the judgement concerning the rightness of action bridges between the moral duty itself and other sources of information about the human being. As Styczeń writes:

> Here comes another example – is *D* affirmed when we care of his religious formation, or when we try to discourage him about religion? . . . As we have seen . . . to form a judgment about the moral duty to affirm *C*, an experience of *C* as a person is sufficient. But this experience is by no means sufficient to form a judgment as to what is the right thing to do with regards to *C*. To

21 Interestingly enough, a similar thought is present in Wojtyła's early work. In *Love and Responsibility*, the author distinguished between the two issues: 'the fact that I should love', which 'has its objective basis in the personal dignity of the recipient of action (the personalistic norm)' and the issue of 'how I should love', which is determined by human nature (Wojtyła 2013, 51, in a footnote). This is just one more sign of the unity I have attributed to the personalist conception of Wojtyła and Styczeń taken together.

22 The original Polish expressions are the following: 'the duty dimension' stands for '*wymiar powinnościowy*', and 'the rightness dimension' stands for '*wymiar słusznościowy*'. Developing this, Styczeń was inspired by an earlier paper by Tatarkiewicz (1931). Styczeń's account, however, is much more clear and more useful.

do the latter, some additional, specific knowledge about *C* is required – the knowledge about him, his internal structure and his place in the real world.

(Styczeń 2012b, 341, footnotes removed, translation by the author)

The distinction between the duty dimension (associated with dignity) and the rightness dimension (associated with the good) seems to explain why moral disagreement occurs, as well as why it does not necessarily nullify the objectiveness of moral judgements. Since there are many different sources of knowledge about the human being, and each individual case has its different history, a different 'place in the real world', it seems natural that people will differ with regards to what ought to be done given the particular circumstances. The objectiveness of the duty to affirm is not threatened by this – everyone implicitly accepts this duty by engaging in a moral debate. The possibility of arriving at the best, the most adequate, the right solution is not excluded either, no matter how difficult it may be.

Let us come back to the alien spaceship case, which was used to (only tentatively!) ridicule the idea of a universally valid intuition of dignity. In order to determine whether or not I have seen an extraterrestrial object, I must interpret my sense perception (the flashing lights in the night sky); I need to have knowledge of natural processes and human activities in the earth's orbit, for example. Analogically, in order to determine what ought to be done in a particular moral case, I should interpret the moral duty that I perceive both in my inner experience and in the outer experience of a moral practice in which I am engaged (in a moral dispute, for instance). Dignity of persons, which is intuited together with the moral duty, and tacitly accepted by the participants to moral practices (including moral disputes), is therefore hard to reject. At the same time, a particular application of dignity (the rightness dimension) may be highly debatable and requires one to reach out beyond moral experience – it invites more knowledge about the case, taken from elsewhere. Interpretation of internal moral experience appears analogical to interpretation of external sense experience in this respect.

However, the duty and the rightness dimensions do not exhaust the structure of moral judgement. There is the third, most fundamental aspect, which bonds morality with ultimate metaphysical questions. According to Styczeń, 'a statement of duty to affirm C for his own sake by A and B, and generally a statement of duty of the person to affirm persons, is nothing but a statement of *realness* of the fact that one really ought to do that which one ought to do' (Styczeń 2012b, 345). In other words, the categorical and overbearing character of the moral duty excludes the possibility of suspending judgement about its real binding force, and therefore the expression 'one ought to do x' is equivalent to 'it is true that one ought to do x' (Styczeń 2012b, 345). In Styczeń's view, then, the aspect of the *real existence of duty* is not possible to detach from moral judgement. It would be artificial and self-defeating: in real moral disputes, as exemplified by the case of the terminally ill friend *C*, the participants must assume that the issue at stake is real; that they do not dispute merely hypothetical or illusory exigencies.

The assertion of the realness of duty is called 'the existential dimension' (*egzystencjalny wymiar sądu moralnego*; Styczeń 2012b, 346). If we agree with this, then morality is not only deeply connected to scientific and common-sense knowledge about the human being, but also to the ultimate metaphysical issues. Moral judgements, at least insofar as they assert realness of duty, call for an ultimate foundation. For Styczeń, that grounding is to be found in the Bible, and in the Christian religion in particular. The relation with God – the most perfect and metaphysically necessary Personal Being – is considered ultimately important in human moral life (Wojtyła 2013, 24; Styczeń 2012b, 233). When viewed from this perspective, the sphere of religion 'appears not as a sector of human activity [that would be] separate from morality, but rather as the deepest and inherent dimension thereof' (Styczeń 2012b, 349, by the author). On the other hand, it is important to bear in mind that the belief in God as the creator and ultimate fate of human persons is not a necessary condition of acknowledging the moral duty – an atheist may have her own ultimate grounding for her moral judgements. The three-tier structure of these judgements secures the independence of the moral duty, and of dignity, which are derived from experience. That is why the personalist conception may meet the requirements of weak metaphysical parsimony and may be put to work in the interpretation of the dignitarian moment in the law, in a universalist manner. Of course, I am far from saying that the notion 'anything goes' applies to the personalist conception, or that we may reconcile it with any set of statements about the world. However, I do believe that the purely philosophical doctrines of Wojtyła and Styczeń may be interpreted in a way that fits many different broader worldviews or 'comprehensive doctrines'. The opinions of ultimate groundings may vary, despite the fact that only one set of statements about them may be true. But disagreements with regards to the ultimate grounding do not make the discourse on the levels of duty and rightness automatically futile.

Conclusion

This chapter was devoted to setting forth the most important elements of the personalist conception of human dignity. Our considerations on human ontology showed the structure of the person that is capable of performing action. This capacity turned out to be marked by two crucial moments: self-determination, and transcendence towards truth. These ontological structures were interpreted as signs of the peculiarity of the *very existence of persons* – the existence that requires treating them as ends in themselves. This led us to the normative dimension of personhood. Dignity was shown as an intuited practical truth or imperative that requires us to affirm all persons, including ourselves.

It is important to emphasise that the reconstruction of the personalist conception offered in this chapter was not meant to be complete. Many crucial questions about personhood and dignity remain unanswered. And many *will* remain, given the limited scope of our inquiry. The philosophical material examined in this chapter could serve as a basis for a detailed and comprehensive metaphysics of personhood, but instead of offering such a metaphysics, I will develop a theory of human dignity in the law which confronts the law with the ontological commitments flowing from this chapter. The presentation of the personalist account had a particular purpose – I examined the threads that will allow us to better understand, and hopefully sort out, the dignitarian moment in the law.

Now, it appears that there are two possible paths in applying our results in interpreting the law. The first is more obvious, and to some extent well-known – it may be called 'the ethical interpretation' of the personalist conception. It would go briefly as follows: human dignity, understood as a basic *moral* prerequisite of any social cooperation, would be shown as fundamentally connected to the good of the person. Expressing this in the language of Styczeń, the duty dimension and the rightness dimension of the moral judgement would always be intertwined to the extent that we cannot derive any particular precepts from either dimension taken separately. In other words, judgement about what should be done would always presuppose a question of what is good for the person – what effectively affirms him. Law, as a particular case of social cooperation, would then be shown as fundamentally intertwined with morality – the good of the persons involved, including the common good, would be always present in the law, at least to the extent to which dignity is present therein. Metaphorically speaking, *law* would be another domain of *love*. As far as the ontological structure of the *actus personae* explored by Wojtyła is concerned, the ethical interpretation emphasises its application in moral acting. The structure of conscience, choice, and self-determination, in the face of truth, works mostly in moral situations. The structure of the person in action, then, would be equal to the structure of the moral agent. Only subsequently – under the condition of positive law being in accordance with natural law – would it be also the structure of the legal subject.

Another possible path, more controversial and less explored, may be called 'the praxiological' interpretation. According to this interpretation – as I mentioned in the section on the *actus personae* – moral action would be discerned from *prima facie* morally irrelevant action, but *both types would be of interest and value from the personalist view*. Whereas a moral action assumes moral value judgement as its direct object, a '*prima facie* morally irrelevant' action is focused on some other aim, which may or may not turn out to be morally relevant. While feeding the starving would be an example of a moral action, designing and constructing a building would instantiate a *prima facie* morally irrelevant one. Now, the praxiological interpretation says that the ontological structures of the person that enable moral action are also at work in actions such as constructing a building. Insofar as such actions do not obviously violate moral norms (like constructing a building for some morally illicit purpose would do), *they also are of the personalist value*. In the sphere of work, or even physical labour, it is not only efficiency that matters, but the agency itself, as manifested also in these activities.

This interpretation has serious implications for the normative sphere. If the structure of the *actus personae* is relevant outside the sphere of moral actions, then the personalist value has an extended range. This allows us to consider the possibility that the implicit recognition of dignity – which, according to Styczeń, is present in moral actions and in moral debates – can be discernible outside moral judgements as well, that is, generally in *normative* judgements. Legal norms and moral norms could be then depicted as distinct from each other, but paying tribute to the dignity of the person in their own way. To express this in the language of Styczeń: One could derive particular precepts of affirming persons directly from the duty judgement. That means that in some instances, one could determine what is required by the duty to affirm persons, without the necessity of a judgement on what effectively serves their good (which is, as we remember, covered by the judgement on rightness). Upon this interpretation, while the domain of the moral would still be affirmation or love (duty and rightness always coming together), the proper domain of law would be that of *respect* (coming solely from the duty judgement). Thereby, dignity – the essential prerequisite of any duty judgement – could be shown as inherent to the law itself, and that bond could be established before any considerations on the mutual relations of law and morality. Humans as legal subjects would be bestowed with dignity, in a way peculiar to law, independently from particular judgements about the moral good. This is the path that I will take and elucidate in more detail in Chapter 3, to which we now shall move.

References

Acosta, Miguel and Reimers, Adrian J. 2016. *Karol Wojtyła's Personalist Philosophy*. Washington, DC: The Catholic University of America Press.

Arendt, Hannah. 1998. *The Human Condition*. Chicago and London: University of Chicago Press.

Bengtsson, Jan Olof. 2006. *The Worldview of Personalism: Origins and Early Development*. Oxford: Oxford University Press.

Casas, Pedro García. 2017. 'Wojtylian Critique of Kantian Morality and Proposal of the Unconditional Personalistic Norm'. *Studia Gilsoniana* 6(4): 609–631.

Churchland, Patricia S. 2008. 'Human Dignity From A Neurophilosophical Perspective'. In *Human Dignity and Bioethics*. Edited by Barbara T. Lanigan. New York: Nova Science Publishers, 71–86.

Colosi, Peter J. 2008. 'The Uniqueness of Persons in the Life and Thought of Karol Wojtyla/Pope John Paul II, with Emphasis on His Indebtedness to Max Scheler'. In *Karol Wojtyla's Philosophical Legacy*. Edited by D.N.M. Billias, A.B. Curry, and G.F. McLean, Washington, DC: The Council for Research in Values and Philosophy, 61–100.

Crosby, John F. 1996. *The Selfhood of the Human Person*. Washington, DC: The Catholic University of America Press.

Digest of Justinian. 1985. *Volume 1*. Edited and Translated by A. Watson. Philadelphia: University of Pennsylvania Press.

Dworkin, Gerald. 1988. *The Theory and Practice of Autonomy*. Cambridge: Cambridge University Press.

Finnis, John. 1998. *Aquinas: Moral, Political, and Legal Theory*. Oxford: Oxford University Press.

Finnis, John. 2011a. *Intention and Identity. Collected Essays, Volume 2*. Oxford: Oxford University Press.

Finnis, John. 2011b. *Natural Law and Natural Rights*. Oxford: Oxford University Press.

Gallagher, Shaun. 2018. 'Consciousness and Action'. In *The Routledge Handbook of Consciousness*. Edited by Rocco J. Gennaro. New York and London: Routledge, 298–309.
Glenn, Patrick H. 2010. *Legal Traditions of the World*. Oxford: Oxford University Press.
Haworth, Lawrence. 1991. 'Dworkin on Autonomy. Reviewed Work(s): The Theory and Practice of Autonomy by Gerald Dworkin'. *Ethics* 102(1): 129–39.
Husserl, Edmund. 1983. *Ideas Pertaining to a Pure Phenomenology and to a Phenomenological Philosophy. First Book: General Introduction to a Pure Phenomenology*. Translated by F. Kersten. Den Haag: Martinus Nijhoff.
Ingarden, R. 1975. *On The Motives Which Led Husserl to Transcendental Idealism*. Translated by A. Hannibalsson. Den Haag: Martinus Nijhoff.
Jałocho-Palicka, Małgorzata. 2016. '"Osoba i czyn", "The Acting Person" – ingerencje redaktorskie i problemy przekładu. Przyczynek do analizy. ["Osoba i czyn", "The Acting Person": Editorial Interventions and the Problems of Translation]'. In *Wokół antropologii Karola Wojtyły* [*The Themes of the Anthropology of Karol Wojtyła*]. Edited by A. Maryniaczyk, P. Sulenta, and T. Duma. Lublin: Polskie Towarzystwo Tomasza z Akwinu, 155–88.
Jeannerod, Marc. 1997. *The Cognitive Neuroscience of Action*. Oxford: Blackwell Publishers.
Kant, Immanuel. 1991. *The Metaphysics of Morals*. Translated by Mary Gregor. Cambridge: Cambridge University Press.
Kant, Immanuel. 1998. *The Groundwork of the Metaphysics of Morals*. Translated by M. Gregor. Cambridge: Cambridge University Press.
Kotarbiński, Tadeusz. 1965. *Praxiology: An Introduction to the Sciences of Efficient Action*. Translated by O. Oxford: Pergamon Press/Warsaw: PWN – Polish Scientific Publishers.
Kovacs, David Marc. 2019. 'The Myth of the Myth of Supervenience'. *Philosophical Studies* 176: 1967–89. DOI: 10.1007/s11098-018-1106-7
Krąpiec, Albert Mieczysław. 1973. 'Książka Kardynała Karola Wojtyły monografią osoby jako podmiotu moralności [The Book of Cardinal Karol Wojtyla as a Monograph on Person as Subject of Morality]'. *Analecta Cracoviensia* 5: 57–61.
Kupczak, Jarosław. 2000. *Destined for Liberty: The Human Person in the Philosophy of Karol Wojtyła/John Paul II*. Washington, DC: The Catholic University of America Press.
List, Christian. 2019. *Why Free Will is Real*. Cambridge, MA and London: Harvard University Press.
Locke, J. 1999. *An Essay Concerning Human Understanding*. University Park: Pennsylvania State University.
McInerny, Ralph. 1992. *Aquinas on Human Action: A Theory of Practice*. Washington, DC: The Catholic University of America Press.
McMahan, Jeff. 2002. *The Ethics of Killing: Problems at the Margins of Life*. Oxford: Oxford University Press.
McPherson, Tristram. 2019. 'Supervenience in Ethics'. In *The Stanford Encyclopedia of Philosophy (Winter 2019 Edition)*. Edited by Edward N. Zalta. https://plato.stanford.edu/archives/win2019/entries/supervenience-ethics/.
Mises, Ludwig Von. 1966. *Human Action: A Treatise on Economics*. San Francisco: Fox & Wilkes.
Moń, Ryszard. 2019. *Tadeusz Styczeń*. Kraków: Ignatianum University Press.

Popović, Petar and Maj, Piotr. 2016. 'The Personalistic Value of the Human Act in the Philosophy of Karol Wojtyła'. *Anthropotes* 32(2): 357–384.

Richard of Saint Victor. 2011. *On the Trinity*. Translated by R. Angelici. Cambridge, UK: James Clark & Co.

Riley, Stephen. 2017. *Human Dignity and Law*. London and New York: Routledge.

Rothbard, Murray N. 1998. *The Ethics of Liberty*. New York and London: New York University Press.

Scheler, Max. 1973. *Formalism in Ethics and Non-Formal Ethics of Values*. Translated by M.S. Frings and R.L. Funk. Evanston: Northwestern University Press.

Schlick, Moritz. 1939. *Problems of Ethics*. Translated by David Rynin. New York: Prentice Hall.

Sensen, Oliver. 2011. *Kant on Human Dignity*. Berlin and Boston: Walter de Gruyter.

Singer, Peter. 2005. 'Ethics and Intuitions'. *The Journal of Ethics* 9(3/4): 331–352.

Styczeń, Tadeusz. 1973. 'Metoda antropologii filozoficznej w "Osobie i czynie" kardynała Karola Wojtyły [The Method of Philosophical Anthropology in 'The Acting Person' by Cardinal Karol Wojtyła]'. *Analecta Cracoviensia* 5: 107–15.

Styczeń, Tadeusz. 2012. *Etyka niezależna. Dzieła zebrane, Tom 2* [*Independent Ethics. Collected Works, Volume 2*]. Edited by Kazimierz Krajewski. Lublin: Towarzystwo Naukowe KUL.

Styczeń, Tadeusz. 2012a. 'Problem możliwości etyki jako empirycznie uprawomocnionej i ogólnie ważnej teorii moralności. [The Issue of the Possibility of Ethics as an Empirically Authorised and Generally Valid Theory of Morality]'. In *Etyka niezależna. Dzieła zebrane, Tom 2* [*Independent Ethics. Collected Works, Volume 2*]. Edited by Kazimierz Krajewski. Lublin: Towarzystwo Naukowe KUL, 17–250.

Styczeń, Tadeusz. 2012b. 'Etyka niezależna? [Independent Ethics?]'. In *Etyka niezależna. Dzieła zebrane, Tom 2* [*Independent Ethics. Collected Works, Volume 2*]. Edited by Kazimierz Krajewski. Lublin: Towarzystwo Naukowe KUL, 247–373.

Styczeń, Tadeusz. 2012c. 'Problem ogólnej ważności norm etycznych w aspekcie epistemologiczno-metodologicznym z uwzględnieniem indukcyjnych nauk o człowieku. [The Issue of General Validity of Moral Norms in the Epistemological-Methodological Context, Taking Into Consideration the Inductive Sciences on Man]'. In *Etyka niezależna. Dzieła zebrane, Tom 2* [*Independent Ethics. Collected Works, Volume 2*]. Edited by Kazimierz Krajewski. Lublin: Towarzystwo Naukowe KUL, 373–400.

Tatarkiewicz, Władysław. 1931. 'On The Four Types of Ethical Judgements'. *Proceedings of the Seventh International Congress of Philosophy* 398–401. DOI: 10.5840/wcp7193169

Taylor, Jameson. 2009. 'Beyond Nature: Karol Wojtyla's Development of the Traditional Definition of Personhood'. *The Review of Metaphysics* 63(2): 415–54.

Weigel, George. 2005. *Witness to Hope: The Biography of Pope John Paul II*. New York: HarperCollins Publishers.

Williams, Thomas D. and Bengtsson, Jan Olof. 2020. 'Personalism'. In *The Stanford Encyclopedia of Philosophy (Spring 2020 Edition)*. Edited by Edward N. Zalta, https://plato.stanford.edu/archives/spr2020/entries/personalism/.

Wojtyła, Karol. 1959. *Ocena możliwości zbudowania etyki chrześcijańskiej przy założeniach system Maksa Schelera*. [*Evaluation of the Possibility of Constructing a Christian Ethics on the Assumptions of Max Scheler's System of Philosophy*]. Lublin: Towarzystwo Naukowe Katolickiego Uniwersytetu Lubelskiego.

Wojtyła, Karol. 1979. *The Acting Person*. Translated by A. Potocki. Dordrecht: D. Riedel Publishing Company.

Wojtyła, Karol. 2006. *Wykłady lubelskie*. [*The Lublin Lectures*]. Lublin: Towarzystwo Naukowe KUL.

Wojtyła, Karol. 2008a. 'Subjectivity and The Irreducible in the Human Being'. In *Person and Community: Selected Essays*. Translated by T. Sandok. New York: Peter Lang, 209–17.

Wojtyła, Karol. 2008b. 'The Human Person and Natural Law'. In *Person and Community: Selected Essays*. Translated by T. Sandok. New York: Peter Lang, 181–95.

Wojtyła, Karol. 2008c. 'The Problem of Experience in Ethics'. In *Person and Community: Selected Essays*. Translated by T. Sandok. New York: Peter Lang, 105–27.

Wojtyła, Karol. 2008d. 'The Person: Subject and Community'. In *Person and Community: Selected Essays*. Translated by T. Sandok, 219–61, New York : P. Lang.

Wojtyła, Karol. 2008e. *Person and Community: Selected Essays*. Translated by T. Sandok. New York: Peter Lang.

Wojtyła, Karol. 2011. *Man in the Field of Responsibility*. Translated by K.W. Kemp and Z. Maślanka-Kieroń. South Bend, IN: St. Augustine Press.

Wojtyła, Karol. 2013. *Love and Responsibility*. Translated by G. Ignatik. Boston: Pauline Books & Media.

3 Law

The status of personhood and the dignitarian moment

Introduction

After all the considerations we have gone through, it is high time to lay out my own theory, namely, the Status of Personhood Theory (the SPT) of human dignity in the law. The SPT is understood as an attempt to explicate and explain human dignity appearing within the law, with the use of the personalist philosophical conception. As such, the SPT is 'my own' in a considerably weak sense. The status of personhood is certainly not something completely new to lawyers and scholars – *it is not* to be discovered or established. However, despite a certain familiarity that we may feel 'under the skin', the bonds between the legal appearances of dignity on the one hand and human personhood explored by means of phenomenology on the other are far from obvious. Hitherto, the reliance on human personhood in the law has been rather conjectural or simply assumed, without sufficient conceptualisation. For some, such a conceptualisation would be inevitably futile or even dangerous. It is not uncommon in the contemporary discourse to regard human dignity in the law as closer to *a commonly accepted convention* rather than 'flesh-and-blood' reality. For others, dignity in the law may be important as an 'article of faith', but it remains essentially inexplorable (Enders 2019). In the face of this, one may say that the burden of explaining why, in the eyes of the law, human individuals are to be treated as 'persons' endowed with inherent dignity remains undischarged. The SPT takes up this challenge. To do so with proper methodological rigor, it takes its root in the law – in the dignitarian moment described in Chapter 1, which is to be interpreted with the use of the personalist conception presented in Chapter 2. The current chapter is therefore an attempt to integrate the preceding two. This task may be fulfilled by *explicating* 'human dignity' in the legal sphere (*explicandum*) as 'The Principle of the Status of Personhood' (*explicatum*).[1] The further goal is to demonstrate that the SPT as a whole sheds new light on the dignitarian moment in the law and offers a sufficient *explanation* of this legal phenomenon.

1 The procedure of explication was described in Chapter 1.

DOI: 10.4324/9781003252733-4

The SPT, at its core, associates human dignity with the acknowledgement of special standing that characterises the human persons vis-à-vis legal norms and procedures, which boils down to a decent relation with other persons mediated by the law. The theory claims that the law *recognises* certain radical capacities of human persons, and *prioritises* persons, or at least assigns special importance to them. The priority or importance is attributed to persons themselves, not to their capacity or accomplishment. The latter means that although the radical capacity for action plays an important role in the SPT, human individuals incapable of it (due to age or disability) are also under the dignitarian protection. The SPT claims that the law not only *strives* (obviously, with many imperfections), but also *ought to* strive towards such affirmation of all persons equally. The theory is thus centred around a status-expressing *principle* – The Principle of the Status of Personhood. The PSP is of legal and cosmopolitan character. It serves as a bridge between natural human personhood on the one hand, and dignity appearing in the law on the other. As such, the PSP is proposed not only as the best explication of human dignity in the law, but also as a part of the law's fabric which helps to explain and systematise the dignitarian moment.

The general strategy of the SPT is to examine the connection between natural human personhood and legal appearances of human dignity. This has a solid basis in the dignitarian moment itself, especially when the *ontological referral* (present in the foundational function of human dignity; see Chapter 1) is taken seriously enough. Namely, the ontological referral suggests that certain uniquely human characteristics are at play in the law's commitment to human dignity (although the law does not specify these characteristics in much detail). In response to the general foundational claims, various *regulative* or *heuristic* legal usages of human dignity strive to specify quite a lot (in a manner that is not free from inner tensions or even contradictions). Human dignity serves as protecting both human autonomy and human vulnerability, basic biological needs as well as intellectual integrity, and so on. It seems highly reasonable to expect that these different regulative and heuristic applications may be integrated and systematised once the ontological referral has been properly scrutinised and understood.

This is the moment in which *philosophical reflection* enters into play, as an indispensable supplement to the law speaking for itself. To explicate the complex entanglement of human dignity and the law, and to better understand the phenomenon, one must have recourse to philosophising (albeit in accordance with the exigencies of weak metaphysical parsimony and sceptical realism; see Chapter 1). A natural question that arises here is the following: which, or whose, philosophy should one draw from first? To put it more strongly: how could one possibly determine the direction or starting point of such philosophical considerations, in the face of bottomless, cumulated philosophical reflection? Here, admittedly, one must rely on intuition, and this is what the SPT has done in selecting the personalist conception of Wojtyła and Styczeń. However, intuition is not necessarily tantamount to *arbitrary* choice. In Chapter 2, I followed Wojtyła's claim that 'action constitutes the specific moment whereby the person is revealed' (Wojtyła 1979, 11). If the problem of human dignity in the law finds its fundamental point of reference in the human person as its subject, then one may hope that revealing certain truths about the person as such will help in understanding the person's dignity as protected by systems of law. This is the time to verify this underlying hope.

Taking these matters for granted, the question that initiated my inquiry as a whole should now be asked again, in a more specific manner. My initial methodological commitment was the human condition. The assertion that human dignity serves as a bridge between the law and the human reality of utmost significance inspired us to ask how this 'bridging' might be possible. At the present moment, that initial question may be reformulated: *Is there a principled way to obtain a meaningful (as well as communicable and verifiable) insight into law's workings that would deeply correspond to the structure of human personhood, as revealed by the personalist conception?* The structure of this chapter is determined by this question.

I begin with considering how the *suppositum humanum* – the person who *is not* reducible to her social or biological conditions, and is endowed with her own, internal subjectivity – can figure in legal inquires (Section 1). I argue that if the irreducible character of the human person (corresponding to the special entitlement to affirmation) is something real, it should spontaneously manifest itself in the sphere of law. The underlying respect for the personhood of everyone subject to the law, observable in the dignitarian moment, is precisely such a manifestation. In Section 2, I claim that only a realist theory can respond to the challenges that await human dignity in the law, and I explain in what sense the SPT is such a realist theory. I make use of the idea of wide reflective equilibrium: the consistency between legal judgements and principles, the experience of personhood in action, as well as the background personalist ontology of the person allows me to claim the truth of the theory. Against this background, Section 3 explicates human dignity in the law as the PSP. I begin with identifying the dignitarian interests of the human individual which are protected by the law. I claim that there is no one such interest – there is an open-ended list of interests. The most important on this list are freedom from degradation, self-determination, and integration – the dignitarian protection in most cases concerns either one of these three or their combination. Examples from law are evoked in support of this thesis. The rest of the section is devoted to the actual explication of the PSP as a status-expressing principle, and making a case of the wide reflective equilibrium that the SPT seeks.

1 The *suppositum humanum* in legal inquiries

The study of the personalist conception conducted in Chapter 2 arrived at the notion of the *suppositum humanum* – a concrete person, reducible neither to the social world nor to his own nature, 'someone' as opposed to 'something'. That unique and irreducible character of the human person may be available in direct intuition, or as a result of metaphysical reflection upon the revealed truth of man as *imago Dei*. The personalist conception does not deny that, but at the same time it offers an additional epistemic grounding, namely, the study of action (the *actus personae*) as an indirect way to study the person as such. In particular, Wojtyła's careful inquiry allows him to distinguish human conduct from human behaviour (1979, 255). While behaviour is *explainable* by reference to various natural or social determining factors, *human conduct* (as a series of actions) is *justifiable* in terms of relation to moral norms and (moral and non-moral) truths that the agent accepts in conscience as relevant reasons to act.

This bears consequences of primary importance for us: if behaviour is connected to any norms, they boil down to 'norms of adaptation' (Wojtyła 2011, 31), that is, rules of adjustment to psychological or social conditions of one's activity. As such, behaviour does not reveal the subjectivity (or irreducibility) of the acting person. After all, beings we would not call persons, such as ants or cockroaches, also adapt to external conditions, and in this sense 'behave'. Human conduct, by contrast, is *inevitably* connected to normativity and truth, whether the agent is ready to accept it or not. The truth in this context means not only certain facts in the external world, but also the self-related truth about the concrete, acting person. To act in a properly human/personal way means not only to respond to what one (in his best judgement) takes to be true; it is also to *determine oneself*, as the author of such and such actions. This means that the *actus personae* must be *something that is one's own*. Once a human activity loses the mark of authorship pertaining to a concrete agent – weighing reasons, deciding what to do, and thereby determining himself – it ceases to count as action. In this particular sense, the agent is revealed in his own *actus personae*: The meaning of his conduct, accessible to himself and to others, becomes possible to grasp.[2] While this does not mean that action is the only element of human reality that has dignity (it is the whole person that has it), it is a particularly strong *sign* of it; one that is, indeed, hard to deny or ignore.

Now, if that irreducible character of the human person (corresponding to the special entitlement to affirmation) is real, it should also spontaneously manifest itself in the sphere of law. This is the main underlying idea of the SPT. As it will be argued, various legal recognitions of human agency, subjectivity, and vulnerability are precisely such manifestations. According to the SPT, they add up to the special status of the *suppositum humanum* in the law, namely, to the dignity of the person. Speaking metaphorically, the human subject is 'showing through' the law, whatever the nature of law may otherwise be, and this is particularly clear in the dignitarian moment. If this is true, then the SPT is a reconstruction of what already has been happening in the law, or, to be more precise, *what has been done* by the means available to legal activity. On the other hand, the SPT offers an explanation of *why it has been done*.

2 So, for example, deeds of a war hero are understandable as *deeds* only when done by a concrete person known by name. According to Hannah Arendt, this has inspired the erection of the monuments of the 'Unknown Soldier', which was the best possible way to restore dignity to the anonymous 'agents of the war' (Arendt 1998, 181).

Although the programme just sketched may appear 'ambitious' and vast, it is important to notice that it is also considerably limited. Although it would be indeed desirable to develop a *personalistic theory of law* based on the aforementioned ideas and postulates, that is beyond the scope of this book. Although I believe that the SPT could very well serve as a starting point for such a theory, I will leave that potential unexplored. Thus, I will continue to abstain from taking a stance in debates between rival theories of law, particularly between positivism and natural law theory. The problem of situating the SPT within the panorama of legal theories will come back in the conclusion of this chapter. But essentially, the SPT will be presented in a way that assumes as little as possible about broader legal theory. In other words, the *suppositum humanum* is treated as a relevant reality which is independent from law, but should be taken into account in real legal activities as well as in theorising them. This approach should be discerned from treating the good of the person (or, in other words, love for persons) as a theoretical assumption about law as such. The following paragraphs will explain this difference in more detail.

1.1 The 'praxiological' and the 'ethical' interpretation of human dignity in the law

At the end of Chapter 2, I indicated two alternative interpretations in applying the personalist conception to legal inquiries – the ethical and the praxiological readings, which yield two slightly different visions of the *suppositum humanum*. Upon the ethical reading, the ontological structure of the acting person really matters only in moral actions (the actions directly pursuing or failing to pursue a moral end), and the structure of the acting person is ultimately the structure of the 'moral subject'. Upon the praxiological reading, the structures of action matter for *prima facie* morally neutral contexts as well, that is, the contexts of actions which have practical ends as their direct concern. While these two views differ in emphasis rather than in substance, the upshot of this difference in theorising human dignity in the law is of key importance. The explication of human dignity as 'the status of personhood' must commence in explaining the legal implications of the reality of the *suppositum humanum*. I will attempt to do it in what follows, in the manner of a praxiological rather than an ethical reading.

A brief discussion on the different types of norms, sketched by Wojtyła in his later book, *Man in the Field of Responsibility*, can serve as a starting point. The author assumes that norms have analogical character – that is, they express real duties of different kinds (Wojtyła 2011, 30).[3] As he writes:

> The characteristic feature of legal norms is that they serve the so-called public order, which cannot be directly identified with *bonum commune* (the

3 Wojtyła maintains that norms are not simply utterances that would be exhausted in their concrete linguistic expression. Instead, duties are first and foremost part of reality, particularly of real relations between persons.

common good) of society, although the public order should strive toward such an identity.

> Just as it is right and necessary for the public order protected by law to strive toward identity with the common good as the fundamental element of social morality, so too is it right for law to be *fundamentally connected with morality*. Nevertheless, those two realities differ from one another – there is in in the world of norms and duties, a basis for distinguishing between them. A legal norm is always a norm coming 'from the outside', rooted in the authority and power of government. In addition, what lies in the very nature of these norms is a concern for the common good (in maximalist approach), or, above all, a concern for public order.
>
> (Wojtyła 2011, 32–3, translation modified, emphasis original)

Although Wojtyła himself certainly adhered to the natural law tradition, which is suggested in the aforementioned passage and confirmed by his works as Pope John Paul II, these brief remarks leave space for developing divergent jurisprudential interpretations – the personalist conception developed by Wojtyła and Styczeń does not directly discuss law.

For purposes of the SPT, I take into consideration two alternative interpretations, corresponding with the ethical and the praxiological reading of the personalist conception as a whole, mentioned in Chapter 2. The first, 'ethical reading', would amount to a natural law position. Under this interpretation, the law, as an instrument of pursuing the common good, is regarded as one of the means to attain *effective affirmation of persons*. In other words, upon the ethical reading, all legal activity presupposes some basic human good intrinsic to it, one that it must not fail to pursue, or, more precisely, to provide the necessary conditions for pursuing it. Thus, law not only has a moral aim, but also a moral structure at all times, it requires cognition of, or at least deliberation on, what brings value and fulfilment to human life. In the personalist language, we could say that under the ethical reading, law is a form of love – a human activity through which human persons achieve full affirmation for their own sakes. The *suppositum humanum*, understood as a holder of rights and duties, is regarded chiefly in the moral plane. Human dignity, analogically, is understood as a moral value, expressing both the fundamental, existential quality of the human being as well as his moral entitlement to effective affirmation. This yields a 'maximalist' approach mentioned in the previous passage – the public order of laws should serve not only to maintain a human community, but also to ensure that all persons comprising the community have fair and optimal conditions that enable them to achieve fulfilment.

The alternative, 'praxiological reading', although perhaps more complicated, is more 'minimalistic' in tenor. It differs from the ethical reading chiefly by emphasising the distinction between legal and moral norms, alongside the analogical distinction between the common good and public order, as laid out in the previous passage. Although Wojtyła does not specify the meaning of the public order, we can probably understand it as peaceful functioning of a society and maintenance of its basic structure. The distinctive, minimalist aim of law, as related to public order, would then be to assure peaceful, or decent, functioning of a human community which respects the status of personhood of all the persons involved. Fulfilling this task is a moral end only indirectly, in the sense that persons living under the public order may or may not achieve fulfilment, and may or may not become morally good persons. Securing a public order may be regarded as analogical to constructing a building. A home is probably inevitable for a family to develop a virtuous common life, but a home is essentially only a prerequisite, 'a scene', which can host both felicity and despair. The public order assured by an effective system of laws serves a similar, 'minimal' purpose – providing the space of respect for human personhood. This differs considerably from a 'maximalist' requirement that the fulfilment of the members of the community, and thus the common good, should be attained to the greatest possible extent (necessary and sufficient conditions are to be assured).

Drawing from this distinction, the praxiological reading of the personalist conception attempts to find a place for human dignity as purely legal, in addition to the moral or political facet it may otherwise have (or, as I believe, really has). If the personalist conception leaves space for autonomy of law, then it also leaves space for the autonomously legal sphere in which human dignity manifests itself. Following Wojtyła's distinction between the common good and the public order, the SPT is concerned with the latter. To be sure, this should not be conflated with *reducing* human dignity to a legal principle. The praxiological reading scrutinises how human dignity may function as autonomously legal, but it must not mean that it can be conceived as exclusively legal (similarly, Riley 2019, 447). The praxiological reading is a matter of focus and emphasis, not necessarily of substantive claims. The assumption underlying this focus or emphasis is that persons may be affirmed not only in actions that are *par excellence* moral (that is, which are directly tied with moral duties and shape the moral fulfilment of the agent)[4] but also in other human activities, *prima facie* morally irrelevant. Such actions, despite not directly pursuing moral value or virtue, have *personalist value*, a value of forming and recognising the human being as a person (the notion of personalist value, as proposed by Wojtyła, was discussed in more detail in Chapter 2).

4 Here of course, I refer to the personalist conception of morality – moral duty is, at bottom, a normative relation with other persons, arising in a 'sourcing moral situation' (Styczeń 2012a, 42–7). Human actions performed in other situations also have a moral aspect, but it is not of direct concern. According to some alternative accounts on morality, the distinction between moral and *prima facie* morally irrelevant situations may not make sense at all. It is possible that ultimately, morality is 'co-extensive with the field of voluntary intentional action' (Haldane 2011, 379). At the same time, moral relevance may come in degrees. Cooking a soup with friends, for instance, may ultimately have a moral concern – fostering friendship – although the direct relevant aim is the soup itself, as well as spending a pleasant evening.

To avoid misunderstanding: This is not to say that human actions may be essentially separated from morality, in a way that could render them valuable regardless of their moral demerit. In the personalist view, plainly evil actions cannot be valuable in any sense. However, the personalist value is separable from the moral value, and the former may appear in actions that are *prima facie* morally neutral (provided they are not evil). As explained before, maintaining public order is an example of such action (or rather, a sequence of actions performed by public officials and citizens). Upon the praxiological reading, human dignity is an indispensable, transcendental prerequisite of a decent public order assured by a system of law. Legal processes, regardless of whether we mean making, applying, or 'making use' of law as a litigant or a petitioner, may or may not directly pursue moral values. But what remains an intrinsic, personalist element of any of those activities is the special status of the human person as the agent who is being recognised and self-confirmed by the very act of engagement or participation in these practices. As the SPT will claim, this status is at the bottom of all dignitarian concerns in the law – the concerns recognising the personhood of human legal subjects. Therefore (to be explained further in due course), the praxiological reading explicates human dignity as 'status' rather than 'value'.

Upon the praxiological reading, the way in which the law (the main substrate of public order) affirms persons may be called 'respect', as distinguished from 'love'. It is assumed that the personalist norm, according to which the person ultimately owes love to other persons, may be perfectly fulfilled only in moral practices. It is the moral action that is bound with the duty to realise the good of the person to the greatest available extent. Therefore, a moral assessment of actions consists in assessing the degree to which they affirm, or fail to affirm, persons. The role of law in this sphere seems considerably limited. Law can serve as a tool or arena of moral action (when legally defending a morally important interest, for example). But this is certainly contingent, occurring perhaps only in unusual circumstances or in hard cases. However, the personalist conception does not exclude the possibility that other social practices, such as law, may affirm persons in their own, genuine way. If that were true, then the law could affirm persons *not only as a vehicle for moral values, but also in an autonomous way*. And this is really the case, according to the SPT. While law is obviously not always perfectly moral (and perhaps morally neutral in some instances), it may affirm persons in the genuine way of 'respecting personhood'. In the sense adopted here, 'respecting personhood' is tantamount to *recognising the intrinsic importance of the human person by paying attention to her self-governance on the one hand, and her basic vulnerability on the other*. Importantly, 'respect' may be, in certain cases at least, assured without assuming a precognition or a consensus on what precisely is the ultimate human good, or what gives value to human life. Upon this reading, human dignity is not only a moral value (which in certain situations may bear moral duties for a legal activity), but also an autonomously legal value of respecting human personhood. The first, initial formulation of human dignity as the *status of personhood* would be then quite simple, saying namely that it consists in *the underlying respect for the personhood of everyone subject to the law.*

Given the inner complexity of this idea, and the obvious ambiguity of nearly every word used in this initial formulation, it cannot be clear at this point. To characterise it in more detail, I must return to the dignitarian moment set out in Chapter 1. So, starting from the next section, I will be engaged with more precise examples, which will lead us to the full explication of the status of personhood in Section 3. However, perhaps this initial formulation should be accompanied by a legal example. Most jurisdictions adopt the principle of *nullum crimen sine lege*, according to which no one can be lawfully considered a felon without having committed an action that was effectively criminalised by the law, no later than at the moment of actually committing this action. Regarded from the view of the SPT, this is a dignitarian principle, respecting the personhood status of those to whom the penal law is addressed. Importantly, this principle does not determine which deeds should, and which should not, be criminalised – it requires merely that people can be reasonably expected to know what the lawful scope of their decision-making power is under a jurisdiction. In this sense, the principle of *nullum crimen sine lege* is tantamount to recognising humans who are subject to a criminal law as responsible, and responsive, agents. In the personalist language, one could say that in this case, law makes room for the personalist value of human action (and genuine responsibility for it) rather than directly encapsulating moral values. This is what the praxiological interpretation, and thus the SPT as a whole, emphasises.

1.2 The praxiological reading and the autonomy of human dignity in the law

It is true that this interpretation may seem to be completely at odds with the tradition of personalism, which has always been closely intertwined with the natural law theory, and hence with the fundamental *moral* value of the human being as bearer of dignity. In my view, despite its underlying commitment to human dignity as a moral value, the personalist conception allows us to 'take a step back' and focus exclusively on the personalist value of human action, along with the way in which that personalist value is manifested in the law. This is the basis for the autonomously legal notion of human dignity that the SPT advocates for. It will also allow us to explicate different 'layers' of dignity which do not necessarily have to be directly bound with moral values. The ethical reading, and thus the direct moral engagement of law endorsing human dignity, remains possible. The praxiological reading does not preclude the ethical reading but reveals the additional, autonomously legal manifestation of dignity. I should emphasise that this is *my own* proposal, which may to a certain extent be steps away from the original thought of Wojtyła and Styczeń.

Whatever one may think about the SPT's relation to the original personalist conception, it is possible to draw support and inspiration for the former coming from the latter. In order to reveal that inspiration, I should now recall the example of the two friends engaged in a moral dispute we discussed in Chapter 2 (the example used in Styczeń 2012b, 340–1). As you may recall, the moral disagreement of the two friends, *A* and *B*, concerned the issue of whether or not to reveal truth to the terminally ill friend, *C*. Despite having the same knowledge about *C*'s close-to-death health condition, the two friends disagree with regards to whether the truth or a lie will best serve his interest (as it was hoped by one of the interlocutors, hiding the truth could save a last hope for recovery). For purposes of further argument, let us call these actors Alan, Bonnie, and Chris. Now, what is of crucial importance is that the heavy moral disagreement between Alan and Bonnie is based on their common commitment to serve Chris's dignity as a person. Despite being in dispute with regards to what exactly they ought to do, they implicitly agree that it is their duty to affirm the dignity of their ill friend (in this case, to serve his best interest). As one may recall, this example points out the threefold structure of any moral judgement, which consists of: (i) the duty dimension (the duty to affirm persons), (ii) the rightness dimension (the contention of what ought to be done), and (iii) the existential dimension (the ultimate grounding of the moral judgement). While Alan and Bonnie both endorse the duty dimension, they disagree with regards to the rightness of their mutually exclusive proposals to hide or reveal the truth to Chris. We can also imagine that Alan and Bonnie endorse different ultimate groundings for their judgements on rightness. For instance, Alan might be a Kantian, and Bonnie might be a Benthamite Utilitarian. Moreover, even if they finally found agreement on what they ought to do, they could still differ with regards to their judgements' ultimate grounding. This clearly indicates that the three elements of the moral judgements are, to a certain extent at least, independent from each other.

Now, the threefold structure of moral judgements (in which each dimension has some degree of independence) may help to specify what I mean by *prima facie* morally irrelevant activities. As we see, the specific moment of the moral ought comes to its full expression in the rightness dimension. The alternative, concrete imperatives – Alan's 'We ought to tell him the truth!' and Bonnie's 'We ought to hide the truth from him!' – assume a precognition or belief on what is good for a person in such circumstances. In order to form and justify these imperatives, the two discussants need to assess their knowledge about human psychology and health in general, and perhaps about some particulars regarding Chris's character or his firm beliefs. Such an assessment, according to the personalist conception, must be made with the view of affirmation of the person (in this case, Chris) to the fullest available extent. As such, moral judgements make sense only when related to 'sourcing moral situations' (in Polish, *macierzyste sytuacje moralne*), that is, those pertaining to the core personal and moral interests, accompanied with the apodictic, unconditional duty to perform certain actions (Styczeń 2012a, 38).

Now, the idea behind the praxiological reading of the personalist conception is the following: In the case of certain human activities, the full affirmation of persons is either impossible to achieve or irrelevant, and hence the duty to act in a certain way is not as apodictic and unconditional as it is in moral situations.

Despite this *prima facie* moral irrelevance, some actions performed in these situations are still bound with the recognition or affirmation of persons. Consider, again, the case of constructing a building. On the one hand, the architects and builders certainly pursue something that serves some human good, so their deeds may be judged as morally good or morally bad (for instance, gross professional negligence could threaten lives, which would be plainly evil). On the other hand, the conduct of architects and builders is not a direct realisation of a moral urge coming from rightness – their work and labour does not automatically drag them into a 'sourcing moral situation', into a genuine moral dilemma, as was the case of Alan and Bonnie in our example. It does not mean that their activity is not rational or reasonable. The architects and builders must make thousands of *practical judgements* during their activity, accordingly to what may be called 'technical norms' of production. The direct concern of these norms is the good of the produced work rather than that of persons (Wojtyła 2011, 31). Despite that feature, the praxiological reading claims that practical judgement – and hence the conduct that follows it – contains a duty dimension analogous to that which we encounter in moral judgements. Certainly, in practical judgements, the duty to affirm persons is present only in an indirect way, that is, *despite the lack of urges* born out of 'sourcing moral situations', and moral rightness characterising them. What is this indirect way? First, the architects and builders must care not to violate the basic moral interests of any persons involved, so they must show some degree of professional diligence, as I said earlier. But there is more than that to be highlighted. By the very fact of engaging in a productive activity, they fulfil themselves as efficacious agents – in this case, as *homo faber*, not as moral agents. Second, their conduct assumes that they participate in a common project, bearing a concrete influence on a particular human community or communities, through a new building being established. For instance, should it be a downtown building, its establishment interacts with the city itself, with all complex human relations that happen in a city. In the case of a house, the building conditions the complex dynamics of a family that will inhabit it. As we see, even a *prima facie* morally neutral activity of production is connected to the basic affirmation of persons, and in fact it does affirm persons on different levels, depending on circumstances.

The prior analysis opens a possibility for an attempt to conceptualise, remaining within the philosophical framework offered by Wojtyła and Styczeń, an autonomously legal account on human dignity. Legal activity would be interpreted as *prima facie* morally neutral, and nevertheless recognising the personalist value of human existence. According to my methodological commitment, this can be attempted only as following the law. My gradual presentation of the SPT will therefore come back to the dignitarian moment described in Chapter 1. On the side of the personalist conception, the crucial role will be played by the *suppositum humanum*, seen not only at the moral, but on the broader praxiological and existential plane which reveals human efficacy and integration as the proper underpinning, and missing explanatory factor, of human dignity in the law. As I will claim, this underpinning is of a plainly factual nature. It boils down to the reality of the human being which law needs to take into account.

Before we proceed further, I should emphasise that the ethical reading is not considered contradictory or rival to the SPT. Again, this is a difference in focus or emphasis and not in substance. First of all, the ethical interpretation may be incorporated into the SPT itself, insofar as it is inevitable to explicate these elements of the dignitary moment which entangle the law and morality to the degree which makes it hard to distinguish between them. In other words: if legal notions are not enough, moral notions will have to enter into play. This may be the case, for example, in legal cases involving bioethics. In presenting the SPT, I will agree with Adeno Addis that human dignity 'is the respect we show to people in virtue of their humanity, nothing more and nothing less' (Addis 2019, 330). According to the SPT, this may mean essentially two things. In *prima facie* morally irrelevant situations, we show respect to our fellow humans by treating them as responsible, self-determining agents, as in the case of *nullum crimen sine lege*. In other, essentially moral situations, the legal means are used to defend the human being from degradation or humiliation that not only denies them fulfilment, but also destroys the very basic conditions of such fulfilment. An example is punishing war crime or torture. These two understandings are not mutually exclusive, and the SPT considers both to be true. The primary emphasis, however, will be given to the former situations, in which human dignity appears as autonomously legal.

2 The realism of the SPT: the ontological referral and reflective equilibrium

In Chapter 1, the dignitarian moment in law was described. Despite the manifold and often contradictory usages of 'dignity', what appears to be the focal and close to universal endorsement is *the foundational function*. In most jurisdictions (national and international) – chiefly as an upshot of the UN Charter and the UDHR – human dignity is mentioned among the foundational commitments of legal and political order. It serves as an organising principle and source of basic rights. Arguably, the underlying premise of this is *the ontological referral*: often, the law refers to a special property, or existence of a special kind, which fundamentally characterises the human being. Just to recall the paradigmatic example, the UDHR states that human beings 'are endowed with reason and conscience and should act towards one another in a spirit of brotherhood' (1948, Article 1). Many legal systems introduce similar clauses into their own constitutions, subsequent legislation, and judicial reasoning. Aharon Barak offers numerous examples of the latter, which add up to an assertion that for judges, 'dignity means humanity' (Barak 2013, 363, examples provided in a footnote). Quite often in such instances, the law is formulated in a way which suggests that human dignity is not simply stipulated by the law but is rather something to be respected and protected, but existing independently of its legal recognition. Although the degree of such 'openness' to extra-legal values may vary, this suggests that the ontological referral is really being made in the law, and is not merely my assumption or speculation.

Despite that fact that the content of the ontological referral is far from any closer specification in the legal texts, the legal practice has merged the foundational function with more concrete, *regulative measures* required (or allowed) by human dignity as a legal norm. In a less radical manner, human dignity has been presumed to offer some *heuristic* guidance in law's application. From a jurisprudential point of view, however, any move from the abstract foundational principle or the highest legal value towards more specific measures, entangled in particular contexts, is doubtful. Too much seems to rely on the unspoken intuitions. That is why, in the first decades after World War II, the prevailing view was to regard the human dignity clauses (present in international law and national constitutions) as part of 'the human and temporal creed which lies at the root of common life and which is but a set of *practical conclusions* or of *practical points of convergence*' (Maritain 1966, 111, emphasis original).[5] In this spirit, German constitutional jurisprudence regarding Article 1.1 of the 1949 Basic Law, following Theodor Heuss's remark, regarded human dignity as a non-interpreted thesis (Dreier 2004, 166). According to Christoph Enders, the non-interpretational character of the human dignity provision may mean not only that its deeper theoretical justification is not a legal concern; it may also mean that it actually *has been interpreted or developed legally*, by the subsequent list of basic constitutional rights (Enders 2019, 286). One option to deal with the fuzzy application of human dignity would be then simply to abandon applying it as a legally binding norm. Human dignity could be treated as a highly abstract, purely logical postulate regarding the human capacity to hold rights.

However, such minimalism is simply no longer an option. The reasons for this may be found already in Chapter 1, if not elsewhere – when presenting the dignitary moment in law, I emphasised the vast, regulative usage of dignity in various cases. Legal practice clearly abandoned the minimalistic reading of human dignity, treating it exclusively as a 'mysterious' foundation of law. Thereby, law entered the hazardous sphere in which 'inviolable' human dignity interacts directly with other competing interests, claims, and rights (Baldus 2016 analyses the case of Germany in this respect). In addition to what has been said in Chapter 1, another important feature of human dignity operating within laws is its 'diffusive' nature. 'Dignity' operates not only at the level of basic rights, but also as a protected

5 As Maritain wrote:

> Thus it is that men possessing quite different, even opposite metaphysical or religious outlooks, can converge, not by virtue of any identity of doctrine, but by virtue of an analogical similitude in practical principles, toward the same practical conclusions, and can share in the same practical secular faith, provided that they similarly revere, perhaps for quite diverse reasons, truth and intelligence, human dignity, freedom, brotherly love, and the absolute value of moral good. (Maritain 1966, 111)

A similar intuition underlies divergent theories of political liberalism, or public reason, although only Martha Nussbaum, to my knowledge at least, acknowledges the contribution of Maritain (Nussbaum 2008, 251).

interest in private law or labour law. An example of this comes from Romania. As part of the struggle to transform the country's legal culture according to the EU requirements, the notion of 'dignity' was introduced into the new civil code in 2009, which resulted in an improved protection of individuals by means of private law (Pop 2019, 757). The Polish history of an analogous transformation process is somehow reversed – dignity jurisprudence was first developed in the private law scholarship, which was subsequently used in debates concerning the 1997 Constitution and its commitment to dignity (Venice Commission 1998, 9–10). These and similar examples give us reason to say that human rights/constitutional rights are not the only issue; dignity also regulates the sphere of actionable private law interests. More generally, should a theory of human dignity take its 'diffusive' nature into account, it must result in hard questions concerning the mutual relations between the dignity well-known from human rights law and constitutions, and its counterparts in private law, labour law, or criminal law.

In my view, the key quest – enabling a reconciliation of these extremely diverse usages of dignity – is to find *a wide reflective equilibrium* between the regulative and heuristic functions of dignity on the one hand, and the ontological referral on the other. If one is able to demonstrate that the ontological referral is not empty or hopelessly vague, then one will be able to provide the common point of reference for divergent legal contexts in which human dignity appears. The method of wide reflective equilibrium allows one to juxtapose and confront particular normative judgements with the ontology of the person. Let me now comment a bit on how I envisage the application of that method. Importantly, reflective equilibrium has been developed and applied mostly within normative political and moral theory (theory of justice). In its 'wide' version, to recall the classical formulation by Daniels, quoted in Chapter 1, the method of reflective equilibrium strives to find coherence between one's considered moral judgements, moral principles, as well as background theories (Daniels 1979, 258). In our case, which is that of jurisprudence, the moral judgements and principles need to be somehow replaced, or at least accompanied, by *legal* judgements and principles. The 'background theory' under consideration will be the personalist conception presented in Chapter 2. Since I assume the praxiological reading of said conception, the set of beliefs under consideration will not cover moral principles and judgements, at least not *prima facie*. It may happen, though, that moral notions will have to be introduced, if the legal notions alone will not suffice to produce a coherent and complete theory. As an essentially procedural and coherentist method, reflective equilibrium does not have a 'foundation' – background theories, which could be expected to serve as one, do not have absolute priority (DePaul 1986, 60), and particular judgements are not 'derived' from them, or from principles. Every belief, regardless of where it resides in the triple set of judgements, principles, and background theories, should be confronted with other beliefs and might need an adjustment, or even abandonment, as a result of such confrontation. Some statements, however – such as the very affirmation of human dignity – are hardly removable. The reason for this, as explained by Styczeń in his analysis of moral disputes, is that assuming dignity is a necessary condition of any sensible normative argumentation. Even if seeking reflective equilibrium is a one-person exercise, it is an exercise of reason and must deal at least with hypothetical interlocutors offering counterargument. If everyone counts as a possible interlocutor, it is hard to deny dignity to some arbitrarily chosen groups or individuals.

My approach differs considerably from the prevailing view on the method of reflective equilibrium. In particular, I reject regarding reflective equilibrium as a mere description of our moral sense, as well as a mere construction of a programme of action for practical purposes. The former view seems to be a possible interpretation of the first proponent of the method in political theory, that is, John Rawls. At times, Rawls made an analogy between the sense of justice and sense of grammatical correctness (Rawls 1971, 46). If that analogy was fully adequate, then reaching a reflective equilibrium would have to be understood simply as finding a *correct description* of how our sense of justice works. This would exclude considerations of whether the beliefs in equilibrium are true or false. The latter, constructivist view was most prominently held by Ronald Dworkin. In his view, instead of seeking the 'truth' of principles of justice, one should rather assert 'that men and women have a responsibility to fit the particular judgments on which they act into a coherent program of action' (Dworkin 1975, 28). In opposition to both accounts, the SPT assumes that the truth of background theories, and the rightness of judgements and principles, must play a decisive role. This may be called a truth-seeking equilibrium, as opposed to 'mere descriptive' or 'constructivist' accounts. This is a complex idea which we do not have to scrutinise in detail. Suffice it to say that it urges anyone responsible for practical judgements (a political or legal theorist, a judge, or a legislator), to take into account *the relevant beliefs she holds to be true*. She is obviously obliged to take every possible precaution *not* to rest on false beliefs, and take to be true only those beliefs which one has good reasons to hold true. Equilibrium may only be really wide, and really attached to 'responsibility', if the question about truth remains at the heart of the considerations.

Despite that commitment to truth, the adopted method is non-foundational, and hence the SPT is not simply derived from the personalist conception. However, *the natural personhood of humans* – its structure and conditions – remains of crucial importance. This is the realism I am pursuing. According to a truth-seeking reflective equilibrium method, legal judgements and principles simply should not disregard the relevant aspects of reality. Thus, a theory of human dignity must pay attention to personhood and its structure. It should scrutinise the impact that natural personhood and dignity has on the artificial, legal capacity and dignity that law ascribes to humans. In other words, the SPT aims to describe the general situation of personal agents vis-à-vis legal norms. Admittedly, this position is very uneasy. It requires an attempt to speak that which has been considered either divisive, or simply unspeakable – the concrete, anthropological content of human dignity. Given the demands of metaphysical parsimony commonly imposed on law and legal considerations, this 'speaking out' must be made in a restrained manner, assuming as little as possible with regards to the ultimate grounding of the content of the ontological referral.

This is somewhat paradoxical: The aim is to reveal things, but the methodological restraints urge to do so in a manner that is independent from ultimate speculative grounding. All these difficulties can be, hopefully, overcome with the use of the personalist conception of Karol Wojtyła and Tadeusz Styczeń set forth in Chapter 2. When interpreted in the praxiological spirit and merged with the reflective equilibrium method, the personalist conception can bridge the human condition and the law in a realistic and, at the same time, metaphysically parsimonious manner.

In order to emphasise the realistic character of the SPT, let us consider the alternative interpretation of the dignitarian moment, namely, the 'political' one. It could be argued that increasing legal engagement with human dignity emerged chiefly, or perhaps exclusively, because of our political commitment to the human community *we aspire and are urged to be*, but not necessarily *in fact are*. In other words, the process expresses our aspirations and longing, with not much to discover or take into account on the side of human reality (that is, human structure or existence). According to Bernhard Schlink, for instance, human dignity:

> is a *Sehnsuchtbegriff*, a concept that encompasses our longing for a better and fairer world where the recognition and protection of humans is not up for grabs and cannot be overpowered or outmaneuvered or argued down. The longing, again, is vague, and it will never be fulfilled and will often be frustrated. But the concept is important. It brings together people of good-will who all share that longing, though they may disagree on what human dignity means, demands, and prohibits.
>
> (Schlink 2013, 634)

From an historical perspective, this view has some plausibility. After all, the moments at which the discourse on human dignity becomes most vivid are the circumstances of grave violations of human rights, or atrocities of war such as the Holocaust. However, paradoxically, it makes dignity very fragile, dependent on particular historical circumstances, a convergence of views and the 'good faith' of most important actors. By no means can this be taken for granted.

In contrast to the political interpretation, the SPT strives to demonstrate that the dignitarian legal commitments are more than just a longing or a response to heartbreaking events. In other words, it strives to demonstrate that the dignitarian moment in the law (obviously accompanied with the longing for better, decent arrangements) has a deeper basis, a basis that is deeply embedded in law as well as in persons. Despite undeniable examples of the law failing to meet the demands of dignity, or misrepresenting them, there is a profound correspondence between the ontological structures of the human person and the legal recognitions of human dignity. In this sense, there is a deep correspondence between facts concerning persons, and principles expressing their dignity. The SPT claims that a person's self-determination, transcendence, fulfilment, and integration – all examined in Chapter 2 – are real, and therefore they influence the functioning and structures of law, in one way or another, with more or less success.

Here, another appearance of human dignity in the law must be mentioned, what I have called the meta-legal level. In Chapter 1, I agreed with Jeremy Waldron that the human being is law's indispensable component, not only in terms of what we have reasons to achieve, but also in terms of what we are actually doing with the law, or in terms of how law really functions (Waldron 2011). This fact should be taken into account when striving to reach wide reflective equilibrium in applying human dignity. However, in certain respects, Waldron's account seems too self-limited. Namely, he seems to believe that scrutinising natural personhood (as it was pursued in Chapter 2 of this book, for example) is not necessary, or perhaps even not relevant for law. His works describe an historical process of equalisation of status (Waldron 2012). However, Waldron seems reluctant to examine the transcendental or essential conditions – features of human beings – which would explain that process. As Dan-Cohen says, Waldron's view is that 'universal and equal dignity is better anchored in evolving social practice than in Kantian metaphysics' (Dan-Cohen 2012, 5). Waldron's later work on human equality (considered to pertain to the same cluster of ideas) confirms this. Namely, he seems to claim that no sharp theoretical choices about the crucial human characteristics are needed to establish the basis for equality. Rather, different human capacities 'come together in complex narratives' and reinforce a common commitment to equality (Waldron 2017, 127). In this sense, Waldron is closer to the 'political' interpretation of the dignitarian moment, and thereby rejects the crucial importance of the ontological structures of human personhood, at least in the sense of trying to speak out what is central and most important to it. Instead, he suggests that the ultimate grounding for human dignity and equality may be, at the end of the day, theological in nature (Waldron 2017, 185).[6] As should be already obvious, the SPT stands in opposition to this attitude. While theological grounding is tremendously important at the more comprehensive or deeper plane, it is beyond the scope of the SPT. The SPT is focused on the natural, radical capacity for action (observable in inner experience and in analysis of human practices), which is considered to be the strongest mark of personhood, and hence the *ratio cognoscendi* of human dignity. In my view, the meta-legal appearances of human dignity in the architecture of law constitute a strong reason to hold this belief true.

Taking all this into consideration, the next section will provide an interpretation of the ontological referral (arguably, a direct analytical consequence of dignitarian provisions) as a reference to the personal activities of humans, with the main emphasis on action. The analysis of personhood provided in Chapter 2 revealed self-determination and transcendence on the one hand, and integration on the other, as the key ontological features of the human being. As a result of

6 Although Waldron considers the theological grounding as legitimate and important, he remains ambiguous as to what is the basis for human dignity or equality. Discussing the issues of profound disabilities, he develops his own account in naturalist terms (Waldron 2017, 240–4), leaving the theological grounding as a possibility.

this scrutiny – interpreting law through the lenses of the personalist conception – the dignitarian moment will be shown as the indispensable substrate of a public order (a rightful relation between persons). Human dignity will be thus shown – on the one hand – as rooted in the ontology of the human person, but – on the other hand – as fundamentally in need of embodiment in legal arrangements of public order. This is the main task of the STP, to be fulfilled in the rest of the chapter.

3 Human dignity as the status of personhood

In what follows, I will argue that human dignity in the law is a status-expressing principle. It protects different human interests, to different extents and in different legal contexts. The protected interests deeply correspond with the status of personhood, the status which all humans have equally. Hence, *the Principle of the Status of Personhood* will be proposed as the explication of human dignity in the law. According to the methodological credentials scrutinised in Chapter 1, the planned explication will be offered as a partial definition, with no intention to deny the existence of the open-ended cluster of meanings that might possibly appear in the family. However, the status of personhood will be considered as the focal meaning, the common point of reference, important to all other possible meanings.

To pursue this explication, we must shift our interest back to the law. In Chapter 1, my attempt was to systematise functions of human dignity. The important result of this initial engagement was the recognition of the importance of personhood (the ontological referral). Our re-engagement with the law will need to take another perspective. Before formulating the PSP, which I think is the best available explication of human dignity in the law, I shall identify the basic dignitarian interests that the law identifies and protects. In this sense, I will be examining the way in which the human being is 'showing through' the dignitarian law. If the ontological referral is to be put into equilibrium with more particular applications of dignity, then one needs to identify the spheres of personal legal interests protected by dignity. As I will argue, these different spheres overlap with each other, but *integrity* should be understood as the focal sphere (as already compellingly argued by Addis 2019). What follows is an explication, partly stipulative in character.

3.1 Dignitarian legal interests of the human person

Before attempting to identify the key interests protected by dignity, I should make one reservation: the term 'interest' is used in a loose, non-technical sense, interchangeably with 'protected area' or 'sphere'. In particular, it does not presuppose an interest theory of rights. In my view, one can propose a theory of human dignity without engaging in a detailed discussion regarding the *function* of rights, in which the 'interest theory' and the 'will theory' are most important standpoints (Wenar 2020, s.2.2.2). However, the SPT (and, most likely, every other theory of dignity) is a theory providing a *justification* of rights. The latter aspect of bonds between human dignity and rights must be addressed in due course. At the same time, I will bracket-off the debate between the interest theory and the will theory of rights. Obviously, the SPT may not imply a strong version of the will theory – the dignitarian protection does not cover only conscious adults effectively expressing their will. Given the possibility of different variations of both theories of rights, or even some forms of combining the two together, that issue remains open.

3.1.1 Freedom from degradation

The first, most obvious, and commonly accepted sphere of dignitarian legal protection may be called 'freedom from degradation'. Indeed, the word 'protection' really fits here – the norms are of *prohibitive* character, the prohibitions being put on slavery, torture, human traffic, war crimes, or extreme poverty. In short, law protects people against different forms of denying their most fundamental quality of 'being human', understood intuitively (as opposed to being subhuman, a beast, nothing but a threat, or a mere means to an end, to borrow from Margalit 1996). The 'degradation' that is in question here is therefore unambiguously grave, often connected with the use of physical violence, and always connected to a clear-cut objectification of the human being. Such prohibitive norms appear in international human rights law and adjudication, as well as in national constitutions, legislation, and adjudication (especially in criminal law). They may protect the individual against abusive exercise of state power (for instance, by excluding cruel punishment, or requiring decent conditions for prisoners and detainees), as well as abusive practices of other people (such as human trafficking or forced sterilisation). In such cases, as well as in the case of protection against extreme poverty, the state authorities are obliged to introduce proper means and take actions, rather than just refraining from certain abusive practices.

At the present stage of inquiry, we need neither recall the legal examples from Chapter 1 nor introduce additional material. We may also postpone dealing with the controversial or borderline cases. The core meaning of 'degradation' is uncontested, and numerous conventions, constitutions, criminal law codes, and other similar instruments being put to work around the globe may be taken for granted as protecting human dignity. What is important in the perspective of the SPT is situating freedom from degradation within our discussion about the autonomously legal notion of human dignity. It is, namely, important to say that freedom from degradation obviously transcends the limits of law. Prohibitions on degrading treatment are legal, as part of law's fabric. At the same time, they constitute a necessary moral prerequisite of any sort of community, so the moral (and the political) dimensions are intrinsically entangled with their legal counterpart. Earlier in this chapter, I indicated that the personalist conception may have two distinct and equally plausible interpretations: the ethical, and the praxiological one. These interpretations overlap when degradation is at stake. The reason for this is that freedom from degradation does not assume any detailed conception of human flourishing or fulfilment. It is, rather, a necessary condition of peaceful common functioning, and any further debates about law and morality must assume that freedom. Recall Styczeń's crucial distinction between judgements asserting *the basic duty* to affirm persons on the one hand, and judgements concerning the *rightness* of some more particular measures on the other. Seen in light of this distinction, assuring freedom from degradation appears as the basic duty, a non-derivable axiom of both: the common good (the domain of ethics) and public order (the domain of law). To clarify with an example: Disputes about education require detailed knowledge about human beings (who are to be educated), and thus require full judgement concerning rightness. Freedom from degradation, in contrast to that, is a basic condition of a community within which any debates can be held, and thus requires 'only' acknowledgement of the basic characteristic of 'humanity' of others, without further specification.

Taking these points for granted, freedom from degradation will reveal paradoxically little detail about the ontological referral and its relations to 'public order'. Despite the crucial importance of that freedom for maintaining human dignity and human rights, its basic character makes it uncontested, and in this sense 'unproblematic'. It should therefore be kept in mind, but for now, there is no need to analyse it any further. Only after some more specific interests – self-determination, privacy, and integrity – are depicted will we be able to provide some guidelines in the borderline or hard cases of freedom from degradation (to be revisited in Chapter 4).

3.1.2 Self-determination in a dynamic relation to truth

Another dignitarian interest, that of individual autonomy (self-determination, or self-control), seems to be problematic at the root. In what follows, I will *at first* use the terms 'autonomy', 'self-determination', and 'self-control' interchangeably. In due course, in this section, I will distinguish between the three and argue for self-determination (in the technical sense) as the most plausible candidate for the protected dignitarian interest. The general idea, commonly associated with human dignity, is quite straightforward and widely shared: law should allow people to make important choices regarding their lives. In other words, law treats human persons as agents – beings capable of reasonably setting their own ends, and entitled to govern their own affairs the way they perceive as best. When one applies that general idea to a specific case, however, one is very likely to meet opposition and disagreement. Autonomy, although vague, is commonly adopted as a background assumption, an aim of laws, or both. The scope of its rightful exercise in a system of law, however, seems to be heavily dependent on the more comprehensive vision of humanity, morality, and constitutional identity of a particular community.[7] The panorama becomes even more complex if we recall that

7 Kommers (2011) argues that differences in abortion policy, and different interpretations of autonomy present in constitutional jurisprudence, result from differences in 'regime values',

the notion of dignity is evoked to justify paternalism, that is, to restrain personal autonomy not for the sake of others, but for the sake of the person whose choices are being restrained.[8] Therefore, the SPT needs not only to present the dignitarian interest of self-determination, but also to cope with the conceptual vagueness and normative indeterminacy attached to it. Why would the same key premises lead different people and different authorities to different conclusions? Is there any hope that appealing to human dignity will help in resolving conflicts regarding autonomy? And, finally, is the picture of human dignity as a 'practical point of convergence' still plausible in contemporary circumstances?

To attempt to answer these questions in a way that is coherent with the SPT, *self-determination* must be distinguished from autonomy and self-control. Adopting self-determination as the proper or most plausible dignitarian interest requires argumentation. Before we get into details, let me propose an initial perspective. In my view, it should be considered that it is a natural tendency of legal and political scholarship to *highlight* disagreements. It is therefore much more probable that the theorist analysing the bonds between human dignity and autonomy will overemphasise some divisive points, rather than fail to notice them or give them due consideration. In my view, this comes from overlooking the fact that whilst disagreements really happen in the law, and constitute the genuine problem for any theory of human dignity, they are also rare. If one focuses exclusively on adjudication of human rights, for example, one's view is somewhat distorted – it is natural that using autonomy and dignity in highly debatable cases will yield disagreement, or at least serious doubts. But what if we consider the bigger picture, and ask about dignity in legal processes in a more general manner? In my opinion, in that case we would see commitment to human dignity and human autonomy in the everyday business of countless lawyers, judges, and citizens making use of the law or even simply obeying it. As I will argue, the self-determination recognised in day-to-day legal practice is much less contested in comparison to the judgements of the highest constitutional and human rights courts. If we take this seriously, disagreement about the hard cases will still appear as real and difficult but, at the same time, as not *essential* to dignity-based legal practices. This is clearly observable at the meta-legal level, in divergent areas of law which rely on human agency. As some have correctly claimed, the recognition of self-determination and agentic structures of persons are inherent to the very idea of the rule of law (Riley 2017, 178).

---

that is, different constitutional identities. Each of what he calls 'fraternal democracy' (characterising Ireland), 'social democracy' (adopted in Germany), and 'liberal democracy' (present in the United States) renders different positions of the state in relation to restraining the individual choices (Kommers 2011, 452–4). The paper obviously does not cover the shift in Ireland on the matter of abortion which resulted in adoption of the Thirty-sixth Amendment of the Constitution Act 2018, according to which 'Provision may be made by law for the regulation of termination of pregnancy'.

8 The most famous case is dwarf-tossing in France. A detailed examination of the admissibility of paternalism in penal law, on dignitarian grounds, is provided by Kleining (2017).

When regarded from this perspective, the hard cases concerning the rightful extent and legitimate regulation of autonomy appear as situated at the borderlines of our semantic and normative beliefs about dignity. Therefore, they may be properly assessed only after the normative and semantic core of the connection between human dignity and self-determination has been made explicit. In what follows, the day-to-day recognition of human agency will serve as the paradigm case.

For one of many possible examples of what I am after, let us briefly reflect on human dignity in France. What almost automatically comes to mind is the famous dwarf-tossing case, upon which I commented in Chapter 1 (Council of State of the French Republic 1995). To recall, the Council of State (the highest administrative tribunal) explicitly recognised human dignity as a component of public order, and upheld the paternalistic ban on dwarf tossing competitions by a local authority. That final judgement was upheld in the international forum, by the Human Rights Committee. The fact that goes almost unnoticed, however, is that in spite of numerous scholarly commentaries, the case has had surprisingly little real impact on the law. Indeed, French judges have shown self-constraint in the direct application of dignity, especially the paternalistic elements inherent in the idea. Since 1995, courts have used dignity to justify analogous bans – for example, on displaying dead human bodies and body parts in a commercial exhibition (Court of Cassation of the French Republic 2010). Insofar as the general picture of French adjudication is concerned, however, human dignity has been used as the 'last resort' rather than an omnipresent principle with vast normative implications (Cossalter 2014). As Régis Lanneau explains, this 'timidity' is a result of the judicial culture in France which, accordingly to its republican principles, leaves vast freedom for the legislative branch of government (Lanneau 2019, 266–9). Does this mean that French law does not really recognise human dignity as a fundamental principle, despite the 'lip service' having been paid to it by the legal bodies, especially the Constitutional Council (1994)? Such a conclusion would be obviously too quick. The controversial cases such as the ban on dwarf-tossing may appear as challenges and problems for human dignity and autonomy, but certainly they do not exhaust the issue. Rather, as I mentioned earlier, they are the borderline cases of something much more common and much less contested.

First, the notion of human dignity is present in many legislative texts in different branches of law. In France, these include the general principles of the civil code (Article 16), a considerable part of the penal law,[9] as well as specific biomedical issues and the condition of prisons (for details, see Cossalter 2014, reporting on more than 50 cases of legislation evoking human dignity). On that background, one may say that daily legal activities in this jurisdiction implicitly

9 Book V of the French Penal Code covers crimes against the dignity of the person (Articles 225-1–225-26). Among others, Book V comprises crimes connected to human autonomy, such as servile work or human traffic.

endorse human dignity by respecting the boundaries that it imposes on action. Certainly, some issues are disputed, but there is a general consensus on the framework of actions which must not encroach on dignity of persons. Second – which is more important, and not limited to France – the dignitarian commitment is present on many occasions in which the law does not necessarily evoke dignity, but implicitly rests on the agency of the addressees. In Chapter 1 (chiefly following Jeremy Waldron's analysis), I indicated law's reliance on self-application, its use of general standards, and its argumentative structure (best observable in lawsuits). All these aspects allow us to say that without assuming rational human agency at the background, the law would simply fail to make sense as an institution. Human dignity – chiefly related to autonomy of the agent – is present as a meta-legal commitment.

Some details and examples of the meta-legal level have already been presented in Chapter 1. Let me supplement what has been said there by highlighting another point, namely, the implicit recognition of rational agency which is (arguably) present in standards of legislation, as well as in the guidelines for good public administration (the latter having been previously mentioned in Chapter 1). These two elements are important indicators of the rule of law[10] and have considerable impact on day-to-day legal processes. I will comment only on the European standards, although it would be interesting to see if and how similar ideas work in other, especially non-Western, contexts.

An interesting document influencing European countries is the Rule of Law Checklist – a report adopted by the Venice Commission to serve as a tool of 'an objective, thorough, transparent and equal assessment' of the rule of law in the member states of the Council of Europe (Venice Commission 2016, paragraph 24). In this document, the Commission stated that:

> the notion of the Rule of Law requires a system of certain and foreseeable law, where everyone has the right to be treated by all decision-makers with dignity, equality and rationality and in accordance with the laws, and to have the opportunity to challenge decisions before independent and impartial courts through fair procedures. The Commission warned against the risks of a purely formalistic concept of the Rule of Law, merely requiring that any action of a public official be authorised by law.
>
> (Venice Commission 2016, paragraph 15)

The rule of law obviously demands more than simply any rule by any laws, according to the Venice Commission. Dignity is mentioned as a separate criterion,

10 In the report of the Venice Commission, we read that 'The Rule of Law has been proclaimed as a basic principle at universal level by the United Nations – for example in the Rule of Law Indicators – and at regional level by the Organization of American States – namely in the Inter-American Democratic Charter – and the African Union – in particular in its Constitutive Act. References to the Rule of Law may also be found in several documents of the Arab League' (Venice Commission 2016, 10).

without further specification. One may reasonably assume that the document refers to the proper weight that should be assigned to all individuals subject to the law. Also, the decision-makers under the rule of law should not compromise someone's interest for arbitrary reasons, or completely disregard their perspective on issues involved in a decision. If dignity is understood along these lines, the commitment thereto permeates the whole document, in the sense of promoting and securing human self-determination in accordance with publicly known, non-retroactive laws. This is observable also in the standards of legal change. A new law needs not only to be ordained in accordance with constitutional procedures. It also needs to be presented as a set of *publicly justifiable* provisions. In order to assess that, the report invites concrete, practical questions. For example, one should ask whether or not the proposed legislation was 'debated publicly by parliament and adequately justified (e.g. by explanatory reports)', or whether the general public had 'access to draft legislation, at least when it is submitted to Parliament'. The guidelines also require that the public should 'have a meaningful opportunity to provide input' at various stages of the legislative process (Venice Commission 2016, paragraph 50, table 5).

All this seems to tacitly accept an underlying premise: that the people whose conduct the law is to regulate have a capacity that is more complex than simply 'following the rules'. This capacity is, namely, obeying the laws by *making sense* of them (both in terms of interpreting law's provisions and having one's own reasons to obey law and order). This is arguably a more dignified way of obedience, which may be achieved only once a *ratio legis* has been properly presented and discussed by the relevant public. Of course, in the circumstances of modern states, it is impossible to ensure that everyone factually agrees on all the laws they should obey, or even that everyone has opportunity to assess the justification of all the laws. However, the essential minimum in this regard is that at least those affected the most, and those expressing their interest, have their voice properly heard. If such a system of standards works well enough, one can reasonably believe that most laws are justifiable to the minimum extent, even if one has reasons to disagree with the adopted legislation (Rupniewski 2019). All this, as it seems, puts the very notion of *legalism* in connection with human reasonable agency, and thus dignity.

Analogically, it is a widely accepted standard of good administration to explain the decisive factors of a case to the parties. As I already mentioned in Chapter 1, the European Code of Good Administrative Behaviour requires public institutions to provide a justification regarding a clear statement of the relevant facts of the case, as well as the legal basis. Similarly, the Polish Code of Administrative Procedure adopts a general *principle of persuasion* (*zasada przekonywania*), according to which:

> Public administration bodies should explain to the parties the basis for the rules used to decide a case, so that a decision may be implemented by the parties without the need for coercive measures.
>
> (Code of Administrative Procedure [Poland] 1960, Article 11)

This principle allows us to perceive the legalism of public administration in a dignitarian manner. On the one hand, public administration procedures are not contracts – public bodies enjoy a superior authority that allows them to create or change someone's legal situation *with their one-sided decision*. On the other hand, these decisions are limited. Not only does the obvious requirement of finding a legal basis for each decision set the limits. The principle of persuasion allows and requires officials to actually explain their decision (either in the formal justification or informally during the process) in terms of its overall reasonableness, not just its coherence with the law. Again, this protects the status of the parties as active and reasonable agents.

The SPT treats these and similar examples as the paradigm case for dignitarian protection of autonomy (or, more precisely, self-determination in the technical sense). Like the principle of *nullum crimen sine lege*, the standards for legislation and the principle of persuasion in administrative processes rest on the assumption of active, responsible and responsive human agency. And this is a dignitarian commitment. As David Luban argues, commenting on the famous canons of 'inner morality of law' proposed by Lon Fuller, when the law is constrained by such canons, it serves human dignity in the sense of preventing despotic humiliation, and fostering respecting relations with and within a polity (Luban 2010).

Now, the question arises – how specific should we be in determining the necessary background theory of human personhood, in order to make sense of that dignitarian commitment? It seems that – in the face of the ontological referral – we cannot simply abandon or circumvent the issue, taking metaphysical parsimony as an excuse. Rather, we need to explicate what judges and legislators should really respect and protect when regarding human dignity and autonomy in an intimate, and yet somehow tense, relation. Or, perhaps, we could stop at the intuitive understanding of autonomy, used interchangeably with self-control or self-determination? The SPT answers in the negative to that second question also. A truth-seeking reflective equilibrium, as well as sceptical realism, urges us to at least attempt to find the ontological structures of the human person that fit here to the greatest available extent. To do otherwise would be tantamount to disregarding the necessary conditions for that which human dignity in the law strives to protect. In order to attempt to find that structure – or, rather, to argue for a particular, personalist interpretation of it – I will now distinguish between three attitudes: self-control, autonomy, and self-determination. Given the vast literature on the topic, and extreme diversity of possible accounts, I will use 'self-control' and 'autonomy' in the stipulative sense, taken up for the limited purpose of our discussion. Here, we are not in search of the historic usage of words by philosophers, but rather of the particularly personalist way of understanding self-determination.

The attitude that is directly connected to empirical observation, and is in a sense the least demanding, is *self-control*. From the external perspective, a person who controls herself is like a tossed coin – others cannot predetermine the exact course of her behaviour. From the internal perspective, a self-controlling person acts on her genuine preference and is able to resist preferences that urge her to do things which are inconsistent with her broader plan of action. In sum, self-control means to be free from automatic subjection to external and internal forces, such as internal stimuli or commands coming from other agents. For example, a hungry person being able to patiently stand in a line for food is resisting the stimulus to 'eat now!' and thus controls himself. He also does not blindly follow the commands of others (such as 'you will eat right now!') and is not easily manipulated (as in the case of 'don't you think you are hungry?').

Autonomy is, in a sense, more demanding and not that easily verified by empirical observation. The reason for this is that it requires the agent not only to act according to his own preferences, but also to abide by self-imposed laws. An autonomous person not only has a consistent plan of action and is ready to execute it. He also accepts this plan as coming from his own, genuine, and deep motivations of a certain kind. In sum, being an autonomous agent means acting on the basis of self-given rules, coming from one's own reason, or will, or both. Additionally, autonomy may cover more than just a programme of action. It may involve the situation in which the agent independently develops his own general worldview and the set of values attached to it.

Self-determination is intimately connected to the personalist conception presented in Chapter 2. It differs from the two former attitudes especially in one crucial aspect: conditioning the vertical transcendence of the agent, namely, the constitutive reference to truth. It should be recalled that the vertical transcendence of the person in action consists in the fact of 'outgrowing oneself' by exercising self-governance. The self-governance Wojtyła talks about, however, is not merely a conscious determination of one's conduct (as it is in the structure of self-control). Rather, self-governance in the personalist sense is exercised in the circumstances of the inevitable responsibility for truth. In other words, the agent does not simply pursue programmes of action. Rather, she *transcends herself* in pursuing these programmes because of her being able to judge them in the face of relevant truths. The transcendental character of action is therefore conditioned by the fact that the agent is able *to judge herself and her actions in conscience*. This is done in the light of relevant truths about the world, her values, and her own personal interiority (Moń 2019, 55–9). While autonomy means acting according to one's own authentic values, higher-order desires, or self-imposed moral laws, *self-determination is best understood as truthfulness, in the sense of responsiveness to, and responsibility for, truth relevant for an action*. As Wojtyła explains:

> The relationship between responsibility and agency indicates that any duty contains [a moment of] an opening of the person towards values. Responsibility, as an intrapersonal fact that man has the experience of in an intimate relation with his conscience, seems to presuppose the specific dynamism of the will noted in the preceding chapter. The analysis of choice and decision with their own originality then led us to the conclusion that the will consisted in the ability to respond independently to value rather than in the ability to strive for an object because of its value. The ability to respond to values integrates in its own special manner man's acting and impresses it with

> the mark of personal transcendence. Following it comes responsibility, which is most intimately connected with the action, because it is action that carries in it the response to values that is characteristic to the will.
>
> (Wojtyła 1979, 170, translation modified)

In light of the preceding, self-determination means that the individual is an author of his own life. In a sense, he is also an author of himself, since becoming such and such a person happens through his own actions.[11] However, these two elements of authorship are inherent also to autonomy, and to a lesser extent, self-control. The distinguishing element of self-determination consists in its integral connection to responsibility, and thus, to conscience. The norms according to which we act are therefore not merely self-imposed, but also self-recognised. According to Wojtyła:

> Conscience plays a creative role in what concerns the truth of norms, that is to say, of those principles of acting and behavior which form the objective core of morality or law. Its creativity goes beyond simple recognition of the norm or injunction that generates the sense of obligation resulting in passive obedience. The experience of rightness is preceded and integrated by the experience of truthfulness.
>
> (Wojtyła 1979, 165)

This passage suggests that the moment of autonomy, understood as being the genuine source of the rules upon which one acts, is somehow also inherent to self-determination.[12] However, in the personalist conception, that bond between the individual decision-affirmation of the norm on the one hand, and its binding force on the other, is inevitably mediated and determined by the objective moment: the truth-rightness of that norm. According to Wojtyła, that particular structure of self-determination, understood as an 'intrapersonal reality', is the necessary condition for the social principles (including laws) which rest on human responsibility (Wojtyła 1979, 169).[13]

The SPT claims that self-determination (in the sense just presented) is the best candidate for the special human attitude which is recognised in the law under different labels of 'autonomy', 'self-control', or 'rational human agency'. Especially when dignity is also at play, the law recognises and protects *the capacity for action*

11 Wojtyła calls this 'the intransitive effect of action' (Wojtyła 1979, 149–50).

12 It is worth noting that a similar role of conscience is present in Kant (1991, 233–34), despite the emphasis he puts on autonomy.

13 I abstain from a detailed examination of the issue of the complex relation between facts, norms, and values. Although the discussions regarding this problem have been sophisticated and important, they do not have primarily importance for our inquiry. While the relation between facts and norms, as well as between moral norms and values, seems underdeveloped in Wojtyła's work, Styczeń took pains to argue that his theory of moral judgement escapes the naturalistic fallacy (for a brief overview, see Moń 2019, 50–3).

motivated by the agent's firm beliefs about the relevant truths. This is observable on divergent occasions. In the courtroom, we have testimony in which the witness is responsible to reveal the truth about relevant facts. In parliament, the MPs and members of the public admitted to hearings argue for or against a bill in the face of its real background, genuine rightness, and prospective outcomes. In administrative decisions, the authorities are obliged to persuade the parties and justify their decisions to them. Admittedly, on certain occasions, one is not able to determine what exactly is under dignitarian protection. The crime of human trafficking, for instance (recognised as a crime against dignity in Poland and France) seems to hit the self-control, the autonomy, and the self-determination of the victim equally. The reason for this is that particular crime is also connected to degradation – it treats the victim as a mere end, or as subhuman, which makes it an outrage upon all those human capacities. But in examples such as the principle of persuasion in administrative law, or standards of good legislation, or even reliance on someone's testimony, self-determination is clearly in the foreground. Self-control is insufficient, since all it does is endow the agent with his own programme of action. The law clearly requires more than just that. Autonomy, to the contrary, is a plausible alternative. The argument against it is as follows: If autonomy were the proper dignitarian interest, the main task of the laws would be ensuring maximum external freedom to everyone, in a libertarian manner. But in the dignitarian moment, as we have seen throughout Chapter 1, the law does much more than just that. Instead of ensuring the framework for harmonising as many worldviews and programmes for action as possible, it strives to find a basis of *common* life in which the dignity of all is safeguarded. And it protects not only human independence and autonomy – equally important are the moments in which dignity protects human dependence on others, and their vulnerability. Self-determination, deeply connected with responsibility not only for oneself but also for others, seems a much better match.

Also, especially in legal activities such as legislative and administrative decision-making, we see that the law appeals to the agentic capacity to engage with common values rather than produce values that are genuinely one's own. The values and reasons for action in administrative decisions, for instance, are not the autonomous creation of the officials or the parties. Rather, they are elements of a public order, given for everyone's consideration as reasons for action. In the contemporary complex world, it is unrealistic to assume that everyone who obeys the law shares the same motivational basis and endorses its justification to an equal extent, or in an equal manner. The harmonisation of autonomous agents would have to either assume their consensus on reasons, or consider their system of laws as a mere *modus vivendi*. In contrast to that, the standards of the modern rule of law create a possibility for a third way. Namely, there may be a public order that is justifiable to a minimum sufficient extent, which is assured by the procedural elements as well as substantive basic rights. I think this is an adequate description of our jurisdictions. Again, this is not easily merged with autonomy, which requires acting on reasons that are genuinely one's own. Self-determination is a better match, since it is consistent with the agent not only *consenting*, but also *having responsibility* to transfer some aspects of his decision-making power and creation of values to other members of the community.

Reliance on self-determination as distinguished from autonomy and self-control has been the important stipulative aspect of this section. The next section will present integrity, which will supplement the previous arguments for self-determination. I am taking the liberty not to pursue the problem of hard cases in this section. This important and problematic issue will be approached after the status of personhood is sufficiently explicated and explained. The hard cases issue will come back in Chapter 4. What is important at this stage is *specification of the ontological referral.* The figure of the subject of dignitarian protection and recognition is now the figure of an active individual, capable of and responsible for 'making sense' of the world – his individual life as well as the institutional-legal life of the community, vis-à-vis relevant truths and true values.

3.1.3 The integrity of the person

The juxtaposition of the two former dignitarian interests – freedom from degradation and self-determination – may appear troublesome. Indeed, tension is something that comes first to mind. *Freedom from degradation* suggests that the person is vulnerable and dependent on others. Although dignity fosters norms of prohibitive character here, the paradigm case for a legal-institutional intervention in this respect will be *aid. Self-determination* seems completely different. The person is regarded as author and master of his deeds, and consequently of his own self. As a result, *non-interference* rather than aid will be normally claimed to protect dignity when connected to self-determination. The third and crucially important dignitarian interest, to which we are now moving, is *integrity.* As I will argue, highlighting integrity may provide coherence in the theory of human dignity we are striving for. Rather than contradict each other, human vulnerability, manifested in the possibility of degradation and humiliation, and relative human independence in determining one's conduct and character, reinforce and explain one another when they are regarded from the perspective of integrity.

I already mentioned integrity (with qualifications such as 'bodily', 'mental', and 'personal') in Chapter 1, when talking about the humanitarian aspect of the regulative function of human dignity. The paradigmatic example was torture. As I argued (following others), torture does not consist simply in inflicting pain and suffering. Rather, the pain and suffering involved in torture are atrocious precisely because of being essentially connected to denying the basic standing proper to the victim. Moreover, the perpetrator often intends the victim to subjectively feel this kind of humiliating helplessness. The purpose is to leave the victim devoid of any control over themselves. Therefore, the assaulted sphere can be best captured by the expression 'bodily integrity'. The person is not only 'being coerced' and 'feeling pain' but is attacked at some deeper level. But what does this deeper level precisely mean? The first and vague intuition would be as follows: An infringement of the human body is in fact the infringement of something beyond the body – the person herself or himself – a being capable of an 'intentional relation to the world' (Bernstein 2015, 118). However, this experience of humiliation and deprivation is essentially attached to the bodily conditioning of human action and human responsiveness (Bernstein 2015, 119).[14] How can those two aspects be reconciled?

This is where the personalist conception is helpful. Wojtyła's account of *integration* in *The Acting Person* may explain why bodily integrity is fundamentally linked to integrity as such (personal integrity). The general lines are as follows: Although Wojtyła's investigation is focused primarily on rational individual agency (*actus humanus/actus personae*, as opposed to *actus hominis*), he also concludes that these agentic activities *do not exhaust* human subjectivity. In other words, the structure of the *actus personae* does not embrace human subjectivity and human dynamism taken as a whole, and conscious acts are only one aspect of it. Thus, as we have seen in Chapter 2, the *actus personae* is not a condition of dignity, but rather *the sign* of it. Let us supplement this with an example (which is mine, not Wojtyła's), namely, pregnancy. As a process during which a child develops in the mother's womb, pregnancy is not an instantiation of human conduct (at least in the technical, personalist sense). From the perspective of the pregnant woman, especially at the early stages, sustaining a pregnancy is not a series of activities which would have a 'man-acts' (or, indeed, 'woman-acts') structure. They are not performed in vertical transcendence, do not constitute self-determination, and do not involve self-governance. Instead, the process of pregnancy *happens* in the pregnant women – its 'something-happens-in-man' structure reflects a certain 'passiveness' of the one who sustains this process.[15] When uninterrupted from the outside, the process of pregnancy relies on the bodily dynamisms. Although an enormous effort of the body is involved (which is sometimes heavily felt by the woman), these efforts are not results of her will, and they happen, for the most part, beyond her consciousness. For, while she might have detailed knowledge of what is happening in her womb, and may deliberately make choices that impact the pregnancy (such as abstaining from alcohol), she has little access in terms of being conscious of the actual development within her. Despite this sort of passiveness, the process of sustaining pregnancy is no less 'personal' or less 'dignified' than performing conscious and wilful actions. Quite to the contrary – the common experience, at least in standard circumstances, shows that pregnancy is very highly valued (special protection of pregnant women has been observed across cultures and times) and is regarded as something deeply personal, something which is not alien to the pregnant woman but rather influences most of her actions and alters the picture of her own self. In real life, then, the biological dynamism of pregnancy cannot be detached from the personal self-determination of a pregnant woman who makes certain decisions, and who acts as pregnant.

14 In the passages I refer to, Bernstein writes about rape. In this particular aspect, I assume that rape and torture share essential characteristics.

15 These two were juxtaposed in Chapter 2.

In more general terms, the two distinguishable human dynamisms – 'something-happens-in-man' and 'man-acts' – unite in the experience of the person, as well as in his general ontological structure. As Wojtyła writes:

> We may say that man's actions and all that happens in him are not only mutually opposed but also distinctly correlated in the sense of a certain parity of both facts or both structures. For speaking of acting we may say 'man acts', and of what takes place in him we may say it 'happens in man', so that in either statement man stands as the dynamic subject. Man's actions just as much the things that happen in him provide – all in their own way – the realization of the dynamism proper to the human being.
>
> (Wojtyła 1979, 62)

This entails that 'the biological' is also 'the personal', in the case of the human being. In other words, there is no distinguished sphere in the human being which 'makes' him a personal being. Rather, the biological nature and the personal structure persist within the same integrated and concrete person. Wojtyła offers a detailed phenomenological analysis of how the elements such as the reactivity of the body, bodily movements, and emotivity integrate as subordinated to self-determination in the acts performed by the person (Wojtyła 1979, 206–54). A detailed analysis of this is beyond the scope of our inquiry. For our purposes, it is enough to say that the person must be regarded as 'a synthesis of the efficacy and the subjectiveness of the human ego' (Wojtyła 1979, 191). In other words, the experience of the person in action reveals two *interdependent* aspects: the passiveness of someone who sustains certain processes, and the activeness of that very same person who is the efficient cause of a significant part of these processes. So, for example, a philosopher 'taking pains' to explicate human dignity in the law experiences a mix of weariness, helplessness, excitement, and satisfaction. All these are psychosomatic processes that happen in the philosopher. At the same time, all these processes are irrevocably connected to that very same philosopher acting – in this case, conducting a complex intellectual inquiry. Self-determination and action on the one hand are in constant interplay with certain subjective conditioning and 'activations' on the other.

The integration of the person sheds light on the otherwise unclear notion of bodily integrity. It also explains how the bodily dimension is intimately tied to other aspects of personhood. If we revisit torture (hopefully, for the last time in this book), we will see that the particularly grave atrocity involved in it arises from the fact that the subject of torture is an integrated person – someone who is capable of transcending or 'outgrowing' themselves in relation to the objective truth, and someone yet fundamentally conditioned by their body. The torturer exploits all the vulnerability inherent to the bodily condition of the victim precisely to nullify her standing as an agent. In this sense, torture does not boil down either to an outrage upon self-determination or upon the bodily functioning of the person. It is an attack on both spheres working together. More generally, integration of the person is the factor which situates her suffering on a different plane in comparison to the suffering of sentient beings which do not have the personal structure of self-determination and integration. Causing pain for the sake of pain, or causing it only to pursue your own end, is always a very bad thing to do. However, when such conduct hits a person, it involves not only the evil of causing pain (disregarding sentience), but also the evil of denying or disregarding personhood. Maltreatments of different kinds which do not involve physical pain can also have that twofold nature. For instance, if we deny someone's freedom of conscience and suppress their religion, we not only attack the interest of that person to hold a religion (or a set of firm beliefs). Another sphere we hit simultaneously is the integrity of that person, who now needs either to abandon their beliefs under the threat of force, or get involved in a hypocrisy.

Taking into consideration the preceding analyses, the link between integrity and dignity may be established. According to the personalist conception, the dignity of the person consists in all other persons being unconditionally obliged to affirm him or her. The duty of affirmation binds, and must be fulfilled, in real-life situations – in relations between 'muscle-and-blood' persons. Tadeusz Styczeń emphasised the difference between the sourcing moral situations in which one concrete person owes affirmation to the other concrete person, from more abstract, and not necessarily moral, appraisals of (even the highest) values that a person may embody. In his view, persons as addressees of affirmation matter *in their wholeness and concreteness, not in selected aspects* (Styczeń 2012b, 166). Thus, a gravely immoral conduct harms not only a particular interest of a person, such as his interest in well-being and lack of pain. Additionally, and more importantly, it is an assault of the whole person in her dignity. Dignity is not 'a particle' which is to be found in persons, but rather that which permeates the person as an integrated whole. Therefore, dignity and integrity go hand in hand, involving manifold personal spheres in their dynamic interplay and their unification that happens in the human person.

This deeply corresponds with the law. A growing number of scholars, although making no reference to the personalist account, acknowledge integrity as the focal subject of the dignitarian legal protection. As Daniel Bedford observes, in Great Britain and Northern Ireland, 'dignity is most referred to by judges to capture situations where harm is done to the whole, integrated person' (Bedford 2019, 338). As a consequence, the indignities or violations of human dignity do not implicate one particular dimension or condition, but rather are 'experienced across the different dimensions of the human being' (Bedford 2019, 338–9). Importantly, Bedford's contention does not stem from a philosophical interpretation of the concept of dignity, but from direct engagement with the British case law. In a similar vein, Adeno Addis argues that dignity – this time not tethered to one jurisdiction, but analysed across jurisdictions – is best understood as integrity. He argues for 'integrity as wholeness' (Addis 2019, 330), which he understands as generally unrestricted and protected development of bodily well-being, identity, and attitudes, as well as social interactions and commitments. Again, he gives numerous examples from case law in the global context. In what remains in this section, I will provide an analysis of selected cases in which different aspects of personal integrity are at stake. As I will try to show, partly in opposition to Addis and Bedford, in cases involving integrity, the law protects something more than simply the completeness or wholeness of the person. Namely, I will argue that the law protects *the very structure of integration* which makes possible the completeness or unity of the person. As a result, I will argue that integrity is best understood once placed within a theoretical framework provided by the personalist conception of Wojtyła and Styczeń.

The case which we will examine first is *Price v. United Kingdom*, heard by the European Court of Human Rights (European Court of Human Rights 2001). The court dealt with claims against the United Kingdom, alleging the government's failure to recognise and adequately respond to the disabilities of a person in detention, thus breaching Article 3 of the ECHR. To recall, the wording is as follows: 'No one shall be subjected to torture or to inhuman or degrading treatment or punishment' (ECHR 1950, Article 3). In *Price*, the applicant suffered from thalidomide-caused phocomelia (a congenital disorder that consists in malformations of limbs), severely limiting her mobility, as well as additional health problems. She was committed to prison for several days for contempt of court during civil proceedings. During her detention, the applicant faced problems connected to the lack of proper access to a toilet, inappropriate sleeping arrangements (which forced her to sleep in her wheelchair), and the cell being too cold for a person with limited mobility. In sum, 'the facilities were not adapted to the needs of a disabled person' (European Court of Human Rights 2001, 27). Importantly, the conditions of detention would have been fully acceptable for a person without severe disabilities. The failure of the government did not consist in maintaining a detention facility beneath the general decent standard, but in neglecting to respond to the special needs and special situation of the applicant (although there was *some* response, it was deemed unsatisfactory). What is also important, the Court held that this constituted 'degrading treatment' under Article 3 of the ECHR despite the lack of direct intention to debase or humiliate the detainee (European Court of Human Rights 2001, 30).

Price v. United Kingdom shows us how the understanding of 'degrading treatment' has been broadened by the Court, which may appear a little puzzling at first glance. In earlier cases, especially in *Ireland v. the United Kingdom* from 1978, 'degrading treatment' was understood in a more straightforward manner, that is, as referring to systematic and abusive practices of state authorities which were less harsh than torture, but of still serious character. Among the 'five techniques' held to be in breach of Article 3 in *Ireland*, there were deprivation of sleep, food and drink, and 'hooding', that is, 'putting a black or navy coloured bag over the detainees' heads' (European Court of Human Rights 1978, 96). According to the Court, these practices were 'degrading since they were such as to arouse in their victims feelings of fear, anguish and inferiority capable of humiliating and debasing them and possibly breaking their physical or moral resistance' (European Court of Human Rights 1978, 167). This is quite different from the situation in *Price*. In this latter case, the government's conduct is closer to 'negligence' of some sort and is certainly far from systematic and intentional abuse. In the Court's own words, the problem was that 'the police and prison authorities were unable adequately to cope with the applicant's special needs' (European Court of Human Rights 2001, 26). However, the section on the circumstances of the case available in the judgement shows that *the applicant was not left without any help*. She was offered hot drinks, blankets were wrapped around her to keep her warm, she received assistance in accessing a toilet, and a visit from a doctor was arranged. As mentioned, there was no evidence of intentional abuse of the applicant, and she was moved to an adjusted facility at the first occasion, that is, after a night spent at the local police station (European Court of Human Rights 2001, 7–19). It is worth noting that despite being a justifiable standard, this is also quite demanding. Even before *Price*, the dynamic interpretation of Article 3 led the Court to push forward the standards of detention. For instance, in *Kudła v. Poland* the judgement required, *inter alia*, the 'health and well being' of the detainee to be 'adequately secured' (European Court of Human Rights 2000, 94), which justified holding the Polish government's failure to provide a detainee with adequate psychiatric treatment as a breach of Article 3. More recent cases bring new examples. In *Slyusarev v. Russia*, the government was considered engaged in degrading treatment by failing to return a detainee's spectacles (or provide him with a new pair) for five months while in detention. According to the Court's opinion, it was a deprivation 'serious enough to fall within the scope of Article 3' (European Court of Human Rights 2010, 36). One may legitimately ask whether the boundaries of 'degrading treatment' have not been pushed too far. This is not to say that the aforementioned cases are minor or unimportant. The real issue is how, and why, the understanding of 'degradation' is understood increasingly broadly to cover cases closer to negligent rather than intentionally abusive conduct of the authorities.

In my view, the key to interpreting *Price v. United Kingdom* and similar cases is the bond between dignity and integrity. The recurring formula of non-degrading detention standards used by the European Court of Human Rights seems to go beyond 'degradation' understood as depriving the detainee of basic human status and treating him or her as a mere means, a mere number, or subhuman. Instead, in relation to detainees:

> the State must ensure that a person is detained in conditions which are compatible with respect for his human dignity, that the manner and method of the execution of the measure do not subject him to distress or hardship of an intensity exceeding the unavoidable level of suffering inherent in detention and that, given the practical demands of imprisonment, his health and well-being are adequately secured by, among other things, providing him with the requisite medical assistance.
>
> (European Court of Human Rights 2000, 94)

In other words, although detention is supposed to constitute some kind of hardship, it should leave the detainee a 'safe space of his own', that is, leave basic security and well-being untouched. In the case of a person with disabilities or other health problems, this must translate to special treatment and care for her or his needs. In my view, as a result of this progressive interpretation of Article 3, we face two distinct legal situations, despite both having the same foundation in the notion of degrading treatment. In the more straightforward application, such as that found in *Ireland v. the United Kingdom*, the abusive techniques used by the police are indeed close to torture, and hence, arguably, deny the human status of the detainees. Note that in *Ireland* the aim of 'the five techniques' was not simply to detain people for practical purposes of due process of law, but rather to break their resistance by creating unusually hard and stressful conditions. Thus, the sphere or interest protected in this case was quite clearly 'freedom from degradation', in the meaning set forth in Section 3.1.1 of this chapter. In the new, more demanding reading presented inter alia in *Price v. United Kingdom*, Article 3 also covers situations in which the demeaning of the applicant is real and relevant, but at the same time less harsh and less straightforward. I argue that the interest of 'integrity' better captures the stakes of such situations.

In particular, I should first emphasise that the 'progressive' reading of Article 3 is partly motivated and justified by an appeal to human dignity in its heuristic function – the Court interprets the situation not only in terms of the applicant's suffering or hardship, but also her dignity. While in the majority opinion this seems to be largely implicit (there is no mention of dignity or integrity, only of 'special needs' of the applicant), the separate (yet concurring) opinion of Judge H. S. Greve is more straightforward. As Judge Greve writes:

> It is obvious that restraining any non-disabled person to the applicant's level of ability to move and assist herself, for even a limited period of time, would amount to inhuman and degrading treatment – possibly torture. In a civilised country like the United Kingdom, society considers it not only appropriate but a basic humane concern to try to improve and compensate for the disabilities faced by a person in the applicant's situation. In my opinion, these compensatory measures come to form part of the disabled person's physical integrity.
>
> (European Court of Human Rights 2001, separate opinion of Judge Greve)

In my view, the notions of integrity and dignity are indeed in place here as reasons for special care that is the applicant's due in the commented case. Moreover, the personalist account on 'integration of the person' seems to be helpful in explicating what exactly 'integrity' may mean in this context and why it is important.

The personalist take on this issue should become clear once confronted with an alternative. For Adeno Addis, who does not lean on the personalist conception, integrity means 'wholeness or completeness' (Addis 2019, 330). He differentiates completeness or wholeness from moral integrity, which signifies a person's adherence to their moral code (Addis 2019, 229). To defend this explication, Addis refers to the definitions provided by dictionaries, according to which integrity is '[t]he quality or condition of being undivided' (2019, 330, in a footnote) or '[t]he condition of having no part or element taken away or wanting' (2019,

330, in a footnote). It seems, however, that while these dictionary definitions capture important aspects of integrity, its link to dignity remains unexplained. It is likewise unexplained how the integrity of human persons differs from integrity of buildings, for example, the completeness of which also may require legal protection (with obviously different legal instruments and intensity). For Addis, the human characteristic of integrity is based on social recognition. In his view, 'a person is complete or whole to the extent that the various dimensions of her identity – physical, social, and psychological – are respected and protected' (Addis 2019, 332). From the personalist perspective, it seems as awkward as saying that 'persons are alive to the extent to which their lives are properly protected'. In other words, regarding social recognition as a *necessary and sufficient condition* of integrity – which is what Addis and others seem to be doing – is fundamentally flawed because it reverses the order of ontological structures of the person on the one hand and social processes on the other. While it is quite true that our lives to a large degree depend on others, no one would say that being alive consists in receiving the proper care. In the personalist perspective, *integrity* is similar to life in this respect. Although it obviously requires social recognition to emerge, its *sufficient* condition is the ontological structure of the person (however, social and legal recognition may turn out to be the *necessary* condition in some instances). As we have seen in this section, the structure of integration is one of the crucial aspects of the ontology of the person. While Wojtyła analysed it in only one particular function of establishing unity between the person and his actions, the conclusions we can draw from his results are more general. Namely, it seems that *being integrated* is an indispensable mark of being a person. In other words, persons are characterised by the special dynamic unity in which different aspects of their lives are in constant mutual feedback but also find the unity in complexity.[16] Taken in this broader perspective, integration allows us, or even requires us, to perceive different aspects of the dynamic personal being as intimately connected to each other, to the extent to which an assault or appreciation directed at one aspect is in some sense directed at all other aspects. So, for instance, rape hurts not 'only' the body, but also the deepest aspects of self-determination and self-respect of the victim. Or, to give another example, respect that we have for a deceased person finds different manifestations in how we treat their no-longer-sentient body.

When we return to *Price v. United Kingdom* and reflect on the issue of disabilities from this perspective, they will not appear as simple deprivations or uneasiness that a person needs to cope with. Rather, the disabilities of a person appear as *the internal conditions which the acting person overcomes in her integrity*, when making sense of the world, producing the image of herself, and pursuing her own

16 Marek Piechowiak argues that this thinking of persons dates back to Plato (Piechowiak 2019, 255). The SPT abstains from offering an ultimate metaphysical interpretation, which Piechowiak finds in the existential category of dignity understood not as essence, but as particular existence of persons (Piechowiak 1999).

projects. In this sense, disregarding these conditions while a person is in detention is not simply to impair her, or to produce additional inconvenience. Rather, falling short of properly responding to the special conditions of disability *is tantamount to disregarding the whole person*. As Judge Greve writes:

> The applicant's disabilities are not hidden or easily overlooked. It requires no special qualification, *only a minimum of ordinary human empathy*, to appreciate her situation and to understand that to avoid unnecessary hardship – that is, hardship not implicit in the imprisonment of an able-bodied person – she has to be treated differently from other people because her situation is significantly different. . . .
>
> In my opinion, everyone involved in the applicant's imprisonment – the judge, police and prison authorities – contributed towards this violation. Each of them could and should have ensured that the applicant was not put into detention until special arrangements had been made such as were needed to compensate for her disabilities, arrangements that would have ensured that her treatment was equivalent to that of other prisoners. The failure to take these steps foreseeably gave rise to violations of the applicant's personal integrity – physical and psychological – as well as to inhuman and degrading treatment.
>
> (European Court of Human Rights 2001, separate opinion of Judge Greve)

As we see, integration is of crucial importance for the dignity of the person, since it allows us to understand that certain maltreatments which could be viewed as 'merely negligent' conduct are in fact degrading. Of course, that degradation is different from the one involved in systematic and intentionally grave abuse, which we encounter in atrocities such as war crimes, torture, or human trafficking. However, in cases such as *Price v. the United Kingdom*, these degradations are real and relevant precisely because the recipient of that conduct is marked with dignity. She is a person who constantly 'integrates herself', in relation to the external conditions as well as to her own, internal conditions. The perspective of that person matters, and her special situation must be followed with special measures.

Understood in this way, integrity is indeed the focal dignitarian interest. Although I think it would be a mistake to argue that it is *the only* interest, it is somehow central and connected to all other interests. Freedom from degradation would mean something different if it was not referring to *integrated* persons capable of self-determination. However, self-determination alone – that is, self-determination detached from integrity – could lead to overemphasising rational individual agency and overlooking the meaning and weight of the bodily aspects of human personhood. Thus, integrity overlaps with all other interests, showing how they are interlinked rather than opposing each other. It also shows the moment of personhood which is connected to *fulfilment*. The person is an integrated whole in the sense of striving toward fulfilling its personal potential.

This many-faceted nature of integrity has resulted in its application across different jurisdictions. The reference to integrity has been made in connection to diverse dimensions of human personhood – from the genetic integrity of an embryo to social and interpersonal commitments or different social relationships. As far as the former is concerned, it is worth briefly commenting on the preliminary ruling of the Court of Justice of the European Union (CJEU) in *Brüstle v. Greenpeace*.[17] In its judgement, the CJEU (2011) provided a strongly protective interpretation of one of the provisions of Directive 98/44 on the legal protection of biotechnological inventions. Article 6(2)(c) of said Directive, stating that 'uses of human embryos for industrial or commercial purposes' shall be 'considered unpatentable', raised some doubts in the proceeding of the German Federal Court of Justice. The German court was not sure, among other things, about how broadly the notion of 'embryo' should be understood, for the purposes of interpreting Directive 98/44. The CJEU replied, in short, that the term 'embryo' should be interpreted as broadly as possible, to include any human ovum after fertilisation, or otherwise stimulated for division and development (CJEU 2011, ruling). Interestingly, the European Court referred to the intentions of the European legislature. As the CJEU said:

> In that regard [that is, the purpose of the Directive], the preamble to the Directive states that although it seeks to promote investment in the field of biotechnology, use of biological material originating from humans must be consistent with regard for fundamental rights and, in particular, the dignity of the person. Recital 16 in the preamble to the Directive, in particular, emphasises that 'patent law must be applied so as to respect the fundamental principles safeguarding the dignity and integrity of the person'. . . .
>
> The context and aim of the Directive thus show that the European Union legislature intended to exclude any possibility of patentability where respect for human dignity could thereby be affected. It follows that the concept of 'human embryo' within the meaning of Article 6(2)(c) of the Directive must be understood in a wide sense.
>
> (Court of Justice of the European Union 2011, 32 and 34)

This is a very interesting (and quite unique) case of recognising the integrity of the human body at the very basic, preliminary stage of its development. Apparently,

17 The procedure of 'preliminary ruling' consists in the CJEU of answering a question posed by a court of an EU member state, regarding interpretation of the European law (which binds the member state judges who should interpret domestic law in accordance with European law). In this case, the question of how widely 'embryo' should be understood was posed by a German court.

the CJEU uses human dignity as integrity in order to justify its broad, highly protective interpretation of the Directive – the purpose is to eliminate the slightest possibility of infringement on human dignity. From the personalist perspective, this is welcome. As mentioned earlier, the structure of integrity is present in the human person from the beginning of her biological life. In a certain sense, it even persists after her death, which is the rationale for maintaining rules for a dignified conduct regarding human remains. (International Committee of the Red Cross 2020).

On the other extreme, we find 'integrity' applied in cases when the dignitarian interest in question is connected to social commitments and interpersonal relations. The most famous example comes from the U.S. Supreme Court jurisprudence, which, in *Obergefell v. Hodges*, has extended the right to obtain a marriage license to same-sex couples. As we have seen in Chapter 1, the majority opinion was partly justified by the striving to guarantee 'the humanity and integrity of homosexual persons' (Supreme Court of the United States 2015, opinion, 7). Although the constitutional basis in *Obergefell* was the Fourteenth Amendment to the U.S. Constitution, where we find no mention of human dignity, the influence of the latter seems to have been decisive. One could even argue that the appeal to human dignity not only justified a certain understanding of the prior rights (the right to equal protection of the law), but also created a substantive change within legally protected rights, in this case, within the law of marriage (Waldron 2016, 3). The idea behind the dignitarian justification seems to be that when a long-lasting interpersonal commitment of homosexual individuals is unrecognised by the law, then they themselves are regarded as not having equal dignity. The dignity of the person is, again, although in a completely different context, deemed deeply connected to the person's integrity, along with autonomy. In this and analogical decisions, the integrity in question is characteristic not of the basic bodily level, but rather of the sphere of commitments and social relations. These commitments constitute the person's very identity, or authenticity, and are not easily detached from the person's deep moral convictions (Addis 2019, 362). Respecting or disrespecting deep personal commitments is tantamount to respecting or disrespecting the whole, integrated person.

Now, the personalist conception has been used to justify the special position of traditional marriage in human life (Wojtyła 2013) and would certainly be used to oppose stretching the institution so that it includes homosexual unions. However, such argumentation would be quite complicated and would require us to engage with considerations beyond dignity and integrity, such as the social functions of marriage, the good of the children, and the like (although the dignity and integrity of homosexuals would certainly count and would have to be maintained). Here, I am not advocating for any position and simply suspend judgement. What is of interest now is not that specific issue taken in its full complexity, but rather one element of the logic behind the decision. When assessed from the personalist point of view, the connection between integrity and dignity made in *Obergefell* seems to be quite correct. While it may be the case that, for some other reasons, homosexual unions should be treated differently from heterosexual ones, it is generally true that deep personal commitments must be respected by the law. Consider a less complex case concerning homosexuality, namely, criminalisation of same-sex intimacy. Even if some citizens (those of the Catholic religion, for example) consider same-sex intimacy sinful, they may still have strong reasons to consider criminalisation an excessive response (which obtains, to be sure, only in the case of consenting adults). The *excessive* character of such criminalisation would come from the high possibility of such criminal law harming the integrity of some persons. And this is independent from one's general moral judgement about homosexual intimacy, or even from its being 'intrinsically disordered' (Catechism of the Catholic Church, 2357).[18] Even if one deems it 'intrinsically disordered', another person's view may be different, although well-considered. Acceptance of one's own homosexuality heavily influences one's commitments, identity, and conditions for self-respect. Denying that by the means of criminal law has come to be widely considered contrary to basic constitutional principles. These principles include respect for personal commitments insofar as these commitments do not harm others. Dignity is an important addition to this harm principle: It points at the fact that by respecting the commitments of one's fellows, one does not simply 'leave them alone', but rather respects their integrity and personhood.

To conclude this section, I shall summarise the most important 'stipulative' results of our analysis of integrity as a dignitarian interest regarded from the perspective of the SPT. First, while it seems untrue that integrity exhausts human dignity – there is too much diversity within dignity law to find only one, exclusive concern – it is certainly the central dignitarian interest. Without due emphasis put on integrity, it would be hard to regard the others as cohesively interlinked. In particular, integrity helps to reconcile human vulnerability (represented by the possibility of degradation) on the one hand, and human independence (represented by self-determination) on the other. Integrity is, in one way or another, connected to both. As the examples have shown, it may shape our understanding of a completely helpless, 'bare' human life at the very early stage of development, as well as the important life decisions of a fully-fledged, self-determining agent. If this contention is true, it quite clearly provides strong reasons to abandon the views according to which the core of human dignity lies in self-determination. While integrity obviously serves as a justification for some of the basic liberties, including negative liberties (especially when our social or religious or interpersonal commitments ought to be respected), it should not be conflated with them. As clearly shown in this section, integrity of the person may require help or special caring for somebody's needs, revealing human inter-dependence rather than individuality and the duty of non-interference that follows from it.

18 While the Catholic teaching on homosexuality clearly deems the inclination as objectively disordered, and treats homosexual acts as sins, it also requires to treat homosexuals 'with respect, compassion, and sensitivity' (Catechism of the Catholic Church, 2358).

Second, 'integrity', as protected or recognised in the law, seems to deeply correspond to the ontological structure of 'integration' which characterises the person regardless of their actual state or point of development. If that is correct, then it is hard to agree that integrity is ultimately constituted socially. It is true – common sense and scientific evidence converging – that a human child will not grow up to be an integrated person without the minimum attention and recognition that she must receive from others (primarily but not exclusively in the family). But this is only a necessary condition, just as nutrition is a necessary condition for maintaining a child's life. Alongside that necessary condition, the *sufficient* condition of integrity is constituted by the ontological structure of 'integration'. It is this very structure that allows people to develop, to act, and interact at the social *niveau*. As the preceding examples have shown, the law often stands for the special sort of unity of the human person, a unity in which different spheres and capacities appear as mutually influencing and reinforcing each other. The person is integrated at different levels, from bare biological functioning to social and moral commitments. The law does not create this unity, but rather expresses respect for its outcomes and thereby *secures the space for fulfilment*.

Third, if integrity, as respected and protected by the law, is indeed based on 'integration', it cannot not be easily detached from *moral* integrity. According to Wojtyła, the structure of integration of the person in action is always somehow connected to truthfulness, and this connects it to reflection upon, and responsibility for, the objective validity of moral norms (Wojtyła 1979, 163). For Styczeń, dignity yields the basic duty to affirm persons, which is not conditioned by their moral integrity. In other words, affirmation is due for all, not only to those of high or even minimum moral standards. However, since the affirmation of persons is the affirmation of them as whole and concrete, *it includes affirming them as moral agents*, that is, as agents that are subject to the duty to abide by certain moral requirements. On top of that, the personalists contend that moral integrity in fact serves the best interest of the person. Moral *disintegration* – falling short of properly responding to moral norms or values – is clearly a problem, or simply a sort of human disorder (Wojtyła 1979, 193). Such a perspective opens the possibility of paternalistic uses of human dignity, which has been deemed controversial. I will return to this problem in Chapter 4, since the problem of paternalism is more complex and exceeds the issue of integrity. What is important at this stage is to bear in mind that the structure of integration in fact invites at least some form of paternalism, understood as acting against the individual's actual preferences or desires for the sake of his (allegedly greater) good. It is considered possible that a person simply fails to recognise it or even, despite recognising his own good, acts against it, as a result of disintegration. A major question for the SPT, then, is how much paternalism is acceptable for a public order. Certainly, some degree is.

3.1.4 Towards the Principle of the Status of Personhood

As one can see from the preceding subsections, the SPT adopts a pluralistic view on dignitarian interests. In other words, it does not try to find one exclusive domain or sphere within which all legal manifestations of human dignity would have to fit. However, the three interests just described– freedom from degradation, self-determination, and integrity – appear as most important. They are also most frequently evoked by scholars, judges, and the fabric of law itself. While one could identify additional spheres or interests, these would be variations on, or some combination of, the three just mentioned.

For instance, *privacy* is commonly perceived as directly connected to human dignity (Floridi 2016 argues for this in the context of protection of personal data). The American Convention on Human Rights stipulates that '[e]veryone has the right to have his honor respected and his dignity recognized', which entails that '[n]o one may be the object of arbitrary or abusive interference with his private life, his family, his home, or his correspondence, or of unlawful attacks on his honor or reputation' (1969, Article 11). The Inter American Court has used Article 11 to hold the Mexican government responsible, *inter alia*, for not properly investigating and punishing rape (2010, 94). The atrocity of rape has been already mentioned in our typology, as an outrage upon freedom from degradation, and upon bodily/personal integrity. Other violations of privacy may be less harsh, and thus not directly involving degradation, albeit still connected to the social integrity of the person. If we remain within the Inter-American Court, the right to privacy (Article 11) has been regarded as closely connected to integrity and liberty, enjoyed, for instance, within a household (2011, 145–7). Analogies could be found in other jurisdictions. In short, then, privacy seems to be captured by the three interests depicted, and there is no need for extensive, separate engagement with it.

The situation is similar in the case of *basic/existential conditions of fulfilment* (the social minimum). Different jurisdictions connect the issue of a social or existential minimum to dignity. It seems to be widely considered as a responsibility of a political community maintaining public order.[19] A paradigmatic example of the explicit connection between dignity and basic material conditions of fulfilment comes from the jurisprudence of the German constitutional court. The court said:

a) Article 1.1 of the Basic Law declares human dignity to be inviolable and obliges all state power to respect and protect it. If people do not have the material means necessary to guarantee a dignified existence because they are unable to acquire means from gainful employment, from their own assets or from payments by third parties, the state is obliged, within its mandate to protect human dignity and to maintain the social welfare state, to ensure that material means are available to those in need . . .
b) The direct constitutional benefit claim to the guarantee of a dignified minimum existence does only cover those means that are absolutely necessary to maintain a dignified life. It guarantees the entire minimum existence as a comprehensive fundamental rights guarantee, that encompasses both

19 Addis (2019, 346–56) gives numerous examples from all around the world.

> humans' physical existence, that is food, clothing, household items, housing, heating, hygiene and health, and guarantees the possibility to maintain interpersonal relationships and a minimal degree of participation in social, cultural and political life, since a human as a person necessarily exists in social context. (Federal Constitutional Court of Germany 2012, 63–4, references removed)

As we can see, the court interprets the establishment of the welfare state as a duty to help those in need, without distinguishing citizens and other human beings (the judgement was made in the context of the rights of asylum seekers, which is why this aspect is emphasised by the court). However, this duty to help is understood in the particular context of the person seeking fulfilment in social contexts. The duty of the state to help is not about bare survival. From the personalist perspective, this is not a surprise – it is the adequate response of the public order to the facts of natural human personhood. One of these facts is the striving toward fulfilment as a person (as opposed to mere survival).

Taking privacy and material conditions of fulfilment into consideration, one should treat the list of dignitarian interests as open-ended, and possibly changing over time. Given the dynamic character of persons themselves, and the changing conditions of life, certain interests may lose, or gain, their significance. One could speculate, for instance, on how our attitude to privacy will change together with technological developments. What is important for our purposes, however, is that having identified the three focal dignitarian interests, we can move further toward a principle which unifies all the interests and helps us reflect on the processes of change within them: the Principle of the Status of Personhood. In what follows, I will argue that this principle serves as the common point of reference for all dignitarian interests. Additionally to that, it helps to capture the connection between the workings of law and the human reality in question.

3.2 The Principle of the Status of Personhood as an explication of human dignity in the law: the status of personhood as a status-expressing principle

In this section, based on everything that has been so far said in this book, I will explicate human dignity as a status-expressing principle. So far, my analysis has been neutral with regards to the legal-theoretical category that human dignity would have within the SPT. And these categories have been, admittedly, not sharply distinguished. Now, I shall explain in what sense the SPT explicates the focal meaning of 'human dignity in the law' as a principle, and why this principle is regarded as expressing and protecting status. Taking into consideration the previous scholarship, it seems that a theorist of human dignity in the law is faced with three possibilities: human dignity may be explicated as a value, as a principle, or as a right. None of these three notions is free from legal-theoretical controversies and equivocations. Lawrence Solum seems to be right in saying that we can 'slice and dice legal norms various ways' (Solum 2009, introduction). I am not going to jump into the well of the very detailed analysis of these three terms, bearing in mind the fact that each legal culture has its own genuine tradition in this regard, and my explication aims at crossing these borders. But the SPT needs, at least, to catch a glimpse of its own image appearing at the bottom of the well. Some categorisation is needed, then, but only to an essential minimum, as offered in the following.

In his penetrating, comparative analysis of human dignity in constitutional law, Aharon Barak distinguishes between human dignity as a constitutional value and human dignity as a constitutional right (2015). As his analyses suggest, conceiving of human dignity as a constitutional value may be considered universal, at least insofar as the purposive interpretation of constitutional law has been assumed.[20] However, the issue of whether human dignity may be considered a right, separable from human dignity as a value, differs from one jurisdiction to another and depends on the particulars. While, for example, in Germany or Israel, human dignity is recognised both as a value and as a right, there are constitutions in which the existence of human dignity as a separate right is rejected.[21] A good example of such rejection comes from the jurisprudence of the Canadian Supreme Court. In one of its judgements, the Court observed:

> Respect for the inherent dignity of persons is clearly an essential value in our free and democratic society which must guide the courts in interpreting the *Charter*. This does not mean, however, that dignity is elevated to a free-standing constitutional right protected by s. 7 of the *Charter*. Dignity has never been recognized by this Court as an independent right but has rather been viewed as finding expression in rights, such as equality, privacy or protection from the state compulsion . . . Respect for a person's reputation, like respect for dignity of the person, is a value that underlies the *Charter*.
>
> (Supreme Court of Canada 2000, 77–80)

As we can see, the Supreme Court of Canada affirms the value of human dignity as something that is (and ought to be) subsequently pursued through, or manifested in, a set of free-standing rights, among which there is no separate and free-standing right to human dignity.[22] Such differentiation between legal

20 According to Barak, the purposive interpretation of a constitution is informed by 'assessing the role, the function and the purpose that the constitution fills at the time of interpretation' (Barak 2015, 70).

21 For a treatment of the German constitutional architecture, see Barak (2015, 225–40). It is remarkable that even though a majority of scholars view human dignity as a separate and free-standing right embedded in the German constitution, this right (conceived as absolute or 'untouchable') is much narrower in scope than human dignity as a value, which is also present in the German Basic Law. Spain, Canada, and the United States are given as examples of jurisdictions that reject human dignity as a free-standing right (Barak 2015, 13).

22 It is worth to mention that the Supreme Court of Canada showed even greater skepticism towards the usefulness of dignity in its later jurisprudence (2008). In this judgement, *R. v. Kapp*, the majority affirmed that claims to equality were more appealing and less confusing than claims to dignity.

values and legal rights adopted by the Canadian Supreme Court seems to be very widely shared among scholars. Neomi Rao, for example, relies on a similar understanding:

> Legal and social values are often associated with goals and purposes – they establish a direction for policymaking and may place demands and limitations on state action. Broadly phrased values rarely require specific actions, but they serve as guidelines or goals to be met either by individuals or the state. As a constitutional value, human dignity places a general obligation on the government to protect and promote human dignity, which may translate into any number of policy implications.
>
> By contrast, a right typically defines relationships between the individual and the state and constitutes a set of entitlements, either to be free from interference (in the negative sense) or to demand particular goods or services (in the positive sense). ... Rights are often provided for with greater specificity in order to place both citizens and the government on notice as to what is required.
>
> (Rao 2008, 223, footnotes removed)

In Rao's dichotomy, rights are regarded as directly authoritative, in the sense of directly empowering the bearer to demand specific things from specific actors (a claim-right), or, alternatively, empowering the bearer with a sphere of liberty of conduct.[23] Thereby, Rao assumes that rights have determinate legal content, and in this in sense have a structure close to 'rules'.[24] Although the nature of rights, and especially constitutional rights, has been conceptualised rather differently by others with regard to that last feature,[25] I will follow Rao here, for the sake of simplicity. I will understand 'a right' as a legal rule assuming a form of determinate

23 From the point of view of Hohfeldian legal logic, then, Rao seems to speak of rights in terms of specific claim-rights, having certain duties as correlatives, as well as liberties, correlating with no-rights on behalf of some other agents. (Referring to Hohfeld's legal logic, I am relying on Visa Kurki's helpful summary, 2019, 55–62). To illustrate, Rao's 'rights' cover a right to social minimum that a citizen may demand to receive from the state (claim-right), as well as a liberty of free speech, which is connected to the situation in which the state is not in the position to demand, for instance, that a certain writer does not publish her book (no-right).

24 Here, Rao refers to Dworkin's famous distinction between rules and principles (see Dworkin 1977, 24).

25 For instance, Robert Alexy conceptualises constitutional rights as principles, that is, as 'optimization requirements' (Alexy 2002, 47). The optimisation requirements are opposed to rules, that is, 'norms which are always either fulfilled or not' (2002, 48). If Alexy is right, then Rao's contention that 'rights operate more like rules' (Rao 2008, 223) should be judged as mistaken. However, as I have said, these issues to a large degree depend on stipulation and choice. It is also important to note that for Alexy, constitutional rights have the form of optimisation requirements only *prima facie*. When properly adjudicated in particular circumstances, they specify rules, 'derivative constitutional rights'. In these cases, strictly

claim-right or liberty. A value, by contrast, is a consideration or commitment underlying legal rights. Although this is a little unclear in Rao's writing, it seems that the 'demands on state action' that she writes about are not specified enough to directly yield legal rules. They do not have determinate legal content and addressees, but rather serve as a general consideration or argument which is moral, social, or political in its nature.

Granted, the right to human dignity would translate to a claim-right or a liberty, with more or less determinate content (or, perhaps, a cluster of claim-rights and/or liberties). Human dignity taken as a value would be less specific and would yield postulates for law, to be pursued either through lawmaking or adjudication (no concrete legal relations between particular legal persons or entities would flow directly from it). As one can easily see, then, human dignity as a value is much more flexible. For this reason, the value of human dignity may be shared across different jurisdictions, in spite of their differences in the architecture of rights and rules. Indeed, this does not stop at the constitutional or human rights level – human dignity may be (and in fact has been) conceived as an underlying value in penal, civil, or labour law. Taking this into consideration, *the value of human dignity* may appear to fit well into the general framework of the SPT. Recall that the SPT aims at interpreting 'the dignitarian moment' – a cosmopolitan phenomenon not limited to one particular jurisdiction. The adherence to the value of human dignity is also cosmopolitan in nature. In contrast to that, the very existence, the content, and the scope of *a free-standing right to human dignity* (especially when a 'right' is understood as a determinate 'rule') may depend heavily on the particulars of a jurisdiction. The SPT will therefore abstain from explicating the right to human dignity. However, the very emergence and recognition of particular rights in a number of legal systems (and on different levels) must be kept in mind as important and legitimate.

As I already mentioned, the dichotomy between values and rights (understood as rules) is not necessarily exhaustive. *Principles* are also on the table, as a separate category, and I see good reasons to explicate human dignity as a principle, not *merely* as a value. In short, these reasons are the following: No matter how important values may be, they always, in one way or another, depend on a value-judgement. Even if one believes in an objective order of values, incorporating these values into law is dependent on the valuing actors (say, judges or legislators) and not on the law itself. Values find their concretisation in an ethos, for example of legal professionals, and we can speak about an ethos of adjudication, legal representation, or legislation. It is important to have these, and their structure should be guided by human dignity as the crucial value. While true, this is also not enough from the SPT's perspective. Our description of the dignitarian moment suggested that at least public authorities (if not other actors) are often

speaking, principles figure as reasons for a rule, rather than being transformed into rules through judicial reasoning (2002, 56–60).

bound by human dignity in a more rigid, or more constraining, way. Our considerations on human personhood scrutinised through phenomenology suggested that this binding force of human dignity deeply corresponds to the structures of action, self-determination, and integration present in personhood. By contrast, a belief that human dignity in the law is ultimately reducible to value is another way of saying that this is a mere expression of the longing for a better and more respectful governance, and not of some truths about personhood which are critically important for law. Also, our commitment to reflective equilibrium goes against relying only on the value of human dignity. In my interpretation, reflective equilibrium requires a search for underlying principles *that integrate our beliefs* rather than merely stating that there is some degree of cohesion between different beliefs. If human dignity is explicated as a legal principle, it may be given an objectively constraining content which does not depend on a floating political consensus and choices of values. At the same time, it is more flexible and broader than a right to human dignity. Instead of being tantamount to a cluster of claim-rights and/or liberties, it is supposed to function as the underlying rationale for the cluster of claim-rights, liberties, and possibly other legal norms, all connected to personhood to some degree. If the Principle of the Status of Personhood in this form is sound, then it deeply corresponds to the ontological structure of human personhood scrutinised by the personalist conception. As such, it is able to integrate our beliefs about structures of human (natural) personhood on the one hand, and our beliefs concerning the structure of law on the other.

To avoid misunderstanding, I should recall that human dignity as a concept is regarded as open ended, interpretative, and having a family-type meaning. My reliance on the *principle* of human dignity, therefore, does not claim exclusivity. Human dignity obviously is also a legal value, and could be explicated as such. Human dignity simultaneously may be a certain specific right or rule, depending on the jurisdiction. It is also possible that some sort of cosmopolitan right, for instance the right not to be degraded, is also in place. These manifold manifestations should be respected, and the hope for finding 'the one and only' correct manifestation in the legal domain must be abandoned. Human dignity has simply assumed too wide and too complex a variety of forms. However, while I am not claiming exclusivity, *I do claim a certain hierarchy in the family of meanings.* Some of them are focal – they constitute a widely shared point of reference for other manifestations and have greater affinity with most of the other meanings in the family. Explicating human dignity as the Status of Personhood is considered to be a 'master explication', that is, one with the potential to integrate other meanings of human dignity, and other possible explications. What is more, and especially important, I regard the PSP as inevitable to *bring values and rights/rules associated with human dignity into a systematic unity*, at least in the circumstances of modern jurisdictions.

Before I set out the specific principle, I will first show in a little more detail how principles differ from values, and what this entails for the interpretation of dignity in the law. Emphasising this difference may help achieve clarity in explication, as well as an equilibrium among different substantive conceptions of human dignity which appear in legal contexts. Some people do not see it this way. Neomi Rao asserts that '[c]onstitutional "values" such as human dignity *are really principles* that set out general guidelines or possibly aspirations for action by the state and also for the interpretation of rights' (Rao 2008, 223, emphasis added). Here, Rao strikes me as conflating values and principles, which seems too quick, and produces some unwelcome consequences. In my view, it may lead to greater, not lesser, *normative indeterminacy* of human dignity in the law. In another paper, Rao contends that there are irreconcilable conceptions of dignity which 'reflect different ways of thinking about what constitutes dignity as a legal matter' (Rao 2011, 189). Moreover, she thinks that 'moving forward with dignity as a legal concept requires choices' (Rao 2011, 192). In her view, the courts should choose a conception they adhere to and exclude the others. This clearly puts values in the first place, and requires value judgement as an anchor for determining the content of the law shaped by human dignity. A scheme of reasoning (or, rather, of a particular part of the larger picture of legal reasoning) would then go as follows:

Value Judgement → Purposive Interpretation of Law → Determination of Law's Content.

What is problematic in this scheme is not that the interpreter takes the values 'out of nowhere', or arbitrarily determines their content and hierarchy. Often, especially in constitutions, the law explicitly refers to values, and sometimes even suggests their hierarchy, so there may be good legal grounds to adopt and prioritise human dignity as a value. However, if the reconstruction proposed in this scheme is correct, then it is the interpreter who chooses, within the limits of *purposive* interpretation, which value, or at least which understanding of that value, should be applied in a relevant case. In my view, if such choices are proven to really be the ultimate ground of the law evoking human dignity, it is much more likely to draw us back rather than to help us to move forward. It is reasonable to expect that court rulings or legislation do not ultimately depend on somebody's choices. Legislators have greater discretion here (and quite clear legitimation to choose between available values), but their discretion is limited not only by a constitution, but also by demands of reasonable justifiability (Rupniewski 2019). It is then natural to expect, both in case of adjudication and legislation, that decisions are, at a minimum, *adhering to fundamental, justifiable principles of public order.*

Granted, the alternative account of human dignity in the law, the one I am advocating for, relies on a broad understanding of legal principles, namely, the understanding of principles as highly general legal norms constituting the underlying rationale for more specific norms, that is, legal rules or rights. In this understanding, principles are part of law's fabric, which distinguishes them from values. Law may commit to or evoke values, but principles simply *are* the law, along with other types of norms. Principles thus have a direct binding force, which means that they are regarded as concrete dispositions or directives, addressed to concrete legal agents. The peculiar character of principles as legal norms consists in their highly general content, and high systemic importance. The principle-based legal reasoning, as distinguished from value-based reasoning, commences with a principle. It is also not tethered to a particular, purposive theory of legal interpretation and may be incorporated into different theories. It may be illustrated by the following scheme:

> *Principle → Interpretation of Law (different theories possible) → Determination of Law's Content.*

This is not to suggest that the interpreter should not make value judgements. In particular, the interpretation of law involving human dignity simply cannot escape doing so. The idea (and hope) is, however, that principles may guide value judgements, if such judgements are necessary for an interpretation of law. A reference to the background principle may thus help to find out the common point of reference for the competing values involved in the issues of human dignity. As we have seen, the value of self-determination may be in tension, contradiction even, with the value of bodily integrity (as in the famous dwarf-tossing case). Other, similar collisions seem inherent to the complex cluster of values associated with human dignity. In my view, it is not enough to say that reference to human dignity requires one to choose among them. Rather, we should seek a reasonable equilibrium within the cluster of ideas and values. If, in a given case, we affirm self-determination, we must not do it *at the expense* of bodily integrity, and the commitment thereto should be sustained in some form. Even in cases in which officials intervene to shield a person or group against degradation, they must take into consideration the dignity of perpetrators, and so on. Principles may help to reach such interpretative equilibria. The SPT perceives the Principle of the Status of Personhood as playing such a role.

What remains in this chapter is to set forth the concrete content of the PSP, comment on it, and attempt to scrutinise, in some detail, how it works in the law. The proposed principle is based on the Personalist Postulate we have already seen in Chapter 2. To recall, the personalist postulate connects the law with incommunicable personhood, stating that:

> *PP. Before the law, persons are not regarded as replaceable specimens or as mere instances of some ideal or type, but rather as having intrinsic importance, each standing as incommunicably his or her own.*

Importantly, the PP was drawn from the philosophy of personalism, not from the law. However, our re-engagement with the law in the previous section allows me to claim that the personalist postulate remains in equilibrium with the dignitarian legal protection. The 'intrinsic importance' and 'incommunicability' endorsed by the personalist philosophy finds its way into the law as an open-ended list of dignitarian interests, with a special emphasis on freedom from degradation, self-determination, and integration. The law, by protecting these divergent dignitarian interests, protects the status of personhood ascribed to all human beings, and to all other (possible) non-human persons. The status of personhood may be synthetically expressed in the PSP, stating that:

> *PSP. Before the law, each person equally must be respected as an integrated whole, radically capable of self-determination, and striving towards fulfilment.*

Since the PSP expresses basic respect, it is logically connected to the *prima facie* priority of persons. Under most circumstances, the considerations referring to the basic standing of persons take precedence over other considerations. The main reason for this is quite simple: as self-determining agents, capable of a special sort of integration leading to personal fulfilment, persons are most adequately considered to have an individual perspective of their own, and that perspective should count, and should have weight. Thereby, the PSP is wide in scope: it does not focus exclusively on autonomy or self-determination, as has often been conceived in status theories. Instead of deferring to one decisive capacity, the principle refers to an open-ended range of dignitarian interests, with the focal role of self-determination, integrity, and freedom from degradation taken together, in their complex dynamics and interdependencies. Therefore, according to the SPT, the dignity-based relations between persons at the institutional level do not boil down to mutual recognition of rational agency. The principle does not apply exclusively to persons as capable of expressing an informed consent after rational deliberation, and does not protect the status of personhood as simply the status of a rational agent. The SPT argues that what really should be, and really has been, protected by dignity law are the persons themselves, understood as multi-dimensional, dynamic wholes. This is reflected in the law in the form of complex relations between dignitarian interests and rights, understood as *responses to the status of personhood*.

Some additional important aspects and characteristics of the PSP should be elucidated, in order to complete our explication. First, let me clarify why I think that human dignity as a principle protects or manifests *the status* of personhood, rather than the *intrinsic or absolute worth* of persons. The distinction between status and value may be quite blurry, especially when both are considered to situate the person in a distinguished and privileged place in the public order. High social status is normally attached to valuable positions in society, so these two categories often converge, or even merge, in real-life situations. A legal status may be detached from value as connected simply to a function, as in the case of diplomatic status, for example. It also can be attached to certain deficiencies or problems rather than to excellence, as in the case of lunacy. However, if the law protects passengers of a hijacked civil aircraft against deliberate striking down, it is hard to determine if it is protecting their basic status as persons, or their absolute worth.[26] Despite these ambiguities, for the purposes of this discussion, I will

26 Although the German judges used the language of value, it can be argued that protecting the passengers from degradation was tantamount to also preserving their fundamental status.

follow Stephen Riley, according to whom human dignity as value 'would relate to axiology and requires an account of what we should value and how, particularly how the value of agents and their ends should feature in our deliberation' (Riley 2019, 440). This formulation should be read as embracing many different possible theories of value. In particular, one may think of a purely teleological account of value as 'something to be promoted', as well as a broader account, such as the one presented by Thomas Scanlon, who contends that values may also have a structure of deontological prohibitions (Scanlon 1998, 85). Indeed, one could argue on the one hand that human dignity *as a value* requires legal actors to maximise human well-being (a teleological account), but on the other, one may say that individual choices are intrinsically valuable, and hence one's choices should take precedence over one's well-being (a deontological account). Since the SPT does not explicate human dignity as a value, I will not press this complicated issue any further. But it is important to bear in mind that the value of human personhood may often consist in some combination of the intrinsic good of human capacities and deontological considerations. In contrast to the value of human dignity, the status of dignity, to follow Riley again, can be thought of as 'concerned with structural and institutional defences of basic respect' (Riley 2019, 441). Again, this account may be intertwined with asserting the *value* of human rational agency. However, the underlying value of agency is distinguishable from the institutional framework based on respect for agency. My theory is similar in this aspect, although instead of relying on rational agency alone, it respects natural personhood understood as a broader category (characterised in Chapter 2). In the SPT, then, the moral value of human persons (their dignity as value), and the pursuit thereof, is distinguished from relations between human persons which respects their dignity. Therefore, *the status of personhood is directly and intimately attached to the norm, the principle that requires respectful relations between persons mediated by the institutional law.*

Against this background, the SPT explicates human dignity as a structural principle protecting the basic equal status of persons in a dignity-based public order. The principle of status of personhood works on two levels: first, it establishes certain relations between persons and the law, and second, as a consequence, it establishes dignity-based relations between persons.[27] Thus, the PSP has a very wide range of addressees: It binds every agent (institutional, corporate, or private) whose relations with other human persons are mediated by the law. The employer, the state official, the judge, or the parent may turn out to be bound by this principle, depending on circumstances. Since the principle is deeply rooted in modern law, it is in fact operating in the background of most

27 My account is thereby different from Jellinek's understanding of status, which he considers to be a relation between the individual and the state (Jellinek 1892, 109). The reason for this may be that Jellinek's theory was focused on public law, especially the constitutional law which assumes the profound character of the state. The SPT, in contrast, aims at conceptualising the status that transcends particular branches of law, and is even more fundamental than constitutional statuses proposed by Jellinek.

legal relations. In some of them, it is brought into light by the circumstances, especially when the basic standing of somebody has been threatened. Despite that wide, open-ended range of addressees, the PSP does not necessarily apply in all possible legal situation in which one needs to assess or weigh the value of human persons. Rather, it is focused on the transcendental prerequisites of basic respect for persons *qua* persons in the law, in a dignity-based public order.

My reliance on status may appear puzzling in the context of the scholarship on human dignity up until now, as well as in the context of the standard understanding of status. The scholarly re-engagement with dignity understood as status or rank (status or rank were, arguably, present in the law since its early beginnings) was influenced by the works of Jeremy Waldron. In his view, an historical process of an 'upwards equalization of rank' underlies human dignity present in modern law (Waldron 2012, 33). As already explained, Waldron's agenda was, *inter alia*, to separate the conceptualisation of human dignity in the law from the issues of ontology of persons or theory of morals (Waldron 2012, 20).[28] Consequently, for most adherents, a status account 'requires a theory of entitlement, not ontology, and it should produce principles for action, not values to be realized' (Riley 2019, 441). One may thus legitimately ask whether it is sensible to introduce ontology of personhood into a status theory. Another problem with status is that it is normally conceived of as fully dependent on the law, or on social convention. In the standard (and quite intuitive) view, a legal status is *conferred* by the state, and may be lost by legal or social means (Kittel 2021, 15). This may be problematic for the SPT, which claims that respect for personhood is a transcendental prerequisite of public order (at least the public order of a particular type), and not merely its product. Finally, status has been understood as serving 'the legal classification of society' (Graveson 1953, 124), or the regulation of 'legally abnormal' persons (1953, 111), so the idea of status that is equally possessed by all persons may appear a contradiction in terms. Despite these possible problems, my theory insists on a conception of status that is not fully dependent on the recognition of the state, but is simultaneously connected to the ontological structure of persons. And it is not used to distinguish between legal classes of persons, but situates the natural human personhood within law, thereby expressing the fundamental equality of all natural human persons.

Since that second feature – the equality of status – is easier to explain, and in fact is already quite well-established in the scholarship, I will deal with it first. The other problem – the relations between the status of personhood, the structure of natural human personhood, and the legal or political recognition of persons in law – is much more complicated, so the full response to them will be given later, in Chapter 4. Some partial response will nevertheless come in the next section. In order to deal with both problems, we need to reconsider the distinction between

28 Waldron does not aim to refute it. As he writes, 'a conception like the one I have been developing does not in any way preclude the independent operation of a principle of the sacred value of human life' (Waldron 2012, 29).

the praxiological reading and the ethical reading of human dignity in the law, laid out the beginnings of this chapter. This reconsideration is also crucial to determining how the philosophical inquiry carried out in Chapter 2 is to be applied to the interpretation of the dignitarian moment in the law, and how exactly status of personhood should be understood. To recall, the ethical reading focuses on *moral* action, and the affirmation that human persons should achieve at the level of their (individual and common) good. The praxiological reading accepts the importance of morality but supplements the ethical reading by pointing at a relatively autonomous sphere of *prima facie* morally irrelevant contexts or practices which nonetheless constitute a space for expressing respect for the dignity of the person. The recognition of personhood, when marking legal institutions in a dignity-based public order, is precisely such a context. Now, when the law is interpreted with the praxiological reading at hand, one can regard the respect for personhood as manifested independently from, or simultaneously to, the pursuit of the good through legal activity (including the common good). The manifestation and protection of respect is the job that status of personhood (human dignity in the law) is primarily doing, according to the SPT.

In real life, the manifestation or protection of personhood on one hand and caring for the good of the person on the other are obviously mixed. However, I contend that the good of the person and the respect for personhood are distinguishable. It is especially clear in cases in which the law assigns special status to the addressees of norms independently in some way from the issue of their good or fulfilment. As I have already indicated, the principle of *nullum crimen sine lege* can be considered an example of this. It is probably true that all actually existing systems of penal law could be improved in terms of their moral merits. The very question of the extent to which penal law should promote certain virtues or lifestyles is highly debatable. Despite these deficiencies and controversies, virtually all criminal law systems adopt the *nullum crimen* principle in some form, which is also protected internationally (Rauter analyses this in detail; 2017, 42–68). Thus, independently of what one thinks about the broader moral merits of criminal justice systems (i.e. how they protect human goods worth protecting), they all share the important *dignitarian* merit – they express respect for their addressees by punishing only the behaviour publicly proclaimed to be unlawful. One may find many analogous examples in other areas of law, for instance in civil lawsuits. The claimant may pursue his claims independently of their moral quality (suing somebody may be morally good or morally bad, depending on circumstances), and while the lawsuit is pending, both parties stand on equal footing and have equal procedural means at their disposal, even if the defendant actually committed the wrongful act. In this sense, the unique personhood of each party manifests itself in the complex architecture of the civil procedure, independently of moral merits (the good) that may or may not be involved in a lawsuit. In contrast, one may point at countless situations in which the law has direct moral aims. The law may embody human goods, such as marriage, or may assure that some goods are provided (through economic and social rights, for example). What must not come out of our sight, however, is that when these particular goods are protected or even created by the law, the principle of dignity is also at play. Law assigns special importance to certain goods, but that importance is, at bottom, ***the good of the person participating in or achieving that good.*** For example, when law promotes well-being or forbids inflicting pain, it does this for the sake of the individual persons involved, not for the sake of the well-being or the lack of pain taken in itself. In such cases, then, the basic standing of human persons is assumed and pursued along with the pursuit or the protection of their good.

Granted, the SPT is based on the praxiological reading of human dignity in the law, which emphasises the importance of the respect for natural personhood, manifested either ***along with*** pursuing the moral values through law, or even ***independently*** of that pursuit. In all these diverse cases, the law acknowledges the basic standing of all human persons. In this sense, ***the status of personhood determines the legal condition of every human person which is fundamental for a public order.*** Instead of being a particular configuration of rights, duties, privileges, or incapacities (other statuses, such as being a minor, may be like this), the status of personhood is rather the condition of everyone's having the equitable share in a public order. The status of personhood is therefore identical with the dignity of everyone, not particular classes or individuals. Undermining the dignity of anyone is tantamount ***to undermining the very possibility of public order properly understood.*** The status of personhood is then ***a simple legal characteristic***, situating all persons (each one separately!) in the legal condition of due and equal concern.[29]

Despite this 'equalisation', the status of personhood does not make everyone identical to others. Quite the contrary – the principle of status of personhood requires responses. They should be carried out in a way that recognises the importance, or weight, of the specific situation and conditions of the person concerned. Protecting the dignitarian legal interests, either via human rights law, constitutional law, or other means, is tantamount to protecting the status of personhood and therefore constitutes precisely such a response.

To clarify that last point: I prefer to regard particular dignitarian protections as *responses to* the status of personhood understood as a simple property, rather than as *incidents of* the status of personhood as a cluster property. The reason for this is equality. If personhood (in the sense adopted by the SPT) is equal for all persons, then it must be mirrored by a simple legal characteristic of every person, not by a cluster property that has an unlimited number of variants. As Visa Kurki explains, a cluster property is one 'whose extension is determined based on a weighted list of criteria, none of which alone is necessary or sufficient' (Kurki 2019, 93). Thus, different individual entities can meet the criteria of holding a cluster property in different configurations, and to different degrees. As Kurki argues, ***legal personhood*** (something quite different from the status of personhood that the SPT talks about) 'consists of interconnected but disseverable incidents', and hence '[t]here

29 The final formulation of this paragraph was shaped in discussions with Eduardo Charpenel.

is no exact border between legal personhood and nonpersonhood' (2019, 94).[30] It might be tempting to think in a similar way about human dignity in the law, given the diverse contexts in which it appears. According to this view, the manifold dignitarian protections and interests could be seen as incidents of the basic status, and all these taken together would be somehow referring to the underlying idea of human dignity. However, this would miss the whole point of dignity in the law, at least insofar as the status of personhood is to be accompanied by the *principle* of status of personhood. As the SPT argues, human dignity in the law is tantamount to the Principle of the Status of Personhood rather than to the bare status itself. Since none of the numerous incidents alone can count as decisive for what the principle requires, the status of personhood as a cluster property would render the principle meaningless. If the status of personhood is regarded as the basic standing of a person and nothing more, and different 'incidents' thereof are in fact legal responses to it, then the principle has a very general, but very clear meaning – it requires treating everyone with respect proper to persons, *in their entirety*.

3.3 *The Principle of the Status of Personhood, wide reflective equilibrium, and the issue of explaining the dignitarian moment in the law*

As far as *explication* is concerned, our job in this book is done. Arguably, the recognition of the Status of Personhood has been a global phenomenon, and the PSP can be thus regarded as a cosmopolitan, implicit legal principle. Many questions about the Principle's exact position in a legal system, and its place within broader legal theory or the theory of adjudication, are still unanswered. Some of them will be dealt with in the next chapter. At this stage, however, I judge the concept of human dignity in the law as the Principle of the Status of Personhood to be clarified to a sufficient extent. In order to present the SPT in its complete form, though, another big issue must be reconsidered, namely, the *explanation* of the dignitarian moment. In particular, the task is to explain why the dignitarian moment emerges, and why its best conceptualisation is the law's implicit cosmopolitan commitment to the PSP.

To avoid misunderstanding: 'Explanation' is here understood as finding the crucial factor or set of factors without which a phenomenon (its appearance and its dynamics) is unintelligible. This type of explanation is less demanding and less ambitious than the classical scientific explanation that requires deductive reasoning and evokes general (scientific) laws. Although multiple alternative models are trying to soften or replace these criteria (Woodward and Ross 2021), Bartosz Brożek seems to be right in suggesting that it is hard to get rid of this classical

30 It is important to note that Kurki's understanding of legal personhood is a novel one. In short, before this book, legal personhood was perceived as capacity to hold rights and/or duties. He transformed this traditional notion with his bundle theory.

form of explanation in science (2016, 40). In the humanities, the situation may be different. For example, Patrick L. Gardiner argues that the explanation in history does not allow general laws, and a historical occurrence is most often an 'outcome of a particular complex of factors' (1959, 89), and hence historians tend to '*assess* rather that to *conclude*' (1959, 95, emphasis original). The explanation I am after is even more loose, since it does not necessarily involve a typical causal analysis.[31] For the purposes of this inquiry, having explained something may mean merely that certain facts or processes must be regarded as true in order to 'make sense' of some other facts or processes. In what follows, then, I am interested in a weak, *pro tanto* explanation which is different from the deductive-nomological scientific explanation as well as from the causal-historical explanation. It also should be distinguished from an ultimate explanation which may be offered only by metaphysics. With regards to the latter, my theory claims weak metaphysical parsimony (as stated in Chapter 1). Despite the parsimony, and *because* of its weakness (recall what has been said in Chapter 1 about sceptical realism), I nevertheless argue that our understanding of law must not be fully detached from reality. In particular, the proper explanation of the legal phenomenon of dignitary moment should not be detached from the extra-legal reality of persons which is available to us in experience. To be sure, that 'availability' comes only with the wide, personalist-phenomenological conception of experience, which has been accepted in the SPT. The figure of personhood that the SPT relies on is therefore not complete: It tries to capture certain observable aspects of real human personhood, yet without ambition to capture its full essence. I thus propose to talk of the ontology of personhood, rather than the metaphysics of personhood, and it is the former which explains the PSP to the extent required for my investigation in this book. It also does not directly rest on a complete theory of law.

All this means that the explanation offered in this book is (for better or worse) provisional in nature. It is assumed that it may be revised, or even completely abandoned, if some relevant facts about persons are considered proven (such as, for example, the lack of free will in any meaningful sense). Likewise, the explanation I am offering does not necessarily rest on a complete theory of law. It is, rather, trying to bind together beliefs regarding the structure of personhood and the processes within the law. Admittedly, when one has good reasons to hold a belief about law that does not cohere with my explanation, one of the two beliefs must be adjusted. Therefore, the explanation I am pursuing is best understood as finding a wide reflective equilibrium between the ontology of personhood scrutinised by the personalist conception and the dignitarian moment, with its central element – the Principle of the Status of Personhood. This reflective equilibrium is

31 Gardiner compellingly explores the particulars of the type of explanation done by historians in terms of complex causal relations of events (1959, 65–96). Although, most probably, such reconstruction of the dignitary moment would also be possible, this is not my aim in this book.

truth-seeking. It is claimed the (partial) theory of personhood explains the legal phenomena; it does not just happen to cohere with them.

With all these reservations, the Principle of the Status of Personhood – a cosmopolitan, status-expressing principle – should be regarded as an inevitable legal response to the self-determination and integration (the latter involves striving for fulfilment) that *we observe in real human persons*. The dignitarian status is therefore not simply a product of recognition that persons may and should enjoy in the law. The ontology of persons *precedes* recognition and explains and reinforces the legal status of personhood. In this regard, the structures of personhood, examined by the personalist conception, constitute the crucial set of factors mentioned earlier: Without them, the endurance and development of the dignitarian moment in the law would not be understandable, even at the minimal level. The PSP, then, not only summarises the law pertaining to dignity, it also points at real personhood and requires to keep its heavy importance for the law in mind. This may be formulated in terms of wide reflective equilibrium. The latter is supposed to unify our beliefs and enable a deeper understanding of each one against the others. As a result of this, one will hopefully be able to better understand the references to human dignity within the law in light of the ontology of personhood; but given the importance of law for human life, the ontology of personhood will also become better understood in light of the deep understanding of law's commitment to human dignity.

In my view, the key to find the equilibrium and the explanation we are after lies in Karol Wojtyła's account of person and action. It might appear paradoxical, since *The Acting Person* does not contain a single mention of the word 'dignity' and does not theorise law. But his account is obviously not neutral with regard to these problems. The SPT accepts Wojtyła's insights into personhood as true, and finds correlations between these insights and the dignitarian moment in the law. It has been already made explicit at the level of the dignitarian interests, which correspond with the crucial elements of the structure of personhood in the Wojtilian account. Self-determination, integration, and the natural striving towards fulfilment as a person were identified as the focal elements of personhood, as far as the legal protections commonly (and globally) associated with human dignity are concerned. They are also revealed as the crucial elements of natural human personhood in Wojtyła's *opus magnum*.

Let us now try to go even deeper with this, and explain why natural human personhood requires us to think of a public order as a structure respecting everyone's equal status of personhood. And vice versa: why the law's respect for everyone's status of personhood – the upward equalisation of rank – is a process deeply rooted in human-personal ontology. In my attempt to explain this, I shall rely on the Wojtilian account on 'the personalist value of the action'. As mentioned before, Wojtyła regards action as a peculiar moment revealing the person as such. The action, in the technical, personalist sense, takes place only in contexts engaging the structures of personhood (self-determination and integration striving towards fulfilment). These contexts situate the person in a special position and manifest the person's special kind of worth. In my interpretation, the worth of this special kind is closely related to the basic status or standing of the human person. If we have good reason to think that the law is one of the contexts in which that standing manifests itself, then the basic *legal* status of the human legal subject may be explained in realist terms, as an indispensable response to natural human personhood that has been made in the law. I contend that this is the proper perspective one should take on the PSP. In order to show the reasons to think this way, we will have to consider the possible personalist value of legal activity. To do this, I will start from the personalist value of the action, and see what this means for human dignity in the general, philosophical sense. Then, I will examine how human dignity in general is related to human dignity in the law, that is, to the PSP. The crucial passage regarding the personalist value (previously quoted in Chapter 2) goes as follows.

> [T]he performance itself of an action by the person is a fundamental value, which we may call the *personalistic* – personalistic or personal – value of the action. Such a value differs from all moral values, which *belong* to the nature of the performed action and issue from their reference to a norm. The personalistic value, on the other hand, inheres in the performance itself of the action by the person, in the very fact that man acts in a manner appropriate to him . . .
>
> The 'personalistic' value of the human action – that is, the personal value – is a special and probably the most fundamental manifestation of the worth of the person himself.
>
> (Wojtyła 1979, 264, emphasis original)

Two things are important in this passage. First, the inherent value of the person is *underlying* the action. The capacity to act must not be perceived as conditioning the value of human persons. The fundamental value of persons (human dignity in the most general sense) is independent of its manifestations, and may be manifested in different ways. Despite being especially important, the moment of genuinely personal action is only one of these ways. It is therefore a mistake to say that a single key property, or even a cluster of properties, is something that 'makes up human dignity' (Ackermann 2012, 87). It is especially clear if we interpret this passage from Wojtyła in light of the meta-ethical theory of his disciple, Tadeusz Styczeń. For the latter, the dignity of the person – the foundation of morals – should be understood as an entitlement to special affirmation that every person enjoys, which is not derived from any of their further characteristics but rather accessible in direct intuition, as a basic norm (Styczeń 2012b, 331). In this context, Wojtyła's account on human action cannot be understood as the 'basis' of human dignity. It is simply its indicator.

Second, the personalistic value of the action and the agent is of *fundamental* character: It is not simply one moral value among others. What exactly does this mean? Consider a good or right deed, such as providing the necessary care to somebody in desperate need. What Wojtyła argues is the following: Such a deed is aimed at a certain good (the well-being of the needy person) and is performed according to a norm ('you ought to help persons in need'). In addition to these two aspects, however, one may discern a third element – the very basic fact that somebody, a responsible agent, acts in a genuinely personal way when performing this deed. This third element reveals the personalist value of the action, and tells us something important about the acting person's worth (again, as an indication but not as a necessary condition of that worth). If the personalist value of the action is a manifestation of the fundamental value of persons, there is a close relation between the action and the dignity of the person. The position of dignity among values is peculiar because it characterises the agent herself or himself – someone whose own value judgements determine their conduct.

This is perhaps the reason why the understanding of dignity as an intrinsic value of the person must be such that it coheres also with her status or standing. As explained in Chapter 2, the affirmation and respect that is the person's due flows from the dignity of the person. Dignity is something that 'permeates' the person as a whole and is accessible through intuition. Even if human dignity in the general, philosophical sense is the fundamental or intrinsic value of the person (Styczeń 2012b, 261), it is hardly indistinguishable from the person's special status. That special status in the general sense (not the status in the law) could be regarded as *equality vis-à-vis others*, and the entitlement to a special kind of concern and affirmation (Moń 2019, 55). Consequently, it is not simply an inherent value of 'something to be promoted'. Contrast that with the value of nature, or of human artefacts. Let us assume that they have some kind of intrinsic value, that we should protect or promote them just for what they are and not for their utility to humans or other sentient beings. In that case, we would have duties (including moral duties) to maintain beautiful historical monuments or intact forests. But as non-persons, neither historical monuments nor intact forests would have dignity. Their intrinsic value (which, I think, should be accepted as a possibility), would have to be given another name. The reason is that, alongside the intrinsic value they are supposed to have, they certainly do not have the basic standing that characterises all persons as self-authenticating sources of claims, as authors and masters of their lives shaped partly by their own judgement.

Taking this for granted, the basic intuition of dignity (as the personalists argue, this intuition is accessible to all moral agents) may help to explain the basic status or standing of human persons in the law (conceived of as an explication of their dignity). The starting point is that a person acts in a particular manner, involving transcendence in action, performed with reference to relevant truths. Recall that the praxiological reading of the personalist conception claims that activities of the personal structure are observable not only in 'sourcing moral situations', but also in the *prima facie* morally irrelevant contexts, such as constructing a building. As I have argued, the law should be regarded as another example of this, insofar as the routine-based cases are involved. Judges, attorneys, administrative officials, and prosecutors are generally bound to respect human personhood, even in situations that are not marked by moral dilemmas or strong moral urges. Even in such situations, they are bound to make principled, justifiable decisions within a framework of law, taking into good consideration the perspective and position of all affected individuals. An example of such legal conduct could be issuing a declaration of inheritance acquisition. Even if we imagine that everything is quite clear in terms of facts and law (we know who inherits what), the officials must respect everyone's status equally and show equal concern for all the affected parties when scrutinising the case. This seems a common and not trivial aspiration of our legal orders. In addition to that, the framework of laws itself must not be simply something that happens to have been enacted or recognised. Rather, the standards of legislation show us that systems of law result from complicated lawmaking processes in which the legislator is bound (at least in terms of public morality) to recognise the status of personhood of the parties involved. The addresses of the proposed laws generally should be treated as self-authenticating sources of claims, capable of understanding the complexity of the legislative process, and having certain procedural tools to influence its course.

On top of these numerous, 'routine-based' situations, the law may be connected to the status of personhood also in a more exceptional and dramatic way, which has a strong ethical dimension. Expressing this in the personalist language, one may say that some legal situations are also sourcing moral situations – situations that affect the core of personal and moral interest, protected by the means available to legal activity. In these cases, dignity is protected in both forms: as the moral value of human persons, and as their basic status. This is especially clear in the cases of degradation, in which the status and value of personhood is denied to some individuals. Prosecution of human trafficking or war crimes is an obvious example of this type of protection of dignity. Here, the moral dimension of protecting the fundamental value of personhood fully converges with protecting the dignitarian status of victims. However, as already suggested in this book, *the violation of status* is the constitutive factor of these atrocities. Their grave character consists not only in inflicting great pain and suffering, but also in the radical denial of human self-determination and integrity, treating others as subhuman or mere objects. Arguably, the main object of such maltreatments is the basic status of human persons, and the remedies aim at restoring it.

All this, at different levels, and with different degrees of reference to moral worth and moral rights, refers to the status of personhood as the basic standing that each person enjoys within a dignity-based public order. That status is followed by legal protections of different sorts, including, but not limited to, the human rights law. Unlike in other theories, though, the SPT's account of basic status does not detach it from the value of persons, and hence from the anthropological concerns. Instead of seeing the dignity-status as a construction or mere convention, it explains the dignity-status in terms of the underlying theory of personhood. For instance, freedom from degradation is intelligible only in the face of the reality of personhood, that is, in the presence of *someone* – the personal being to whom the basic standing is being denied.

Despite that affinity with the reality of the person, the status of personhood in law (the PSP as a legal principle), along with particular responses to that status as stipulated by the law, *is not directly derived from the personalist conceptual framework*. The dignity of the person (a real standing of particular character) as someone radically capable of action is something that should be, and to some extent has already been, reflected in legal arrangements. Many final determinations of legal rights and duties are therefore informed by the status of personhood, and hence – albeit only indirectly – affected by the reality of personhood. What we observe as a result of this is a complex equilibrium between the underlying theory of personhood, the principle of status attached thereto, and particular judgements (judicial or legislative decisions). This type of wide reflective equilibrium, in the truth-seeking interpretation, has both dimensions – the explicative, and the explaining. The reference to the personalist conception of Wojtyła and Styczeń helps to explicate human dignity in the law as a special standing that is recognised and 'embodied' by the law in the form of the PSP. In addition to explication, the personalist account also helps to explain dignity's appearance and growing recognition.

One final remark, and one more question to be asked. How wide, or how deep, is the equilibrium in the SPT? It is especially important in the order of explanation – we are entering a new sphere here, which is much more neutral with regards to more general statements about law. The status of personhood is not something merely conferred by a convention. It is rather a 'natural' response to the reality of personhood (independent from any philosophy theorising it). Here, within the order of explanation, we may be tempted to think of the status of personhood as a foundation of law in general, not only a prerequisite of a dignity-based public order. This could be a starting point of the more general, personalist theory of law (which would be probably best understood as a variant within natural law theory, especially in the Thomistic tradition). But this would exceed the limited purposes of this book, and I am not going to pursue this issue any further. As far as explication goes, I have identified the principle of human dignity as referring to a status. The particular *rules or rights* connected to the principle are regarded as responses to that status. These are not thought of as postulates of a complete legal theory. Rather, they are explicated as the proper interpretation of the dignitary moment in the law (and not the law as such). In contrast, the *explanation* of the dignitary moment in personalist terms takes us away from the law and urges us to look at its foundations. These foundations do not boil down to social convention. In this sense, the SPT, as far as the explanatory part is concerned, is non-positivistic in tenor.

Conclusion

In this chapter, I have explicated human dignity in the law as a status-expressing principle – the Principle of the Status of Personhood. I argued that the best way to understand the PSP is to postulate its existence as an implicit, cosmopolitan principle which serves as the focal point of reference for the dignitarian moment in the law. The PSP unifies and integrates divergent uses of the idea of human dignity, and may help in assessment of these uses. This includes, but is not limited to, the fundamental rights. The PSP is the common denominator also in other areas of law, insofar as these areas express respect for human personhood and secure its status. Thus, when properly acknowledged and applied, the PSP may contribute to a principled unity of the law, giving structure to the public order based on the acknowledgement of fundamental equality of the dignitarian status.

Importantly, the SPT claims that the emergence and implicit recognition of the PSP is not an historical accident, and especially that it is not a result of a merely superficial, ideological agenda. The reasons why the legal history turned toward its wider and wider recognition deeply corresponds to natural human personhood; the structures of the person, especially the structures of the person in action, sufficiently explain this process (as a *pro tanto* explanation). While this explanation is certainly not exhaustive, it gives strong reasons to perceive the law and human reality as strongly interlinked through the PSP.

Commenting on the content of the PSP, one should emphasise that is not directly oriented toward the good of the person, but rather toward her personhood as such. The reason for this is that it protects the basic status, or standing in the political sense, of the human person. The dignitarian legal recognition of that status consists in respecting everyone in their particular vulnerability, as someone radically capable of self-determination and integration despite that vulnerability. It also urges us to treat everyone as striving towards fulfilment, in the special sense attributable only to persons. It awaits adequate responses to the human condition, including but not limited to human rights. These responses, however, require scrutiny and prudence, which is not available in the PSP taken in itself. In this sense, one can say that the PSP is a guiding principle, but not necessarily the master principle which contains all the answers needed when human dignity is at stake in legal activity. This last claim will be pursued further in Chapter 4.

Finally, one should bear in mind that although I have explicated human dignity as a principle with particular content, I am not claiming that this is the only possible explication. Taking into consideration the rich 'family' of related meanings, human dignity most probably appears also in other forms within the law. An especially important and promising alternative thread would be to explicate human dignity as a free-standing right, and possibly an absolute, cosmopolitan right to freedom from degradation. This is however, another story that would require separate studies.

References

Ackermann, Laurie. 2012. *Human Dignity: Lodestar for Equality in South Africa.* Cape Town: Juta.

Addis, Adeno. 2019. 'Dignity, Integrity, and the Concept of a Person'. *ICL Journal* 13(4): 323–72. DOI: 10.1515/icl-2019-0015.

Alexy, Robert. 2002. *A Theory of Fundamental Rights.* Translated by J. Rivers. Oxford: Oxford University Press.

Arendt, Hannah. 1998. *The Human Condition.* Chicago and London: University of Chicago Press.

Baldus, Manfred. 2016. *Kämpfe um die Menschenwürde*. Berlin: Suhrkamp Verlag.

Barak, A. 2013. *Human Dignity: The Constitutional Value and the Constitutional Right*. Edited by Christopher McCrudden. 361–80.

Barak, A. 2015. *Human Dignity: The Constitutional Value and the Constitutional Right*. Translated by D. Kayros. Cambridge, UK: Cambridge University Press.

Bedford, Daniel. 2019. 'Human Dignity in Great Britain and Northern Ireland'. In *Handbook of Human Dignity in Europe*. Edited by P. Becchi and K. Mathis. Cham: Springer, 319–62. DOI: 10.1007/978-3-319-28082-0_15.

Bernstein, J.M. 2015. *Torture and Dignity*. Chicago and London: University of Chicago Press.

Brożek, Bartosz. 2016. 'Explanation and Understanding'. In *The Concept of Explanation*. Edited by B. Brożek, M. Heller, and M. Hohol. Krakow: Copernicus Center Press, 11–43.

Cossalter, Philippe. 2014. 'La dignité humaine en droit public français: L'ultime recours'. *Revue Générale du droit, Etudes et Réflexions* 4: 1–26.

Dan-Cohen, M. 2012. 'Introduction: Dignity and Its (Dis)content'. In *Dignity, Rank, and Rights*. Authored by J. Waldron. Edited by M. Dan-Coen. Oxford and New York: Oxford University Press.

Daniels, Norman. 1979. 'Wide Reflective Equilibrium and Theory Acceptance in Ethics'. *Journal of Philosophy* 75(5): 256–82. DOI: 10.2307/2025881.

DePaul, Michael R. 1986. 'Reflective Equilibrium and Foundationalism'. *American Philosophical Quarterly* 23(1): 59–69.

Dreier, Horst. 2004. 'Menschenwürde'. In *Grundgesetz Kommentar, Band I: Article 1–19*. Edited by Horst Dreier. Tübingen: Mohr Siebeck, 139–231.

Dworkin, Ronald. 1975. 'Original Position'. In *Reading Rawls*. Edited by N. Daniels. Stanford: Stanford University Press.

Dworkin, Ronald. 1977. *Taking Rights Seriously*. Cambridge, MA: Harvard University Press.

Enders Christoph. 2019. 'Human Dignity in Germany'. In *Handbook of Human Dignity in Europe*. Edited by P. Becchi and K. Mathis. Cham: Springer, 281–318. DOI: 10.1007/978-3-319-28082-0_14.

Floridi, Luciano. 2016. 'On Human Dignity as a Foundation for the Right to Privacy'. *Philosophy & Technology* 29: 307–312. DOI 10.1007/s13347-016-0220-8.

Gardiner, Patrick L. 1959. *The Nature of Historical Explanation*. Oxford: Oxford University Press.

Graveson, R.H. 1953. *Status in the Common Law*. University of London: The Athlone Press.

Haldane, John. 2011. 'Is Every Action Morally Significant?'. *Philosophy* 86(3): 375–404. DOI: 10.1017/S0031819111000192.

Jellinek, Georg. 1892. *System der Subjektiven Öffentlichen Rechte*. Freiburg: Akademische Verlagsbuchhandlung von J.C.B. Mohr.

Kant, Immanuel. 1991. *The Metaphysics of Morals*. Translated by Mary Gregor. Cambridge: Cambridge University Press.

Kittel, Laura. 2021 'Human Dignity in the Universal Declaration of Human Rights: "Old" or "New"?'. In *The Inherence of Human Dignity. Volume 1: Foundations of Human Dignity*. Edited by B.W. Busey and A.J.L. Menuge. London and New York: Anthem Press, 13–31.

Kleining, John. 2017. 'Paternalism and Human Dignity'. *Criminal Law and Philosophy* 11: 19–36. DOI 10.1007/s11572-014-9358-6.

Kommers, Donald P. 2011. 'Autonomy, Dignity and Abortion'. In *Comparative Constitutional Law*. Edited by T. Ginsburg and R. Dixon. Cheltenham, Northampton: Edward Elgar, 441–59.

Kurki, Visa. 2019. *A Theory of Legal Personhood*. Oxford: Oxford University Press.

Lanneau, Régis. 2019. 'Human Dignity in France'. In *Handbook of Human Dignity in Europe*. Edited by P. Becchi and K. Mathis. Cham: Springer, 259–80. DOI: 10.1007/978-3-319-28082-0_13.

Luban, D. 2010. 'The Rule of Law and Human Dignity: Reexamining Fuller's Canons'. *Hague Journal on the Rule of Law* 2(1): 29–47. DOI: 10.1017/S1876404510100025.

Margalit, Avishai. 1996. *The Decent Society*. Translated by N. Goldblum. Cambridge, MA and London: Harvard University Press.

Maritain, Jacques. 1966. *Man and State*. Chicago: University of Chicago Press.

Moń, Ryszard. 2019. *Tadeusz Styczeń*. Kraków: Ignatianum University Press.

Nussbaum, Martha. 2008. 'Human Dignity and Political Entitlements'. In *Human Dignity and Bioethics*. Edited by Barbara T. Lanigan. New York: Nova Science Publishers, 245–64.

Piechowiak, Marek. 1999. *Filozofia praw człowieka*. [*The Philosophy of Human Rights*]. Lublin: Towarzystwo Naukowe KUL.

Piechowiak, Marek. 2019. *Plato's Conception of Justice and the Question of Human Dignity*. Berlin: Peter Lang.

Pop, Maria Lia. 2019. 'Human Dignity in Romania'. In *Handbook of Human Dignity in Europe*. Edited by P. Becchi and K. Mathis. Cham: Springer, 745–69. DOI: 10.1007/978-3-319-28082-0_34.

Rao, Neomi. 2008. 'On The Use and Abuse Of Dignity In Constitutional Law'. *Columbia Journal of European Law* 14(2): 201–56.

Rao, Neomi. 2011. 'Three Concepts of Dignity in Constitutional Law'. *Notre Dame Law Review* 86(1): 183–271.

Rauter, Thomas. 2017. *Judicial Practice, Customary International Criminal Law and Nullum Crimen Sine Lege*. Cham: Springer.

Rawls. John. 1971. *A Theory of Justice*. Cambridge, MA: Belknap Press of Harvard University Press.

Riley, Stephen. 2017. *Human Dignity and Law*. London and New York: Routledge.

Riley, Stephen. 2019. 'Human Dignity as a Sui Generis Principle'. *Ratio Juris* 32(4): 439–54. DOI: 10.1111/raju.12258.

Rupniewski, Michał. 2019. 'Public Reason, Background Culture, and the Justification of Legal Change'. In *The Philosophy of Legal Change*. Edited by M. Chmieliński and M. Rupniewski. London and New York: Routledge, 31–45.

Scanlon, Thomas. 1998. *What We Owe to Each Other*. Cambridge, MA and London: Belknap Press of Harvard University Press.

Schlink, Bernhard. 2013. 'The Concept of Human Dignity: Current Usages, Future Discourses'. In *Understanding Human Dignity*. Edited by Christopher McCrudden. Oxford: Oxford University Press, 631–36.

Solum, Lawrence. 2009. *Legal Theory Lexicon: Rules, Standards, and Principles*. https://lsolum.typepad.com/legaltheory/2009/09/legal-theory-lexicon-rules-standards-and-principles.html

Styczeń, Tadeusz. 2012a. 'Problem możliwości etyki jako empirycznie uprawomocnionej i ogólnie ważnej teorii moralności. [The Issue of the Possibility of Ethics as an Empirically Authorised and Generally Valid Theory of Morality]'. In *Etyka niezależna. Dzieła zebrane, Tom 2* [*Independent Ethics. Collected Works, Volume 2*]. Edited by Kazimierz Krajewski. Lublin: Towarzystwo Naukowe KUL, 17–250.

Styczeń, Tadeusz. 2012b. 'Etyka niezależna? [Independent Ethics?]'. In *Etyka niezależna. Dzieła zebrane, Tom 2* [*Independent Ethics. Collected Works, Volume 2*]. Edited by Kazimierz Krajewski. Lublin: Towarzystwo Naukowe KUL, 247–373.

Waldron, Jeremy. 2011. 'How Law Protects Dignity'. NYU School of Law, Public Law Research Paper No. 11–83. DOI: 10.2139/ssrn.1973341.

Waldron, Jeremy. 2012. *Dignity, Rank, and Rights.* Edited by M. Dan-Coen. Oxford and New York: Oxford University Press.

Waldron, Jeremy. 2016. 'What a Dissenting Opinion Should Have Said in Obergefell v. Hodges'. NYU School of Law, Public Law Research Paper No. 16–44.

Waldron, Jeremy. 2017. *One Another's Equals: The Basis of Human Equality.* Cambridge, MA and London: Belknap Press of Harvard University Press.

Wenar, Leif. 2020. 'Rights'. In *The Stanford Encyclopedia of Philosophy* (*Spring 2020 Edition*). Edited by E.N. Zalta. https://plato.stanford.edu/archives/spr2020/entries/rights/.

Wojtyła, Karol. 1979. *The Acting Person.* Translated by A. Potocki. Dordrecht: D. Riedel Publishing Company.

Wojtyła, Karol. 2011. *Man in the Field of Responsibility.* Translated by K.W. Kemp and Z. Maślanka-Kieroń. South Bend, IN: St. Augustine Press.

Wojtyła, Karol. 2013. *Love and Responsibility.* Translated by G. Ignatik. Boston: Pauline Books & Media.

Woodward, James and Ross, Lauren. 'Scientific Explanation', In *The Stanford Encyclopedia of Philosophy (Summer 2021 Edition).* Edited by E.N. Zalta. https://plato.stanford.edu/archives/sum2021/entries/scientific-explanation/.

Cases

Constitutional Council of the French Republic. 1994. Conseil Constitutionel. 27 July 1994, no. 94–343/344 DC.

Council of State of the French Republic. 1995. Conseil d'Etat. 27 October 1995, no. 136727.

Court of Cassation of the French Republic. 2010. Cour de cassation, civile, Chambre civile 1, 09–67.456. 16 September 2010.

Court of Justice of the European Union. 2011. *Brüstle v. Greenpeace eV.* C-34/10. 18 October 2011.

European Court of Human Rights. 1978. *Ireland v. the United Kingdom.* 5310/71. 18 January 1978.

European Court of Human Rights. 2000. *Kudła v. Poland.* 30210/96. 26 October 2000.

European Court of Human Rights. 2001. *Price v. the United Kingdom.* 33394/96. 10 July 2001.

European Court of Human Rights. *Slyusarev v. Russia.* 60333/00. 20 April 2010.

Federal Constitutional Court of Germany. 2012.18 July 2012.1 BvL 10/10. Official translation. www.bundesverfassungsgericht.de/SharedDocs/Entscheidungen/EN/2012/07/ls20120718_1bvl001010en.html.

Inter-American Court Of Human Rights. 2010. Fernández Ortega et al. v. Mexico. 30 August 2010.

Inter-American Court Of Human Rights. 2011. *The Barrios Family v. Venezuela*. 24 November 2011.
Supreme Court of Canada. 2000. Blencoe v. British Columbia [Human Rights Commission] SCC 44 (CanLII), [2000] 2 SCR 307.
Supreme Court of Canada. 2008. R. v. Kapp SCC 41 (CanLII), [2008] 2 SCR 483.
Supreme Court of the United States. 2015. *Obergefell v. Hodges*. 135 S. Ct. 1732. 576 U.S.

Legal and political documents

American Convention On Human Rights. 1969. Adopted at the Inter-American Specialized Conference on Human Rights. 22 November 1969.
Catechism of the Catholic Church. www.vatican.va/archive/ENG0015/_INDEX.HTM
Code of Administrative Procedure [Poland]. 1960. Ustawa z dnia 14 czerwca 1960 r. kodeks postępowania administracyjnego. Dz. U. 1960 Nr 30 poz. 168. Translation available at: 553www.asylumlawdatabase.eu/sites/default/files/aldfiles/EN%20-%20Code%20of%20Administrative%20procedures%20Poland%20.pdf
ECHR. 1950. Convention for the Protection of Human Rights and Fundamental Freedoms (ETS No. 005). Rome, 4 November 1950.
International Committee Of The Red Cross. 2020. *Humanity after life: Respecting and Protecting the Dead*. Advisory Service On International Humanitarian Law. www.icrc.org/en/document/humanity-after-life-respect-and-protection-dead
UDHR. 1948. The Universal Declaration of Human Rights. United Nations General Assembly resolution 217A (III). 10 December 1948.
Venice Commission. 1998. European Commission For Democracy Through Law. The Principle of respect for human dignity. CDL-STD(1998)026. Montpellier, 2–6 July 1998.
Venice Commission. 2016. European Commission For Democracy Through Law. Rule of Law Checklist. CDL-AD(2016)007rev. Strasbourg, 18 March 2016.

4 Politics

Institutions and the status of personhood

Introduction

If we imagine this book as a musical composition, this chapter would be more of a coda, although extensive and important. While Chapter 1 was devoted to the setup, the central themes were 'played out' in Chapters 2 and 3. The essential presentation of the Status of Personhood Theory may be considered complete. However, the overall message of the project may have been lost in the technicalities. Although misunderstanding is always possible, the hitherto highly abstract level of our inquiry invites perhaps too much. The idea behind this chapter, then, is to clarify the meaning of the Principle of the Status of Personhood by showing what it entails – to 'widen up' our reflective equilibrium by developing the SPT further in more concrete, institutional contexts. In the more technical language from Chapter 1, the job to be done in this chapter is to include the PSP, our *explicatum*, into a broader system of propositions and contentions related to institutions. The investigations conducted in this chapter are grounded in the reality of *participation*, that is, in the ability of the human person to engage in genuinely common projects and strivings, which may lead to personal fulfilment. The details will come as the chapter unfolds.

If one accepts the Principle of the Status of Personhood as the ground, multiple paths of further inquiry become available. It seems that there are, essentially, three such paths. First, one could attempt to develop a full *personalist theory of law*, a theory unfolding from the PSP. Although my inquiry in Chapter 3 ended with some non-positivist conclusions, they came quite late (at the level of explanation), and were not particularly extensive, leaving some space for ambiguity. On the one hand, I said that human dignity was foundational for the law in general, but this was understood as an interpretative claim regarding the actual, really functioning law (the dignitarian moment presented in Chapter 1). On the other hand, the way I evoked wide reflective equilibrium may have suggested that human dignity was foundational to law in the stronger sense, namely, foundational to the very existence and concept of law. If one were to press this stronger claim further, a detailed argumentation in the field of general legal theory would have to be conducted. The basic standing of every human person in the law (expressed by the PSP) would have to be presented as the ultimate source of

DOI: 10.4324/9781003252733-5

legal validity. Law as such would be regarded as a result of dignity-respecting relations between persons. Rudiments of such theories have already been proposed, although that field is certainly not crowded, and much work needs to be done.[1] The second, alternative path of developing the SPT further would be to contribute to the Catholic-personalist political theory, in dialogue with its 'modern classic' (Mounier 1952; Simon 1951), and the contemporary representatives (Rhonheimer 2013; Walsh 2016). That would be quite natural, in the face of the Catholic roots of the SPT's philosophical branch. It is also important to bear in mind that Cardinal Karol Wojtyła directly contributed to Catholic social teaching as Pope John Paul II, in his great encyclicals, and it would be interesting to examine whether or not the SPT coheres with that legacy (Sadowski 2021 provides a helpful overview). Finally, there is the third path: Without engaging in a comprehensive discussion about the fundamentals of law or politics, one could apply the SPT directly to the interpretation of legal institutions, especially those connected with the judicial and legislative specifications of human dignity. Such examination would have a selective and limited focus – the direct implications of the PSP for the institutions as we know them.

In this book, I choose to take the third, most abstemious path. The development of a fully-fledged political doctrine or a fully-fledged legal theory must wait, although I hope this book constitutes a good foundation for both. The main reason for choosing the third path is its proximity to what has been done so far. Developing a comprehensive personalist theory of law is a separate task, the topic for an independent, extensive inquiry. With regards to the Catholic political theory or social thought, it must be emphasised that this book has applied the personalist conception in a fairly unusual and perhaps paradoxical manner, 'setting aside' its Catholic underpinnings and motivations. Most studies in Wojtyła's academic philosophy have been conducted from a perspective which, in one way or another, includes the context of his later papal teaching (Aguas 2014; Kupczak 2000). The works of Tadeusz Styczeń should also be read in the context of his Catholic faith. In my own view, too, personalism as a general philosophical doctrine is most promising in its Catholic or Christian version, which inherits Aquinas's belief in the substantive, hylomorphic nature of the human person and finds its ultimate grounding in the existence and love of God. The aim of this

1 Michał Barański suggests that law should be conceptualised as 'emerging in interaction between persons' (Barański 2016, 153, translation by the author), and that the rightful sphere of personal freedom determines also the scope and content of law. However, this is only a brief remark, formulated as a conclusion of Barański's interpretation of the work of Antonio Rosmini, a nineteenth-century Italian personalist thinker. It is remarkable that similar threads have been taken up also outside the Catholic-personalist tradition. For example, Christoph Hanisch interprets the Kantian tradition (chiefly via Korsgaard 2008) in a way that leads to similar conclusions. As he writes, 'the juridification of human relationships is part of the answer to an inescapable human activity, namely, action and identity-constitution in the presence of others' (Hanish 2015, 452–3). I will point at certain disagreements that the SPT has with Korsgaard's constitutivism later in this chapter.

book, however, was not to engage in discussions about the ultimate grounding and full metaphysical interpretation of personhood. As Chapter 1 explained, we have remained at the level of *pro tanto* explanations, keeping the focus on the 'empirical' material available in legal documents and court judgements, as well as in the phenomenology of person and action. The aim, then, was not to interpret the personalist conception as a whole, in the context of the complete lives and work of its creators. It was rather to borrow from them, engage in a creative dialogue, and go wherever that dialogue was leading. I took up selected threads and philosophical tools offered by Wojtyła and Styczeń (Chapter 2), and then used them in an independent inquiry in the sphere of law (Chapter 3). Therefore, while some congruence between the SPT and the Catholic legacy (especially that after the Second Vatican Council) can be reasonably expected, it will not be scrutinised in this chapter. The interpretation of law in Chapter 3, which led me to formulate the PSP and to find its place in the law, was deliberately restrained. It was guided by the methodological commitment to weak metaphysical parsimony (explained in Chapter 1). I am going to keep that minimalist track, to the extent that doing so is sustainable. I will also attempt to show the limits of this attitude in adjudication.

Taking that self-restraint into account, the reflection in this chapter is developed from the idea of *decent law*. It is inspired by the notion of *the decent society* proposed by Margalit (1996). His fruitful intuition was to focus on the basic institutional conditions of non-humiliation, rather than finding the 'positive' requirements for safeguarding human dignity (1996, 84). Starting from the basic moral intuition that cruelty is 'the ultimate evil', Margalit goes on to argue that *humiliation* is a special, symbolic sort of cruelty that only humans can be subject to (1996, 85). A decent society is a nonhumiliating society: One that avoids, at the institutional level, treating humans as non-humans, subhumans, or mere numbers (1996, 89–112). In Margalit's view, the exigencies of decency are less demanding that these of justice, and I defer to this view. I also agree with him that justice *remains* an attractive ideal, and it is separate – decency is not simply the 'second-best' version of justice, or justice with some injustice in it (1996, 284). To be sure, I am not referring to the ideal of decency simply to top up the pot already full of technical terms. My aim is, rather, to express a certain minimalism which characterises the development of the SPT that I pursue in this chapter. If human dignity in the law is understood as the basic status, and different applications of human dignity are responses to that status, there emerges a moral-political question of *the best possible response*. The answer to this question would have to entail a detailed discussion about the justice, and the good, of the alternative proposals. These are important discussions, and they should be held both in real political life and in books written by scholars. But I am not going to delve into them here. What I am trying to isolate in this chapter is, rather, the institutional background that makes these discussions sensible. This background cannot be merely procedural, as some would have it. What we need is a *substantive* basis: A set of institutions and practices that gives strong reasons to believe that everyone's status of personhood is respected, in situations in which people who obey the institutions nevertheless disagree with regards to the justice or the good these institutions are supposed to embody. Speaking metaphorically, the law which justifies a belief in its decency must not fail to *see humans*, although it may err in terms of understanding what their dignity requires in particular circumstances. Granted, the main aim of this chapter is to isolate and depict the conditions of law recognising humans as real persons, rather than as mere numbers, or animals with a set of capabilities, or mere legal constructions.

It must be emphasised that my concept of decency differs in some respects from the one proposed by Margalit, mainly because it operates at a different level. For Margalit, decency is an ethical ideal, the opposite of cruelty. The decency of law as I understand it is a legal-political ideal. It regulates our acting together with others, and our being together with others, insofar as this is mediated by legal institutions. Following Wojtyła's account, especially in the praxiological reading, asking about decency is 'pre-ethical'; it does not directly concern moral norms. Instead, it focuses on the structures of human action and its personalist value (Wojtyła 1979, 284). As I argued in Chapter 3, law may respect human agency, and human personhood more broadly, independently of pursuing the good of the affected persons. The political question about recognising personhood within legal institutions will be asked precisely in this personalist-praxiological plane, not in the moral plane. Let us consider an example. One may strongly oppose certain forms of welfare state and high taxes. One may perceive the welfare mechanisms adopted in a state as an obstacle to the real flourishing of its beneficiaries, and the high progressive taxes may appear unjust. At the same time, the law that has introduced the bad welfare state and the unjust taxes may be regarded as decent, even from the internal perspective of the opponent. For example, the opponent may recognise that the legislative process has been conducted according to high political standards, and the content of that law is clear. Moreover, the officials generally keep the letter of law, and systemic corruption is avoided. In this example, the political and legislative decisions may invite *opposition* (either normative or teleological considerations may enter). But in general, the decency of these contested institutions is maintained, which may be precisely the reason why the opposition itself is sensible – more sensible than, say, emigration.[2]

Granted, the direct opposite of decency of law is not humiliation (as a form of cruelty) – it is rather *ignorance*. The *indecent law*, as I understand it, ignores the status of personhood of certain individuals or groups. This ignorance may or may not overlap with the moral evil of humiliation. For example, a system of public law which completely failed to fight the atrocity of human trafficking would not only ignore the status of the victims, but also humiliate them. Human trafficking is essentially a humiliating and inherently evil practice. The state, if doing nothing, would contribute to that cruelty. At the other extreme, we may think of a law – for example, some technical regulation – which was enacted in

2 Wojtyła analyses the attitude of opposition in some detail (1979, 286–7). We will come back to it in due course.

a hurry, failing to keep the standards of legislation. The majority in a parliament might have been under pressure of time, and simply enacted the draft as prepared by governmental bureaucrats. No actor of civil society was properly heard, albeit many had expressed their interest. The affected group (say, some group of entrepreneurs) was strongly opposing the new legislation, but their voice was not taken into consideration during the drafting. In this hypothetical case, the status of personhood of some people would have been affected, at the legal-political level. But it does not necessarily mean that they suffered humiliation. We can even imagine that the final, long-term result of the new regulation was beneficial to the affected group and the whole society (yes, bureaucrats are sometimes able to prepare good laws!). The demerit of law in this example would nevertheless be real. It would be a matter of bad political manners or weak standards, rather than of direct violation of a moral norm, but still that flaw would be dignitarian in character. One could say that the legislative institution failed to properly respond to the status of personhood of some representatives of civil society during the legislative process. As we can see, sometimes the ignorance of law may have mostly symbolic value, as a matter of bad manners rather than serious moral flaws. In other cases, however, when ignorance converges with cruelty, the moral flaws are particularly outrageous: The law not only misrepresents the good of the affected persons, but also denies them their basic dignitarian standing. This means that decency of law, although it is a legal-political ideal, is not deprived of moral relevance.

In the face of the preceding, the structure of the chapter is as follows. Section 1 elucidates the idea of the decent law, as well as its connections with the personalist idea of genuine participation. The particular importance of this section is that it shows the PSP as expressing not only the independence of the individual persons before the law, but also their mutual interdependence. The decent law 'sees' humans in all their complex involvements in communities, with all their vulnerabilities. Section 2 deals with adjudication, particularly with the normative indeterminacy of human dignity in the law, which is sorted out in the spirit of the decency of law. Here, I lay out the most important ideal for adjudication – the equality in dignity. Subsequently, I offer an account on both the easy and the hard cases. Section 3 briefly characterises the most important implications the PSP yields for legislation. In particular, I deal with the dilemmas connected to constructing the contours of legal personhood, as well as with the problems connected to the 'engineering' role that the law increasingly plays in modern jurisdictions. I maintain that all the challenges met by legislators must be dealt with in a way which does not forget the status of the direct authors and recipients of the law – that is, the human persons.

1 The status of personhood, participation, and the idea of decent law

1.1 The Principle of the Status of Personhood and genuine participation

Although Karol Wojtyła does not directly discuss political or legal institutions, I will draw from his work once more, presenting the requirements that the PSP imposes on institutions. The requirements or implications of the status of personhood must be examined in the spirit of wide reflective equilibrium, which in our case means interpreting the PSP in connection with the background theory of the human person. Especially the last chapter of Wojtyła's *The Acting Person*, focused on the issue of 'acting together with others', that is, on ***participation***, contains the insights that are critical to the proper understanding of my theory of human dignity in the law (Wojtyła 1979, 261–99). It is important to emphasise at the outset that Wojtyła does not analyse participation from the sociological perspective, but as another characteristic of the person – somebody who strives for, or achieves, genuine personal fulfilment in cooperation with others (1979, 269). As such, participation allows the person to 'share in the humanness itself of every man', that is, to recognise others as neighbours (1979, 295, emphasis removed). The two claims concerning the social (or the interpersonal)[3] relations are particularly important in this regard. Namely, Wojtyła contends that the multiple situations in which people are working together generally do not (the factual claim), and ought not to (the normative claim) undermine the personal dimension of the human being, and the personalist value of the action (1979, 272). Of course, the factual claim does not take anything for granted. As Wojtyła writes,

> the limitation of the personalistic value may sometimes go so far that we can hardly speak of 'acting together with others' in the sense of the 'authentic' actions of the person. Under certain conditions 'acting' (as the synonym of 'action') may change to denoting something that only 'happens' to a particular man under the influence of other human beings. An extreme example of this is so-called 'mass psychology', when a large group of men may begin to act in an uncontrolled way and so affect the behavior of individuals.
> (1979, 270)

What Wojtyła argues for is, therefore, not the structural necessity but the realistic possibility of the action that is both genuinely common and genuinely personal. That possibility correlates with the norm, and hence the normative claim. Although Wojtyła does not give this norm an explicit name, we could call it a Principle of Genuine Participation.[4] According to this principle, different communities – unions established by persons 'acting together with others' – should safeguard the subjectivity of each member, that is, 'the self-determination of the person, and so her agency, as well as the transcendence and the integration of the person in action' (1979, 272, translation modified).[5] Although Wojtyła avoids the word

3 Wojtyła distinguishes between these two. The interpersonal relations occurs when one *I* meets the other *I* (*thou*), while in the social relations, the individual *I* participates in society, that is, in the social *we* (2008, 240–52).

4 In somewhat different sense, Wojtyła talks about the common good as connected to the 'principle of correct participation' (1979, 282). I will come back to the issue of the common good in due course.

5 It is important to note that the 1979 English edition omits the expressions 'transcendence' (*transcendencja*), and 'integration' (*integracja*) which are present in the Polish edition.

'dignity', the meaning is clearly dignitarian in the personalist sense of endorsing the '"specific gravity" of a personal being' (Wojtyła 2008, 237).

The Principle of the Status of Personhood (which the SPT equates with human dignity in the law), should be read against this background. It should be understood as a particular case of the more general Principle of Genuine Participation. In this chapter, I will be focused on the PSP as a principle of public order, which is distinguishable from the common good of a political community. This is not to say that the PSP does not have relevance in theorising common good. Quite the contrary, I believe that the PSP is a structure-giving principle in this case as well. However, a closer look at this issue would be tantamount to entering the sphere of (social) ethics, which is beyond our direct interest. Despite this limitation, the distinction between public order and common good will become important only in the next subsection, where I will examine the decency of law as part of a public order in more detail. In this subsection, I will offer a more general, underlying picture of relations between persons and communities, which sets the scene for the more specific issue of the decency of law. 'Community' is here understood loosely, and comprises 'public orders' as well as other multiple forms of human association. In this loose sense, I will talk about community and society interchangeably. In the next subsection, I will provide a more technical and restricted meaning of 'community' and 'public order', in the context of the decency of law.

We can now move to the general picture of how the individual is related to the community, according to the personalist conception. Our phenomenological description of the structures of personhood and action (presented chiefly in Chapter 2) was focused on the individual person and her individual capacities of self-determination, transcendence, and integration. There were good reasons to focus on the individual person and set the social dimension aside. The personalist conception argues that personhood is not a mere construction or function of society, but has its real substrate in each and every human being – their ontological structure. Personhood is an immanent characteristic referring to the human being as a whole, simply because humans are personal beings. Thus, the community does not 'create' or 'constitute' personhood, at least not in the strong sense. Wojtyła argues that the constitution of the self (the *I*) in relations with the other (*thou*) really does occur, but it is a matter of consciousness and lived experience, and not of reality in the metaphysical or ontological sense (2008, 242). Just as it would be quite awkward to say that we 'create' a healthy body by nourishing it, we should not say that persons are 'created' by the recognition in a community. As a consequence, we should say that not only *action*, but also the very *existence* in community is ultimately the existence of individual persons, not of the communities in which the persons participate. As Wojtyła writes,

> [a]ctions, which man performs in all his different social involvements and as a member of different social groups or communities are essentially the actions of the person. Their social or communal character is rooted in their personal character, and not the vice versa.
>
> (1979, 263)

As we see, the ontological structure of the person is the basis for humane societies or communities. A lot has been said about this structure in Chapter 2. Here, let us only recall that the most important characteristic of the person which reveals itself in action is the *transcendence in reference to truth*. The human agent does not only want certain things to happen and does not simply choose her course of action – she is also able to judge, in conscience, the rightness or reasonableness of her wants and her actions. In this sense, the choice preceding the action is made according to the truths which are relevant in a particular case, since the rightness of actions is determined by how adequate they are in the relevant conditions (similarly: Wojtyła 2008, 234). In this sense, the agent is always – and this is the extent to which we can talk about genuine human action – able to transcend the conditions in which she acts, through her conscience. Also in this sense, the structure of the acting person is independent from the underlying social conditions. Wojtyła says that this capacity has a solid ontological basis in the *suppositum humanum*, and is a mark of the spiritual nature of the human person (1979, 258). At the same time, Wojtyła leaves the issue of metaphysical explanation of this phenomenon open (2008, 233). This is also our course of action, as explained before.

Despite the independence of the ontic basis for individual subjectivity, which is inherent to the person, mutual recognition in relations with others is one of the most important conditions for the development of individual subjectivity and agency. This naturally 'opens up' the human person to relationships with others; relations which mutually confirm the personhood of the participants (Wojtyła 2008, 240–6). In normal circumstances of life, then, communities are a natural background or scene for genuinely personal fulfilment, and many forms of personal fulfilment may come only through activities in a community. However, participation in a community is not simply a means to achieve fulfilment. Quite to the contrary, sometimes personal fulfilment *serves* genuine belonging to the community. For example, a patriot subordinates his goals to the common good of his homeland, which he considers superior. This subordination can be authentic only insofar as the patriot has been a developed person with certain moral character and integrity. In this sense, his development serves his homeland. On the ontological plane, community is 'accidental with respect to each subject individually and to all of them together' (Wojtyła 2008, 238).[6] At the same time, the peculiar

6 One of the important legal implications of this is that attempts to grant 'dignity' to groups are deeply mistaken. Dwight Newman analyses this problem in some detail (2021). Although he does not directly refer to the personalist framework but relies on the idea of the inherent worth of persons, the SPT coheres with his arguments against group dignity (which, as such, does not exclude the possibility of collective rights or group agency). Most importantly, Newman argues, group dignity undermines the well-embedded belief that dignity is at bottom 'beyond human construction' (2021, 99). Fundamental human equality is also at stake, if dignity can be attributed to groups in a way independent from the individuals comprising it (2021, 100). The doctrine of participation seems to offer a plausible framework to grant high recognition to communities, and even apply human rights instruments to them, without

character of social bonds in a given community may make it an end in itself, possibly requiring high sacrifices, as well as high recognition in the law.

Considering all of these factors, the personalist account attempts to reconcile the two opposing propensities of the human condition. On the one hand, the person is 'constituted' (in the weak sense of the lived experience of constitution) through relationships. Fulfilment – the process of becoming a fully developed person – occurs most naturally in the interpersonal or social environment. Often, a community becomes the space in which 'the human *I* more fully and more profoundly discovers itself precisely in a human *we*' (Wojtyła 2008, 250, emphasis original). On the other hand, communities of the sort that humans are able to create, and genuinely communal actions that humans are able to engage in, inevitably require the structure of the *actus personae* as their ontological basis. Therefore, 'acting together with others', when genuine participation is safeguarded, does not annihilate the irreducibility of each participant. This twofold vision of the human being contains tensions: The human being is simultaneously rooted in, and relatively independent from, the community in which he participates. As a result, the personalist account accepts the importance of the communal or social sphere, and the natural entanglement of the individual in relations with others, which should be practically reconciled with individual self-determination, and the individual dignitarian standing of each and every participant.

The SPT is a specification of this very general picture in the political and legal sphere. Accepting the background theory of human participation situates the SPT in a position which is neither individualistic nor holistic, in terms of political theory. Individualism, understood as a vision of the human being in which other persons are mere limitations to individual external freedom, and the community is simply an aggregate of individuals, is explicitly rejected by Wojtyła (1979, 272). The individual, although of fundamental value, and having basic status, should not be regarded as a 'supreme and fundamental good' in every instance (1979, 273). As explained earlier, the common good may take precedence over individual goods. That precedence, however, is not grounded in the fact that the common good outweighs the individual good. Rather, the precedence is established in terms of *the nature of the social bond between persons forming the community.* The individual perspective always counts as a consideration of a particularly high weight. This entails that the rejection of individualism in the personalist way does not boil down to the claim that the good of individual persons should be subordinated to the good of the community. This would amount to 'anti-individualism' or 'totalism', as Wojtyła calls it (1979, 272). Both individualism and totalism (or holism, to use a more common name for the same doctrine), commit the same mistake: They fail to recognise the real structure of the person in action with others. Individualism misunderstands joint actions, thinking of them in terms

conferring dignity. The protected interest, upon personalist understanding, is the particular strength and importance of social bonds, but that boils down to the participants and not to the groups themselves.

of a coordinated pursuit of individual preferences (Wojtyła 1979, 274). Holism perceives the individual in a similar way, as striving only toward individual good, and in this sense as an 'enemy' of the community (1979, 274). This presumes the community is a real, direct subject of 'interest' and action, thereby ignoring the fact that the individual transcendence of each participant is the ultimate foundation of every genuinely human community (1979, 277). As a result, both individualism and holism fail to properly take into account the participation of the human person in their axio-normative considerations. Personalism argues that in many instances, the individual and the social reinforce each other and do not stand in a straightforward opposition, which is reflected in the normative sphere.

This has important implications for understanding the Principle of the Status of Personhood. On the one hand, it pertains to individual persons: Each person separately, or incommunicably, has dignitarian standing. On the other, the PSP is not strictly individualistic and is not intended simply as the protection of individual freedom against the external, unjustified interference of the state or society. The true meaning of the PSP refers to participation. The sphere in which an individual personality actualises itself, or in which it may achieve fulfilment, is the basic entitlement of every human person (Wojtyła 1979, 273). The PSP says that every human being, in a community mediated by the law, ought to have a genuine opportunity of acting together with others in a way which recognises and respects his individual subjectivity. The ultimate purpose is thus the protection of dignitarian standing in our relations to one another, which may or may not translate to the relation between the individual and the state or society. Against this background, not only rights, such as freedom of conscience, but also duties, such as the duty to protect one's country (or not to invade another), find their ground in the dignitarian standing of every person. Thus, despite the non-individualistic character, the SPT is far from the holistic belief in the independent interest of the society or the state. Even commitments to a common good (including the duty to sacrifice oneself to protect the country against invasion, for example) ultimately refer to the persons involved in the community, and not to supra-individual 'entities'. The deepest intention of the PSP is therefore to protect the basic standing which is the prerequisite of further conditions of individual personal fulfilment through genuine participation. Whatever one thinks about the conditions of fulfilment more specifically, that fulfilment can be attained only in humane relations with others. This is what the PSP strives to protect in the law. And this is what makes my theory a personalist one.

1.2 Decency of law and the public order

The substantive connection between participation and the status of personhood, outlined in the previous subsection, has a variety of implications one could unfold in different fields of inquiry. Here, we are confined to the issue of the decency of law, which is the crucial basic commitment of a dignity-based public order. As already stated, asking about the decency of law is equivalent to investigating the basic framework of respect for personhood within legal institutions. In other words, the inquiry concerning decency focuses on the principles of a polity whose laws respect human dignity at the most basic, and thus relatively thin, level. A legal order that respects personhood may take many forms, and many alternative decisions can be made with regards to public policy. The configuration of rights may differ within and between jurisdictions. The decent law, which I will be scrutinising in this chapter, is the ideal that provides a substantive basis and dignitarian framework for the alternative configurations of rights, duties, and public policies. It allows one to find personhood within the diversity of legal-political cultures, and in different – perhaps even contradictory – institutional arrangements. If the presentation of this basic framework is compelling, one can reasonably hope that the Status of Personhood Theory proves its universalism, as well as a certain flexibility. As a consequence, the SPT could defend itself against charges of conflating ideology with scientific scrutiny. But universalism itself is perhaps not enough to consider the separate reflection upon decency of law worth pursuing. After all, all theories of dignity claim universalism. Thus, the other advantage of focusing on decency is the *argumentative potential* that the STP may gain. To give just one example: I claimed that human 'autonomy', often praised as the subject of dignitarian recognition and protection, should be understood as self-determination in transcendence, that is, as subordinated to truth. This is very likely to meet with opposition, since many may see it as an arbitrary imposition of a contestable 'comprehensive doctrine' on the political sphere, as famously argued by Rawls (2005). The SPT argues that this would be a misunderstanding of the political-legal institutions that respect dignity. The commitment to self-determination and the transcendence of the human person is not a matter of a contestable conception of the good, or a metaphysical worldview. Quite the opposite is true – the commitment to self-determination and participation lies at the very heart of a decent public order, as part of the conception of the political. It is a part of the dignitarian framework which enables disputes and reasonable disagreement regarding the right and the good. It does not belong solely to one of the competing conceptions but is rather the shared background – sometimes shared unconsciously. The personalist conceptualisation still may be controversial and debatable, *not as a comprehensive metaphysical doctrine, but precisely as the political conception of a dignity-based public order*. The doctrine of the person the SPT endorses lies at the heart of the personalist conception of the rule of law.

In Chapter 3, I distinguished between the two different functions of law that are related to human dignity. First, the law may respond to the dignity of the person by effective affirmation: protecting the good of that person, or at least safeguarding entitlements necessary for individual pursuit of the good. Second, the law may express the basic status of the person. This second function is the domain in which the decency of law manifests itself with particular clarity. It is true that the law which effectively and adequately affirms persons is decent as well. But decency is most noticeable when it obtains *despite* deficiencies or disagreement with regards to effective affirmation (that is, the goodness or the justice of law). The PSP certainly requires responses, and that means the law ought to provide human goods, or at least grant rights and create conditions that enable the individual pursuit of the good. But the direct content of the PSP is more minimalist – it requires respect for persons as capable of self-determination, striving toward fulfilment, and forming an integrated whole. The question of what should be done in particular circumstances is more comprehensive and requires further debate. This debate, though, must meet the condition of respecting personhood. In the next section. I will propose a conception of dealing with the normative indeterminacy of human dignity in the law, and that discussion will benefit from distinguishing between the *decency of law* and the *effective affirmation of persons in the law*. For now, let us focus solely on what the former requires.

The distinction between effective affirmation of the person and respecting his personhood is analogous to another distinction, namely, that between public order and common good, sketched in Chapter 3. This is a proper place to develop this further. The general scheme would be such that the justice or the goodness of law is connected more directly to the common good of a united political community, while the decency of law is the main commitment of a public order. The latter is understood as a political association that is not in consensus as regards the common good or justice, but the members of that association are nevertheless connected by the bonds of participation (I call this bond 'civic fellowship', to be defined later in this subsection). To be sure, public order and common good may very well be two sides of the same coin, or two distinguishable aspects of the same empirical political society. Contemporary Poland, for example, can be considered a united community in some respects, and a public order in others (and, unfortunately enough, none of them in too many other aspects). Public order and common good should be distinguished for the same general reasons I gave for distinguishing between effective affirmation of the person and respecting her status of personhood. My claim, which may appear controversial from the point of view internal to the personalist tradition, is that human dignity suffices to establish a public order, but not a united political community. The common good requires more than the commitment to the status of personhood – it requires an adequate response to that status.

The idea of public order borrows from Wojtyła's analysis of participation but departs from it in one specific, albeit important, aspect: it emphasises the persistence of deep political disagreement, and accepts its consequences. For Wojtyła, a political community (the state) has its axiological ground in the common good (1979, 282). This entails that truly communal relations between persons may be established in the circumstances of a general consensus with regards to its common good. For example, in a loving family, spouses generally agree on what is good for their children. They may disagree about the specific means to achieve that good. For instance, they may debate whether their child with a musical talent should be first taught to play violin or piano, or which school she should attend. But it is quite clear, for all the members of the loving family, that the common good comprises the growth of the children. For better or for worse, everyone tries to contribute to that good in their actions. That is why a loving family is a community, both in the ethical and in the praxiological sense. Perhaps a country can be like this, too. If a homeland has been ruined during a war, for example, the survivors will most likely unite in efforts to rebuild. This process may re-constitute the nation as a genuine ethical-praxiological community, resembling a family.

However, in most cases of ordinary politics, political communities are marked by deep disagreements, and thus with a lesser degree of unity. The disagreements are 'deep' in a twofold sense. First, the disputes regard not only the means to achieve the common good (as in the family case), but also *the very shape of the community in question*. This is not analogous to the question of what musical school a child should attend. The questions are more fundamental: 'Should we get married in the first place?' Or, 'Should we have musical schools at all?' It is true that in most countries there is a general long-term consensus as to constitutional identity, as well as to basic liberties and rights. But still, this allows for numerous and contradictory paths for handling public affairs and thereby shaping the content of the common good. Second, the disagreements are deep because opponents generally sincerely believe in what they argue for, and are ready to support the expressed views with complex justifications. This has been articulated quite rightly by Jeremy Waldron. As he observes:

> No doubt, each politician or political activist has confidence in her own principles and her own proposals; she thinks they are supported not just by her will or interest but by the objective balance of reasons. But that does not preclude disagreement: every political activist thinks of their convictions in this way (in this 'objective' mode) and still they are opposed to one another. (Waldron 2016, 94)

Waldron himself is quite far from the personalist tradition. But his observation – which strikes me as obviously true, especially after the caveat that there may be doubts and it is not always true – may be accommodated into the personalist framework. One could even argue that the analysis of the person in action, and in participation, obliges us to think this way. It is tempting to regard our political opponents as not merely mistaken, but also twisted by a cynical ideological agenda, manipulated by media, or representing the interest groups we despise. In real life, there are certainly cases like this. However, if the transcendence of the person in action is to be taken seriously, and the dignity of the person distributed equally among us, we should treat our opponents, at least *prima facie*, as representing some 'objective balance of reasons'. Their views stand in need of genuine consideration, and deserve dialogue (Styczeń 2012b, 440; Wojtyła 1979, 287). Again, not all political statements and movements will turn out to be sincere and reasonable. But some of them certainly will, even after sceptical scrutiny. This means that political communities have a particularly complex relation to their common good, in comparison to more simple communities such as a family.

Taking the preceding for granted, my proposal is as follows. Accepting deep political disagreements as persistent and real obliges us to regard a polity united by the rule of law as a *prima facie* public order. The notion of public order is only briefly mentioned by Wojtyła, in the context of distinguishing morality from legality (2011, 33). In our elaboration, we should see if and how a public order as the primary aim of law differs from the common good as the primary aim of social ethics. Public order, in the sense adopted by the SPT, is an ideal of non-arbitrary, decent jurisdiction which 'sees' everyone as human, and takes their personhood seriously. The very same polity may become, or may *have already* become in some respects, a community united by ethical commitments. But even if this does not occur, *there are genuine bonds of participation* within that polity. Public order may be thus understood as a praxiological community, but not yet an ethical community.

In order to explicate this in more detail, let me first consider the personalist meaning of the common good. An important Wojtilian thought in that regard is that one should not understand the common good in simplistic, teleological terms as merely the goal of the many, external to the community (1979, 281). While common action is obviously animated by common aims or interests, the essence of the community is rather related to the 'subjective moment' of joint actions, namely, the genuine participation of the members. True communities are not established merely through common aims and contingent joint efforts to pursue them, but *by principle*, that which allows 'the person acting together with other persons to perform authentic actions and fulfill himself through these actions' (1979, 282). At the same time, genuine communities are committed to true good. As Wojtyła writes:

> First of all, then, the 'common' relation of many I's to a common good, by virtue of which this multiplicity of subjects appears to itself (and others as well) as a specific *we*, and indeed *is* that *we*, is a particular expression of the transcendence proper to the human being as a person.... Objectively, transcendence is realized in a relation to truth and to the good as 'true' (as 'befitting', *honestum*). The relation to the common good, a relation that unites the multiplicity of subjects into one *we*, should likewise be grounded in a relation to truth and to a 'true' good.
>
> (Wojtyła 2008, 249, footnote removed, translation modified, emphasis original)

In short, a political community united by the common good is established by the fact that its members have found consensus, grounded in objective truth, with regards to the *bonum honestum* they choose to jointly pursue. For instance: if an enactment of some labour regulations is sustainable, just, and serving the labourers, then we can say that in this respect a polity is united by the common good, once the enactment has been completed. It constitutes the genuine community. In such a situation, each member may reasonably believe to have chosen 'what others choose and because they choose, and that his choice will be *his own good* that serves the fulfilment of *his own* person' (Wojtyła 1979, 283, emphasis original). Seen in this light, the labour regulation is not simply a political compromise between opposite interest groups, say, the capitalist and the labourers. It is rather a common establishment of the dignity-based social relations that benefit all the participants.

Now, the notion of public order is an answer to the question – 'and what when we do not find consensus, or the consensus we have reached is based on false premises or erroneous judgement? Have we simply failed to comply with our dignitarian principles?' This is a difficult question, but it must be asked in the face of empirical political circumstances, often marked not only by the lack of consensus but also by public expressions of hostility. The possibility of public order, as another way of exercising participation and at least partial fulfilment of persons, brings an optimistic answer. The ideal of public order may help to overcome hostility by safeguarding the fellowship of the opponents. Moreover, if our political functioning is established through the rule of decent law, we can continue our debate. We can reasonably hope to find a new, rightful consensus, or improve the existing one. This is possible, and likely, if we respect each other as citizens, and give each other the political space for dialogue. We may disagree, but we will do so as fellows, not as foes. These are the essentials of the ideal of the decent law in a principled jurisdiction respecting the status of personhood.

This ideal might be alien to the original personalist conception, which is deeply rooted in the perennial philosophy, sharing its relative optimism as regards finding the truth, and the true good. Perhaps, from the personalist perspective, there is no need to distinguish between the norms of public order and the norms of common good, given their mutual affinity. Recall that Wojtyła writes that 'it is right and necessary for the public order protected by law to strive toward identity with the common good' (Wojtyła 2011, 33). By contrast, moral or political disagreement has been taken as one of the main premises of modern, liberal theories. As a result, many liberals adhere to the principle of state neutrality (itself taking many forms), the principle to some extent replacing the common good. In my view, however, introducing the issue of disagreement into the SPT is not simply *liberalising personalism*. There are some aspects of the personalist thought that allow us to develop the theory from within, in the direction of recognising the importance of disagreement. The other commitments of this conception, however, render results different from the standard liberal solution. It is important to note that Wojtyła and Styczeń, each in their own way, did recognise the persistence of disagreement. Styczeń emphasises that the dignity of the person invites and sometimes even bolsters debates about the good, either in particular circumstances or in a more general sense (2012b). For Wojtyła, the common good should have an inner dynamic, and thus some of its realisations will meet with opposition in the community. The proper opposition, however, is not directed at tearing the community apart, but at improving the social relations based on participation. It may make a community more authentic, since it triggers processes of change which may help to eliminate partisan or arbitrary views and policies (1979, 287). As Wojtyła writes:

> The one who voices his opposition to the general or particular rules or regulations of the community does not thereby reject his membership . . . Different interpretations of opposition are of course possible, but here we adopt the one that sees it as generally a solidarity attitude; far from rejecting the

> common good or the need of participation, it consists on the contrary in the confirmation of all this. Opposition aims then at more adequate understanding and, to an even greater degree, the better means to achieve the common good, especially from the point of view of the possibility of participation. The divergent examples of standing in opposition we know from experience, expressed in the course of man's existing and acting 'together with others', show that those who stand in opposition do not intend thereby to cut themselves off from their community. On the contrary, they seek their own place and a constructive role within the community; they seek for *that* participation and *that* comprehension of the common good which would allow them a better, a fuller, and a more effective share of the communal life.
>
> (Wojtyła 1979, 286, translation modified)

Quite clearly, opposition is an expression of disagreement. If we reflect specifically on how disagreement works in the public sphere, a more nuanced picture may be developed. Namely, one can more sharply distinguish between the situation in which the disagreement regards *the means to achieve the common good* on the one hand, or the opposition concerning its *more adequate understanding* on the other. As we see in the previous passage, Wojtyła focuses on the former. The idea of decency of law amplifies the latter. The disputes about understanding the common good are also debates about the shape of the interpersonal bonds, or about institutions that embody or realise the common good.

Consider, again, the case of the family, and dilemmas about the education of children. The spouses fully endorse, and understand in similar ways, the growth of their children as integral to the common good of their family. Such a loving family is a true community, characterised by *solidarity*. Despite the parents having their disagreements about the specific means to achieve the common good, it is the latter that 'properly conditions and initiates participation' – in this case, the participation in family life (Wojtyła 1979, 284–5). This is what solidarity is about, according to Wojtyła. The problem with the political-legal sphere is that very often our disagreements there are so deep that genuine solidarity is hard to achieve. Again, this is *not only* because the opposite standpoints express opposite interests or purely partisan agendas. This is *also* because the matters to be solved in the public sphere are complex and may be approached from many different angles. It is inevitable, in a plurality, that the different backgrounds, worldviews, and values, as well the ambiguity of the concepts people use in their discourse, will yield dissent. This is the sphere in which the famous 'burdens of judgement' apply in the most vivid way (Rawls 2005, 54–58). But perhaps the burdens of judgement are not the only reasons for this. The additional reason is that, in the law or in legal activity broadly understood, we rarely have direct interest in really recognising the other as human, in the strong personalist sense. In normal circumstances of life, our legal relations are those between co-workers, contractors, or citizens, but none of these must be like a family. The social bonds mediated by law are very often ones that simply assume greater distance between persons, in comparison to the social bonds mediated by love or friendship.

The ideal of decent law is the SPT's response to the obstacles to achieving genuine solidarity, which requires consensus as to the shape of the common good, and also requires deeper connections between people 'as human beings' rather than as contractors, competitors, employees, and the like. Modern political-legal bonds between people are inescapably characterised by disunity, which is even stronger given the fact that they are very often at work in transnational or supranational contexts. Thus, the controversies very often concern the very shape of the common good, or the proper understanding of its rudiments. And there are social groups with directly conflicting interests, each group having the right to care for their own. This does not mean that the efforts to achieve solidarity are necessarily hopeless, or should be abandoned in the name of 'neutrality'. Nonetheless, the problem of obstacles remains, which has important implications for human dignity in the law. Namely, a theory of human dignity – and that is hopefully what the SPT provides – should conceptualise the institutional expression of dignity *which remains despite the lack of consensus in the public sphere, and despite the lesser unity of social bonds mediated by law.*

My proposal is to focus on a relation between human legal subjects that can be called *civic fellowship*, as a parallel to solidarity. The law which establishes a dignity-based public order – that is, the law effectively regulated by the Principle of the Status of Personhood – expresses mutual respect, and thus the mutual recognition of dignity. It allows citizens to treat each other as fellows, not simply as competitors or foes. This is the task of the decent law, and thus the primary task of the PSP in a pluralist polity, as well as in transnational legal relations. It does not presuppose or necessarily require consensus as regards the common good. *Fellowship in dissent, and despite certain disunities*, is enough for decency. If debates continue, and the consensus is lacking, the decent law ensures that the fellow opponents are not engaged in a war, but in participation. They disagree, but they do not disregard each other. They may have contradictory interests, but their interest is not the only perspective they have. This underpins the familiar basic rights that protect not only the debate itself, but also the ones who have lost in the debate (Waldron 2016, 96). To be sure, if the consensus is reached, and a polity in question becomes a genuine political community, the PSP still regulates its law: it still protects the genuine participation of the members by protecting their standing. The only point that I am making here is that even when consensus is lacking, the commitment to the status of personhood may still be present, insofar as the conditions of decency of law (establishing fellowship in public order) are met. And even if law does not always bind us in perfect unity, it nevertheless is indispensable for certain kinds of participation.

This brings us to the final dimension of the decency of law, namely, the way in which the decent law may be considered a platform of *sharing in the humanness of others*. It is perhaps not the most obvious way of thinking about law. Other, more intimate communities of love or friendship seem better suited for this, and for good reasons. Law may be sometimes simply soulless, trivial, or too technical to take seriously the idea that it connects people at some deeper level. The existence of construction law or traffic regulations speaks for itself in this respect.

Or consider financial law. Perhaps few other things may seem less humane, in the sense of the level of technicality, than the 'math' that is involved in the process of financial transactions between corporations, directed at generating profit. Moreover, when the law enters more natural or affectionate interpersonal relations, it is very often connected to the decay of solidarity between persons rather than to its growth. Consider the law of divorce, or remedy claims. Solidarity is certainly the most perfect way in which the community of action and existence can be embodied, but, as already said, it is not realistic to hope that it will always accompany activities in the legal sphere. However, the presence of the PSP at the background of the law – and that is what I have argued for in this book – allows us to think that whenever the law establishes a framework for human cooperation, it also establishes the bonds characterised by genuine participation. This is another expression of the meta-legal level I wrote about at the beginning of this book. The participation may take the form of fellowship and, in the more optimistic scenario, may also express our solidarity. If the dignitarian requirements of the PSP are met, we can say that the law which conditions our cooperation or simply our co-existence respects all involved as human persons. The financial law, for example, contains mostly highly technical and complex regulations, such as these of derivative contracts. However, behind these regulations, there are real people working together in complex processes. It is their deep dignitarian interest to have good reasons to consider themselves fellows in an authorised and lawful activity, rather than merely blind servants to the capital, or, even worse, as partners in crime. Thus, in striving to achieve the decent shape of the financial law, a legislator indirectly serves the people involved in the business, helping to maintain their civic fellowship. But the idea of decent law goes even further. It does not focus only on human agency and the independence that is connected to it. As the other side of the same coin, the PSP yields certain requirements regarding those who are lacking, in terms of individual or social endowment. For example, welfare services are not considered to be simply a charitable concession to the poor, but rather as an entitlement of the least advantaged, covered by human rights. The decent law responds to the condition of the worst off simply because it recognises them as fellow humans, the neighbours of all others in society, and not as the poor with whom society must deal to maintain stability. According to the SPT, welfare policies are best understood as backed with dignitarian concerns. The ongoing disputes regarding the scope and shape of these policies should keep that in mind. A decent public order recognises the imperfections or disabilities of the persons and responds to them for the sake of the beneficiaries. The decent law, therefore, is not exclusively based on rational individual agency: It also expresses the mutual interdependence of persons in the human world. The decent law would not make sense if humans generally were not rational agents capable of self-determination; but the necessity of decency very often comes from human interdependence, incompleteness, and the fragility of the human condition.

Let me summarise our investigation into the decency of law by stating the set of crucial elements of this ideal, which correspond to the PSP. To recall, I am assuming that human beings are for now the only 'persons' that count as protected by this principle, and hence that have interest in the decency of law (conditions for the decent law protecting some other sentient animals, for example, could be overlapping, but certainly the set would look differently). Here they are: First, under a decent legal order, human beings are treated *as rightfully and naturally setting their own ends and pursuing them*. They are not only entitled to but also responsible for this. Second, in doing so, human beings are treated *as capable of self-determination, which involves following the truth* in the sphere of normative considerations (rightness). It follows that particular laws are addressed to them as persons, that is, as agents who are capable of 'making sense' of the legal provisions and of following them for their own sake. This capability of finding and following the truth also requires that the conduct of individuals must be interpreted by officials as the pursuit of that which individual persons take to be true. Third, *human beings are equal in dignity, regardless of their factual state, and must not be treated as replaceable specimens, but as unrepeatable, irreducible individuals*. This means that every human person is the neighbour of others, sharing human vulnerability and interdependence in striving for genuine fulfilment. Finally, the decent law does not allow us to leave anyone behind, and *it requires adequate responses to the human dignity of each person*, although all the responses cannot be based solely on decency. Rather, decency *plus* prudential delving into the relevant circumstances and truths can produce an adequate response. In short, the decent law *acknowledges and protects* the status of personhood at the basic level. The true common good, and the truly just law, *responds* to that status in a rightful and adequate way, providing full affirmation to the person. That is why the public order and the common good are not mutually exclusive, but rather are two different dimensions of the same dynamic and complex social reality.

2 Normative indeterminacy and the principles of adjudication

With the concept of the decency of law at hand, we can now attempt to approach one of the most persistent problems regarding human dignity in the law, namely, that of *normative indeterminacy*. The underlying hope for the SPT, and especially replacing the expression 'human dignity in the law' (the *explicandum*) with the Principle of the Status of Personhood (the *explicatum*), was to sort things out. Assessment of the success hitherto is perhaps best left to the reader. Testing the PSP in adjudication is something that must be done to complete the theory. I will not recall in detail the numerous worries regarding indeterminacy which have been expressed by many philosophers. The main challenge is that human dignity, when referred to in adjudication, is too rich with potential meanings, which invites arbitrary applications. What is considered as particularly troublesome is the potential incorporation of contested philosophical, moral, or religious ideas into the law. In what follows, I will outline my response to this challenge because, needless to say, the SPT argues that human dignity in the law – when understood as the PSP – makes sense and is useful in legal activity, and that the arbitrary imposition of anything that is not deeply embedded in the law itself may be avoided. Thus, my attempt in this section is to identify a set of considerations that: (i) directly follow the PSP, (ii) are relevant to judges, (iii) are rational, and (iv) help to arrive at intelligible judicial decisions.

2.1 Basic assumptions concerning adjudication

My intention *is not* to work with any particular theory of adjudication, which is a distinct and well-developed field of scholarship (for an overview, see Lucy 2002). However, the ideas presented in this subsection make sense only along with certain assumptions that I will now make explicit (unfortunately for possible opponents, I cannot defend these assumptions here in detail). First, following Lucy (2002, 207), I am assuming that adjudication is supposed to be, and in fact can be, rational and legitimate. As far as legitimacy is concerned, I assume that the *prima facie* task of judges is to apply the law as it exists, rather than create new law. This is certainly not an absolute rule, since in most jurisdictions judges have some authorisation to be creative; for instance, they have freedom to fill the gaps within the body of law. Moreover, while judicial lawmaking is obviously a legitimate source of law in the common law tradition (Sharpe 2018, 78), it is also increasingly being accepted in the continental European systems, especially in constitutional courts (for a comparative survey, see Florczak-Wątor 2020). Despite the long tradition in the former, and the recent developments in the latter, a judge deciding a case in either system is never simply free to legislate, or to decide the case only on the basis of what the law should be. She must take into consideration what the law actually is at the moment of making a judicial decision (Sharpe 2018, 80). Beside this initial assumption, I will not be focused on the legitimacy of adjudication in more detail. I will offer some modest conclusions regarding judicial discretion with regards to human dignity, but this will reflect the implications of my doctrine of rational justification, rather than a separate account of legitimate judicial authority.

Granted, I will be occupied mostly with the issues of *rational argumentation* in favour of judicial decisions implementing human dignity. I am assuming that the *rationality* behind adjudication very often requires judgement. The characteristics of judgement may be different, depending on the difficulty of the case. As Neil MacCormick compellingly argues, 'the process of legal justification is sometimes purely deductive and logical in character', which means the relevant legal rules can be expressed in the form 'if p, then q' (MacCormick 1978, 36–7), and the justification consists here in subsuming the facts to the rules. In short, deductive justification is available in cases in which 'there is a relevant, clear, and unambiguous proposition of law applicable to the case' (Lucy 2002, 213), plus 'it is . . . the case that the "facts" found are unequivocal instances of "p"' (MacCormick 1978, 37). At first glance, such cases (which can be called 'easy') might seem not to require any judgement. And MacCormick's original analysis of deductive reasoning does not employ the notion of judgement. However, it seems to me that what a judge in such cases needs to do, which is logically prior to the deductive justification of his decision, is to *assess* the facts, to *find* them unequivocal. This can be called *evaluative judgement*.

The second possible situation, and the second type of judgement, is more complex and more interesting. In some cases, deductive reasoning is not enough, because of the ambiguity of law. What I mean is, of course, the issue of 'hard cases'. In short, hard cases consist in a situation in which at least two interpretations of a given proposition of law are *prima facie* equally plausible. The judge must then not only justify his decision under the given rule; he also must justify his choice among the competing versions of the rule (MacCormick 1978, 68). The judgement that is involved in hard cases can be called *interpretative judgement*. What is of interest now is what judges do with all the divergent reasons in favour of a particular interpretation of the law in hard cases. Following and paraphrasing Lucy, we may say that the interpretative judgements require: (i) recognising considerations as *prima facie* reasons in favour of alternative interpretations; (ii) sorting reasons, that is, discerning putative reasons from genuine reasons; and, finally (iii) weighing genuine reasons in favour of one particular interpretation (Lucy 2002, 230–1). As we can see, the interpretative judgement is much more complex than the evaluative judgement. In the latter case, the judge simply assesses the relevant facts. In the former case, the judge is involved with much fuzzier terms, propositions of law which relate to many other propositions, possible consequentialist considerations, as well as general moral or legal principles. All this can guide him either way. This is very often the fate of judges applying human dignity. And that is why they are prone to the critique alleging arbitrary application of a normatively indeterminate concept.

The complex nature of the interpretative judgement leads to my final assumption, namely, that when the law leaves space for interpretative judgement, it also leaves a considerable area of freedom to choose between legally and morally admissible options.[7] Thereby, I reject the famous Dworkinian thesis of 'one right answer' to a hard case. Dworkin believes that when making complex interpretative judgements, the judges strive, or at least should strive, to find 'the best constructive interpretation of the political structure and legal doctrine of their community' (Dworkin 1986, 255).[8] While my rejection of this thesis can be quite controversial, this is precisely what is supported by the personalist theory of the person in action (adjudication certainly counting as action, in the sense adopted by the theory). This should not be conflated with assuming relativism

7 As Finnis (2002, 36) compellingly argues, this is the position accepted in the classical natural law theory. This account seems to be strongly supported by Thomas Aquinas's conceptualisation of the free decision (*liberum arbitrium*). See Finnis (1998, 62–71).

8 It is not fully clear whether Dworkin's position was indeed that rigid. Some argue that he might have meant simply that a judge, from her internal perspective, strives to find a solution she considers the best answer to the hard case, but other judges can find alternative solutions superior (Lucy 2002, 219). Dworkin's later work seems to support the opposite belief: Arguing that there is objective truth in interpretation, Dworkin seems to have claimed that there is also the 'best possible' legal interpretation (Dworkin 2011, 123–44).

or non-cognitivism. The judge, like every acting person, rationally recognises the values and principles that count as possible reasons for a judicial decision, so the decision is made on solid rational ground. Moreover, the judge is able to discern what the objectively genuine reasons *forbid or exclude*.[9] However, the deliberation, the *weighing* of competing genuine reasons for one or another acceptable course of action, takes place in circumstances of *the freedom to decide*. Again, it is not my aim in this book to develop a full personalist theory of adjudication. But I assume that judges in their decisions do, and should, exercise their prudence, as well as their conscience, which is intelligible only if we assume that weighing reasons is not an automatic calculation of premises but the result of a free agent's conscientious deliberation. Deciding on the hard cases involving human dignity, that is, applying the PSP, is best understood as precisely such a practice.

2.2 *The personalist meaning to equal dignity*

With the quest well defined, and basic assumptions at hand, we can now move on to our attempt to find a set of considerations that help to sort out the adjudication invoking human dignity. The first and fundamental consideration is *equality of dignity*. The PSP states, in part, that each person should be respected to an extent equal to others. This fragment requires some more elucidation to make it 'operationalised' in adjudication. Here, a re-engagement with the basis of the PSP will be necessary, since the basis of human dignity has implications for its ultimate normative concerns. In this regard, it must be emphasised that the SPT would be misunderstood if rational agency in general, or self-determination in particular, were taken as a 'range property' that justifies the respect due to persons and ultimately determines the normative core of human dignity in the law. The idea of finding a 'range property' which would play this twofold role comes from John Rawls (one could argue that he theorised human dignity 'in disguise' of equal entitlement to justice). In his view, equal respect is owed to moral persons, that is, to those meeting the twofold sufficient condition: (i) being 'capable of having . . . a conception of their good (as expressed by a rational plan of life)', as well as (ii) being 'capable of having . . . a sense of justice, a normally effective desire to apply and to act upon the principles of justice' (Rawls 1971, 505). These two taken together add up to moral personality which, for Rawls, is a 'range property' analogous to all the points within a circle being equally 'inside' the circle. Individual people differ in the degree to which they develop their moral personality, but they all have it to some extent. Likewise, points within a circle may differ in their positions (say, one is right in the centre, and another nearly touches the circumference), but they are still contained inside it. Thus, in the case of the moral personality, 'any variations in ability within the range are to be regarded as any other natural asset' (Rawls

9 Thomas Scanlon rightly points out this feature of practical thinking. As he observes, recognising some consideration to count as a reason for an action very often results in excluding other considerations that would otherwise count as reasons (Scanlon 1998, 52).

1971, 508). What suffices to count as the bearer of the claim to equality is thus having the range property to the minimal degree. Of course, Rawls's characterisation of moral personhood differs considerably from the personalist account. In particular, Rawls makes no reference to the transcendence of the person (which assumes the relation of the person to the relevant truth). But setting differences aside, it could seem that the SPT endorses an analogical view. Particularly *the transcendence of the person in action* (the characteristic that essentially conditions and constitutes self-determination and thus genuine personal action) could be understood as the range property that requires equal respect for all persons.

Upon this reading, the PSP would ultimately boil down to protecting the agency of the human person, understood both as the basis and as the main dignitarian concern. The different dignitarian interests we talked about in Chapter 3 would be admissible only insofar as they would contribute to, or flow from, the agency of the person. Something similar has been already claimed by many, in the context of human rights rather than the law in general. For example, James Griffin argued that the best account on human rights should be

> centred on the notion of agency. We human beings have the capacity to form pictures of what a good life would be and to try to realise these pictures. We value our status as agents especially highly, often more highly even than our happiness. Human rights can then be seen as protections of our agency – what one might call our personhood.
>
> (Griffin 2001, 4)

This passage should not be read as saying that rational individual agency is the only subject of protection – many more particular interests and rights can be derived from it. For example, the right to welfare is included in the menu of human (and not merely civic) rights, because 'our picture of human agency' is such that 'certain supporting goods are integral to it' (Griffin 2008, 180). But the multifarious protections are all rooted in agency (or personhood understood as the capacity for agency), accompanied with 'practicalities', that is, 'the conditions for a human right' (2008, 38). The SPT could be understood as a modification of Griffin's account or, perhaps more accurately, as a deep disagreement *within the same general framework*. For Griffin, agency (the agency he calls 'normative'), is 'specifically our capacity to choose and to pursue our conception of a worthwhile life' (2008, 45). Should the SPT be understood within this framework, a disagreement with Griffin would be that the choice and pursuit of a valuable life is only one aspect of something that is more profound: the transcendence of the person in action. Also, our analysis of participation would have to be taken into account, which would require defining normative agency in a manner which takes human interdependence much more seriously than simply saying that deep personal relations are valuable in a human life (this is what Griffin (2008, 116) says).

But as I stated, *all this would be a misunderstanding of the SPT as a whole.* The reason for this is that the SPT *is not* on the same page with any theory that ultimately grounds human dignity (and human rights) in a particular characteristic of the human person that was chosen to count as the most valuable characteristic.

As I have already suggested, transcendence, self-determination, or any other distinctive capacity of the person which is revealed in action, *is best understood as a signifier of dignity, not as its ultimate basis or condition*. A well-recognised threat of attaching human dignity rigidly to one distinguished human feature is the possibility of missing important dignitarian considerations that do not directly flow from the presence of this feature. For example, S. Mattew Liao argues that freedom from pain, among others, is a non-agentic interest of each human being that must not be disregarded by any theory of the groundwork for human rights (Liao 2010). In my view, however, the urgency of the problem lies somewhere else – not in the concerns about *the scope* of dignity, but in the issue of *equality of the basic status*. If we take rational individual agency as the ultimate ground of human dignity, we may simply lose those who, in their present state, are not prospective agents, either as a result of decline or severe disability. A good example comes from the following passage by Alan Gewirth. In his rationalistic account,

> the ultimate purpose of the rights is to secure for each person a certain fundamental moral status: that of having rational autonomy and dignity in the sense of being a self-controlling, self-developing agent who can relate to other persons on a basis of mutual respect and cooperation, in contrast to being a dependent, passive recipient of the agency of others.
>
> (Gewirth 1985, 743)

In contrast to that, the SPT is committed to the decency of law and the equality of human dignity, and thereby accepts that some members of the human family, whom we have every reason to call 'persons', like people with severe disabilities or those approaching the end of life, *will in certain instances be* 'mere passive recipients of the agency of others'. Their tragically disadvantaged situation does not nullify their fundamental, equal dignity. Quite the contrary: The impairments and dependence on the help of others may bring *the dignity of the impaired* to a particularly strong light. If we should have equal concern for the dignity of each person, then certainly a healthy man leading a flourishing life has inherent dignity to the same extent as the person with severe disabilities. But it is the latter case in which the dignitarian concerns are actualised and require action from others. This is perhaps best observable in ethical practices, such as the help offered to the terminally ill. However, a similar tendency exists also in the law, in the practice of adjudication. A recent example comes from the justification of a decision by the Ontario Court of Appeal,[10] in which Justice Miller observed that:

> A great many persons, by reason of immaturity, decline, or other physical or mental impairment, have little or no present ability to exercise many, if not

10 In this case, the court considered whether or not Ontario's common law definition of death as cessation of neural brain activity may be challenged based on religious beliefs. The appellants demanded, acting on behalf a person with no neural activity but on mechanical ventilation, to sustain her life support, since 'the adoption of neurological criteria to establish the

> most, of the rights and freedoms guaranteed by the Charter. These impairments have no bearing on their status as subjects of Charter rights. Furthermore, at least some of the Charter rights protect not only one's interest in doing, but simply in being. The rights govern how one is to be treated by others. These include, for example, the right not to be deprived of life and the right to equal benefit of the law.
>
> (Court of Appeal for Ontario 2019, 38)

This is the perspective in which the status of personhood is indeed unconditional, and indeed equal to all persons. The question remains open: how should we interpret the PSP and its basis, in order to establish coherence with such egalitarian intuitions?

Instead of relying on one fundamental feature of human beings, one option would be to rely *on a set of valuable features*. Instead of joining monistic-rationalistic accounts, such as those offered by Griffin or Gewirth, we could attempt to find the ultimate meaning of the PSP in a pluralist understanding of the basis of equal dignity. Such a position has been developed by, among others, Pablo Gilabert, in his theory of human dignity and human rights (2018). As he argues, the real reason why humans are 'owed such strong forms of respect and concern' is a set of 'certain features of human beings that warrant the ascription of status-dignity to them' (Gilabert 2018, 126). His proposal is to make a tentative 'reasonable list of the valuable features of human beings' which is best understood as a hypothesis (2018, 127). As such, the list may be revised and supplemented, and the items on the list can be explicated in more detail, as circumstances require. 'One such list', according to Gilabert, 'would include the human capacities for sentience, knowledge, prudential and moral reasoning and choice, aesthetic appreciation, self-awareness, creative production, social cooperation, and sympathy' (2018, 127). This is certainly a remedy to the problem of losing the equality of dignity that inevitably emerges in exclusively rationalist theories. The main advantage of the pluralist account in this context is that even if the strictly agentic capacities are missing (say, the neural structures of a person's brain have been either severely damaged or never properly developed), the individual still has other valuable features from the list. Thereby, the status of persons with disabilities is not questioned, which allows us to think about the necessary support for them, rather than excluding them from the range of persons (2018, 151).

While this view may seem attractive, it inherits *the fundamental misunderstanding* about the true nature and meaning of the equal status of personhood; the misunderstanding which overburdens the rationalist account. Namely, both

---

death of those persons who hold a religious belief that life does not end until the heart stops beating (with or without mechanical assistance) violates such persons' religious freedom' (Ontario Court of Appeal 2019, 6). While the appeal was dismissed, the court offered an extensive framework for future cases, which can eventually allow such challenges to succeed. I thank Amy Ross for drawing my attention to this judgement.

rationalist and pluralist bases of human dignity render the status of personhood *dependent on value judgement*. It is more evident in the rationalist account, exemplified by Griffin. It seems quite unequivocal, from the passage just quoted, that he first assumes that we value our agency, and only in the second step says that it yields the normative agentic status. In other words, the valuing comes first, and the attribution of status follows the value judgement. In the case of Gilabert (and presumably in other pluralist accounts), the situation is perhaps a little more complicated, precisely because of the underlying egalitarian concern to include 'non-typical' human beings. As Gilabert writes,

> we should develop a dignitarian perspective that is truly inclusive of all human beings. To do so, we can proceed in three steps. First, we identify the set of human beings in the broadest possible way. ... We ascribe status-dignity to all of them. At this stage, the ascription of status-dignity is only a promissory note. It expresses our intuition that all human beings count and are entitled to respect and concern. But this reaction needs to be developed and defended. Thus, in a second step, we identify valuable features that are relatively constant amongst most of those we call (adult) 'human beings' and articulate the norms of respect and concern that properly respond to them. (2018, 150)

In my view, this is the point at which Gilabert's position regarding the basis of dignity commences to lose clarity and consistency. In particular, it is becoming unclear what plays the truly decisive role here: Is it our intuitive affirmation of equality of status, or is it the valuable features of human beings that justify its equal attribution? This is especially troublesome in the third step, related to non-typical human beings, such as those with profound disabilities. For Gilabert, we subsume them under the dignitarian status 'by noticing that . . . [they] still have some of the valuable features', despite the impairments (2018, 151). It appears that according to Gilabert the equality of dignity, although somehow rooted in a moral intuition, ultimately depends on our choice (because value judgement is a choice of particular sort) to include all. Gilabert does not talk about a minimum threshold, but it seems reasonable to assume that there is one, since our 'noticing' of valuable features assumes at least a possibility of contending that a particular human being does not hold enough of them. Perhaps Gilabert would not go that far, but some other scholars who ground human dignity in valuable features explicitly say that the value of some persons (say, those suffering from dementia) is mainly symbolic value, not very far from the symbolic value of human *remains* (Wielenberg 2021, 66).

The personalist proposal is radically different from both analysed accounts. Equal dignity, in the personalist perspective, is the fundamental axiom of relating to, or deliberating about, human persons. We affirm (love or respect) other persons in their entirety, insofar as we ourselves are able to deliberate and act *as a person*. Obviously, nothing here is taken for granted. But if one is able to develop and exercise the structures necessary for genuinely personal action (the *actus personae*), the relation with, or deliberation about, all other persons will be marked by the respect or love that takes their equal standing seriously. Importantly, such relations concern concrete, real persons – others whom we respect not for what they are, but simply *because they exist as persons* in our human world. In this sense, equal dignity is not something that stands in need of justification; It is something that is grasped by intuition together with ascertaining the existence of persons with whom we interact. The *axiomatic* nature of dignity was particularly important for Tadeusz Styczeń's moral philosophy, especially his meta-ethics (2012b). He insisted that the moral duty is always, in reality and in common moral experience, directed at concrete persons, as some course of action we owe 'to someone', either an individual or a group (Styczeń 2012a, 166). Despite that concrete and thus individual character, the moral duty is open to universalisation, which consists in endorsing the belief that potentially all persons are covered by the same or analogical moral duty (2012a, 184–98). This means that the intuition of equal dignity is not merely a reaction-to-be-defended, as Gilabert calls it. It is, rather, something deeply embedded in our moral life and moral judgements, insofar as they are made without internal or external distortions. As I have attempted to show in this book, a similar, structural endorsement of dignity is present in other practical considerations. The law affirms persons in the form of 'respect'. That is why the dignity of the person concerned is the axiom of adjudication. And, therefore, the judge keeping fidelity to the Principle of the Status of Personhood does not merely endorse the abstract ideal of equal dignity to all; she also, and most importantly, keeps fidelity to the real persons affected by the particular act of adjudication.

A similar conclusion seems to come from Wojtyła's discussion of participation. An especially important aspect thereof is that it helps the participants to recognise others as true *neighbours*. When engaged in decent practices, one participates in the humanity of others, which by consequence must mean grasping and reaffirming their dignity. As Wojtyła writes:

> First of all, I view it [participation] as a property of the person, a property that expresses itself in the ability of human beings to endow their own existence and activity with a personal (personalistic) dimension when they exist and act together with others. Secondly, I conceive participation in *The Acting Person* as a positive relation to the humanity of others, understanding *humanity* here not as the abstract idea of the human being, but . . . as the personal self, in each instance unique and unrepeatable. Humanity is not an abstraction or a generality but has in each human being the particular 'specific gravity' of a personal being (clearly this 'specific gravity' does not derive in this case solely from the concept of the species). To participate in the humanity of another human being means to be vitally related to the other as a particular human being, and not just related to what makes the other (*in abstracto*) a human being.
>
> (Wojtyła 2008, 237)

As we see, the humanity of others is not tethered to the ideal, but to the real and concrete persons with whom one is in interaction. And the 'gravity' of humanity should be understood, in my view at least, as tantamount to 'dignity'. In this perspective, dignity is equal to all in the radical sense. Talking about some minimum threshold of valuable features that one needs to 'pass' in order to 'justify' one's dignity and rights seems essentially flawed in this perspective. Note that thinking in terms of a minimum threshold is not exclusively characteristic of utilitarianism (which requires actual sentience as the necessary condition for an entity to count in moral considerations). Rawls and his followers (broadly understood, which includes Griffin and Gilabert), insofar as they require the possession of the range property or properties to the minimal sufficient extent, make the same mistake: they look for a 'justyfying' property of dignity that indeed does not need this type of justification.

The particular weight of the error connected to this thinking is that it *reverses the typical dignitarian order of deliberation regarding human persons.* Let us focus on the case of profound disabilities, as a litmus test for a more general account embracing all members of the human family. The capacity-centred account, of whatever variant, rests on an assumption that one is in a position to justify, on behalf of those with profound disabilities, their right to life, for example by saying that their actual condition meets the minimal threshold of sentience. If sentience is not decisive, then some other reasons to continue their life must be proven (Scanlon 1998, 103–7). If that position were to be taken seriously, it would mean, by logical consequence, that the person with profound disabilities bears the burden of proof. This is not how we normally think of humans, precisely because of their status of personhood, which is best understood as the axiom of practical considerations affecting persons. In 'normal' considerations of this kind, we feel obliged to justify any intrusion on the integrity, self-determination, and general standing of persons with whom we interact. This applies also in the urgent need for help, which is the situation which generally results in the moral, and sometimes legal, duty to provide that help. I see no reason to reverse that common attitude in the case of humans with profound disabilities. A similar account has been recently developed outside the personalist tradition. Again, I mean Jeremy Waldron, who seems to share some important insights with personalism. Carefully considering the case of the equality of individuals with profound disabilities, Waldron comes to the right conclusion that we have every reason to think alike in case of minor illness and severe impairments. Both flow from our common human condition, which is that of fragility. Such a conclusion is independent from an ultimate, metaphysical explanation of human nature, and is rooted in seeing human life as a continuum, which may always be interrupted by an unhappy event. As Waldron writes:

> Our capacities and our potential are in the first instance material and biological facts, even if they have spiritual and metaphysical significance (as in Kant's account or as in the religious account). This means that their growth is to be

> understood in the first instance as a biological process. They grow, they are nurtured, and they develop. What is true of growth of these capacities is true also of their decline and decay. . . .
>
> All of us are subject to the contingencies of illness, dementia, genetic failure, and consequent, more or less profound disability. The possibility of these failures and disabilities is part of the human condition.
>
> (Waldron 2017, 242–3)

This attitude can by accepted by the Status of Personhood Theory. Seeing humans as equal to oneself means seeing them as sharing in our common human condition, and possibly our fragile human nature. 'Accordingly', notes Waldron, 'the appropriate reflection on this fragility in the context of any given example of a person who is profoundly disabled must include the content *that could have been me*' (2017, 244, emphasis original). This remark should not be understood as a consideration of a rational calculus of individual advantage. Rather, by saying 'that could have been me', one asserts our common belonging to one human family, and that the profoundly disabled person 'is *one of us*' (2017, 244). Human family, as we here understand it, is not simply constituted by being born into one species. Rather, being a member of the human family means belonging to the world of persons that inherently have their own, personal subjectivity (which may be rooted in their nature but is discernible from it). This is *signified* by the fact of transcendence and integration, observable in the action of fully developed persons, as was elucidated by Wojtyła.

When one thinks in these terms, ascribing the status of personhood equally to all the members of 'the family' has nothing to do with surprise or supererogation; it is simply what a human – or perhaps, *a humane* society – should do. The profoundly disabled (independently of whether or not they are sentient) ought to be regarded as members of that society, who are entitled to special care, rather than exposed to arbitrary exclusion dependent on someone's value judgement. To be sure, this does not mean that the suffering involved in illness or disability does not count in moral and judicial deliberation. So far, I have not attempted to offer any complete bioethical account. Rather, I have been trying to articulate the proper initial position I consider necessary to arrive at correct and rightful judgements in the case of all members of the human family, including but not limited to the members burdened with illness or disability. The initial position alone does not yield judgement, especially in hard cases, but it certainly *excludes* some considerations. In particular, it excludes positions within which the burden of proof works against any member of the human family.

To sum up: At the very ultimate level, the PSP does not 'protect agency'. It also does not 'protect valuable capacities' in the general sense of everything that makes our life valuable enough to attribute dignity to it. In contrast, it protects concrete persons in their wholeness, in their particular internal and external conditions, and in their social involvements. And it does so without exceptions. This is the meaning of equal dignity that is considered the proper basic understanding, which is also helpful in adjudication. With this understanding considered fixed, we can now move to more detailed principles of adjudication.

2.3 Hard cases and easy cases: toward a theory of error

Having elucidated the deeply egalitarian meaning of the PSP, we can now move on to specify further how this principle is to be applied in adjudication. For reasons set forth in Section 2.1, we will have to consider the issue of hard cases separately from easy cases. Our specification will have to be sketchy and should be understood as a framework for possible further developments. Along with some positive guidelines, I will concentrate on the *errors* that a judge can make in adjudicating cases involved with human dignity understood as the status of personhood.

As far as the positive guidelines are concerned, some of them can be drawn for both easy and hard cases, and I will set them forth now. The first suggestion is that referring to natural human personhood is indispensable when trying to grasp the meaning of human dignity in adjudication. The PSP refers to dignitarian interests (freedom from degradation, self-determination, and integration being the most important three), but also refers to the standing of the human person in joint actions with others (that is, in participation). This standing is the foundation of the social-ethical solidarity, as well as legal-political fellowship. If 'human dignity' is understood as the PSP, then judges should interpret the clauses that refer to human dignity as signs of the special concern that is required for human person as such, in the very concreteness of the conditions of individuals or groups. At the same time, it is not an 'arbitrary' imposition on the law of a metaphysical doctrine or a contestable conception of the good. The crucial importance of basic political-legal standing comes with the praxiological (pre-ethical) phenomenological analysis of action, participation, and the human person who is the first subject of law. The second, more technical suggestion is that human dignity in the law – the status of personhood – is a simple legal characteristic, which is why it has been described as the status-expressing principle. This means that *respect for the status of personhood* of the persons involved (the direct obligation that the PSP yields) can be distinguished from *effective affirmation of the particular person*, that is, the adequate normative response to the basic status of that person. It is important for public officials, including judges, to discern whether their job in a given case is the former, the latter, or both.

2.3.1 Easy cases: freedom from degradation

It is time to focus our attention on easy cases. The first question that comes to mind is whether any adjudication evoking human dignity can ever be considered easy. I believe that the affirmative answer is justified. Although human dignity often appears as a heuristic principle which favours one of the two competing interpretations of the law in hard cases, it may also play a role in assessing the facts of a case in which the applicable rule is relatively clear. It should be remembered that easy cases are not necessarily trivial. As Neil MacCormick compellingly argues, it is the logical form – the deductive character of judicial argumentation involved – which makes them easy. At the same time, as I have indicated, easy cases may require *difficult* evaluative judgements. In my view, the judicial application of the PSP is like this when the basic recognition of the status of personhood is at stake. The particularly important dignitarian interest at play here is *freedom from degradation*. It is threatened when one of the elements of the PSP, or the PSP as a whole, is radically and directly ignored or violated by unlawful conduct. The denial of the PSP is tantamount to treating the human person in question as subhuman, a mere number, a non-human. An instructive example comes from the case heard by the International Criminal Tribunal for the Former Yugoslavia, *Prosecutor v. Furundzija*, quoted previously in Chapter 1. In the context of judging war crimes connected to sexual abuse, the Tribunal held that 'the forced penetration of the mouth by the male sexual organ constitutes a most humiliating and degrading attack upon human dignity', which justifies classifying this behaviour as rape (1998, 183). This was said in the context of some jurisdictions differentiating that particular type of unlawful behaviour as a sexual assault less grave than rape (1998, 182). In this case, the court used human dignity – the PSP applies here as the principle helping in evaluative judgements – in order to eradicate any doubts about legally classifying the outrageous behaviour as rape, recognising its gravest character. The positive guideline that comes from this could be formulated in the following way: *Always be sensitive to genuine degradation, the denial of the status of every person involved in your judgement*. Failing this may lead to degradation, a form of cruelty, or, in less dramatic scenarios, to ignorance, the distinguishing feature of indecent law.

Now, what about the negative guidelines? What errors can be committed in easy cases concerning the PSP? In my view, inaccuracy can happen on both extreme sides of recognising freedom from degradation: On the one hand, one may fail to notice a real deprivation of the basic status, and on the other, one may become oversensitive and regard any infringement of rights or interest, or even the mere potential of such, as equivalent to denying that basic status. As an example of the latter situation, one could recall the famous *Omega* case, heard by the Court of Justice of the European Union (the CJEU) in the procedure of preliminary ruling, put forward by the German Federal Administrative Court. The CJEU allowed the German authorities to hold the ban[11] put on laser games which involved 'playing at killing' (2004). The acceptance of the ban constituted an exception to a fundamental principle of EU law, namely, the freedom to provide services across the borders of member states. Omega, the operating company, was running similar 'killing simulation games' in the United Kingdom (an EU member back then). According to the principle of freedom to provide services within the EU across borders, the games should have been allowed in

11 Speaking more technically and accurately, the CJEU provided an interpretation of the EU law which allowed the German Federal Administrative Court to uphold the ban. This is what the procedure of preliminary ruling consists in, in the EU law.

Germany, too. However, the CJEU stated that the protection of human dignity, the foundational constitutional principle in Germany, justified the banning, as a reaction within limits of proportionality, that is, with regard to the principles and aims of the German Basic Law (Court of Justice of the European Union 2004, 36–8).

The case as a whole was perhaps more complicated, as it also concerned the relations between EU law and the law of respective member states, as well as the interpretation of the proportionality principle in limiting fundamental freedoms. The reasoning I want to isolate, however, is quite simple and deductive. Namely, as it can be reconstructed, the court said that if (i) human dignity shall not be infringed, and (ii) killing simulation games infringe human dignity, then (iii) the ban on killing simulations games is legitimate (2004, 34). The CJEU accepted that this may not be recognised equally in all member states; the particularity of the strong adherence in Germany to inalienable human dignity should be acknowledged.

In my view, there are strong arguments to contend that the evaluative judgement behind this reasoning was oversensitive. In particular, the CJEU agreed with the German Federal Administrative Court, saying:

> The referring court [the German Federal Administrative Court] states that human dignity is a constitutional principle which may be infringed either by the degrading treatment of an adversary, which is not the case here, or by the awakening or strengthening in the player of an attitude denying the fundamental right of each person to be acknowledged and respected, such as the representation, as in this case, of fictitious acts of violence for the purposes of a game. It states that a cardinal constitutional principle such as human dignity cannot be waived in the context of an entertainment, and that, in national law, the fundamental rights invoked by Omega cannot alter that assessment.
>
> (Court of Justice of the European Union 2004, 12)

In this passage the court invoked appeals to 'awakening and strengthening an attitude' which results in denying the fundamental right to respect due to every human. However, it may be argued that the criteria of having (or not having) such an attitude are extremely vague, especially in the judicial context. Even if we agreed on what forming such an attitude exactly means, it would certainly turn out to depend heavily on the individual character of the person concerned, as well as on the context of the situation. If this were really to be taken seriously, then a lot of what appears in the media, many computer games, or even a lot of day-to-day social situations could be banned as potentially forming a bad attitude toward some persons, or humanity in general. I am not questioning the status of hate speech here, for example. But I urge a rethinking of the position taken by the courts in *Omega*, given the possibility of such opinions being simply oversensitive. A similar thought can be found in the German legal system too. In judging paintball games (which is another way of 'playing at killing') the Bavarian Administrative Court stated that 'a violation of human dignity . . . comes into consideration if . . . actions call fundamentally into question the human quality of being a subject, and this deed is an expression of the contempt for the value of the human being, which comes with his personal existence [*der ihm Kraft seines Personseins zukommt*] (Bavarian Administrative Court 2012, 33, translation by the author). This is an attitude to which the SPT could adhere – it provides a proper understanding of the strong violations of the PSP. It means that the infringement, if it is to count as a genuine violation of human dignity, should consist in sincere questioning or denying someone's status of personhood, with the real possibility of harm done to that basic standing of any human person. In this context, *Omega* walks a fine line between sensitive and ridiculous.

Let us now turn to the other extreme. The grave example of law's ignorance, that is, legal activity arbitrarily denying the consideration of the status of personhood, is – as I will argue – present in the landmark abortion decision of the Supreme Court of the United States, namely, *Roe v. Wade* (1973). I will not recall the complexities of this case, which, taken as a whole, may be regarded as a hard case within the Fourteenth Amendment jurisprudence. In short, the Texas restrictive anti-abortion legislation was struck down as unconstitutional, chiefly on the basis of the right to privacy – then declared to be covered by the Fourteenth Amendment – enjoyed by every potential mother. What is of my interest here is the fundamental error of refusing to even consider the status of personhood of some prenatal humans (that is, the unborn human beings who are not yet viable outside the womb). This should be distinguished from arguing about the details and scope of the right to life at the prenatal stage, a complex issue which I will not attempt to resolve here. What I argue is, however, that the Supreme Court in *Roe* did not have a chance to resolve it either, because of the grave error it committed. The particular gravity consists here in treating a complex, philosophically loaded issue as if it were a legally easy one. The Court simply refused to take into account the unborn, at least within the Fourteenth Amendment (Supreme Court of the United States 1973, 158). The Court motivated its decision by recalling the fact that 'the unborn have never been recognised in the law as persons in the whole sense' (1973, 162), and that 'the unborn' does not appear in the wording of the Constitution (1973, 157). Moreover, the Court said:

> Texas urges that, apart from the Fourteenth Amendment, life begins at conception and is present throughout pregnancy, and that, therefore, the State has a compelling interest in protecting that life from and after conception. We need not resolve the difficult question of when life begins. When those trained in the respective disciplines of medicine, philosophy, and theology are unable to arrive at any consensus, the judiciary, at this point in the development of man's knowledge, is not in a position to speculate as to the answer. (1973, 159)

As we can see in this passage, the Court assumed that it ought not to impose any philosophical views on the law – since there is a multiplicity of competing theories regarding the unborn human life, the Court should restrain from relying on any of these theories in adjudication. An obvious problem, which I will not press any further, is that the Court in fact did adopt a theory denying human life to a foetus, for the purposes of the constitutional law at least. Although the declared position was to abstain from speculation, the theory adopted tacitly by the court seems to have contended something quite substantial and controversial – that there was nobody, legally speaking, worthy of protection before viability. Another tacit premise here is that it was within the power of the Supreme Court to define who counts as a human person in the eyes of the law, and consequently, to make the unborn human life before viability a legal 'zero' (Noonan 1984, 673).

It is rather uncontroversial (and this knowledge was already available in 1973) that a separate organism, a developing whole with a unique DNA, begins to 'live' (at least in the sense of a structured development that is not random) at the moment of conception. Even if one thinks of conception in terms of a process, it seems obvious that a new organism is alive once the process has been completed. However – and it remains beyond the scope of what science can tell – it is debatable, or at least debated, whether the human person, or a genuinely human life, begins at the very same moment. Some would strongly oppose this claim, on the basis that human life becomes human with sentience, or self-awareness, or something else they deem decisive. The personalist conception, however, *gives reasons to equate the organic human life with the life of the person*. As we may recall, the bodily aspect of human existence in general was included into the personal sphere. The somatic integration was recognised as marking the human person as such, and was thereby strongly related to the integration of the person in action (see Chapter 2). Moreover, the capacity for action, a sign of dignity, was depicted as a radical capacity, that is, the capacity that is 'at the root' of one's being, rather than a mere possibility of doing one thing or another acquired through socialisation or social recognition. One could argue, then, that the irreducible subjectivity of personhood is not attached to the conscious acts of a fully developed person any more strongly than it is attached to the organic functioning of a human being with a DNA code, which is already present in prenatal life.

The problem that I want to emphasise, however, does not directly depend on the issue of when human life begins or how we conceptualise personhood as opposed to 'bare life' (although I personally do not believe that this is a justified opposition). In the perspective of the SPT, the failure of the U.S. Supreme Court did not consist in simply failing to recognise the facts (those available in 1973) of early development of the human being. Also, my argument does not rely on the claim that a human embryo should be recognised as a fully-fledged legal person. According to the ideal of decent law, the court's error was to completely ignore the status of personhood in the *normative* sense, as a principle – the principle that should have been respected in struggling to provide a thorough, reasonable adjudication of the case heard. I am obviously not claiming that the Supreme

Court should have used the PSP, calling it by name and declaring it as an implicit part of the Constitution. Such a claim would indeed reduce the SPT as a whole to absurdity. What I do claim is the following, and this is how the *implicit* character of the PSP should be understood: Any careful adjudicative decision and argumentation, whatever final shape it would have taken, should respect the developing life of an embryo. Independently of what the foetus really is, the PSP urges us to take into account a developing human life. In the context of any public order generally protecting human life with no explicit exclusion of the unborn in the legal text, such an exclusion is arbitrary and in contradiction with human dignity. The indecent character of *Roe v. Wade* was therefore to completely fail to respect or account for the possible bond between the human organism, its normal development, and the life of the person, whatever that bond may really be in detail. If dignity is not attached to any particular capacity but rather to the person as a whole, then any attempt to find a point in time before which one is free to deny that human life has a weight must be considered ignorance. After *Roe v. Wade*, a systemic degradation of some human beings at the constitutional level has become at least a possibility.

This strong claim is not tantamount to concrete postulates regarding the shape of the abortion law in the United States or anywhere else. The legal issue of abortion, to be resolved either through adjudication or through legislation, is a paradigm hard case, involving weighing the competing values and principles of high priority. Although the Court declared that the state may have competing interests, including the protection of the unborn life (1973, 155), there is no sign of any genuine weighing of the protection of life on the one hand and privacy on the other, in the opinion of the Court. Rather, as the dissenting opinion of Justice White claims, after *Roe*, 'people and the legislatures of the 50 States are constitutionally disentitled to weigh the relative importance of the continued existence and development of the fetus' (Supreme Court of the United States 1973, Justice White, dissenting). The PSP encourages dialogue, with the reservation that the interest of the unborn must not be simply ignored in such debates, just as the well-being and equal status of pregnant women, especially in burdensome health conditions, must also be considered.

To sum up, the Court in *Roe* excluded the life of the unborn from constitutional recognition, and did so without any proper weighing. This is a dignitarian fallacy in evaluative judgement which consists in ignoring degradation. The other extreme, exemplified by *Omega*, consists in the court being oversensitive, conflating mere potential for misbeliefs regarding human worth with serious and real degradation – deprivation of status. Both extremes are fallacies committed in 'easy' cases, that is, in a deductive reasoning backed up by evaluative judgement. According to the PSP, proper evaluative judgement (which requires prudence on the side of the judges) is indispensable for the substantive (as opposed to the formal) correctness of otherwise legitimate reasoning. The litmus test for such cases is provided by the personalist meaning of equal dignity, that is, the equality of the status of personhood. The application of dignity is erroneous when it contributes to a distortion of the equality of status rather than trying to restore it.

2.3.2 Hard cases: paternalism

As I said, *Roe v. Wade* taken as whole is a hard case, although the Supreme Court's fallacious evaluative judgement treated it as if it were an easy one. Following MacCormick, hard cases are ones in which a deductive reasoning does not suffice to justify the decision. What is needed is an *interpretative* judgement, which involves weighing of applicable legal principles and values which stand in tension, or even plainly in conflict, in a given case. It thus requires a choice among competing and *prima facie* equally plausible interpretations of the law. In this section, I am going to examine what the PSP requires, or how it may help in such cases. To anticipate, as an overall account, I will argue that the PSP as an isolated principle *says less* than is sometimes expected from human dignity in the law. In particular, I will oppose treating the PSP (and more broadly, human dignity in the law) as some kind of 'magic box' containing all the answers one requires to justify a hard case. The PSP guides interpretative judgements, it is certainly true. Its function, however, is limited to safeguarding the equal basic status of personhood that all human persons enjoy before the law.

I will first be occupied with the problem of paternalism. That problem is crucial not only because it comes directly from the tensions internal to the PSP itself, but also because it helps indicate what I take to be the correct understanding of the basic status expressed by this principle. As mentioned previously in this book, human dignity is sometimes used as a justification for paternalistic government interventions, restricting the legal freedom of choice. This is in tension with other applications of human dignity, in which it establishes and permeates the body of basic liberties. The latter is most probably prevailing in the post-UDHR legal world. The PSP absorbs this tension: On the one hand, it says that every adult human person of sound mind is entitled to become author and master of his own conduct and life by exercising free choice; on the other, it understands human self-determination as subordinated to truth, as well as to social concerns of equality in basic status. How can these two tendencies be reconciled?

Some have interpreted paternalistic decisions as depending on an objective standard of 'dignified behaviour', for example, pertaining to sexuality (Botha 2009, 203). Others have regarded dignitarian paternalism as 'a revival of an ancient, rank-based conception of dignity', which is no longer attached to members of higher classes, but rather to humanity in general (Hennette-Vauchez 2011, 38). These and analogous interpretations are suspicious toward paternalism as possibly undermining the position of the individual who was supposed to be protected by human dignity clauses. According to these worries, paternalism may impose contestable standards or values on individual agents (Rosen 2013, 149–53), or even, paradoxically, question their inherent and inalienable dignity by attaching it to rank (Hennette-Vauchez 2011, 57). The SPT takes a less suspicious view. As mentioned in Chapter 3, my theory regards some paternalistic uses as legitimate, which largely follows from the fact that one of the protected dignitarian interests is self-determination, distinguished from self-control and autonomy. Self-determination means choosing goals and values in conscience, that is, with reference to the relevant truths. The agent is responsive to truth, and therefore can be held responsible for her conduct. Self-determination is thereby attached to responsibility, which includes responsibility for oneself – one's condition, situation, and status. According to the SPT, the litmus test for admissibility of dignitarian paternalism in the law is *the status itself.* Dignitarian paternalism so conceived is not simply acting against somebody's will for his own good, or the quasi-aesthetic quality of dignity in character and conduct. It is, rather, an intervention of public authorities in order to maintain either *someone's own basic status*, or, at a minimum, the equality of the status enjoyed by persons generally.

Numerous examples from the law could be evoked. Since we have discussed the controversial French 'dwarf-tossing' in previous chapters, I will use this as the paradigm case. To recall, the Council of State (the supreme administrative tribunal in France) upheld a ban on 'dwarf-tossing' competitions. The ban was considered to be a justified intervention in defence of public order, and in particular of human dignity as part thereof.[12] One of the participants, a person of short stature used as a missile in the competition, strongly objected to the ban as depriving him of the occupation he had freely chosen. How would the SPT respond to worries that the real self-determination of the consenting participant was sacrificed for the abstract ideal of human dignity? First, let us reconsider the case by tentatively *suspending the fact of clear consent.* Let us imagine that the dwarf-tossing competition was not a planned show preceded by signing a contract, but, say, a spontaneous development of events when a party in a club has gotten out of control. Let us further assume that no direct compulsion was involved (although the facts of consent were at least not clear) and no physical harm was done. It seems reasonable to say that such a situation disturbs the public order, despite the lack of physical harm or compulsion, precisely because certain persons of an exceptionally short stature *were presented and used in an undignified manner.* The problem here is not only an abstract 'negative attitude' which could allegedly have been induced by a laser game in *Omega* (in 'playing at killing'). The tossing competition physically turns people suffering from a genetic disorder into living missiles, that is, into objects thrown at a target, and thereby violates the bodily integrity of such passive participants. Thus, it is possible, although it certainly would depend on the particulars of our modified case, that the person with dwarfism could be entitled to compensation for breaching his bodily integrity, one of the focal dignitarian interests. This paternalistic usage of dignity in administrative law, then, does not necessarily differ from its other applications simply by virtue of objectively defining certain types of conduct as degrading or otherwise contrary to human dignity. The same

12 One could argue that the dwarf-tossing case is, in fact, an easy case since it involves a simple deductive argument; Rosen (2013, 151) would suggest this. In my view, the case is hard because it involves judgement with regard to public order as a whole – it requires an ordering and weighing of values inherent to the public order, with liberty or autonomy being certainly one of its central commitments. The Council of State upholding the ban must have implicitly asserted that the concern with human dignity outweighs individual autonomy and freedom to provide entertainment services.

kind of assessment is done when defining rape as rape or torture as torture. The peculiarity of dignitarian paternalism consists rather in accepting that an individual may voluntarily act against their own dignity, and legal bodies are authorised to intervene. By definition, every such case must be a hard one, since it must justify why, in a particular case, public intervention outweighs the *prima facie* strong duty to respect individual self-determination. In order to defend paternalism in terms of the SPT, and find the constraints thereto, one should explain in what sense an individual can misrepresent, and voluntarily act against, her own status.

The heart of the problem lies in assessing the weight of consent. It certainly has great power within law, transforming theft into a donation, for example, or rape into ordinary sexual intercourse. However, if human dignity in the law expressed nothing but respect for consensual relations, it would be redundant, as inseparable from liberty. I have sought to demonstrate that self determination is not the whole story behind human dignity. As I argued, the status of personhood is a simple legal characteristic of every (human) person. Despite being simple, that characteristic requires multiple and multifarious responses. The PSP certainly calls for fostering individual freedom, but this is only one action within a wide range of possible actions that are legitimate or required with reference to the status of personhood. Under certain circumstances, respecting it may involve simply supporting one's biological functioning (in case of a car crash victim), or arranging for *compulsory* education (in case of minors). As Pablo Gilabert rightly suggests, not everything that human dignity norms are concerned with is covered by the exercise of free choice (2018, 147). But I am inclined to go even further than that: Nothing in the wording of the PSP suggest that rights are the only possible legal form in which that principle takes effect. Precisely because the SPT explicates human dignity as basic *status*, there is no contradiction in attributing not only rights, but also duties based on the same principle. The status of a parent, for example, yields certain rights and certain duties at the same time. Likewise, the equal status of personhood may generate duties and responsibilities, along with the familiar catalogue of human rights. One such duty is to maintain one's own status, that is, to abstain from conduct that systematically and seriously undermines it. In other words, one is generally not entitled to act as if one did not actually have the status of personhood. This is a strong reason for deeming the public intervention in the dwarf-tossing case legitimate.

Granted, the paternalistic use of the PSP should be generally assessed, and possibly justified, with a view to maintaining the basic status of persons. Human trafficking is an obvious example of the public duty to intervene. As noted in Chapter 1, it is a practice that is normally prosecuted even if the persons being 'traded' are consenting (perhaps even paying to arrange the trafficking), precisely because the context in which that practice is being organised and pursued is degrading – the human persons are systemically treated as subhuman, or as commodities. More controversial cases are also in place. Some of them come with the issues attached to the delicate sphere of sexuality and liberty within that sphere. In the already-mentioned Canadian case, *R v. Butler*, the Supreme Court upheld anti-pornography legislation, despite the fact that the persons involved expressed their consent to participate in the production of scenes containing violent sexual behaviour. The court stated that

> in the appreciation of whether material is degrading or dehumanizing, the appearance of consent is not necessarily determinative. Consent cannot save materials that otherwise contain degrading or dehumanizing scenes. Sometimes the very appearance of consent makes the depicted acts even more degrading or dehumanizing.
>
> (Supreme Court of Canada 1992, 479)

Although it may be tempting to say that the Court was simply imposing a sexual morality on the law, this is not necessarily the case. Similar to the human trafficking scenario, some practices concerning the production of obscene material may be degrading to the models involved in the process, depicting them as if they were not persons entitled to respect for their own sake. The purchase and distribution of such material may also be a serious threat to safeguarding the equality of status in a given society, just as open and legalised exploitation of forced labour would certainly be. The argument for dignitarian paternalism in the case of a pornography ban, therefore, does not boil down to the abstract dignity of humanity, nor does it boil down to merely keeping the social standards of sexual practices. Under certain circumstances (including, arguably, the circumstances of *Butler*), the dignity of the models themselves is what crucially matters. Being engaged in depicting violent sexual behaviour that would be assessed as degrading by a reasonable third party may outweigh the entitlement to self-determination that everyone normally enjoys. In this vein, one could argue that the models act contrary to their own status of personhood when consenting to depict violent sexual behaviour. Public authorities are arguably in the position to maintain that status as part of the public order, and thus intervene. In sum, according to the PSP, the denial – including self-denial – of someone's basic status is the threshold above which self-determination may be outweighed by paternalistic concerns.

What possible errors are attached to the paternalistic usage of the PSP? It certainly requires a lot of prudence from judges, given the fact that it often touches upon delicate spheres of human life. One possible error is, again, oversensitivity. We could imagine judges acting similarly to *Omega*, delegalising any practices which contain even a slight trace of denying basic status. Their judgement can be considered erroneous insofar as these 'traces' are not enough to outweigh the general entitlement to self-determination. A similar yet distinguishable error would be to impute one's personal views, or maybe even views generally held in a society, to what is required by an ideally dignified behaviour. A lot of ordinary human practices could be considered 'below human dignity' in the sense of not living up to the ideal. In such cases, however, one rather approves some form of 'dignitarian virtue' or moral integrity attached to one's dignity as a human person. While acting against virtue or lacking moral integrity may and perhaps should meet *moral* condemnation, it certainly does not suffice to justify a paternalistic *legal* intervention. Only the systemic and sincere denials of the status of personhood, connected to the real harm to equality of that status, properly justify a paternalistic adjudicative decision.

Each case certainly involves a separate, careful scrutiny and prudent judgement according to the circumstances. What may help in arriving at such prudent judgement is the assessment of infringement of bodily integrity. For instance, the important difference between *Omega* (the laser 'killing game' case) and the ban on dwarf-tossing imposed by the French Council of State is that the latter involved using some human persons *physically* as missiles, displaying to the public their genetically short stature. This undermined their bodily integrity (although with prior consent), as well as, arguably, their equality of status. The latter consists in the fact that the short persons are not players, but are used for the purposes of the game. One may thus argue that while paternalism in the dwarf-tossing case is legitimate, it is not in *Omega*. The latter case does not influence (but rather presupposes) bodily integrity. Although 'playing at killing' may be considered contrary to the dignitarian *virtue*, it does not seriously threaten the equality of basic dignitarian *status*. The decency of law focuses on the latter.

2.3.3 Hard cases of life and death: a challenge for the PSP

The important lesson we learned from the prior discussion is the peculiar way in which the status of personhood is conceived within the SPT. It is not something that can be lost through social, political, or legal deprivation. It does not ultimately depend on social or legal recognition, although it calls for it and, in a sense, 'needs' it to manifest itself fully. It is true that the status of personhood is attributed to human persons via manifold legal protections. However, if judges fail to provide them to some individuals, it does not automatically mean that the law has revoked the basic status. In such cases, the law is, rather, showing ignorance and thus becoming indecent. Therefore, the PSP is an implicit principle that is binding upon public authority in a unique way: Legal activity (including judicial activity) should take the status of personhood into account, because otherwise there will be some persons that can reasonably claim (for themselves, or in the name of someone else) that the law has fallen into fundamental indecency. This is different from simply saying that law has some moral or technical flaws. The imperfection that is at stake in the case of indecency is fundamental; it calls into question the very legitimacy of a legal activity. This means that the status of personhood is something that can be *denied or infringed* by various agents, including public authorities, or even by the bearers of dignity themselves. The inalienable (and inviolable, in the postulate-normative sense) dignity may be, and frequently has been, violated by means of law's ignorance as well. In extreme cases, the individuals themselves may misrepresent their own dignity and either degrade themselves or ignore their own basic status, which is a legitimate cause for public intervention.

Importantly, the entitlement to dignitarian legal protections is not conditioned by metaphysical beliefs regarding what human persons ultimately are. For example, whether or not human persons really have immortal souls is irrelevant at the level of our present analysis. Their overall rank in the hierarchy of beings, if there is such an objective hierarchy, is also not of direct relevance. What matters at our level of theoretical analysis are the capacities of persons, and the dignitarian standing that is their correlate. The capacities (and legal interests following them) are, however, merely signs or indicators of dignity. Dignity in its most essential meaning is an axiom of legal activity that urges everyone to respond to the status of personhood, as circumstances and the scope of authority permit. If you agree that this is metaphysically parsimonious, then not only the easy cases that combat degradation, but also some hard cases, such as the paternalistic interventions just discussed, can be resolved in a metaphysically parsimonious manner. Recall that my justification of paternalism depends neither on convictions regarding the high rank of humanity as such, nor on a vision of what a dignified human life consists of. Rather, keeping the minimalist track, paternalistic intervention is justified when individual conduct seriously threatens the basic status itself – and hence distorts the basis of proper relations between persons mediated by the law. The centrality of status and metaphysical parsimony are even more obvious in easy cases of combating degradation. The great debates regarding the ultimate fate and meaning of humanity lose urgency in the face of human trafficking or war crimes. People holding otherwise extremely different worldviews will combat human trafficking together, in perfect accord. The SPT's explanation of this is that they all implicitly share a commitment to the status of personhood.

In this section, I admit that such metaphysical parsimony and minimalism does not always suffice in dignity adjudication, and sometimes will not produce consensus. The troublesome nature of hard cases within dignity jurisprudence consists in the reality that sometimes judges are put in a position that may, in fact, engage metaphysical presuppositions or require comprehensive moral judgement regarding the good, or regarding the fundamental moral duties of persons. At least in Western jurisdictions, these factors are commonly considered problematic in adjudication, unless the law itself urges or invites the judges to employ them. The problems generated by human dignity come from the fact that many explicit provisions evoking 'dignity' may reasonably be, and indeed have been, considered such an invitation. But in fact, the situation is even worse: Remaining silent is very often tantamount, in practical terms, to taking a particular (possibly partisan) stance, as we have seen in our analysis of *Roe v. Wade*. This is a real trouble for the SPT, especially because it claims that the PSP is a *cosmopolitan* principle. The question of possible clashes between competing metaphysical and comprehensive moral views, as well as particular legal traditions and constitutional identities, becomes even more pressing.

I have already touched upon the issue of abortion law in the previous section, so I will engage with it once more in order to illustrate the problem that hard cases pose to the SPT. In *Roe v. Wade*, the U.S. Supreme Court refused to take into account the standing of the foetus and granted pregnant women a right to privacy shaped in a way that authorises decisions regarding termination of early pregnancy. Let us now set aside the fundamental flaw of ignorance that I talked about in the previous section, and reconsider the meaning implicitly given to dignity in this judgement. This is certainly a meaning closely attached to the reproductive autonomy of a pregnant woman. As already mentioned in Chapter 1, the subsequent and similarly seminal judgement, *Planned Parenthood v. Casey*, confirmed the precedent stipulated in *Roe*, adding the dignitarian argumentation of the autonomist sort. According to the majority opinion in *Casey*, choices regarding family life and reproduction are intimate and personal, thereby connected not only to autonomy (freedom), or privacy, but also to dignity itself (Supreme Court of the United States 1992, 916).

If we leave the United States for a moment, and examine analogous judgements in continental Europe, we will find completely different concretisations of dignity. A widely known example comes from the Federal Constitutional Court of Germany, which presented a clearly opposite view regarding dignity in its first abortion judgement in 1975 (not far in time from *Roe*). The German Court invalidated a 1974 statute liberalising abortion. As a result of this judgement, criminal sanctions for termination of pregnancy in most cases, except direct threats to the health or life of the pregnant woman, were upheld.[13] Justifying the decision, the Court affirmed the fundamental right to life, explicitly guaranteed by Article 2 of the German Basic Law, contending that the constitutional protection of 'the most fundamental and most original human right' is granted also to the unborn human life (Federal Constitutional Court of Germany 1975). To defend this position, the court engaged the dignitarian argument. This was quite natural and straightforward in the German context – the Basic Law starts with the human dignity provision giving structure to the constitutional order as a whole. In particular, the Court held that human life as such is followed by dignity: 'Where human life exists, human dignity is present to it; it is not decisive that the bearer of this dignity himself be conscious of it and know personally how to preserve it' (Federal Constitutional Court of Germany 1975, quoted in Jonas and Gorby 1976, 641). This was not a moral or metaphysical claim. The Court contended that its ruling was deeply embedded in 'an objective ordering of values', stipulated by the fundamental constitutional principles inherent to the Basic Law (Jonas and Gorby 1976, 642). The German case was certainly a hard case requiring a careful balancing, especially the rights and dignity of pregnant women, which the Court provided, at least to some extent.[14]

It is obvious that in deciding *Roe*, and especially in confirming its general framework in *Casey*, the U.S. Supreme Court applied dignitarian concerns in completely the reverse manner. The idea that human prenatal life could be endowed with dignity and a self-authenticating entitlement to protection seems to be completely alien to the Court, at least to the Fourteenth Amendment jurisprudence. It is remarkable that the dissenting opinions in *Roe* and *Casey* did not

13 For some detail and background, see Kommers (1994, 4–7).

14 Reva Siegel criticises this decision, saying that it failed to balance the right to life against 'deliberative autonomy' of women (2013, 514). However, there was some balancing in place (see Kommers 1994, 8).

seriously question the central claim of the majority opinion in *Roe*, according to which a foetus is not a person (and thus enjoys no dignitarian standing, one should add). Nothing even close to the German constitutional duty to protect life was suggested (albeit individual states may turn out to have an *interest* in such protection). For instance, Justice Stevens, partly dissenting with the majority in *Casey*, wrote that 'Roe is an integral part of a correct understanding of both the concept of liberty and the basic equality of men and women'. According to Stevens, 'a developing organism that is not yet a "person" does not have what is sometimes described as a "right to life"'. Justice Stevens accepts this contention as 'a fundamental premise of our constitutional law governing reproductive autonomy' (Supreme Court of the United States 1992, Justice Stevens dissenting). Even the dissenting opinions in *Roe* (Justice Rehnquist and Justice White) did not speak in the duty-to-protect-life manner. Rather, they suggested that the complicated issue of protecting unborn life, and the ordering of competing values involved in this, should be removed from the federal-constitutional level. According to the dissents, it should be left to democratic processes in the individual states. No guidance for these processes was provided by the Court, which most probably comes from the American constitutional architecture securing the relative autonomy of the states. The fate of (anti-)abortion law in Germany was quite different. Although the subsequent judgement was issued in 1993, the essential commitments of dignity and right to life remained intact from the 1975 ruling. Abortion remained formally illegal, although the threat of criminal sanctions was made considerably weaker, or even apparent – counselling and waiting periods were enough to avoid the illegality of abortion (Kommers 1994, 15–25).[15] Although the social views and practices have changed over the years into a much more abortion-friendly environment, the German constitutional law still expresses respect for the unborn human life at least in principle.[16]

Now, it is tempting to claim that such strong normative discord between the United States and Germany indicates something that undermines the feasibility of any attempts to find a cosmopolitan dignitarian principle, especially in the practice of adjudication. It is important to note that the American and German legal systems may be far from one another, but at least they belong to one Western culture, broadly understood. The picture would become even more troubling if we left that relatively safe area. This may be a fatal problem, excluding the PSP from play, or at least rendering it a political or moral principle that has at best an indirect effect on law. One could thus argue, following McCrudden's placeholder argument mentioned in Chapter 1, that a dignity-based legal reasoning becomes intelligible only within a particular community and interpretative tradition (McCrudden 2008, 723). Along these lines, one could say that the strongly autonomist understanding adopted in the United States reflects its

15 Siegel emphasises that the perception of women changed into more respect for her ability to make a conscientious decision (2013, 517)

16 Official statistics report nearly 200,000 abortions in Germany in 2020 (Statista 2021).

liberal legal culture, while the peculiar position of dignity in the German Basic Law follows the German experience with Nazi atrocities, as well as the Christian background which was quite important in 1975 West Germany. Consequently, one could argue that the dignity provisions serve only as signifiers of vague political and moral aspirations of peoples or states – the determinate content feasible for adjudication is always produced along the way. This is a fairly sceptical position, but the scepticism can be even more radical. Friedrich Toepel claims in a recent paper that judges who incorporate moral norms of dignity into their legal reasoning inevitably commit a logical fallacy. According to Toepel, the inference from (the existence of) a norm in one system to (the existence of) another norm in another system is as illicit as the more familiar and straightforward derivation of norms from facts (Toepel 2021, 187). Thus, in applying 'dignity' as a legal norm which takes its content from Christian ethics, for example, or liberal secular ethics, judges make a fallacious crossing between normative systems. There are many good reasons to disagree with Toepel.[17] The least controversial one is that when a legislator explicitly refers to dignity, perhaps using only the word with some additional characteristics ('inalienable' or 'inherent', for example), he seems to authorise judges to determine its meaning, and that must somehow relate to moral or metaphysical contentions. Even when no explicit reference to dignity is made in the legal text, the judge, arguably, may acknowledge its implicit presence in law's fabric, although that is much more controversial. Setting that disagreement aside, another of Toepel's claims is certainly hard to deny – judicial engagement with dignity produces practical problems, because '[u]niversal acceptance of a certain meaning cannot be taken for granted on account of the variation of moral codes from one society to another' (2021, 190). According to Toepel, hard cases emerge because even universally accepted principles tend to produce disagreement 'at the edges' (2021, 190). The cases of life and death certainly lie at these edges.

Unfortunately enough, the presence of human dignity in adjudication is too profound, and disagreement too likely to persist. It is therefore not reasonable to circumvent or ignore the problem of hard cases. Saying that dignity is given meaningful content only within particular jurisdictions will not suffice, simply because single legal communities are also almost never univocal with regard to dignitarian issues. Legal traditions, in themselves, also do not give guidance. They are rather 'bran tubs' – what will be taken out from the bran tub largely depends on the interpreter (Glenn 2010, 142). For instance, the historical background offered by the U.S. Supreme Court in *Roe v. Wade* is an example of a selective

17 For instance, one could argue that Toepel assumes certain controversial meta-ethical commitments, such as that there is a variety of moral systems that are on equal footing. For his reply to this charge, see Toepel (2021, 194–5). I doubt, however, whether 'moral systems' even exist in a way Toepel describes them, as merely sociological phenomena and complete systems of norms (many natural law theorists compellingly argue that natural law is not a system of norms, for example). Toepel's claim that moral systems 'see the world from their own perspective' (2021, 195), seems especially controversial in this regard.

interpretation of the tradition to support the pro-choice decision. Toepel's postulate to eradicate dignity from the law and particularly from adjudication does not help either, at least in the current circumstances of the growing rather than declining judicial interest in human dignity. One cannot change the direction of a river's flow with a stick, according to one old Polish proverb. But the STP as a whole claims that the growing interest *is not unfortunate* in itself. It has a reasonable and stable basis in the reality of persons. Regarded in this light, the judges' efforts in adjudicating dignity do not necessarily boil down to introducing either a contestable morality or a political agenda into law. Instead, one should regard these efforts as the recognition of everyone's equal status of personhood, along with the complexities of the person's life. This what the judges strive to take properly into account, when acting in good faith. The judges themselves may be regarded as the acting person trying to respond to truths about human persons – truths that are so fundamental that they do influence the shape and dynamics of law, even if unmentioned explicitly in the legal text. In order to do this job in a careful and legitimate manner, judges (and scholars) must cope with the normative indeterminacy of human dignity. I have been trying to provide a framework for this, and the next subsection will be my final word in this regard, as far as this book is concerned.

2.3.4 Towards a general framework for the adjudication applying the PSP

Let us first sum up what has been said so far. First, when the PSP is applied to adjudication, it serves as an indispensable component of justifying decisions that pertain to the basic dignitarian status. The justification of a judicial decision 'starts' from this principle, in the sense of the logical structure of an adjudicative decision. The PSP is often either implicit or functioning under the broader name of human dignity. A thorough adjudication takes this principle into account simply by taking into account the persons concerned. With the PSP at hand, the judge interprets the law and gives it a determinate content. Arriving at the decision is therefore preceded either by an *evaluative judgement* in easy cases, or by an *interpretative judgement* in the hard ones. What is common to hard and easy cases, when properly adjudicated, is the recognition of the status of personhood equal to all. Failing in these judgements or, even worse, being ignorant that they are required, a judicial interpretation becomes guilty of ignorance and thus indecency – or, at least, indecency may be reasonably claimed.

Now, according to the SPT, and the idea of decent law inherent to it, two types of situations should be discerned. In one type of situation – one could call it 'the basic dignitarian protection' – the judge *acknowledges* the status of personhood and *protects* the person at the basic level. In the other situation – let us call it 'the specific dignitarian protection' – the judge strives to acknowledge that status adequately or fully, that is, to *provide the best possible response*, in the situation of conflicting interpretations of law. My hypothesis is that while the basic dignitarian protection occurs in both hard and easy cases, the troubling and distinctive feature of hard cases is that they often require the best possible response to the status of personhood and specific dignitarian protection. At times, as illustrated by our discussion of paternalism, specific dignitarian protection can focus on the values of public order and somehow retain metaphysical and moral parsimony. Other cases, like the cases of life and death I touched upon in the previous subsection, inescapably open up the discourse to the truth about the nature of persons in the metaphysical sense, or the comprehensive account on the good and the moral duties of persons. Hard cases are, unfortunately enough, a space in which metaphysical and moral parsimony ceases to be easy, even though judges may be very reluctant to explicitly admit it.

The earlier clarification of possible configurations in which the PSP plays the crucial role, either called by the name of human dignity or not, may help us to approximate some general principles of dignity adjudication which may assist judges to cope with its normative indeterminacy.

First, the easy cases – the cases in which only the basic dignitarian protection is provided – do not produce major problems. The judge's job here is to combat degradation. What is required from the judge is thus the proper sensitivity allowing proper evaluative judgement, acknowledging that the degradation has taken place. The adjudicative decision aims at restoring basic status to the victims of degradation. Possible errors can consist of oversensitivity and seeing degradation everywhere, or, at the other extreme, making degradation go unnoticed. The evaluative judgement certainly requires some prudence from judges but does not produce tragic conflicts. The details would depend on the jurisdiction, but in most jurisdictions, judges should be able to refer to the hypothetical judgement of a reasonable third party functioning in the society in question. If such a reasonable third party would see degradation, the judge is also bound to see it.

Second, there come the hard cases (involving specific dignitarian protection) which can be resolved in a metaphysically and morally parsimonious way. They involve an interpretative judgement, but do not drag the interpreter into the most troubling moral and metaphysical questions regarding persons. Perhaps one could call this type of hard cases 'semi-hard', to distinguish from the other type on which I will focus in the next paragraph. The judicial activity in the 'semi-hard' cases assumes the recognition of personhood at the basic level, just like in the easy cases, but requires some additional consideration. This consideration is needed to adjudicate among the competing dignitarian interests. To illustrate the difference: the prosecution of human trafficking is an easy case of basic dignitarian protection because its job is to restore the basic status of victims which is questioned and violated *tout court* by that illicit practice. In contrast to that, the paternalistic intervention in the French dwarf-tossing case instantiates a hard case (and specific dignitarian protection) because the judges and officials had to reconcile at least two dignitarian interests in tension – self-determination on the one hand, and integrity of status on the other. Possible mistakes in such an adjudication may consist in failing to recognise some important dignitarian interest involved, at the expense of another. So, for example, the judge could overemphasise self-determination at the expense of the integrity and equality of status, or the other way round. The maintenance of proper and respectful relations in the society seems to be the final goal of such adjudication. Again, a hypothetical test of a reasonable third party can be helpful.

Third and finally, the heaviest cases involve the answers to the most troubling metaphysical and moral questions about the ultimate nature, fate, and duties of persons. Abortion is certainly one such case. We can label these 'the hard cases proper'. Here, the PSP taken in isolation is perhaps not completely hopeless, but the role it plays is considerably limited. It is crucial to understand that normative indeterminacy is not something to be completely removed from hard cases, especially from the hard cases proper. The interpretative judgement involved in them leaves, by the very nature of interpretation, certain discretion to judges. The justification of such a judgement is not tantamount to demonstration (such as this known in mathematics, for example). It is argumentative in nature: It reveals the reasons for a particular interpretation, despite the fact that additional reasons may always enter, and the weighing of reasons may be different. In my view, many overuses of dignity in adjudication come from failing to reflect upon the limits of dignity and take them into account. The SPT acknowledges these limits, not in the sense that dignity must be limited or balanced, but rather in the sense that it does not suffice to produce all decisions. In other words, dignity as the PSP is not decisive in itself: It does not contain the answers to all the troubling questions. For instance, once we have accepted that the foetus has dignitarian standing (we have strong reasons to do so in the face of the personalist meaning to equal dignity), we are still in need of balancing, or at least taking into consideration, heartbreaking situations such as pregnancies resulting from rape, or the terminal illness of the foetus. In all cases, including a 'standard' pregnancy, the equal standing of the potential mother, her perspective, and her health must be taken into account. The limited role of the PSP in such cases is to make sure that all the interests are taken into consideration. One-sidedness in hard cases proper is the basic and quite commonplace error. Taking proper care to consider all the parties – their interests and their perspectives – is merely the starting point. The rest depends on the conscience of judges and their legitimacy to make hard decisions, which varies among jurisdictions and competing theories of the judicial branch.

3 Decent law, social engineering, and the principles of legislation

As mentioned quite a few times in this book, the PSP is an implicit principle that functions in different spheres of legal activity. Adjudication is certainly the most troubling sphere – that is why it required the extensive discussion offered in the previous section. The last (and brief) section of this book will focus on a considerably less complicated matter. We will touch upon *the basic principles of democratic legislation* suggested by the SPT. The relative 'lightness' of this issue may be assumed, chiefly because the normative indeterminacy of human dignity, which was so problematic for adjudication, becomes an asset in legislation. As we have seen at the beginning of this chapter, the PSP invites public discourse regarding the best response to the exigencies of the status of personhood that everyone possesses equally. Legislative bodies are a natural home for such discussions: Debates held within them are far less restricted when compared to judicial proceedings.

Recall the illustration of the two friends, proposed by Tadeusz Styczeń, engaged in the moral dispute concerning the third person, their ill friend. Although Alan and Bonnie (I assigned these names to them in Chapter 3) held opposite visions of how to best serve their ill friend Chris, their affirmation of him as a person was the common background making the discourse sensible, and giving it at least a hint of hope for consensus. The dispute between Alan and Bonnie can also be regarded as a metaphor for legislative debates, to the extent to which legislation is a transparent and reasonable process. In a decent public order, a great deal of public discourse is concentrated on the effective affirmation of persons. Although, in the interpretation of the SPT, the public discourse seeks truth about persons, it is a genuine dialogue respecting disagreement, which is an important virtue of contemporary legislators. The process is conducted in the spirit of civic fellowship, which assumes that full consensus may never be achieved, but nonetheless others are regarded as neighbours, not as foes. Decency of law – the law taking into consideration the equal dignitarian status of the persons concerned – is enough to establish such bonds. This ideal may be realised in different institutional settings. Although a democratic-liberal framework is well-suited for this, other options are not excluded, such as a hierarchical society with 'decent consultation hierarchy' as conceptualised by Rawls (1999, 61–3). I am not making a separate case for liberal democracy as such, nor for any particular configuration of institutions within a democracy. The commitment to the PSP is envisaged as a possible enhancement of any decent political setting, an enhancement that urges the legislators to take seriously the priority of persons, as well as the unique bond between the law and natural human personhood.

Legislation is in itself an enormous topic which should be, and has been, studied for its own sake. Some contributions compellingly argue that a careful look at legislation shifts the general understanding of law itself, especially in the Anglophone world traditionally focused on judges (Wintgens 2016). For now, the SPT does not provide an independent account on legislation comparable to ones just quoted. Our reflection will be occupied with the two most important implications for legislation: (i) the priority of natural persons in the architecture of legal personhood; and (ii) a calling for caution in treating the law as a device of social engineering.

3.1 Toward dignitarian unity of a legal system: legal personhood

According to the SPT, the emphasis on human dignity in the law has occurred for a reason: It is a result of law's increased sensitivity and openness to responding to the reality of human persons. The peculiarly personal capacities have always been recognised by the law to some extent. Admittedly, the law in hierarchical societies, such as ancient Rome, did not recognise everyone as a fully-fledged legal person. At the same time, the human subject, endowed with free choice and capable action, held the pivotal role in the legal system grounded, *inter alia*, on the law of persons. Today, having achieved the equality of status among humans, many legal communities host deliberations about extending comparable concern to non-human beings. The most remarkable effort is to endow higher animals with legal personhood in order to better protect them – to make them legal subjects rather than mere objects of law (Wise 2010). Human dignity, and human personhood, is not the only 'dignitarian' concern imaginable in contemporary legal discourse (Nussbaum 2020). In this context, we may ask: When judges or legislators disregard the complex needs and capabilities of non-human animals, are they guilty of the same ignorance or indecency as when they disregard the status of personhood held by humans? To generalise: Is attribution of dignity to non-human agents a legitimate and prudent political choice?

The SPT answers these questions in the negative and defends anthropocentrism in the law. It argues that there is something special about the human status of personhood which prevents us from placing other concerns on equal footing (although these concerns taken in themselves may be very pressing). At the same time, the anthropocentrism advocated here does not by itself exclude fundamental legal protections for non-human beings – it accepts all possible concerns legislators may have, including those not directly pertaining to the affirmation of, or respect for, persons. Legislators themselves are acting persons, which makes them *responsible* for all sorts of things (and certainly not only for persons), and authorises them to responsibly use the available means. In particular, there is no contradiction between accepting the central commitments of the SPT and extending legal personhood to beings or organisations other than human beings. This is especially so when legal personhood is perceived as a 'cluster property', which means that it is gradable and consists of a set of separate but interrelated incidents, as was famously and rightly proposed by Kurki (2019, 91–120). The SPT coheres with the view that certain non-human beings may be granted certain incidents of legal personhood but not others, and still be considered 'persons' for some purposes of law. This is a distinct matter, left in the first place to legislators, whose official and publicly known task is to make and change the law as they see fit (Waldron 2016, 126).

What the SPT does advocate, however, may be hard to swallow for some people. According to the results of our inquiry, and our wide reflective equilibrium, only human beings (in the earthly world as we know it) are persons in the stronger, ontological sense. In the face of that fact (but not as a direct inference from it), the equal attribution of *fully fledged legal personhood*, along with *the status of personhood understood as dignity*, makes sense only for humans. The ontological fundament which we examined in Chapter 2 must be in place, in order to sensibly speak of 'persons in the law' in the full sense. Having interpreted the law with the ontological ground (the background theory), we observed that the Principle of the Status of Personhood protects a dynamic set of related dignitarian interests. The particular connection between freedom from degradation, self-determination, and integration (along with other possible interests) occurs only in the case of human persons. Self-determination in the personalist sense – that is, free authorship of actions marked with vertical transcendence – is also the distinctive feature of human persons. To a certain degree, it has already been recognised as such by the law. As far as I know, no one advocates for freedom of conscience for giraffes or dolphins, for example, despite the multidimensional legal protection they may otherwise deserve. In sum, the anthropocentrism I am defending means two things. First, 'the status of personhood' as conceptualised by the SPT must be distinguished from 'legal personhood' or 'legal subjectivity' as theorised contemporarily. Second, the equal and fully-fledged legal personhood should be attributed to all human beings (with some possible qualifications, such as minority age or lunacy) and to human beings only. Corporations, non-human animals, rivers, or AI algorithms may enjoy legal personhood to some extent. But the ultimate point of reference in all these cases must be natural human persons.

Given that, the SPT postulates 'dignitarian unity' as a virtue of a public order and thus a system of law. This dignitarian unity may be achieved when legislators bear in mind the status of personhood, and abstain from changing the law in a way which blurs that status. In my view, a lot of contemporary chaos in the law results from exactly this: forgetting that the law in general has real *authors and ultimate addressees*, namely, the natural human persons. The banality of this statement does not prevent it from being somehow forgotten or even straightforwardly rejected. For some, expecting the law to mirror the nature of persons is wrongheaded: It 'misconceives the very character of the legal endeavour' (Naffine 2009, 2). In the contemporary discourse, especially in the context of the linguistic turn in philosophy and the sympathy to legal positivism in jurisprudence, there is a widespread tendency to talk primarily about how a world is depicted in legal language (or how the law constructs its own language-based world). But at the same time the fundamental, and quite reversed, question – how adequately the law and legal language corresponds to the real world – tends to be avoided. For example, Tomasz Gizbert-Studnicki, while examining how everyday language and legal language are related to each other, asserts that '[t]he inhabitants of the legal world are not human beings but legal subjects' and therefore 'personhood cannot be considered a distinctive characteristic of individual persons or human assemblages' (Gizbert-Studnicki 1992, 154, translation by the author). Many people have followed similar paths. Yet the results collected in the last two chapters of this book produce the opposite picture. While 'legal subjects' of whatever kind may be created in the law, they would be meaningless if it were not for the pre-existing natural human persons. So, for example, the legal subject called 'party to a contract' would be incomprehensible if human persons did not have wills and beliefs regarding what is in their best interest. Non-human animals as possible legal subjects would not enter the discourse if human persons were not capable of compassion and did not recognise themselves as responsible for the suffering or well-being of animals, and so on. Therefore, the SPT does not conflate a jurist with a metaphysician. All that needs to be done in legal activity is to respect the status of personhood. The natural human personhood will then manifest itself in the law spontaneously.

An important postulate to achieve dignitarian unity is that if 'artificial' entities such as corporate agents or AI entities are created in the law, they should not be regarded as creations established for their own sakes. Rather, they are best perceived as legal tools of natural persons to achieve different ends (such as separating business from personal assets, which was essential to the legal infrastructure of modern capitalism). And if any 'dignity'-based rights or interests were to be ascribed to such artificial entities, it would be only an analogy to the rights or interests law recognises with regards to natural human persons. Similarly, if legal subjectivity or personhood, and thus some sort of 'dignity', were ascribed to non-human animals, it would have to be viewed as analogical to human dignity and human personhood, which is the obvious parading case here. The personalist figure of the legal person, as central to the law in general, *is the figure of the human in an interaction with legal norms, or, in other words, the human operating in legal contexts and activities.* The SPT urges us to bear in mind, in all legislative debates and procedures, that the law should ultimately mediate and foster decent relations between persons.

3.2 *Legislative standards for decent law and the threats of 'law as engineering'*

Lastly, I want to sketch out another important postulate for legislation coming from the SPT – abstemiousness in social engineering through law. This postulate comes from the general conclusion we can draw from the discussion about legal versus natural personhood, held in the previous section (Haldane, 2011). If the bond between the two personhoods is taken seriously, then the status of personhood in the law should be treated more like an axiom of legislative activity and not merely one of the many results. As Graveson has written, '[s]tatus is a condition imposed by the State, but imposed according to settled principles of law' (Graveson 1953, 114). Although he certainly was not a personalist, he proposed a useful metaphor that I intend to interpret in a radically personalist way: 'Status is the legal shadow of a human personality: remove either that personality or the light of the law which creates it, and the shadow vanishes' (Graveson 1953, 124). The radical interpretation of this metaphor says that the law 'produces' the status of personhood in a way similar to the sunlight 'producing' a shadow. The differences are obvious – no legal process goes exactly like a physical one. While a ray of sunlight cannot 'choose' not to produce a shadow when contacting a person, the legislator can create laws which deny personhood to some – slavery being the paradigm example.[18] However, at least in the long run, the natural personhood of slaves will 'show through' the unjust system of enslavement anyway.[19] Although a slave will

18 Graveson emphasises this as well. As he writes, 'legal personality may or may not be granted to any particular class of persons. Unlike its natural counterpart, it is conferred on the individual by the supreme power in his own community' (Graveson 1953, 111).

19 A brilliant example of this is given by Marcia L. Colish. One of the reasons why slaves were granted some incidents of legal personhood was that they had skills in business operations.

be legally deprived of a family, for example, the enslaved persons will nevertheless lead family lives and recognise mutual duties and rights coming from this. As history shows, they will be able, in many instances, to maintain their self-respect and dignity despite the lack of legal recognition. Indeed, dignity needs 'the light of law' to manifest itself fully. But it is not simply an artefact created through legislation. It is merely *manifested* through legislators properly responding to natural human personhood.

Against this background, nothing prevents legislators from reacting to the challenges of common concern they perceive as pressing. Not all legislative processes must be directly aimed at respecting or adequately affirming persons. For instance, restrictive regulations (or the total ban) on industrialised livestock agriculture would be directly motivated by the well-being of animals – and that is perfectly consistent with the PSP. Although such regulation does not pursue the PSP directly, it also does not have to violate it. In general, then, the SPT does not preclude using 'rational and efficient methods to change social life', which can be named 'social engineering' (Podgorecki 1962, 177). Such an attitude seems common to modern legislators, as well as scholars, who accept the means-end analysis as paradigmatic for the law (Posner 1975 serves as a paradigmatic example). Different instruments of rationally steering and managing social affairs, such as nudging (as opposed to directly telling people what to do), are discussed and widely accepted by legislators and academics (Mathis and Thor 2016).

Although practices of social engineering are not excluded in principle, the SPT sends an important warning in this regard. Many people have expressed their worries and scepticism toward social engineering through the law, and for good reason. Probably the most profound discontent comes from Friedrich August von Hayek, who argued that treating the law primarily as rules of rational organisation of society miscomprehends the real structure and dynamics of law. According to Hayek, law is an evolving scheme of spontaneous cooperation and coordination rather than a product of rational design (Hayek 1982). From a different and more recent perspective, Brian Tamanaha warns that the overuse of instrumental rationality in the law can lead to an erosion of its very integrity (Tamanaha 2006, 219). To these worries, the SPT adds another personalist one, which is the concern for genuine participation. As we remember, genuine participation is the situation in which the person, as a community member, is able to engage her self-determination and other personal capacities, and hence maintain the personalist value of her actions. Social engineering through law can threaten this, simply because the instrumentalist approach to the law regards human beings as 'units', or 'mere individuals', which the legislator moves on a grid toward the indented pattern. The SPT's worries do not regard the economic or political implausibility of this, nor its impact on the law. The main concern is, rather, the negative impact *on persons themselves*, which is a possibility. I cannot

The owners would then use their slaves as agents, which required endowing them with some legal capacity (Colish 1974, 121).

make the full case for these worries here, but it is important to at least flag this implication of the SPT before this book ends.

Now, since this is the final chapter, instead of opening a separate section collecting the conclusions from it, I will proceed directly to the General Recapitulation, embracing the most important conclusions of the book as a whole, including this chapter.

References

Aguas, Jove J. S. 2014. *Person, Action, and Love: The Philosophical Thoughts of Karol Wojtyla (John Paul II)*. Manila: UST Publishing House.

Barański, Michał. 2016. *Antonia Rosminiego personalistyczna koncepcja prawa*. [*Antonio Rosmini's Personalist Conception of Law*]. Warszawa: Wydawnictwo Semper.

Botha, Henk. 2009. 'Human Dignity in Comparative Perspective'. *Stellenbosch Law Review* 20(2): 171–220.

Colish, Marcia L. 1974. 'The Roman Law of Persons and Roman History: A Case for an Interdisciplinary Approach'. *American Journal of Jurisprudence* 19: 112–27.

Dworkin, Ronald. 1986. *Law's Empire*. Cambridge, MA and London: Belknap Press of Harvard University Press.

Dworkin, Ronald. 2011. *Justice for Hedgehogs*. Cambridge, MA and London: Belknap Press of Harvard University Press.

Finnis, John. 1998. *Aquinas: Moral, Political, and Legal Philosophy*. Oxford: Oxford University Press.

Finnis, John. 2002. 'Natural Law: the Classical Tradition'. In *The Oxford Handbook of Jurisprudence and Philosophy of Law*. Edited by J. Coleman and S. Shapiro. Oxford: Oxford University Press, 1–60.

Florczak-Wątor, Monika, ed. 2020. *Judicial Law-Making in European Constitutional Courts*. London and New York: Routledge.

Gewirth, Alan. 1985. 'Rights and Virtues'. *The Review of Metaphysics* 38(4): 739–762.

Gilabert, Pablo. 2018. *Human Dignity and Human Rights*. Oxford: Oxford University Press.

Gizbert-Studnicki Tomasz. 1992. 'Język prawny a obraz świata. [Legal Language and an Image of the World]'. In *Prawo w zmieniającym się społeczeństwie. Księga jubileuszowa Profesor Marii Boruckiej-Arctowej*. Edited by G. Skąpska. Kraków and Toruń: WUJ and Adam Marszałek, 149–61.

Glenn, Patrick. 2010. *Legal Traditions of the World*. Oxford: Oxford University Press.

Graveson, R.H. 1953. *Status in the Common Law*. University of London: The Athlone Press.

Griffin, James. 2001. 'I – The Presidential Address: Discrepancies between the Best Philosophical Account of Human Rights and the International Law of Human Rights'. *Proceedings of the Aristotelian Society* 101(1): 1–28.

Griffin, James. 2008. *On Human Rights*. Oxford: Oxford University Press.

Haldane, John. 2011. 'Is Every Action Morally Significant?'. *Philosophy* 86(3): 375–404. DOI: 10.1017/S0031819111000192.

Hanish, Christoph. 2015. 'The Legality of Self-Constitution'. *Ratio Juris* 28(4): 452–69.

Hayek, Friedrich August von. 1982. *Law, Legislation, and Liberty* (*in three volumes*). London: Routledge & Kegan Paul.

Hennette-Vauchez, Stephanie. 2011. 'A Human Dignitas? Remnants of the Ancient Legal Concept in Contemporary Dignity Jurisprudence'. *International Journal of Constitutional Law* 9(1): 32–57.

Jonas, Robert E. and Gorby, John D. 1976. 'West German Abortion Decision: A Contrast to Roe v. Wade West German Abortion'. *Marshall Journal of Practice & Procedure* 9: 605–84.

Kommers, Donald P. 1994. 'The Constitutional Law of Abortion in Germany: Should Americans Pay Attention?'. *Journal of Contemporary Health Law & Policy* 10(1): 1–32.

Korsgaard, Christine. 2008. *The Constitution of Agency: Essays on Practical Reason and Moral Psychology*. New York: Oxford University Press.

Kupczak, Jarosław. 2000. *Destined for Liberty: The Human Person in the Philosophy of Karol Wojtyła/John Paul II*. Washington, DC: The Catholic University of America Press.

Kurki, Visa. 2019. *A Theory of Legal Personhood*. Oxford: Oxford University Press.

Liao, S. Matthew. 2010. 'Agency and Human Rights'. *Journal of Applied Philosophy* 27(1): 15–25.

Lucy, Wiliam. 2002. 'Adjudication'. In *The Oxford Handbook of Jurisprudence and Philosophy of Law*. Edited by J. Coleman and S. Shapiro. Oxford: Oxford University Press, 206–67.

MacCormick, Neil. 1978. *Legal Reasoning and Legal Theory*. Oxford: Clarendon Press.

Margalit, Avishai. 1996. *The Decent Society*. Translated by N. Goldblum. Cambridge, MA and London: Harvard University Press.

Mathis, K. and Thor, A. 2016. *Nudging – Possibilities, Limitations and Applications in European Law and Economics*. Cham: Springer.

McCrudden, Christopher. 2008. 'Human Dignity and Judicial Interpretation of Human Rights'. *The European Journal of International Law* 19(4): 655–724. DOI: 10.1093/ejil/chn043.

Mounier, Emmanuel. 1952. *Personalism*. Translated by P. Mairet. Notre Dame: Notre Dame University Press.

Naffine, Ngaire. 2009. *Law's Meaning of Life*. Oxford and Portland: Hart Publishing.

Newman, Dwight. 2021. 'Against Group Dignity: Contemporary Human Rights Instruments and Their Attributions of Dignity to Groups'. *The Inherence of Human Dignity, Volume 2: Law and Religious Liberty*. Edited by B. W. Busy and A. J. L. Menuge. London and New York: Anthem Press, 93–106.

Noonan, John T. Jr. 1984. 'The Root and Branch of Roe v. Wade'. *Nebraska Law Review* 63(4): 668–79.

Nussbaum, M. 2020. *Brief of Amicus Curiae Professor Martha C. Nussbaum in Support of Plaintiffs-Appellants*. Court of Appeals of the State of New York, Case No. 2020–02581.

Podgorecki, Adam. 1962. 'Law and Social Engineering'. *Human Organization* 21(3): 177–81.

Posner, Richard. 1975. 'The Economic Approach to Law'. *Texas Law Review* 53: 757–82.

Rawls, John. 1971. *A Theory of Justice*. Cambridge, MA: Belknap Press of Harvard University Press.

Rawls, John. 1999. *The Law of Peoples*. Cambridge, MA and London: Harvard University Press.

Rawls, John. 2005. *Political Liberalism*. New York: Columbia University Press.
Rhonheimer, Martin. 2013. *The Common Good of Constitutional Democracy*. Translated by W.F. Murphy. Washington, DC: Catholic University of America Press.
Rosen, Michael. *Dignity: Its History and Meaning*. Cambridge, MA: Harvard University Press.
Sadowski, Mirosław. 2021. '*Dignitas Humana* and *Bonum Commune* as the Cornerstones of Human Rights in the Teaching of John Paul II'. *Teka Komisji Prawniczej PAN Oddział w Lublinie* 14(2): 449–62. DOI: https://doi.org/10.32084/tekapr.2021.14.2-32
Scanlon, Thomas. 1998. *What We Owe to Each Other*. Cambridge, MA and London: Belknap Press of Harvard University Press.
Sharpe, Robert J. 2018. *Good Judgement: Making Judicial Decisions*. Toronto, Buffalo, London: University of Toronto Press.
Siegel, Reva. 2013. 'Dignity and the Duty to Protect Unborn Life'. In *Understanding Human Dignity*. Edited by Christopher McCrudden. Oxford: Oxford University Press, 509–23.
Simon, Yves. 1951. *Philosophy of Democratic Government*. Chicago: University of Chicago Press.
Statista. 2021. Number of legal abortions in Germany from 1996 to 2020. www.statista.com/statistics/1087387/number-of-abortions-germany/
Styczeń, Tadeusz. 2012a. 'Problem możliwości etyki jako empirycznie uprawomocnionej i ogólnie ważnej teorii moralności. [The Issue of the Possibility of Ethics as an Empirically Authorised and Generally Valid Theory of Morality]'. In *Etyka niezależna. Dzieła zebrane, Tom 2* [*Independent Ethics. Collected Works, Volume 2*]. Edited by Kazimierz Krajewski. Lublin: Towarzystwo Naukowe KUL, 17–250.
Styczeń, Tadeusz. 2012b. 'Etyka niezależna? [Independent Ethics?]'. In *Etyka niezależna. Dzieła zebrane, Tom 2* [*Independent Ethics. Collected Works, Volume 2*]. Edited by Kazimierz Krajewski. Lublin: Towarzystwo Naukowe KUL, 247–373.
Tamanaha, Brian Z. 2006. *Law as a Means to an End*. Cambridge, UK: Cambridge University Press.
Toepel, Freidrich. 2021. 'How Not to Interpret Human Dignity: A Common Fallacy'. In *The Inherence of Human Dignity, Volume 1: Foundations of Human Dignity*. Edited by B.W. Busey and A.J.L. Menuge. London and New York: Anthem Press, 185–200.
Waldron, Jeremy. 2016. *Political Theory*. Cambridge, MA: Harvard University Press.
Waldron, Jeremy. 2017. *One Another's Equals: The Basis of Human Equality*. Cambridge, MA and London: Belknap Press of Harvard University Press.
Walsh, David. 2016. *Politics of the Person as the Politics of Being*. Notre Dame: University of Notre Dame Press.
Wielenberg, E.J. 2021. 'Three Sources of Human Dignity'. In *The Inherence of Human Dignity. Volume 1: Foundations of Human Dignity*. Edited by B. W. Busey and A. J. L. Menuge. London and New York: Anthem Press, 63–78.
Wintgens, Luc. 2016. *Legisprudence: Practical Reason in Legislation*. London: Routledge.
Wise, Steven M. 2010. 'Legal Personhood and the Nonhuman Rights Project'. *Animal Law Review* 17(1): 1–12.
Wojtyła, Karol. 1979. *The Acting Person*. Translated by A. Potocki. Dordrecht: D. Riedel Publishing Company.

Wojtyła, Karol. 2008. 'The Person: Subject and Community'. In *Person and Community: Selected Essays*. Edited by Karol Wojtyła and translated by T. Sandok. New York: Peter Lang, 219–61.

Wojtyła, Karol. 2011. *Man in the Field of Responsibility*. Translated by K.W. Kemp and Z. Maślanka-Kieroń. South Bend, IN: St. Augustine Press.

Cases

Bavarian Administrative Court. 2012. Bayerischer VGH. 15 BV 09.2719. 27 November 2012.

Court of Appeal for Ontario. 2019. *McKitty v. Hayani*, 2019 ONCA 805.

Court of Justice of the European Union. 2004. *Omega Spielhallen- und Automatenaufstellungs-GmbH v Oberbürgermeisterin der Bundesstadt Bonn*. C-36/2. 14 October 2004.

Federal Constitutional Court of Germany. 1975. BverfGe 1, 39. 25 February 1975.

Federal Constitutional Court of Germany. 1993.2 BvF 2/90. 28 May 1993. Official translation available at: www.bundesverfassungsgericht.de/SharedDocs/Entscheidungen/EN/1993/05/fs19930528_2bvf000290en.html.

Supreme Court of Canada. 1992. R v. Butler. 1 S.C.R. 452.

Supreme Court of the United States. 1973. *Roe v. Wade*. 410 U.S. 113.

Supreme Court of the United States. 1992. *Planned Parenthood of Southeastern Pennsylvania v. Casey*, 505 U.S. 833.

United Nations International Criminal Tribunal for the Former Yugoslavia. 1998. *Prosecutor v. Anto Furundzija*. IT-95-17/1-PT. 10 December 1998.

Conclusion

At the beginning of this book, I said that my inquiry had four aspects: the reconstructive, the explanatory, the critical, and the transcendental. Developing the Status of Personhood Theory throughout the book, I hope to have visited all four. As far as the *reconstructive* aspect is concerned, I claimed that the appeals to human dignity, post-UDHR and especially in recent decades, are frequent and intense enough to consider them a separate legal phenomenon. I called this phenomenon 'the dignitarian moment in the law', indicating its most characteristic elements and identifying it as the main subject under scrutiny. Led by the intuition that the ontological referral present in the dignitarian moment needs a philosophical elucidation, I engaged with the personalist conception of Wojtyła and Styczeń – the conception that arguably captures the most important truths about persons, their action, and their dignity.

Subsequently, taking the personalist conception as the background theory for human dignity in the law, I explicated – that is, partly reconstructed and partly stipulated – the personalist conception of human dignity in the law. According to this approach, the essential (although not the only) form of human dignity in the law is the Principle of the Status of Personhood. The PSP is understood as an implicit and cosmopolitan legal principle, working differently in different spheres of legal activity. Examples were shown in the final chapter.

As far as the *explanatory* part of the SPT is concerned, I claimed, and hope to have supported by sufficient evidence, that the dignitarian moment in the law is not a mere accident. According to my theory, it is rather an inevitable response to natural human personhood. This claim is not deterministic. I do not contend that the institutions and choices regarding human dignity had to take the shape they actually have taken. The dignitarian moment as we know it is one of many alternatives that may have occurred. *But the reaction as such was inevitable.* According to the SPT, human beings are persons: They are capable of self-determination and integration. Their standing as persons requires respect and affirmation, as well as preventing degradation (denying the basic standing as a person) in the first place. Personhood understood as a fact deeply corresponds to certain norms. In the face of these facts and these norms, the emergence of the dignitarian moment in the law was natural.

Such 'natural' character of the dignitarian response to human personhood as a whole yields another important explanatory result – human dignity does not

DOI: 10.4324/9781003252733-6

supervene on some human capacities we would call 'valuable'. The basis of dignity is neither one crucial property such as rationality, nor a set of capabilities that enable us to live a personal life. In the barest essentials, human dignity is rather *an axiom* of legal activity. It is a way we reason about the law and the public order, when we take the concerns about personhood seriously enough. This is what the PSP urges everyone to do. At the same time, the axiom of dignity leaves a considerable area of freedom. The particular responses to the status of personhood depend on the decisions of participants to legal activity. The participants are the authors of actions in the legal sphere as well. And they are responsible for their conduct.

This leads us to another important aspect of our inquiry, namely, the *critical* one. Freedom to respond to the status of personhood as one sees fit entails responsibility. And that responsibility requires critical tools. In this book, they have been explored in some detail with regards to adjudication, as well as in my brief remarks on legislation. As far as adjudication is concerned, perhaps the most important message is the call for judges to exercise care. The PSP, in itself, *should not* be regarded as containing all the answers that may be needed for the effective, comprehensive affirmation of persons. The judges should be careful not to overlook the fundamental degradation of human persons and are bound to combat all such degradations (and they need not be oversensitive to it). This was called 'basic dignitarian protection', which the judges must provide at all times. The issues of more particular, 'specific dignitarian protection' are more complicated. The extent to which judges are obliged or legitimised to provide this depends on the particulars of a jurisdiction and the adopted political theory of the judicial branch.

Taking into consideration the choices made in Chapter 4, the most troubling aspect of my investigation is the *transcendental* one. In order to fully examine it, we would need to abandon our commitment to metaphysical parsimony. My aim in this book was not to do so, and the further possible developments of a comprehensive legal or political theory were set aside. However, even our self-restrained analysis points to some transcendental conclusions, that is, to conclusions valid not only for *the law in general* but also *for law as such*. If we connect the ontology of the person with the dignitarian moment in the law, the two spheres seem to point at the same direction. This is something more fundamental than the structure of personhood taken separately, or the structure of law taken likewise separately. What I have in mind here is the special existential status of human persons. The person, understood as the irreducibly and incommunicably individual existence, seems to be approached here. This means that the SPT may have metaphysical implications, despite initial, methodological metaphysical parsimony. However, exploring these implications further would require another, independent study with different methodological credentials. The person as such is obviously bigger than the approximation we may have achieved in this book, and remains a mystery. This is the point at which I deliberately stop, for the purposes of this book at least.

The preceding paragraphs have made explicit what I take to be the most important general conclusions of the SPT and of this book, in terms of the reconstructive, the explanatory, the critical, and the transcendental aspects. In what remains, I will point at some more specific conclusions. They will pertain to the three disciplines I have been interacting with in this book: (i) philosophical anthropology, (ii) jurisprudence, and (iii) politics. My aim here is to present the most essential threads of our inquiry and be as brief as possible.

Philosophical conclusions

Chapter 2 advocated for a certain general vision of the human being, based on the accounts of Karol Wojtyła and Tadeusz Styczeń. The most important elements of this vision are freedom and integration, understood respectively as self-determination and a particular kind of unification of the person. In the normative sphere, the crucial element is dignity, understood as the fundamental standing and the personalist value of each human being independent of her actual capacities. This is not an original conclusion; rather, it reaffirms the personalist account as it stands. What I take to be my own contribution to the personalist picture is the significance of law. The law, in the view of the SPT, is not simply a vehicle to realise moral values. Its relation to dignity is more basic. It refers to the personalist value of action and the basic standing of persons. The law gives the human person a special kind of 'space', a space in which her personhood and dignity may manifest itself fully. Again, this is not to say that human dignity depends on legal recognition, in the strong sense of dependence. Human persons have their ontological structure, and the law serves only as a medium of recognition. But that legal recognition is crucial. The most general conclusion for practical philosophy is therefore a moral-praxiological imperative, directed at all persons in public office. They should establish a decent legal order – the order in which human dignity may manifest itself properly. Keeping the metaphor proposed by Graveson, the 'shadow' of dignity is inevitable, but it requires 'the sunlight' of the law. Unlike the real sun and real shadows, the delivery of the proper 'sunlight' depends on the persons in office.

Jurisprudential conclusions

The most important jurisprudential implication of this book is, perhaps somewhat paradoxically, that human dignity as a legal concept has a family-type meaning. One should not hope to find one, exclusive meaning. Within the SPT, I have explicated human dignity as the status-expressing principle. But this was deliberately limited and not exclusive – many alternative concepts of dignity are also admissible. In particular, human dignity as *a cosmopolitan right* could be also included. That right would be *freedom from degradation*. Since freedom from degradation seems to be focal also for the PSP, it seems reasonable to postulate the existence of such a right, possibly in the cosmopolitan legal context. Again, this would require additional studies which are beyond the scope of this book.

Political conclusions

The PSP was explicated as expressing the special bond between natural human personhood and the law. Particular emphasis was put on self-determination: the rational and reasonable authorship of one's own life. Public order in general, and the rule of law as the crucial part of public order, must be conceptualised and assessed against this background. However, the personalist meaning of human agency differs from standard accounts focused on autonomy. According to the SPT, recognising dignity is not equivalent to recognising the capacity to make sense of one's life, produce a plan for that life, and coordinate with the plans of others. Instead of that simplified and somewhat reductionist picture, the SPT connects the individual self-determination with truth, as well as with individual responsibility for that truth. The ideal of decent law embraces this and urges judges, legislators, and other officials to interpret the behaviour of the persons with whom they interact as genuine, responsible, and personal *conduct*. Obviously, not all behaviour will really flow from genuine personal responsibility and convictions, but the burden of proof rests on the officials, not on the persons concerned. Everyone is entitled to have their positions and views taken seriously, at least *prima facie*.

Against this background, the political ideal that is connected to the PSP with particular force is *equality*. It is strongly connected to human dignity because dignity is equal. Equality, going hand in hand with dignity, is likewise an 'axiomatic', intuited truth of the public order. As mentioned earlier, the status of personhood can be compared to a shadow that is produced whenever the law 'touches' the human person. This does not allow anyone to unfairly discriminate between persons in their legal activity. Although not a direct topic of this book, the natural equality of status makes human rights law the focal, though not the only, response to that status. The particulars of our personalist account on that topic await further study. What must be emphasised right now is that disagreement with regard to particular rights and their configuration should be respected. A wide margin of appreciation should be granted. This is not tantamount to a commitment to non-cognitivism or relativism. It only means that finding the truth is never easy and requires a careful examination of every position sincerely presented to the public.

Finally, I must emphasise that I have taken pains to demonstrate that politics is important for human dignity, but not constitutive for it. Human dignity as an ideal does not boil down to a fleeting consensus, dependent on our longing for a better future after World War II. It also is not merely a mask or an empty vessel for an ideological agenda. If the message of this book were to be expressed in a slogan, that slogan would be pretty simple: *Human dignity is real.* It has a real substrate and foundation in the reality of human persons, which is not limited to outstanding individuals but is, rather, our common human experience. As such, human dignity is the crucial element of legal systems as we know them. Much of the future of these systems depends on the proper recognition of the status of personhood. In the turbulent times of technological revolution, social engineering, as well as growing existential threats (from wars to the climate crisis and pandemics), the capacities involved in natural human personhood are not easy to cultivate. Thus, it appears as a genuine possibility that they will simply slide into oblivion. While personhood is transcendental, it is also quite fragile and cannot simply be taken for granted. It is our common responsibility to maintain institutions that will respect and reinforce the personal dimension of the human condition, expressed in the principles and values related to the status of personhood.

Information on the Alexis de Tocqueville Centre of Political and Legal Thought

The Alexis de Tocqueville Centre of Political and Legal Thought is a researched unit within the Faculty of Law and Administration at the University of Łódź.

The Centre draws from the ideas and intellectual heritage of the author of *Democracy in America*. This heritage combines two traditions that dominate today, conservatism and liberalism, with the Christian vision of Western identity and the republican ethos of civic participation. It derives political, institutional, and legal reflection from the analysis of actual social relations and avoids constructing any *a priori*, abstract, and rationalist models of public life. It views the main values of today such as liberty, equality, democracy, the rule of law, efficiency of state authority, civil society, and self-government as being far from harmonious. It leaves room for axiological scepticism, inspires the dissemination of ideas, and demands epistemological objectivism.

In all its endeavours, the Centre treats this heritage as important for both civic attitudes and research projects.

Centrum Myśli
Polityczno-Prawnej
im. Alexisa de Tocqueville'a

Index

abortion rights 11, 35, 208–10, 216–20
absolute worth, dignity as 49–50
Acosta, Miguel 91
Acting Person, The (Wojtyla) 80, 81, 84, 87–8, 94, 139, 166, 181
action 79–80; contrasted with activation 86–7
Addis, Adeno 121, 141–2, 144–5
adjudication 195–7; as application of PSP 220–2; *see also* judgement
administrative law 51
affirmation: entitlement to 57; of persons 92–104, 115; and person-to-person relations 92
African Convention (Human and Peoples' Rights) 36–7
American Convention of Human Rights 38
American Convention on Human Rights 151
anti-individualism 184–5
Aquinas, Thomas 77, 177
Arendt, Hannah 78, 79, 81
argumentation, rational 195–6
Aristotle 69
Article 3, European Court of Human Rights 36, 37, 41, 43, 142–4
artificial intelligence (electronic personality) 18
Assenov and Others v. Bulgaria 37
Atkin, Lord 29
autonomy 11–12, 39–45, 129–30, 134, 135, 136; *see also* self-determination
Aviation Security Act (Germany 2006) 38–9
A. v. The United Kingdom 37

Barak, Aharon 121, 153
Bedford, Daniel 141–2
Bible, Christian, and foundation of moral judgements 104
biotechnical inventions 147
bodily integrity 38
Boethius 68, 69
Brożek, Bartosz 164–5
Brüstle v. Greenpeace 147

Canada: human dignity as a right 153–4; Ontario Court of Appeal 199–200; Supreme Court, *R v. Butler* 47–8, 213–14
Carnap, Rudolf 24, 26–7
Catholic Church: and personalism 67–8; and roots of SPT xi-xii, 177; on same-sex marriage 149
Charter of Fundamental Rights of the European Union 41
Christianity and foundation of moral judgements 104
Cicero 23
Coetzee v. Comitis 42–3
commitment to the human condition 13–14, 58–9
community: and the common good 189, 191; and personhood 182–5
comparative legal interpretation 58
conduct contrasted with behaviour 113
consciousness 82–3; personal 69
consensus and metaphysical parsimony 14–16
constitutions: Germany 33; Ireland 34; Poland 12–13, 33, 40–1, 46; South Africa 42, 46; Spain 33; *see also* U.S. Constitution
Court of Justice of the European Union (CJEU) 147–8, 206–7
Crosby, John F. 70
Cruzan v. Director, Missouri Dept. of Health 41–2

Dan-Cohen, M. 126
Daniels, Norman 57, 123

decent law 178–9, 223, 235; legislative standards for 226–8; and public order 185–94
definitions of terms 22–6; contextual aspects 25–6; equivalence definitions 24, 30; family-type meanings 22–4, 156; of human dignity 22–6; partial definitions 24
degradation, protection from 35–9, 128–9, 137, 138, 169, 205–10, 224–5
Digest of Justinian 71
dignitarian moment in the law: analysis and interpretation 52–6; background and overview 31–2; foundational function 32–4; heuristic function 46–9; meta legal level 49–52, 126; regulative function 34–46; and wide reflective equilibrium 164–70
dignity, equal, personalist meaning to 197–205
dignity, human *see* human dignity
disability rights 142–6, 199, 203–4
disintegration, moral 150
Donoghue v. Stevenson 29
duty: duty dimension of moral judgement 119; moral duty 98–104; realness of duty 103–4
Dworkin, Ronald 23, 24, 30, 31, 124, 196

electronic personality (artificial intelligence) 18
empiricism, rejection of 72
Enders, Christoph 122
entitlement to affirmation 57
equal dignity, personalist meaning 197–205
equality 34, 126, 235
equivalence definitions 24, 30
essence, human 69
ethics 98–9; *see also* moral duty
EU (European Union) law 206–7
European Charter of Fundamental Rights 55
European Code of Good Administrative Behaviour 51, 133
European Convention of Human Rights 29
European Court of Human Rights 36, 37, 142–4
European Parliament 18
evaluative judgement 195–6
evaluative standards 29–30
existential dimension: of moral judgement 119; realness of duty 104
experience: as acting persons 73–4; and comprehension 74–5; and realism 75–6
explication, rules of 26–31

family-type meanings 22–4, 156
fellowship, as parallel to solidarity 192–3
Finnis, John 69
foundational function of human dignity 32–4
France: "dwarf-tossing" bans 44–5, 131, 212–13, 221; judicial culture 131–2
freedom, human 73, 82–7
fulfilment: and action 90–1; conditions of 151
Fuller, Lon 134

Gardiner, Patrick L. 165
Geneva Conventions 36, 37
Germany: abortion laws 218–19; Bavarian Administrative Court 208; constitutional law 122; "dwarf-tossing" bans 44–5; Federal Administrative Court 206–7; Federal Constitutional Court 38–9, 151–2; German Basic Law 33, 207, 217; German Federal Court of Justice 147; human dignity as a right 153; positivistic legal framework 17–18
Gewirth, Alan 199, 200
Gilabert, Pablo 200–1, 202, 213
Gilson, Etienne 69
Gizbert-Studnicki, Tomasz 225
Glenn, Patrick 71
Graveson, R. H. 226, 234
Great Britain 141
Greve, Judge H. S. 144, 146
Griffin, James 198, 200, 201
Groundwork (Kant) 93

Hayek, Friedrich August von 227
heuristic function of human dignity 46–9
Heuss, Theodor 122
holism 185
human action 57, 77–9
Human Condition, The (Arendt) 80
human conduct contrasted with behaviour 113
human dignity: consensus and metaphysical parsimony 14–16; definitions 22–6, 121; degradation, protection from 35–9, 128–9; as

foundational commitment 121; as free-standing right 153–6; function of, as methodological commitment 10–14; and intuition 100–1; law and reality 16–21; minimalist approach to 122–3; and moral duty 98; reality of 235–6; and regulative measures 122; and self-determination 129–138; and status of personhood 169–170; *see also* dignitarian moment in the law
humanitarian aspect of dignity 35–9
human reality 69
human trafficking 43, 128, 137, 179–180, 221
humiliation 138–9, 178, 179–180; *see also* degradation, protection from
Husserl, Edmund 72, 76

ICCPR (International Covenant on Civil and Political Rights) 7
ICESCR (International Covenant on Economic, Social and Cultural Rights) 7
ignorance 179
imago Dei 21, 112
incommunicability 70–1
indecent law 179–180
individualism 184–5
inhuman treatment 35–9
integration 87–92, 224–5, 234
integrity of the person 138–150
Inter-American Court of Human Rights 37–8, 151
International Covenants on Human Rights 7
International Criminal Tribunal, Yugoslavia 36, 206
interpretative judgement 196–7, 211
intrinsic worth 34
intuition 100–1, 111–12, 168
invocatio Dei, Irish Constitution 34
Ireland v. the United Kingdom 142–3, 144
Israel, human dignity as a right 153
I.V. v. Bolivia 37–8

judgement: easy cases 205–210, 221; errors 205; evaluative 195–6, 220; hard cases 196, 211–15, 215–220, 221–2; interpretative 196–7, 211, 220
Justinian, Digest of, 71

Kant, Immanuel 92–3, 98
Kirste, Stephan 16–17
Kotarbiński, Tadeusz 80–1
Krapiec, Albert 79, 84
Kudla v. Poland 143
Kurki, Visa 163–4, 224

language: grammatical correctness and justice 124; Polish language translations 86
Lanneau, Régis 131
law and reality 16–21
law as engineering, threats of 226–8
legislation: democratic 222–3; legislative standards 226–8
Liao, S. Mattew 199
liberty 40
literature and morality 99–100
Locke, John 68
love: contrasted with respect 117; duty to love 97; and person-to-person relations 92
Love and Responsibility (Wojtyla) 97
Luban, David 51, 134
Lublin School (Catholic University of Lublin) xi, 69, 79
Lucy, William 195, 196

MacCormick, Neil 195–6, 205–6
Man in the Field of Responsibility (Wojtyla) 114–15
Margalit, Avishai 178–9
marriage, legal aspects 11, 13, 14–15, 41, 49, 148–9
Matheus de Cracovia xii
McCrudden, Christopher 53, 218
McInerny, Ralph 69
M.C. v. Bulgaria 37
meanings, family-type 22–4, 156
meta-legal level of human dignity 49–52
metaphysical parsimony: and consensus 14–16; strong metaphysical parsimony 16–19; weak metaphysical parsimony 19–20, 30
Metaphysics of Morals (Kant) 92–3
methodology of author's argument 8–9, 76; consensus and metaphysical parsimony 14–16; function of human dignity 10–14; law and reality 16–21
Mexico, and Inter-American Court 151
Miller, Justice, Ontario Court of Appeal 199–200
Mises, Ludwig von 80
moral duty 98–104

moral judgements 101–4; threefold structure of 119–120

National Soccer League 42–3
natural law theory 15–16, 115
non-interference 138
normative indeterminacy 194
normativity, phenomenon of 97
Northern Ireland 141
nullum crimen sine lege 118, 121, 134, 162

Obergefell v. Hodges 41, 49, 148–9; Chief Justice Roberts' dissent 14–15; human reality and the law 11, 13
O'Connor, Justice Sandra Day 42
Omega case 206–8, 215
ontological commitments 19
ontological referral: and dignitarian protection 138; and foundation of SPT 111; human dignity as 33, 53, 55, 65, 66; reflective equilibrium and SPT 121–7
ontology: role of integration 87–92; self-determination and vertical transcendence 79–82; self-possession and self-governance 82–87
opus magnum (Styczeń) 69
Osoba i czyn (Wojtyla) 77

participation, genuine, and PSP 180–5, 227
paternalism 39–40, 130, 131, 150, 211–15
Pawlowski, Tadeusz 26–7
perennial philosophy 69, 70
personal dignity *see* human dignity
personal integrity 38
personalism: background and definitions 67–8; emphasis on action 93–4; empirical basis and relevance 72–7; ethical interpretation 105, 114–18; personalistic norm 97; personalist meaning to equal dignity 197–205; praxiological interpretation 105–6, 114–121, 163
Personalist Postulate 67–72, 97, 158–9
Person and Act (Wojtyla) 77
personhood: background theory of 134; and community 182–5; conceptions of 68–9; legal 223–5; legal definitions 18; and respect 117–18; as status-expressing principle 152–164, 215; *suppositum humanum* 112–14
"Person: Subject and Community, The" (Wojtyla) 89
phenomenology 58; of the human person 66; of normativity 66
Philosophical Investigations (Wittgenstein) 22
philosophy: and foundations of SPT 111–12, 234; of the human person 65–7; as sequence of comprehensions 75
physician-assisted suicide 41–2
Planned Parenthood v. Casey 11, 13, 217–18
Poland: Constitution (1997) 12–13; Constitutional Tribunal 11–13, 15; law of entrepreneurs 48; Penal Code 43–4; Polish Code of Administrative Procedure 133–4; Polish constitutional law 40–1, 123; public order and common good 187
Polish language translations 86
pornography, legislation concerning 47–8, 213–14
positive obligations 45
pregnancy 139–140; *see also Roe v. Wade*
Price v. United Kingdom 142–4, 145–6
Principle of Genuine Participation 181–2
principle of incommunicable personhood 70–71
Principle of the Status of Personhood (PSP): application in adjudication 220–2; background and overview 1, 28, 111; dignitarian moment in the law 164–170; explication of human dignity in law 152–164; foundations of 150–2; genuine participation 180–5; scope of 159
principles, contrasted with values 156–8
privacy 151
private law 50–1
problem of consensus 15
Prosecutor v. Furundzija 36, 37, 206
public order and decency of law 185–194

Rao, Neomi 154–5, 157
rape 151, 206
rational argumentation 195–6
Rawls, John 57, 58, 124, 197–8, 203, 223
realism, sceptical 19–20, 58, 134
reduction 75, 77

reflective equilibrium 57–8, 58–9, 77, 156; ontological referral and SPT 121–7; wide reflective equilibrium 123, 165–6, 170, 181
regulative function of human dignity 34–46; autonomy aspect 39–45; humanitarian aspect 35–9; social security aspect 45–6
Rehnquist, Justice William 218
Reimers, Adrian J. 91
representation, legal, importance of 51
reproductive technology 147–8
respect 92, 117–18
rightness dimension of moral judgement 119
rights: balance between 55–6; human dignity as free-standing right 153–6; interest-based contrasted with will theory 13; system of 48
Riley, Stephen 160
Roberts, John G., Chief Justice 14
Roe v. Wade 208–10, 216–20
Romania, law and dignity 123
Roman law 71, 85
Rule of Law Checklist, Venice Commission 132–3
rules of explication 26–31
R v. Butler 47–8, 213–14

same-sex marriage 11, 13, 14–5, 41, 49, 148–9
Scanlon, Thomas 160
sceptical realism 19–20, 58, 134
Scheler, Max 68
Schlink, Bernhard 125
Second Vatican Council 67, 70
self-control 134–5; *see also* self-determination
self-determination 79–82, 129–138, 194, 211–12, 224–5, 234
self-governance 82–7, 135–6
self-possession 82–7
slavery 128, 226–7
Slyusarev v. Russia 143
social engineering 226–8
social security aspect of dignity 45–6
Socrates 91; Socratic argumentation 100
solidarity 191–3
Solum, Lawrence 152
status: dignity as 49–50; equality of 161–2; reliance on principle of 161–2
Status of Personhood Theory (SPT): Catholic roots of 177–8; ontological referral and reflective equilibrium 121–7; overview 1, 56–9, 110–112; *see also* decent law
Stevens, Justice John Paul 218
strong metaphysical parsimony 16–19
Styczeń, Tadeusz: affirmation and dignity 93, 150, 167; and Catholicism 67–8, 177–8; concept of human personhood 68–9; on dignity 141, 202; empirical basis of personalism 72–7; and ethics 69–70; personalistic norm and morality 97; phenomenological method 66; public order and common good 190; theory of moral duty 98–104; Thomistic framework 67; "two friends" example 101, 119, 223
suffering 35–9
suppositum humanum 112–14, 120, 183

Tamanaha, Brian 227
Thomism 67, 69–70
Toepel Friedrich 219–20
torture 35–9, 128, 138–9, 140–1
totalism 184–5
transcendence: and integration 204; of the person in action 198; reference to truth 87–92, 183; transcendental nature of action 136–7; vertical 79–82, 225
Traverso, Justice Jeanette 42
Trop v. Dulles 46–7, 48, 49
truth, reference to, and transcendence 87–92
truth-seeking 57–8, 66

UDHR (Universal Declaration of Human Rights) 7, 32–3, 34, 45, 121
United Kingdom 142; England and Wales, law of torts 50–1; *see also* Great Britain
United Nations Convention against Torture 35–6
United Nations Convention against Transnational Organized Crime 43–4
United Nations Human Rights Committee 45
Universal Declaration of Human Rights (UDHR) *see* UDHR (Universal Declaration of Human Rights)

U.S. Constitution: Eighth Amendment 47; Fourteenth Amendment 11, 41–2, 55, 148, 208, 217

values: contrasted with principles 156–8; value judgements and personhood 201
Venice Commission 132–3
vertical transcendence 79–82, 225
volition 85–6

Wackenheim, Manuel 45
Waldron, Jeremy 49–50, 51–2, 53, 126, 161, 188, 203–4
war crimes 128, 206
Weinrib, Jacob 47, 55
White, Justice Byron 210, 218
wide reflective equilibrium 123, 165–6, 170, 181
Wittgenstein, Ludwig 22
Wojtyla, Karol: action, fulfilment, and integration 90–2; *actus personae* 77–9, 80–2; bodily integrity and personal integrity 139–140; and Catholicism 67–8; common good contrasted with public order 114–15, 116, 190–1; on community 182–5, 187, 189, 202–3; concept of human personhood 68–9; conduct contrasted with behaviour 113; consciousness, examination of 83–4; empirical basis of personalism 72–7; equilibrium and personhood 166–170; freedom and transcendence 89–90; on integration 139, 145, 204; morality and action 87–9, 91; personalistic value of action 94–7; phenomenological method 66; as Pope John Paul II 97, 115, 177; PSP and institutions 180–2; self-determination 85–7, 135–6; Thomistic framework 67

Taylor & Francis Group
an **informa** business

Taylor & Francis eBooks

www.taylorfrancis.com

A single destination for eBooks from Taylor & Francis with increased functionality and an improved user experience to meet the needs of our customers.

90,000+ eBooks of award-winning academic content in Humanities, Social Science, Science, Technology, Engineering, and Medical written by a global network of editors and authors.

TAYLOR & FRANCIS EBOOKS OFFERS:

- A streamlined experience for our library customers
- A single point of discovery for all of our eBook content
- Improved search and discovery of content at both book and chapter level

REQUEST A FREE TRIAL

support@taylorfrancis.com

Routledge
Taylor & Francis Group

CRC Press
Taylor & Francis Group

FSC
www.fsc.org
MIX
Papier | Fördert
gute Waldnutzung
FSC® C083411

Kolibri 360 GmbH
Ferdinand-Jühlke-Straße 7
99095 Erfurt, Deutschland
produktsicherheit@kolibri360.de